THE HISTORY OF IMMIGRATION
AND RACISM IN CANADA

D1596917

THE HISTORY OF IMMIGRATION AND RACISM IN CANADA

Essential Readings

EDITED BY

BARRINGTON WALKER

Canadian Scholars' Press Inc.

Toronto

The History of Immigration and Racism in Canada: Essential Readings
Edited by Barrington Walker

First published in 2008 by
Canadian Scholars' Press Inc.
180 Bloor Street West, Suite 801
Toronto, Ontario
M5S 2V6

www.cspi.org

Canadian Scholars' Press Inc. gratefully acknowledges financial support for our publishing activities from the Government of Canada through the Book Publishing Industry Development Program (BPIDP).

Library and Archives Canada Cataloguing in Publication

The history of immigration and racism in Canada : essential
readings / edited by Barrington Walker.

Includes bibliographical references.
ISBN 978-1-55130-340-6

1. Canada—Race relations—History. 2. Canada—Emigration and
immigration—History. I. Walker, Barrington, 1970-

JV7220.H48 2008   305.800971   C2007-906218-0

Cover art: "Victoria Chinese Children on Fisgard Street during Chinese New Year"
(image C-06727). Courtesy of the British Columbia Archives.

Book design: Susan MacGregor/Digital Zone

08   09   10   11   12   5   4   3   2   1

Printed and bound in Canada by Marquis Book Printing Inc.

This reader is dedicated to my sons, Miles and Ellis.

TABLE OF CONTENTS

ACKNOWLEDGEMENTS

I want to thank Canadian Scholars' Press and in particular Megan Mueller for first suggesting the idea of a reader in this area. Megan's patience, generosity, energy, and enthusiasm are limitless. Her talents and thoroughness have also saved me from making quite a few embarrassing errors. I would also like to thank the anonymous reviewers for their insightful comments that made this reader much stronger than its initial inception. Any errors or shortcomings contained herein are my own. As always, I would also like to thank my partner, Georgina Riel, for her support during this project. This reader is dedicated to my sons, Miles and Ellis.

Barrington Walker
Kingston, Ontario
2008

A NOTE FROM THE PUBLISHER

*T*hank you for selecting *The History of Immigration and Racism in Canada*, edited by Barrington Walker. The editor and publisher have devoted considerable time and careful development (including meticulous peer reviews) to this book. We appreciate your recognition of this effort and accomplishment.

This volume distinguishes itself on the market in many ways. One key feature is the book's well-written and comprehensive part openers, which help to make the readings all the more accessible to both general readers and undergraduate students. The part openers add cohesion to the section and to the whole book. The themes of the book are very clearly presented in these section openers. Further adding value to the book, the editor has composed annotated further readings for each section.

For the university and college market, critical thinking questions pertaining to each section of this book can be found on the CSPI website at www.cspi.org.

INTRODUCTION

Canadians rarely question the fact that Canada is an immigrant nation. We are a country that celebrates "diversity" and "multiculturalism" as important elements of our national character, and yet our relationship with these much celebrated values is complex and fraught. The scholarly evidence compiled in this reader makes it abundantly clear that today's avowed celebration of "difference" is a relatively recent phenomenon bearing little resemblance to much of our history. But heterogeneity has always been a basic fact of Canadian life since its inception, a vexing problem—an obstacle—for those many and varied actors over time whose goal was to create and maintain Canada as a white settler colony. Indeed, in the post-9/11 era, our nation's commitment to multiculturalism and cultural pluralism is based on quite a fragile consensus, even while, as of this writing, Canadian cities are going through a period of rapid and unprecedented increase in non-white immigration from non-European countries.

The Canada of the early 21st century, a country that has become decidedly urban and increasingly non-white, has thus fostered a renewed interest in the histories of race and immigration in Canada. Many Canadians are curious to know more about the histories of immigration and settlement in Canada, the racial attitudes that shaped the responses of the host society, and how these attitudes both remained similar and changed over time. Compiling this reader has provided me a renewed opportunity to reflect upon the importance of these topics in my own teaching and scholarship and the ways in which it can potentially broaden and deepen our understanding of Canada's past.

The immigrant experience is a topic that has steadily attracted increasing attention from students of immigration history in a growing body of important scholarly work.[1] These developments reflect the growing awareness that issues of race and immigration are not merely obscure sub-fields in Canada's social and cultural histories, but are integral to understanding the country's history as a whole. The readings in this collection are by no means an exhaustive account of the immigrant experience in Canada; a collection of this length certainly cannot claim to tell the stories of everyone who has come to Canada. What is hoped for in this reader is that the

selected pieces are examples of some of the best scholarship in the field of immigration history—both classics and new material—and that this reader will allow readers to think about
this subject in ways that build on previous efforts while striking out in new directions.

Firstly, students of immigration history and Aboriginal history have usually thought of the two
as completely separate entities. At least one of the anonymous reviewers of this reader raised concerns about the rationale of Aboriginal history in a collection on the immigrant experience. This
reader maintains it is crucial to bridge the divide between the two fields. A modest attempt has
been made here to begin bridging this scholarly divide. Early immigration in Canada was absolutely
dependent upon the displacement and colonization of Canada's First Nations. Moreover, many
of the racial attitudes that plagued Canadian society throughout the period covered in this reader
were forged in the crucible of early Native/non-Native relations, resulting in the dispossession
of Aboriginals, colonization, settlement, and a racially and ethnically exclusive project of nation-
hood and nation building that has strong reverberations in our own time.

Secondly, this reader places much importance on the ideas of "race" and racism. "Race" is
the grouping of various peoples based on erroneously conceived "biological" criteria, such as
skin and eye colour or hair texture. Racism is "a negative concept, based on the belief that some
races are inferior to others...."[2] Neither of these powerful ideas was a side effect of immigration policy but, rather, was central to the process of making modern Canada.

This reader is organized both chronologically and thematically and divided into five major
sections. Part I: Natives and Newcomers in Early "Canada" sets the stage for the rest of the
reader. The histories of immigration and racism in Canada did not begin on a blank slate, or a
terra nullius. On the cusp of the Europeans' arrival, First Nations peoples throughout North
America had developed complex and robust societies. The arrival of French and British colonists
in what would become Canada inalterably changed this part of the world. The later newcomers also examined in this part, the white British Loyalists who brought the practice of slavery
with them and gave it renewed vigour after the institution had waned in the last days of colonial New France, would emerge as the dominant social and political culture in Canada. Their
slaves and ex-slaves would have to fight for their dignity and their freedom in ways that por-
tended civil rights struggles over the next two centuries.

Part II: Space and Racialized Communities shows the key relationship among space, racism,
and immigrant settlement in Canada. From the mid-19th century until the turn of the century,
the dominant culture's racial attitudes (increasingly supported by the science of "race" at this
point) were often produced, reinforced, and rendered intelligible when it imposed order on
physical and geographical space.

Part III: Dangerous Others: Non-Citizens and the State explores the Canadian state's tense,
often confrontational, relationship with the working-class foreigners and non-citizens in its midst
and the "radical" ideologies of these outsiders. These outsiders often forged common bonds
within and across ethnic, national, or tribal lines.

Part IV: Gate-keeping: Enemies Without and Within continues the examination of the
Canadian state's relationship with "dangerous" foreigners, with a discussion of its preoccupation
with gate-keeping—deciding who was, and who was not, a member of the imagined community that is Canada—in peacetime and, most urgently, in times of war.

Part V: The Post-War Era: New Rights and New Racisms highlights the paradox of the post–World War II era, an age where the old, overt racisms that plagued Canada's past were nearly relegated to the dustbin of history, and civil rights and human rights gained their ascendancy. There is nonetheless disturbing evidence that newer and more covert racisms, both structural and systemic, have risen to take the place of the old.

It is my hope this reader will address growing interest among students and scholars in the history of racism and immigration in Canada and that it will be a useful tool for classroom instruction for specialists and non-specialists alike. I also hope the interdisciplinary orientation of the readings will prove to be useful not only for historians, but for scholars in fields as diverse as sociology, anthropology, and geography.

NOTES

[1] Examples include: Franca Iacovetta, et al., eds., *A Nation of Immigrants: Women, Workers, and Communities in Canadian History, 1840s–1960s* (Toronto: University of Toronto Press, 1998); Valerie Knowles, *Strangers at Our Gates: Canadian Immigration and Immigration Policy and 1540–1990* (Toronto: Dundurn Press, 1992); Ninette Kelley and Michael Trebilcock, *The Making of the Mosaic: A History of Canadian Immigration Policy* (Toronto: University of Toronto Press, 1998); and Norman Hillmer and J.L. Granatstein, *The Land Newly Found: Eyewitness Accounts of the Canadian Immigrant Experience* (Toronto: Thomas Allen Publishers, 2006).

[2] Leo Driedger and Shiva S. Halli, "The Race Challenge 2000" in Leo Driedger and Shiva S. Halli, eds., *Race and Racism: Canada's Challenge* (Montreal and Kingston: McGill-Queen's University Press, 2000), 3.

PART I

NATIVES AND NEWCOMERS IN EARLY "CANADA"

On the cusp of the arrival of Europeans in the late 16th century in what is today known as Canada, the original occupants of the land—its First Nations—each had their own language, history, culture, mores, and traditions. A rich array of nations had taken root in this part of the world, and this would change when the French and English newcomers, both of whom needed to make made allies of the First Peoples, slowly imposed a new order and a new reality upon the region. The First Peoples' initial, and most extensive, contacts throughout much of Canada were with the French. After the Treaty of Paris (1763), the French ceded their North American empire to the British, who took possession of Quebec (the former administrative centre of New France). Loyal subjects of the British Crown flocked to British North America after the fall of New France—most markedly in the period between the years of 1783 and 1812. These Loyalists (most but not all of whom were white settlers from the British Isles and Britain's American colonies) were both Canada's first refugee movement[1] and the basis of the dominant culture that took root in Canada.

Olive Dickason's chapter surveys the history of Canada's First Peoples on the Northwest coast, the boreal forest, the tundra, and the plains of the Northwest. These cultures, she points out, were "based upon regulated patterns that had evolved over thousands of years" and developed among these different cultures. Nonetheless First People shared a few basic characteristics that comprised—in very broad strokes—an Amerindian worldview.

Robin Winks's classic chapter from his foundational work *The Blacks in Canada: A History* recounts a little-known episode in the history of Loyalist settlement in Canada: slavery. The Loyalists reintroduced slavery into Canada after the fall of New France and indeed gave an institution that was in its last days before 1763 renewed life as many Loyalists—refugees fleeing persecution as they found themselves on the wrong side in the aftermath of the American Revolution—brought their slaves with them into British territory.

The last two chapters of Part I further complicate our understanding of the Loyalists, this great refugee movement into British North America. Peter Marshall's piece revisits a classic historiographical debate about whether settlers who came to British North America after 1788 were so-called "Late Loyalists," or "post-Loyalist immigrants," or settlers. Marshall asks whether we should identify this group as late Loyalists or early immigrants, and his chapter suggests the clues to this question lie in a frank assessment of the common ground that was forged out of the complementary motives of land acquisition and political expediency for American settlers and Upper Canadian elites, respectively.

James Walker tells the story of black Loyalism in Canada, a topic that has sparked heated debate about whether slaves who fled their masters were indeed loyal to the British Crown in any real sense or primarily wanted to be free from bondage. While many white Loyalists brought their slaves into Canada, not all blacks in British North America were their chattels. The black Loyalist movement was also one of the great freedom movements of the early modern era; during the American Revolution, in an effort to strike a mortal blow against American slaveholders, the British Crown offered freedom to slaves who were willing to abscond from their masters and cross British lines. In the aftermath of the war, the British transported many of these blacks to Nova Scotia, where they tasted what can only be called the bitter fruits of their loyalty. Under the British flag they were no longer slaves but not quite free. Many black Loyalists would later cross the Atlantic to the fledgling West African colony of Sierra Leone in search of their freedom.

NOTE

[1]   Ninette Kelley and Michael Trebilcock, *The Making of the Mosaic* (Toronto: University of Toronto Press, 1998), 36.

CHAPTER I

CANADA WHEN EUROPEANS ARRIVED

OLIVE PATRICIA DICKASON

At the time of the first known European contact with North America, that of the Norse in about A.D. 1000, by far the majority of Canada's original peoples were hunters and gatherers, as could be expected from the country's northern location.[1] This way of life, based on regulated patterns that had evolved over thousands of years, grew out of an intimate knowledge of resources and the best way of exploiting them. Anthropologist Robin Ridington has made the point that their technology consisted of knowledge rather than tools.[2] It was by means of this knowledge of their ecosystems, and their ingenuity in using them to their own advantage, that Amerindians had been able to survive as well as they did with a comparatively simple technology.

Because of Canada's extended coast line (the longest in the world), many of them were sea-oriented; however, the great variety in the country's geographical regions (Arctic, Subarctic, Northeast, Great Plains, Plateau, and Northwest Coast) ensured many variations on fundamentally similar ways of life. For the most part, the population was thinly scattered, as this mode of subsistence is land-intensive; the most widely accepted estimate is about 500,000, although recent demographic studies have pushed the possible figure to well over 2 million.[3] The principal population concentrations were on the Northwest Coast, where abundant and easily available resources had allowed for a sedentary life, and in what is today's southern Ontario, where various branches of Iroquoians practised farming. The Iroquoian groups may have totalled about 60,000 if not more, and the Northwest Coast could have counted as many as 200,000 souls, making it "one of the most densely populated nonagricultural regions in the world."[4] Most of these people had been in their locations for thousands of years; as Wright has pointed out, only in the Arctic and the interior of British Columbia had there been comparatively recent migrations (A.D. 1000 and A.D. 700 respectively).[5]

These people spoke about fifty languages that have been classified into twelve families, of which six were exclusive to present-day British Columbia. By far the most widespread geographically were those within the Algonkian group, spread from the Rocky Mountains to the Atlantic and along the coast from the Arctic to Cape Fear; Cree and Inuktitut had the widest geographical ranges. This accords with Rogers's hypothesis, that by the proto-historic period areas that were once glaciated (most of Canada and a portion of the northern United States) had fewer languages than areas that had been unglaciated. While Canada was completely covered with ice during the last glaciation, except for parts of the Yukon and some adjacent regions, the strip along the Pacific coast was freed very early. According to Rogers's calculations, once-glaciated areas averaged eighteen languages per million square miles, and unglaciated regions 52.4 languages per million square miles (2,590,000 square kilometres).[6] Following the rule of thumb of linguistics that greater diversity of language indicates longer occupation, then the settlement of Canada can be judged to be comparatively recent—for the most part, dating to no more than about 15,000 years ago. In any event, the Athapaskan languages spoken in the unglaciated Northwest are more diversified than the Algonkian spoken in the once-glaciated taiga that stretches from the Rockies to the Atlantic coast. Intrusive Iroquoian-Siouan languages have been aptly described as islands in an Algonkian sea. In Canada, as in the two Americas generally, the greater language diversity of the Pacific coast indicates settlement prior to the rest of the country, although this has not so far been backed up archeologically.[7] At the present, one can only speculate about the villages and campsites that have been drowned by rising sea levels following the retreat of the glaciers.

All of these peoples, whether mobile or sedentary, lived within cultural frameworks that met social and individual needs by emphasizing the group as well as the self. This was true even among those peoples, particularly in the Far North, whose groupings were fluid, depending on the season and availability of food. The social organization of Amerindians, like their languages, displayed a wider variety than was the case in Europe. However, with the exception of some aspects of the chiefdoms of the Northwest Coast, the only area in Canada where that type of social organization developed,[8] Amerindians shared the general characteristics of pre-state societies in that they were egalitarian to the extent that their sexual division of labour and responsibility allowed,[9] and they were regulated by consensus. The leaders' role was to represent the common will; not only were they not equipped to use force, they would have quickly lost their positions if they had tried. This lent extreme importance to eloquence, the power to persuade; a chief's authority was "in his tongue's end; for he is as powerful in so far as he is eloquent." Failure in this regard meant loss of position.[10] The Mexica word for ruler translates as "one who possesses speech"; the centrality of the "word" was signalled by the importance of keeping it, once given. This characteristic would later be of major importance in the conduct of the fur trade. Anthropologist Miguel León-Portilla has stressed the centrality of poetry— "flower and song"—for the Mexica, who saw it as arising from the divine, the means for expressing the truth;[11] in the seventeenth century, the Jesuits noted the power of the word and song among the peoples of the St. Lawrence Valley.[12] This can be extended to Amerindians generally. The Amassalik Inuit of East Greenland use the same word for "to breathe" and "to make poetry"; its stem means "life force." Among the Salish, the loss of a power song was tantamount to losing one's soul.

NORTHWEST COAST

Canada's west coast pre-contact peoples largely depended on the sea for subsistence. The Nuu'chah'nulth (Nootka) of Vancouver Island (along with the Quileute and Quinault, and the Nuu'chah'nulth's relatives, the Makah of the Olympic Peninsula in Washington state), were the whalers of the region, using a technology that had originated with the Aleuts and Inuit to the north. The chiefdoms (such as those of the Haida, Nuu'chah'nulth, Kwagiulth, and Tsimshian) were hierarchical, with clearly marked class divisions between chiefs, nobles, and commoners based on wealth and heredity; there was also grading within each class. Present archeological evidence indicates that this stratification developed between 3,000 and 2,500 years ago.[13] Outside and below these classes were slaves, in some villages making up a third of the population. These were usually prisoners of war, but sometimes individuals who had lost status because of debt; one could also be born into slavery, one of the few regions in North America where this happened. In any event, slaves had no rights of any kind and could be put to death at the will of their masters. Overriding class and even tribal distinctions among the northern tribes (Tlingit, Haida, and Tsimshian) was the division of each of these groups into two exogamous moieties,[14] in turn subdivided into clans, which recognized descent only through the female line. Farther south, the Kwagiulth, Bella Coola, and Nuu'chah'nulth had no moieties, reckoned descent ambilaterally, and practised a ritual life that was dominated by secret societies. These characteristics were less in evidence among the most southern of the Canadian west coast tribes, the Coast Salish, although there were considerable differences among their various groups. Their chiefs also had less power; the Salish word for chief translates best as "leader."

In general, social divisions interlocked and sometimes overlapped each other, so that an individual lived in a web of obligations and privileges that operated on the basis of reciprocity. This reciprocity was particularly operative where production and economic matters were concerned; its aim was to reinforce the community. In spiritual matters, individualism prevailed, although even here selfhood was not necessarily perceived as being separate and distinct from others within the group. Identity was acquired as one progressed through life. The elaborate give-away feasts known as potlatches could be used for various purposes, one of which was to provide the mechanism for ambitious persons to rise in the social scale, and another was to distribute wealth.[15] Originally it had a subsistence function, facilitating food exchanges between those groups with surpluses and those with shortages. Property by which wealth was measured could be either in material goods (especially among the northerners) or in immaterial rights such as those to certain songs, dances, or rituals (particularly among the Salish). Despite the emphasis on rank and material goods, more pronounced in the north, the principle of sharing prevailed as far as the basic necessities of life were concerned; a village's hunting, fishing, and gathering territories were divided among its kinship groups and exploited accordingly. Some fishing sites have been in use for thousands of years, such as the one at Kitselas Canyon on the Skeena, "the river of mists," which has been used for at least 5,000 years.

Warfare along the Northwest Coast appears to have been more widespread before and during early contact than it later became, particularly after depopulation as a result of epidemics. In the Far North its principal purpose appears to have been to kill the enemy, but to the south the objective was the acquisition of slaves and booty, especially canoes (those of the west coast were dugouts, the manufacture of which was long and laborious);[16] the Haida were feared slavers, frequently raiding the Salish of southern Vancouver Island and the mouth of the Fraser River. According to archeologist Gary Coupland, among such people as the Tlingit, Tsimshian, and Haida, warfare was aggressive and associated with the origins of ranked society, whereas to the south, among the Coast Salish, it was largely defensive.[17] The Tlingit were the only people of the Northwest Coast to practise scalping.

FARMER/TRADERS OF THE
BOREAL FOREST

Other sedentary groups were the Iroquoians as well as some Odawa (Ottawa) of the St. Lawrence River and Great Lakes—land of the white pine—who had adopted agriculture. The Iroquoians included the Huron and the Five Nations (later Six Nations, usually referred to simply as Iroquois), who became among the best known of Canada's aboriginal societies. These people, as well as the Iroquoians in general, were all farmer-hunters, practised slash-and-burn agriculture, and spoke related languages (apart from the Algonkian-speaking Odawa).[18] They lived in longhouses clustered in palisaded villages that counted up to 1,500 inhabitants each, and occasionally considerably more. This pattern of settlement appears to have developed with the adoption of agriculture and was well in place by A.D. 800.[19] Villages were moved to new sites when local resources, such as land and firewood, became exhausted. This could happen anywhere from within ten to fifty years. For these people, the fourteenth into the fifteenth centuries was a period of population expansion during which some villages expanded and others disappeared, and the "three sisters"—corn, beans, and squash, each introduced at different times—eventually dominated the regional agricultural scene.[20] All of these factors contributed to rapid social transformation. Although the Iroquois had earlier experienced intrusions from the burial mound peoples to the south, their cultures appear to have been indigenous developments, even as they adopted and absorbed traits from others.

As we have already seen, agriculture and pottery were both introduced, so that ideas and techniques from others certainly contributed to the characteristics of the flourishing societies that Europeans encountered.[21]

Sometime during the sixteenth century, or perhaps earlier, groups of Iroquoians organized into confederacies that were to have powerful impacts in regional politics.[22] The northernmost was that of the Huron,[23] an alliance of four nations (with a possible fifth) that clustered around the southern end of Georgian Bay; to the south on the Ontario peninsula was that of the Neutrals, about which even less is known than about the Huron; and in today's United States, in the Finger Lakes region of northern New York state, was the Five Nations. The Huron Confederacy was concentrated between Lake Simcoe and the southeastern corner of Georgian Bay, an area of about 2,331 square kilometres; as far north as agriculture was practicable with a Stone Age technology, it enjoyed 135–142 frost-free days a year and about 190 growing days. By the early seventeenth century, the Huron had about 2,833 hectares (7,000 acres) under cultivation, and it was reported of Huronia that "it was easier to get lost in a cornfield than in a forest."[24] It was the granary for the northern tribes with which they traded, supplying them with such crops as corn, beans, squash, and tobacco, as well as twine for fish nets, in return for products of the hunt, such as meat, hides, and furs. Huron pottery has been found as far north as James Bay. The beauty and bounty of the land were such that when the French first came to their country, the Huron assumed it was because France was poor by comparison.[25]

* * *

Despite this initial position of strength, Huronia would rapidly disintegrate before the realignment of forces brought about by the intrusion of European trade, and the old dominance of the north/south axis would give way to the east/west axis because of the influx of European trade goods from the Atlantic coast.

LEAGUE OF FIVE NATIONS

The territory of the League of Ho-de'-no-sau-nee (People of the Longhouse), as the Five Nations also called themselves, was more extensive than the lands of the Huron, although their population was less. The league's territory stretched from the Mohawk River on the east to the Genesee River on the west, a distance of about 180 kilometres. It was a geographic position that would come into its own after the establishment of European colonies on the east coast, as it controlled the major routes from the coast to the interior. The Iroquois villages were much more scattered than those of Huronia, as each was surrounded by its own cornfields, and each maintained its own language; the languages of the Five Nations (from east to west, Mohawk, Oneida, Onondaga, Cayuga, and Seneca)[26] were more distinct from each other than those of the Huron. Each of the member nations occupied its own villages, usually two or more; each had its own council, as did each tribe, whose council usually met in the group's largest village.

The "Great League of Peace," another of the appellations for the Iroquois confederacy, was governed by a council of fifty chiefs representing participant tribes, although not equally; despite that fact, each tribe had one vote. The aim was to keep peace between them and to co-ordinate their external relations, which had to be by unanimous decision. The system would later be described as a "marvel, only to be accounted for by the fact that the wills of this stubborn people were bent and moulded by the all-controlling influence of patriotism."[27]

Centralization was by no means complete, and member tribes maintained a considerable degree of autonomy, above all in internal affairs. The league had been founded by Dekanawidah, "Heavenly Messenger," said to have suffered from a speech impediment, and his disciple, Hiawatha (Hionwatha), "One Who Combs";[28] its symbol was the White Tree of Peace, above which hovered an eagle, a very wise bird "who sees afar," indicating preparedness for all exigencies. Hiawatha was said to have dedicated himself to peace when he lost his family in an inter-tribal feud. The chairman of the Great Council bore the title Thadodaho (Atotarho), after the warlike chief whom Dekanawidah and Hiawatha had converted to peaceful ways.[29] The Great Peace was not an overriding authority, but a "jural community" charged with maintaining the peace through ceremonial words of condolence and ritual gifts of exchange.[30] The founding of the league has been linked with an eclipse of the sun that was seen in Iroquoia in 1451.

Iroquois social organization included division into phratries and clans, as on the Northwest Coast. Although the men cleared the fields, the women did the farming. They exercised considerable influence and had the right to choose sachems (who, however, were selected from within certain families or clans);[31] they also had the right to order the removal of one who proved to be unsatisfactory. All Iroquoians practised torture and cannibalism within a war context, both of which appear to have been introduced from the south comparatively late.[32]

HUNTERS OF TAIGA AND TUNDRA

All the other peoples of Canada were hunters and gatherers, although there were several who were at least partly agricultural and others who had been influenced by farming cultures. The Odawa in certain areas depended quite heavily on their planted crops, and the closely related Ojibwa (Anishinabe)[33] relied on a largely uncultivated one, wild rice (*Zizania aquatica*). Their care of wild rice stands bordered on farming, to the point where they appear to have been responsible for the spread of the plant beyond areas where it was found naturally. While their dependence on wild rice was much less than that of farmers on their crops—it has been estimated that Iroquoians grew 80 per cent of their food requirements—this is still one more illustration of the large "grey" area between hunting and farming.[34] The Nipissings and Algonquins, both allies of the Huron, did some planting, but they were too far north for this to be other than marginal for their subsistence. The Montagnais of the northeastern boreal forest also appear to have practised some swidden (slash and burn) agriculture.[35] The Gwich'in (Kutchin, Loucheux) and related Han and Tutchone of the Yukon, in common with other hunting peoples, "encouraged" the growth of plants near their encampments, particularly those used for medicinal purposes.[36] In the cultural domain, the Nipissings practised the Huron custom of the Feast of the Dead, a far more elaborate ceremonial than was usually found among northern hunting societies. The Mi'kmaq and Maliseet of the Atlantic coast, specifically today's Nova Scotia, illustrate another type of cultural adaptation: that of an agricultural people reverting to hunting and gathering. According to their traditions, they were descended from a people who had migrated from the south and west; [...] archeology has confirmed a connection with the Adena and Hopewellian mound builders of the Ohio Valley. Mi'kmaq social organization was more complex than that of their northern hunting and gathering neighbours. They called their land Megumaage and divided it into seven districts under a hierarchy of chiefs. The district where Halifax would be established, for instance,

was called Gespogoitg, and Cape Breton Island, Oonamag.[37] Another hunting and gathering people, the Siouan Assiniboine (Stoneys), neighbours and allies of the Cree, had also migrated from the south, where their ancestors had been farmers on the fringes of the Mississippian mound-building complex. Cultural evolution and diffusion are by no means one-way processes involving a fixed sequence of stages.

* * *

NORTHWESTERN PLAINS

On the northwestern Plains, "where the sky takes care of the earth and the earth takes care of the sky,"[38] the population at the beginning of the historic period has been estimated to have averaged less than one person per ten square miles (twenty-six square kilometres). However, there were wide fluctuations, with considerable influxes from surrounding areas during seasonal hunts. The bison hunt provided the basis for cultural patterns.[39] From about 5000 B.C. to 2500 B.C., during a period called Altithermal, higher temperatures and greater aridity decimated the herds of giant bison by cutting down on their food supply. Before the Altithermal, hunters pursued giant bison; afterward, the bison were of the smaller variety with which we are familiar. Both drives and jumps were practised, depending on the conformity of the land; the greatest number of jump sites have been found in the foothills of the Rocky Mountains, whereas pounds were more commonly used on the Plains, particularly along the continental escarpment known as the Missouri Coteau, where sites have been found at Oxbow and Long Creek in Saskatchewan. In Canada, most drive sites have been found in that province, as well as in Alberta.

These forms of hunting called for a high

degree of co-operation and organization, not only within bands but also between them and sometimes intertribally. Impounding, or corralling, was the more complex method, and has been described by archeologist Thomas F. Kehoe as a form of food production rather than hunting—a precursor, if not an early form, of domestication.[40] One of the earliest of the jump sites was Head-Smashed-In in southern Alberta, more than 5,000 years old; it would continue to be used until the 1870s. This was an enormous site, so big that its use was an intertribal affair. Recent archeology has revealed thirty different mazeways along which the buffalo were driven and up to 20,000 cairns that guided the direction of the stampeding herds.[41] Whatever the type of communal hunting, strict regulation was involved; when several tribal nations congregated for such a hunt, regulations were enforced by organized camp police. Penalties could include the destruction of the offender's

dwelling and personal belongings.[42] In contrast, when herds were small and scattered, individuals could hunt as they pleased. In general, campsites were located on lookouts; some of them found in Alberta include several hundred tipi rings, indicating use over a considerable length of time. It has been estimated that there may be more than a million such rings scattered throughout Alberta.[43] Medicine wheels, important for hunting rites, ringed the bison's northern summer range; some were in use for at least 5,000 years.[44] At the time of European arrival on the east coast, the use of bison jumps and drives was, if anything, increasing.

It has been suggested that Head-Smashed-In was a trading centre, perhaps connected with Cahokia networks, providing bison materials such as pemmican and hides in return for dried maize, artifacts, and possibly tobacco.[45]

* * *

NOTES

[1] Canada's ecology, subsistence bases, and population distribution for 1500 are mapped in R. Cole Harris, ed., *Historical Atlas of Canada*, I (Toronto: University of Toronto Press, 1987), plates 17, 17A, and 18. Seasonal Algonkian and Iroquoian cycles are schematized in plate 34.

[2] Robin Ridington, "Technology, world view, and adaptive strategy in a northern hunting society," *Canadian Review of Sociology and Anthropology*, 19, 4 (1982), pp. 469–81.

[3] Russell Thornton, *American Indian Holocaust and Survival. A Population History Since 1492* (Norman: University of Oklahoma Press, 1987), p. 32. Ethnologist June Helm, University of Iowa, divides the Subarctic into the shield with associated Hudson Bay lowlands and Mackenzie borderlands, the cordillera, the Alaska plateau, and the region south of the Alaska range. The first division, that of the Subarctic shield and borderlands, covers approximately three-quarters of the land mass of the Arctic. June Helm, ed., *Handbook of North American Indians, 6: Subarctic* (Washington, D.C.: Smithsonian Institution, 1981), p. 1.

[4] Robert T. Boyd, "Demographic History, 1774–1874," in Wayne Suttles, ed., *Handbook of North American Indians, 7: Northwest Coast* (Washington, D.C.: Smithsonian Institution, 1990), p. 135. Richard Inglis, curator of ethnology, Royal British

Columbia Museum, estimates the pre-contact population for the west coast from California to Alaska at 500,000. (*Vancouver Sun*, 21 November 1987.)

[5] Harris, ed., *Historical Atlas of Canada*, plate 9.

[6] Ruth Gruhn, "Linguistic Evidence in Support of the Coastal Route of Earliest Entry into the New World," *Man*, new series, 23, 2 (1988), pp. 77–79.

[7] See Harris, ed., *Historical Atlas of Canada*, plate 66, on linguistic evidence indicating extremely ancient habitation of the Northwest Coast. The discovery of a longhouse dated to 9,000 years ago near Mission, B.C., appears to be an archeological break-through. See *Alberta Report*, 18, 34 (1991), pp. 50–51.

[8] There is some evidence that chiefdoms had appeared among some of the Iroquois. See William C. Noble, "Tsouharissen's Chiefdom: An Early Historic 17th Century Neutral Iroquoian Ranked Society," *Canadian Journal of Archaeology*, 9, 2 (1985), pp. 131–46.

[9] An offshoot of the sexual division of labour and responsibility was that it prevented celibacy. See Reuben Gold Thwaites, ed., *Jesuit Relations and Allied Documents*, 73 vols. (Cleveland: Burrows Bros., 1896–1901), XVI, p. 163. Another

consequence was the clear definition of roles, a major factor in the harmony that prevailed in the encampments. (Ibid., VI, pp. 233–34)

[10] Ibid.,VI, p. 243;V, p. 195.

[11] Miguel León-Portilla, *Aztec Thought and Culture* (Norman: University of Oklahoma Press, 1963), pp. 71–79.

[12] Thwaites, ed., *Jesuit Relations*, IX, pp. 59–61; XII, pp. 9–11, 225.

[13] Kenneth M. Ames, "Evolution of Social Ranking on the Northwest Coast of North America," *American Antiquity* 46, 4 (1981), p. 797.

[14] "Moiety": half. This division of a community into two halves was for ceremonial purposes.

[15] Descriptions of various aspects of potlatch ceremonialism are found in Stuart Piddocke, "The Potlatch System of the Southern Kwakiutl: A New Perspective," *Southwestern Journal of Anthropology*, 21 (1965), pp. 244–64; Helen Codere, *Fighting With Property: a study of Kwakiutl potlatching and warfare, 1792–1930* (New York: Augustin, American Ethnological Society Monograph #18, 1950); and Frederica de Laguna, "Potlatch Ceremonialism on the Northwest Coast," in William W. Fitzhugh and Aron Crowell, eds., *Crossroads of Continents: Cultures of Siberia and Alaska* (Washington, D.C.: Smithsonian Institution, 1988), pp. 271–80.

[16] Ernest S. Burch, Jr., "War and Trade," in Fitzhugh and Crowell, eds., *Crossroads of Continents*, pp. 231–32.

[17] Gary Coupland, "Warfare and Social Complexity on the Northwest Coast," in Diana Claire Tkaczuk and Brian C. Vivian, eds., *Cultures in Conflict* (Calgary: University of Calgary, 1989), pp. 205–14. The Quinault have a more peaceful explanation: they see social distinctions arising from the fact that wealth tended to concentrate with certain families or groups of families, who were thus favoured for providing chiefs; continuing through many generations, a class was born. See Pauline K. Capoeman, ed., *Land of the Quinault* (Taholah, Washington: Quinault Indian Nation, 1990), pp. 73–74.

[18] Iroquoian languages are related to Siouan and Caddoan. The Caddo, of the U.S. Southwest, were organized into hierarchical chiefdoms at the time of European contact; the Sioux had been connected earlier with the Mississippian Mound Builders.

[19] Harris, ed., *Historical Atlas of Canada*, plate 12.

[20] Succotash, an Amerindian dish that was adopted by early settlers, was made with corn and beans boiled with fish or meat.

[21] A description of Huronia as first seen by Europeans is in Thwaites, ed., *Jesuit Relations*, XVI, pp. 225–37.

[22] On the possible Basque origin of the word "Iroquois," see Peter Bakker, "A Basque Etymology for the Word Iroquois," *Man in the Northeast*, 40 (1990), pp. 89–93. He postulates that the word derives from two Basque elements that together mean "killer people." An earlier explanation for the term is that it is of Algonkian origin and signifies "snake." The Ojibwa referred to both Hurons and Five Nations as "Nahdoways," snakes. Peter Jones, *History of the Ojebway Indians* (London: Bennett, 1861), p. 111.

[23] They called themselves Wendat, People of the Peninsula, and their land Wendake. "Wendat" could also refer to the confederacy. The name "Huron" was given them by the French because of the coiffures of the warriors, which reminded them of the bristles on the spine of a boar. Diamond Jenness, *Indians of Canada* (Ottawa: Acland, 1932), p. 82. Odawa men affected a similar hairstyle. Apparently the term "huron" also referred to manner of dress, implying rusticity.

[24] Gabriel Sagard, *The Long Journey to the Country of the Hurons*, tr. H.H. Langton (Toronto: The Champlain Society, 1939), p. 104.

[25] Gabriel Sagard, *Histoire du Canada, et voyages que les frères mineurs Recollects y ont faicts pour la conversion des infidelles*, 4 vols. (Paris: Sonnius, 1636), III, p. 728.

[26] According to the Huron historian Margaret Vincent Tehariolina, the Huron were an offshoot of the Seneca and thus essentially the same people. Tehariolina, *La nation huronne, son histoire, sa culture, son esprit* (Québec: Editions du Pélican, 1984), pp. 96–97.

[27] "Oka and its Inhabitants," in *The Life of Rev. Amand Parent, the first French-Canadian ordained by the Methodist Church* (Toronto: Briggs, 1887), p. 167.

[28] Hiawatha has been identified as an Onondaga by birth and a Mohawk by adoption, and also as a Huron. Some of the versions of the origins of the league are told by Christopher Vecsey, "The Story of the Iroquois Confederacy," *Journal of the American Academy of Religion*, LIV, 1 (1986), pp. 79–106. Indian historian Bernard Assiniwi gives his version in *Histoire des Indiens du haut et du bas Canada: moeurs et coutumes des Algonkins et des Iroquois*, 3 vols. (Québec: Leméac, 1973), I, pp. 111–24.

[29] Alice Beck Kehoe, *The Ghost Dance* (Toronto: Holt, Rinehart and Winston, 1989), p. 115. Hiawatha's name, "One Who Combs," was earned because he combed the snakes out of Thadodaho's hair. There are several versions of the story, one of which is recounted by Paul A.W. Wallace, *The White Roots of Peace* (Port Washington, N.Y.: Ira J. Friedman, 1968), pp. 11–17.

[30] Daniel K. Richter, "War, Peace, and Politics in Seventeenth Century Huronia," in Tkaczuk and Vivian, eds., *Culture and Conflict*, pp. 285–86.

[31] A report in the *Jesuit Relations* says that the Onondaga alternated men and women as head sachems (XXI, p. 201).

[32] Nathaniel Knowles, "The Torture of Captives by the Indians of Eastern North America," *Proceedings of the American Philosophical Society*, 82, 2 (March 1940), reprinted in *Scalping and Torture: Warfare Practices Among North American Indians* (Ohsweken, Ont.: Iroqrafts Reprints, 1985).

[33] "Anishinabe" (plural, Anishinabeg) means "the people." "Ojibwa" translates as "the talk of the robin."

34 A detailed study of the exploitation of wild rice and its cultural ramifications is that of Thomas Vennum, *Wild Rice and the Ojibway People* (St. Paul: Minnesota Historical Society Press, 1988). See also Kathi Avery and Thomas Pawlick, "Last Stand in Wild Rice Country," *Harrowsmith*, III, 7 (May, 1979), pp. 32–47, 107.

35 Sagard, *Histoire du Canada*, IV, p. 846.

36 Catharine McClellan, verbal communication.

37 An early description of them is that of Jesuit Pierre Biard (1567?–1622) in Thwaites, ed., *Jesuit Relations*, II, pp. 73–81. At Quebec, Jesuit Paul Le Jeune was vividly impressed with the facial painting of Amerindians, as well as by their general appearance when he saw a group of 600 warriors, "tall, powerful," wearing, among other skins, those of elk, bear, and beaver. Thwaites, ed., *Jesuit Relations*, V, p. 23; VI, p. 25.

38 The expression is borrowed from the Navajo Blessingway ceremony.

39 Anthropologists once argued that the Plains could not have been inhabited to any extent before the advent of the horse and the gun. Clark Wissler wrote in 1906, "the peopling of the plains proper was a recent phenomenon due in part to the introduction of the horse and the displacement of tribes by white settlement." Wissler, "Diffusion of Culture in the Plains of North America," *International Congress of Americanists*, 15th session (Quebec, 1906), pp. 39–52. Although Wissler later modified his position, A.L. Kroeber in 1939 was still arguing that the Plains had developed culturally "only since the taking over of the horse from Europeans." Kroeber,

Cultural and Natural Areas of Native North America (Berkeley: University of California Press, 1939), p. 76.

40 Thomas F. Kehoe, "Corralling Life," in Mary LeCron Foster and Lucy Jane Botscharow, eds., *The Life of Symbols* (Boulder, Colorado: Westview Press, 1990), pp. 175–93.

41 Head-Smashed-In has been named a World Heritage Site by UNESCO.

42 Eleanor Verbicky-Todd, *Communal Buffalo Hunting Among the Plains Amerindians. An Ethnographic and Historic Review* (Edmonton: Archaeological Survey of Alberta Occasional Papers #24, 1984), pp. 25–32. At a later date an offender risked being flogged or even (among the Kiowa) having his horse shot.

43 Richard G. Forbis, *A Review of Alberta Archaeology to 1964* (Ottawa: National Museum of Canada, 1970), p. 27.

44 Harris, ed., *Historical Atlas of Canada*, plate 15. See also Brian O.K. Reeves, *Culture Change in the Northern Plains: 1000 B.C.–A.D. 1000* (Edmonton: Archaeological Survey of Alberta, Occasional Papers No. 20, 1983); H.M. Wormington and Richard G. Forbis, *An Introduction to the Archaeology of Alberta, Canada* (Denver, Colorado: Denver Museum of National History, 1965), particularly the summary and conclusion, pp. 183–201.

45 Jack Brink and Bob Dawe, *Final Report of the 1985 and 1986 Field Season at Head-Smashed-In Buffalo Jump* (Edmonton: Archaeological Survey of Alberta, No. 16, 1989), pp. 298–303.

BIBLIOGRAPHY

Printed Documents and Reports

Thwaites, Reuben Gold, ed. *Jesuit Relations and Allied Documents*, 73 vols. Cleveland: Burrows Bros., 1896–1901.

Media (Newspapers, Television)

Vancouver Sun.

Books and Articles

Ames, Kenneth M. "The Evolution of Social Ranking on the Northwest Coast of North America," *American Antiquity*, 46, 4 (1981), 789–805.

Assiniwi, Bernard. *Histoire des Indiens du haut et du bas Canada: moeurs et coutumes des Algonkins et des Iroquois*, 3 vols. Québec: Leméac, 1973.

Bakker, Peter. "A Basque Etymology for the Word Iroquois," *Man in the Northeast*, 40 (1990), 89–93.

Brink, Jack, and Bob Dawe. *Final Report of the 1985 and 1986 Field Season at Head-Smashed-In Buffalo Jump*. Edmonton: Archaeological Survey of Alberta No. 16, 1989.

Capoeman, Pauline K., ed. *Land of the Quinault*. Taholah, Washington: Quinault Indian Nation, 1990.

Coderre, Helen. *Fighting With Property: a study of Kwakiutl potlatching and warfare, 1792–1930*. New York: Augustin, American Ethnological Society Monograph #18, 1950.

Fitzhugh, William W., and Aron Crowell, eds. *Crossroads of Continents: Cultures of Siberia and Alaska*. Washington, D.C.: Smithsonian Institution, 1988.

Forbis, Richard G. *A Review of Alberta Archaeology to 1964*. Ottawa: National Museum of Canada, 1970.

Foster, Mary LeCron, and Lucy Jane Botscharow, eds. *The Life of Symbols*. Boulder, Colorado: Westview Press, 1990.

Gruhn, Ruth. "Linguistic Evidence in Support of the Coastal Route of Earliest Entry into the

New World," *Man* (N.S.), 23, 2 (1988), 77–100.

Handbook of North American Indians, general ed., William C. Sturtevant, Washington, D.C.: Smithsonian Institution, 1978–; Vol. 4, *History of Indian-White Relations*, ed. Wilcomb E. Washburn, 1988; Vol. 5, *Arctic*, ed. David Damas, 1984; Vol. 6, *Subarctic*, ed. June Helm, 1981; Vol. 7, *Northwest Coast*, ed. Wayne Suttles, 1990; Vol. 8, *California*, ed. Robert F. Heizer, 1978; Vol. 15, *Northeast*, ed. Bruce G. Trigger, 1978.

Harris, R. Cole, ed. *Historical Atlas of Canada I*. Toronto: University of Toronto Press, 1987.

Jenness, Diamond. *Eskimo Administration: II. Canada*. Montreal: Arctic Institute of North America, 1972 (reprint). This volume is part of a five-volume series on Inuit administration from Alaska to Greenland published by the Arctic Institute, 1962–63.

Jones, Peter. *History of the Ojebway Indians*. London: A.W. Bennett, 1861.

Kehoe, Alice B. *North American Indians, A Comprehensive Account*. Englewood Cliffs, N.J.: Prentice-Hall, 1981.

Knowles, Nathaniel. "The Torture of Captives by the Indians of Eastern North America," *Proceedings of the American Philosophical Society*, 82, 2 (March, 1940). Reprinted in *Scalping and Torture: Warfare Practices Among North American Indians*. Ohsweken: Iroqrafts Reprints, 1985.

Kroeber, Alfred L. *Cultural and Natural Areas of Native North America*. Berkeley: University of California Press, 1939.

León-Portilla, Miguel. *Aztec Thought and Culture*. Norman: University of Oklahoma Press, 1963.

Noble, William C. "Tsouharissen's Chiefdom: An Early Historic 17th Century Neutral Iroquoian Ranked Society," *Canadian Journal of Archaeology*, 9, 2 (1985), 131–46.

Piddocke, Stuart. "The Potlatch System of the Southern Kwakiuktl: A New Perspective," *Southwestern Journal of Anthropology*, 21 (1965), 244–64.

Reeves, Brian O.K. *Culture Change in the Northern Plains 1000 B.C.–A.D. 1000*. Edmonton: Archaeological Survey of Alberta, Occasional Paper No. 20, 1983.

Ridington, Robin. "Technology, world view, and adaptive strategy in a northern hunting society," *Canadian Review of Sociology and Anthropology*, 19, 4 (1982), 469–81.

Sagard, Gabriel. *Histoire du Canada, et voyages que les frères mineurs Recollects y ont faicts pour la conversion des infidelles*, 4 vols. Paris: Sonnius, 1636.

Sagard, Gabriel. *The Long Journey to the Country of the Hurons*, tr. H.H. Langton. Toronto: The Champlain Society, 1939. (First published in Paris in 1632.)

Tehariolina, Margaret Vincent. *La nation huronne, son histoire, sa culture, son esprit*. Québec: Éditions du Pélican, 1984.

Thornton, Russell. *American Indian Holocaust and Survival. A Population History Since 1492*. Norman: University of Oklahoma Press, 1987.

Tkaczuk, Diana Claire, and Brian C. Vivian, eds. *Cultures in Conflict: Current Archaeological Perspectives*. Calgary: University of Calgary, 1989.

Trigger, Bruce G. *The Children of Aataentsic. A History of the Huron People to 1660*, 2 vols. Montreal and Kingston: McGill-Queen's University Press, 1976.

Vecsey, Christopher. "The Story of the Iroquois Confederacy," *Journal of the American Academy of Religion*, LIV, 1 (1986), 79–106.

Vennum, Thomas. *Wild Rice and the Ojibway People*. St. Paul: Minnesota Historical Society Press, 1988.

Verbicky-Todd, Eleanor. *Communal Buffalo Hunting Among the Plains Indians. An Ethnographic and Historical Review*. Edmonton: Archaeological Survey of Alberta Occasional Papers #24, 1984.

Wallace, Paul A.W. *The White Roots of Peace*. Port Washington, N.Y.: Ira J. Friedman, 1968.

Wissler, Clark. "Diffusion of Culture in the Plains of North America," *International Congress of Americanists*, 15th session (Quebec, 1906), 39–52.

CHAPTER 2

SLAVERY, THE LOYALISTS, AND ENGLISH CANADA, 1760–1801

ROBIN W. WINKS

*B*y the Treaty of Paris in 1763, France ceded the whole of her mainland North American empire east of the Mississippi to Great Britain. An incidental effect of this transfer of power was the legal strengthening of slavery in Canada. On three occasions explicit guarantees were given to slave-owners that their property would be respected, and between 1763 and 1790 the British government added to the legal superstructure so that a once vaguely defined system of slavery took on clearer outlines.

When Pierre François Rigaud, Marquis de Vaudreuil, surrendered at the Chateau de Ramezay on September 8, 1760, he included in the treaty of capitulation a clause, number 47, which affirmed that all slaves would remain the possessions of their masters, that they might continue to be sold, and that they could be instructed in the Roman Catholic faith. The Commander-in-Chief of the British forces in North America, Jeffrey Amherst, who received the surrender documents, accepted the clause, reserving those slaves who had been taken prisoner by the British during the fighting.[1] On the following day Vaudreuil wrote to the French commandant at Detroit to inform him of the terms of the peace and to instruct him to return any slaves taken from the British during the war.[2] Three years later article 47 was incorporated, virtually without change, into the final treaty of peace. In July 1764, the bedraggled Huron allies of the French made their own peace with Sir William Johnson, the Superintendent of Indian Affairs for New York, and Johnson not only ordered that all "negro's, Panis or other slaves … who are British property" should be delivered to the commandant at Detroit, but warned that the Hurons must turn over to the commanding officer any slaves who subsequently might seek refuge with them.[3]

The Treaty of Paris introduced English criminal and civil law to Quebec, depriving slaves of those few protections provided by the informally observed *Code Noir*. But in 1774, with the Quebec Act, Britain restored the earlier French civil law to the province while retaining the English criminal code. The boundaries of Quebec were extended to the Ohio River, bringing under the one administration those few slaves living in the old Northwest. Most important among these were the slaves held at Detroit, increasing in number although, in 1774, slightly short of one hundred in all.[4] In 1791 Quebec was divided into two provinces, and Britain preserved the French laws for Lower Canada while introducing English civil law into Upper Canada. English criminal law was applied in both Canadas.

The English civil and criminal law that was introduced into Quebec in 1763 contained no effective strictures against slavery; indeed, the entire weight of law and custom in the British colonies tended to support the legality of the institution overseas. Lord Mansfield's famous decision, from the Court of King's Bench in the case of Somerset vs. Stewart, which held that slavery could not exist in England itself without specific legislation, did not come until 1772, well after the British administrators in Quebec had made it clear to the French that they would be permitted to retain their slaves. The 47th article of capitulation at Montreal, the same article in the definitive treaty of peace, and George III's proclamation of October 7, 1763, which affirmed those articles, had all given support to the institution. And in the Quebec Act the British Parliament reaffirmed that all His Majesty's subjects within the province could continue to hold and to enjoy their property and possessions. To the east, in Nova Scotia, the General Assembly had given indirect recognition to slavery in 1762 by referring, in an act intended to control the sale of liquor on credit, to "any soldier, sailor, servant, apprentice, bound servant or negro slave." An attempt in 1789 to pass a bill asserting that no one could enslave a British subject "unless they are proved by Birth or otherwise to be bound to Servitude for Life" would fail.[5]

At its first session in 1792, the Parliament of Upper Canada affirmed English law in order to remove certain ambiguities arising out of the act of 1774 and the division of the two Canadas in 1791. When, during the second session in 1793, the Parliament brought in a specific bill to promote the abolition of slavery, it was clear that the mere introduction of English common law was insufficient to this end. While public opinion, and not a few antiquarians and local historians, have held that slavery was illegal in the whole of British North America after the Somerset case, this was not so; for Lord Mansfield's decision, whatever it may be that he said,[6] had no legal effect within the colonies.

But the most important legal protection given to slavery by Britain for the northern provinces was contained in an Imperial act of 1790 to encourage immigration into British North America. Britain permitted free importation into North America, the Bahamas, and Bermuda of all "Negroes, household furniture, utensils of husbandry or cloathing." No one could sell such goods for a year after entering the colonies; and furniture, utensils, and clothing were not to exceed in value £50 for every white and £2 for every Negro slave. Free Negroes were not encouraged.[7] All white settlers over fourteen years old were to take an oath of allegiance; children and Negroes, slave or free, were not expected to do so since they were unable to swear.

The British military governor of Quebec, General James Murray, echoed the arguments of Denonville, Champigny, and Bègon, for he hoped to bring more Negro slaves into the reorganized colony. In November 1763, Murray wrote to a friend in New York asking for "two Stout Young fellows" and—so that they might have "a Communication with the Ladys" and be happy—"for each a clean young Wife." While these four Negro slaves were to be his, he saw broader possibilities: "without Servants nothing can be done"; soldiers would be poor laborers, and the French would work for no one but themselves. Murray hoped, "by setting a good Example," to improve agriculture. "Black Slaves are Certainly the only people to be depended upon, but ... they should be born in one or other of our Northern Colonies, [as] the Winters here will not agree, with a Native of the Torrid Zone." For the right Negro slaves he would "begrudge no price."[8] Wishing to conciliate the French and to create a colony loyal to the British Crown, Murray appears to have allowed French customs and codes to govern slave relations as before. In effect, slavery continued under the British as under the French.

There were Negroes, and slavery,[9] on the eastern seaboard as well. French blacks had been involved in the unsuccessful defense of Louisbourg in 1745, and among the common laborers there in 1747 was a free black laborer, Quash, who received the same pay as his thirty-five white coworkers did, and two free Negro masons.[10] In 1749 the British government offered passage, provisions, muskets, and ammunition to settlers, and free Negroes were included; in 1750 fifteen or more were victualed at Halifax. When the Nova Scotian government opened parcels of the original French lands to settlers from New England in 1759, blacks again were given the same opportunities to come as whites.[11]

The first clear references to slaves occur in 1752. A "negro servant" named Orange was mentioned in a will; and in May an entrepreneur and victualler to the navy at Halifax, Joshua Mauger, advertised several Negro slaves for sale.[12] A Halifax merchant and magistrate, Malachy Salter, asked his wife to buy a Negro boy for him while she was in Boston in 1759, confessing that he was "obliged to exercise the cat or stick [against one of his two slaves] almost every day."[13] Negro slaves were introduced to Liverpool by 1760, to the New Glasgow region in 1767, and to Bridgetown, Amherst, Onslow, and Cornwallis by 1770. In that year Henry Denny Denson of Falmouth held five and possibly as many as sixteen slaves at his Mount Denson home.[14] "A boy and a girl, about eleven years old; likewise a puncheon of choice cherry

brandy," were offered for sale in 1760; and in 1769 an auction was held on the beach at Halifax to sell "two hogsheads of rum, three of sugar and two well-grown negro girls, aged fourteen and twelve." By 1767 there was at least one slave on the Saint John River, a "rascal negro" who, according to his owner, "cannot be flattered or drove to do one-fourth a man's work."[15] In 1768 alone, 2,217 Negro slaves valued at £77,595 sterling were imported into the British provinces of North America, Newfoundland, Bahama, and Bermuda; and while most of these probably went to the Bahamas, many did not. In 1788 "robust able black men" were at work in the Newfoundland fisheries; for thirty-four sloops from Bermuda, each carrying eight to twelve men—three quarters of whom were Negro slaves—arrived at the banks early in the spring. Although at first not feared as competitors because of the widespread belief that Negroes could not stand the climate, they soon excelled the locals at the catch, abandoning the banks only for lack of any place to dry their fish.[16]

The Loyalist migration to the faithful British lands in North America brought the first really major influx of Negroes to the maritime areas, however. Some of the Loyalists had owned large plantations in the rebellious colonies, with household slaves and field hands. Others had owned little more than the clothes on their backs. Loyalists came from all colonies, all professions, and all levels of society, having in common only a conscious commitment to their Crown and a general respect for property. Many took slavery for granted, and those who owned slaves found important work for them to do in the new land—clearing fields, chopping wood against the long winters, and building ships.

Five results of this influx of Loyalists are clear. The number of slaves increased rapidly. The defense of slavery received a number of vocal and well-informed advocates. Negro slaves virtually supplanted *panis* slaves, even in Quebec. Because many of the slaves came from larger plantations where they had been trained to specific skills, the variety of work done by Negroes was greatly expanded. Since a number of the Negroes were freedmen, slave and free Negroes now lived side by side.

But in time the effect of the Loyalist and Negro immigration was the reverse of the initial trend. The slaves, given the example of free Negro agricultural settlers nearby, cannot have continued to assume that black skins automatically decreed servitude. Many of the Loyalists found that they could not afford to maintain gangs of fifty or more field hands, and that once the land was cleared it was not sufficiently productive to require an extensive labor force. Since the Loyalists came from several colonies, they tended to apply to their slaves a pastiche of their previous practices and laws, but without specific enactments; and in doing so, they seem almost always to have applied the softer, less formal of the regulations. Slaves were baptized, given some education, and kept together as families, whatever the practices may have been in the colonies to the south. Most important, a number of the Loyalists already had been moving toward antislavery positions; and once they resettled, they tended to look upon slavery as too closely associated with the new Republic which they had cause to hate. Although the Loyalists temporarily gave new numbers and new strength to slavery in Canada, within two decades those same Loyalists had all but ended the practice.

Judging slavery to be a major weakness of the rebellious southern colonies, the British offered emancipation to all slaves who, during the Revolution, volunteered to serve with their forces. Britain hoped to get thousands of laborers in this way, and also slowly to strangle the southern economy. Fewer slaves accepted the call than the British had hoped, however, and since slaves were valuable property, many British officers were unable to resist the temptation to sell them in the West Indies. In Quebec, too, the desire to turn a small fortune led to illegal seizures, betrayals, and unjust enslavements; but since the numbers dealt with along the northern frontier were small, the problem was also small.

The line between slaves who surrendered to British officers and slaves who were captured and thus taken to be the legitimate spoils of war was one too thin to draw at times. While Montreal was still in French hands, at least one free Negro who had been taken prisoner at Fort William Henry was sold in Montreal as a slave. In 1778 some men stationed in Quebec with the Light Infantry Chasseurs of Brunswick took away and sold a slave belonging to a French merchant, Joseph Despin; and later that year a Negro who had been captured by "the Yankys," twice petitioned the new governor, Frederick Haldimand, for a clear grant of his freedom. In 1780 a number of slaves captured in Kentucky were brought into Quebec via Detroit and sold, although at least ten apparently belonged to a Loyalist; and near Detroit Indians continued to seize Negroes for themselves. In New York two Loyalist groups, the Royal Regiment of New York and Colonel John Butler's Queen's Rangers, together with Indian allies, took a number of slaves as spoils, to sell in Montreal and on the Niagara peninsula; in one raid on Ballston, New York, in 1781, seven or more Negroes were captured. In 1787 a man held by Captain Johan Jost Herkimer, who had settled on the Bay of Quinté after the war, complained that, although he had escaped from the rebels in New York and had served the King, he was kept as a slave; and a Negro with Richard Cartwright, Colonel Butler's former secretary, also told of being enslaved illegally. Indeed, as Captain John Monroe, who was in charge of the expedition against Ballston,[17] later was to declare, "he never considered these captured negroes as ordinary prisoners of war and consequently did not report to the Commander-in-Chief or any other Commanding officer," for selling Negroes was "customary." It is, therefore, impossible to know how many slaves were carried into Quebec during the Revolution.[18]

The Governor, Sir Frederick Haldimand, wished to know. After an unsuccessful attempt to have a group of illegally seized slaves returned at Detroit to their Loyalist owner, in 1781 Haldimand ordered Sir John Johnson, a Loyalist from New York who, together with Butler, had organized many of the raids into rebel territory, to report to him on "all Negroes who have been brought into the Province by Parties in any Respect under your Directions whether Troops or Indians." Johnson himself had owned slaves, including one who had loyally buried his master's silver plate when the Johnson family estate was confiscated, and he had brought fourteen with him. (Sir John's ability to work with Indians was to lead, two years later, to his appointment as Superintendent-General of Indian Affairs.) He filed a census return in July—far too quickly to be credited with anything approaching accuracy—in which he accounted for the disposition of only fifty slaves.[19] But Haldimand cannot have hoped for a true accounting, for Negroes sought refuge in the province throughout the Revolutionary War, and most quite naturally claimed to be free men; nor could effective controls be applied to the sale of slaves around Detroit, especially of those taken captive by marauding Indians, although Haldimand tried to block unauthorized slave entry into the colony. The Negroes had one advantage over whites taken captive by the Indians, however: if the latter might be slain, Negroes were kept alive because they could be sold.

During the war, the British employed Negroes against the enemy in many ways. In the army they were boatmen, woodsmen, general laborers, buglers and musicians. One corps, the Black Pioneers, was formed entirely from free Negroes. Sir Henry Clinton encouraged slaves to desert rebel masters and promised them their freedom if they did so. To regularize such offers, late in the war Sir Guy Carleton, then commander-in-chief of the British troops in North America, guaranteed that all slaves would be free who, upon seeking refuge behind British lines, made formal claim to British protection; and as he supervised the massive evacuation of Loyalists and troops from New York in 1783, he sought out places to which these Negroes might go. The great majority of them were resettled in the British West Indies, and others temporarily in East Florida, but many—slave and free—went to the remaining British provinces in North America.

A final settlement between Britain and the United States had to wait until terms were agreed upon between Britain and France, but in the meantime hundreds of former slaves, who had taken refuge with the British and thought themselves free, now lived in fear of return to and punishment by their putative owners. Carleton decided to transport them elsewhere, promising that if doing so infringed the final treaty, the British governor would compensate the owners; and he ordered that a register should be kept on the name, age, occupation, and former owner of all Negroes. Not all masters were opposed to this arrangement, for in the northern states many preferred the promised compensation to the slaves. In any case, as Carleton pointed out in defense of his decision, the Negroes would have found other ways of getting out of New York "so that the former owner would no longer have been able to trace them," thus losing any chance of compensation. Because of Carleton's registers, we have a clearer record of Negro movement by sea into Nova Scotia at the end of the Revolutionary War than for any other major Negro migration into British North America.

General Washington met with Carleton in May of 1783 to discuss how American property should be preserved, with particular reference to Negro slaves. Carleton insisted that those Negroes who had taken advantage of the proclamations issued in their favor during the war should be embarked if they wished to be, and admitted that some already had been. Washington apparently stood upon the letter of the Provisional Articles of the previous November, the seventh of which had stipulated that "His Britannic Majesty shall with all convenient speed, and without causing any destruction, or carrying away any Negroes, or other property of the American Inhabitants, withdraw all his Armies." In the interim between the date of the Provisional Articles and the conclusion of the British treaty with France, Carleton had arranged for the evacuation. He now insisted that those Negroes who had come to the British lines were, by their act, free and therefore did not fall within the terms of article seven which, although it referred only to Negroes and not to slaves, nonetheless clearly meant only those Negroes who were slaves—a condition they lost upon their formal application for freedom before the British. Washington insisted that the provisional article was binding on this point and that it had prohibited carrying away any Negroes at all, to which Carleton is said to have responded that "no interpretation could be sound, that was inconsistent with prior Engagements of the Faith and honor of the Nation, which he should inviolably maintain with People of all Colours and Conditions." If Britain shared Washington's view, Carleton added, his registers would make full compensation possible: "the Slave would have his liberty, his Master his Price, and the Nation

support [of] its honor." Ultimately they agreed that an American should help oversee the embarkation, and from May until November of 1783, Washington's aide-de-camp stood by in New York as hundreds of Negroes embarked for Nova Scotia.[20]

Despite Carleton's decisive stand, which was approved by Lord North in August, an air of indecision and expediency hung over the preparations for evacuation from the American colonies, since deep into 1782 no one had known which ports in North America Britain might ultimately retain. In August, 4,230 whites and 7,163 Negroes were gathered in Charleston, South Carolina, awaiting transport; and while most expressed a desire to be taken to either Jamaica or St. Augustine, they continued to mill about uncertainly, not wanting to "bind themselves now to any specific spot." Not until March of 1783 did Carleton order the commissary at Halifax to issue provisions for an advance body of 259 white adults, 65 children, and 24 slaves who were to be sent from this group in South Carolina. Many of the whites and Negroes who were sent to Jamaica and East Florida were unable to find work, and faced with the prospect of supplying them with provisions long beyond the allotted time, Carleton transferred some of them to Nova Scotia as well.

Between April 15 and November 30, 1783, Carleton's commissioners at New York inspected every vessel bound for Nova Scotia, save for two that failed to comply with regulations, to learn how many Negroes were being carried away. In the first two weeks they accounted for 328 Negro men, 230 women, and 48 children, all free in British eyes, as well as several slaves accompanying white Loyalists. In June, when the two recalcitrant vessels were inspected upon arrival in Nova Scotia, 165 more free Negroes were registered. They continued to arrive in Nova Scotia in such numbers that in some sections they outnumbered the whites, and by the end of November the British and American commissioners had accounted for 2,714 free Negroes who had gone to the one colony, and an additional 286 were cleared for Nova Scotia in November in the absence of the Americans. Of these three thousand free Negro migrants, 1,336 were men, 914 were women, and 750 were children. Carleton's figures did not include the Loyalists' slaves or the few Negroes who left before mid-April.[21]

Most of the Negroes taken into Quebec were slaves, the property of Loyalist owners fleeing the rebel states, and Carleton's registers can tell us nothing of them. There were slaves in virtually all of the Loyalist settlements, however—along the Bay of Quinté, for example, the Harmen Pruynses from New York, Richard Cartwright at Cataraqui, the Everett family, and Major Peter Van Alstine, who helped found Adolphustown, owned perhaps ten or more each, while several other families brought one or two. John Stuart, Episcopal missionary to the Mohawk Indians, took his slaves with him, as did Captain Justus Sherwood, one of the founders of Johnstown. Thomas Fraser at Fraserfield possessed several slaves, and there were a number at Delta in Leeds County, kept on an island in a lake. The pioneers of Camden and Edwardsburgh were slave-owners. Peter Russell, William Jarvis, James and Robert Isaac Dey Gray, Peter Robinson, and others who were to figure prominently in the early political history of Upper Canada all held slaves in substantial numbers.[22] Russell is said to have owned ninety-nine Negroes, which is unlikely, and his friend Matthew Elliott brought between fifty and sixty.[23] The principal chief of the Six Nations, Joseph Brant, who settled on the Grand River, seventy miles northwest of Niagara, also kept slaves at his estate.[24] The family of William Davis, from North Carolina, arrived with a grandfather clock, some peach stones, some car-

pet, and "several faithful slaves." In the Niagara district alone—where the first slave arrived in 1782—an estimate put the slave population (now chiefly Negro, although a few *panis* remained) at nearly three hundred in 1791.[25]

Many slaves were also taken into the relatively rich lands east of Montreal, soon to be known as the Eastern Townships. One carried his master on his back while the family treasure was drawn up-river in boats; others carried precious seeds, books, the family Bible, and their own young children. Crossing over from New York to Missisquoi Bay in 1782, Colonel Philip Luke brought several slaves who helped fell trees, build houses and barns, clear stumps from the fields, and thus make the tiny settlement of St. Armand possible, so that Luke might get on with an ashery and his business as a general merchant. And since Vermont had outlawed slavery in 1777, those who remained there were forced to sell quickly elsewhere, including across the line into Quebec.[26] In 1784 a census of slaves for what was to become Lower Canada showed only 304,[27] but this number was low, and since manumissions were gaining ground and more slaves were being brought in throughout the year, one may assume the presence of a substantially larger number of Negroes.

But by far the greatest number went to Nova Scotia, and there the majority were free men. Thinking themselves Loyalists, many felt entitled to the same benefits that a grateful King gave to his white subjects. Their descendants, and the descendants of the corps of Black Pioneers, were to remind themselves much later that they, too, were of Loyalist strain; and they would be no more eager to cooperate with non-Loyalist Negroes who arrived from other sources and under other compulsions than United Empire Loyalists in Upper Canada were willing to make common cause with the rude Irish immigrants of the 1840s. Legally secure in all rights except for the vote, these free Negroes wished to stand apart from the enslaved.

* * *

On the whole the Negroes' conditions were not as good in New Brunswick as in Nova Scotia, although for a period of time a shortage of labor meant high wages for the free Negroes. In Nova Scotia the colonial governors between 1782 and 1808, Parr and John Wentworth, sympathized with the Negroes' plight, while the ruling oligarchy at Fredericton was less interested. By 1800 Nova Scotia had moved against slavery as an institution by judicial means, when legal opinion in New Brunswick was still poised on indecision. Not surprisingly, when in 1791 they were offered an opportunity to sail for Africa, 222 Negroes from Fredericton, Saint John, and the river valleys responded positively.[28]

Only on Isle St. Jean—which in 1799 became Prince Edward Island—was slavery genuinely benign, and the number of slaves in the colony was very small. The concession granted by France to the Count de St. Pierre in 1719 included the right to hold slaves on the island, but there is no record of any Negroes there until the coming of the Loyalists. The first muster of disbanded officers, soldiers, and Loyalists, in June 1784, showed sixteen Negro servants. Later in the year other Loyalists moved on to Bedeque Bay. Among them was William Schurman, from New York, who purchased eleven thousand acres of land and in time became one of the colony's leading merchants and general traders. Schurman owned two slaves, brought them up in the Presbyterian church, remembered them in his will, and freed one to go to the United States. At Little York, Colonel Joseph Robinson from North Carolina settled with a number of Negro servants, all in

fact slaves; one of them, who lived to be a hundred and five, was treated with special kindness for having rescued the colonel's wife and children from drowning. The Lieutenant-Governor, Edmund Fanning, a former judge of the supreme court of North Carolina, owned two slaves, and to one he gave both liberty and a farm. Other slaves were brought in from Rhode Island and Massachusetts to Summerside, Prince Town, and Charlottetown, the capital. Not more than five or six slaves appear to have been sold, and most seem to have been baptized and permitted formal marriage.[29]

Slavery received its only legal recognition on the island because of these baptisms. Fearing that Christian slaves might consider themselves free, or that white Christians might so construe baptism, the legislature passed an act in 1781 declaring that baptism of slaves would not exempt them from bondage. Although some casuists argued that slavery had no legal foundation in Prince Edward Island, members of the General Assembly recognized that, while it did not derive its foundation from this act, the act recognized that such a foundation existed; and in 1825, admitting that "Slavery is sanctioned and permitted within this Island" although "entirely in variance with the laws of England, and the Freedom of the Country," the Assembly repealed the act, with the clear intention of abolishing slavery. By this time few slaves can have remained in any case, for most of the Negroes now lived in shacks in Charlottetown, where they worked as occasional laborers, chimney sweeps, puntsmen, and market gardeners.[30]

There is no way to know how many of the several thousand Negroes in the Maritime provinces were slaves and how many were free. The tendency to use the terms *servant* and *slave* interchangeably reflected a growing sensitivity to slavery as a moral and economic issue; it also has led to much confusion. Most "servants" were slaves, but some were free Negro children who were bound out by their parents, and some were adults who entered white households as true servants after failure on their farms. While many baptismal records, wills, receipts, and advertisements for auctions, sales, and runaway slaves have survived, far more data would be needed to go beyond an informed guess. Popular and antiquarian literature relating to the Loyalists is filled with ill-judged estimates about the Negro population, and any exact conclusions relating to numbers are suspect. The data do provide a sufficiently diverse record, however, to make possible generalizations relating to the condition of the Negro during the period of British slavery.

White response to the new influx of Negroes at the end of the Revolutionary War changed the uniform and stable pattern of Negro slavery which the British in Quebec had inherited from the French nearly twenty-five years earlier into a variety of legal, economic, and social experiences. No longer were most of the slaves baptized as Roman Catholics, no longer did most work in houses as domestic servants, no longer were they owned chiefly by merchants and government officials, no longer were the majority of Negroes resident in towns and cities, and after 1793 a single code of laws no longer covered their legal position. Since Vermont, Massachusetts, Rhode Island, Pennsylvania, and within certain limits Connecticut, had abolished slavery by 1784, and it was prohibited in the Northwest Territory after 1787,[31] Negro slaves to the north had an additional sieve through which they could move, an extended area where, temporarily at least, they might seek out freedom. The nature of slavery in British North America thus changed in subtle but perceptible ways after 1783.

Perhaps most significant is the fact that the post-1783 Negroes brought a greater variety of useful skills to the frontier communities than the pre-revolutionary slaves ever provided. Several Negroes, slave and free, had trades, especially as millwrights, blacksmiths, sawyers, caulkers, and coopers. Others were printers: as early as 1766 William Brown, the founder of the *Quebec Gazette*, had wanted a Negro slave as his assistant, and ultimately he acquired three. John Neilson, his successor, William Moore, the printer of the *Quebec Herald*, and Fleury Mesplet, who began the first French newspaper in Montreal, kept slaves to help in their printing shops. Tavern-keepers used slaves as house servants, to make butter, and to wait on table. In Halifax domestics dressed in livery as door attendants, delivered notes, carried tiny boxes of charcoal to church or the theatre so that their mistresses' feet might be warm, and looked after the carriage horses. In Saint John, Negroes carved gates and fences, drove carriages, and a free man, Peter Thomson, kept a tavern there in 1797. In Birchtown, several Negroes went to sea.[32] In Upper Canada in 1799 Negroes built roads for the Loyalists, and at least one company had a black foreman. Two Negroes were contractors: Jack Mosee and William Willis undertook to open a road from Yonge Street, York, westward through "the Pinery"; and although at first the senior surveyor of the province found the road too narrow and improperly cleared, in time it was completed satisfactorily.[33] The skills the Loyalists' slaves possessed are best illustrated by those belonging to Sir John Wentworth of Halifax, after 1783 Surveyor-General of the King's Woods in North America. In February 1784, two weeks after having all of his slaves baptized, Wentworth sent nineteen of them to a kinsman in Surinam. One was a master sawyer, another a rough carpenter, a third an axeman, and three more were sawyers. Six women and four children accompanied the group, with two more adults to follow. None were field hands and but one male was a domestic.[34]

Increasingly Negroes apprenticed themselves to their former masters in order to gain training and yet have some guarantee of continued provisions. In areas where slavery was unpopular—around Pictou, in Nova Scotia, or in portions of Upper Canada—a slave might be freed upon agreeing to remain with the former owner as a paid servant. At Thurlow, in Upper Canada, as late as 1824 a mulatto boy was transferred to a new owner upon condition that he would "well instruct and use him" as an apprentice for ten years. In Nova Scotia a number of the Black Pioneers who were unable to scrabble a living from their bleak lands virtually became sharecroppers or tenant farmers for their white Loyalist neighbors.[35]

* * *

On the whole, slaves appear to have been well treated, even though many were not domestics. Their small number eliminated the need for overseers, the brutalizing effects of slave breeding, and controls arising from fears of armed Negro rebellion. In the tiny communities news of mistreatment traveled quickly. Punishments were tempered by the law and by good sense: when a Negro woman hid stolen butter under her hat, her white owner was satisfied to see her writhe with embarrassment as the butter slowly melted down her face in an overheated room. In 1792 William Dummer Powell, as judge of the Court of Common Pleas of Upper Canada, sitting at L'Assomption (now Sandwich), sentenced a Negro to death for burglary; but in 1795, when a Negro boy of seventeen was convicted of the same offense and was sentenced to death by a jury, Powell appealed to the lieutenant-governor to show leniency because of the age of the offender and

the undesirable effects of slavery upon his character. When William Jarvis, provincial secretary of Upper Canada, caught two of his slaves stealing gold and silver from his desk, they were tried in court with the full protection of the law rather than being summarily punished by their owner. One of the earliest murder trials in New Brunswick was of a Negro woman who killed her husband by thrusting a fork into his temple; she, too, was given the full benefit of the law and, when convicted, was branded rather than executed. During the War of 1812 refugee Negroes slaughtered unprotected cattle to sell the meat to the army, and although the death penalty was prescribed for the offense, none were executed. The ultimate sentence was given against one Jack York, convicted of the rape of one Ruth Stufflemine in 1800—and he escaped. In 1791 in Sydney, Cape Breton Island, a white man struck down a Negro who was trying to force his way into a public dance, and the killer was ostracized until, after a full trial, he was acquitted on the ground of self-defense.[36]

Incidents of genuinely harsh treatment were sufficiently uncommon to become focal points for local gossip and legend. Jupiter, a slave belonging to the Russells, was remembered for being trussed up in a storehouse for a day; near Bath, in Upper Canada, a tree to which a slave had been tied and beaten became a local landmark. At Annapolis a slave died from the effects of a whipping. In Windsor, Nova Scotia, a master killed his slave boy with a hammer, and in Truro an owner cut a hole in the lobe of a recaptured slave's ear and, after passing a knotted whiplash through the hole, dragged the slave to death. Neither master appears to have been punished although both were condemned by their communities. Matthew Elliott fixed a lashing ring to a tree in front of his house in Sandwich, apparently for psychological effect since few if any slaves appear to have been flogged upon it. One slave who was punished in this way belonged to William Brown, the printer, who in 1777 paid five shillings to have the public executioner whip his slave boy Joe in Quebec's marketplace.[37]

There is far more positive evidence of humane treatment. The slaves belonging to James Law, a trader at Fort Cumberland after 1761, were so well cared for, the phrase "as proud as Law's niggers" became a local proverb. Peter Russell paid a schoolmaster to teach the son of one of his slaves to read and write, and his account book shows that he provided well for his slaves; even to the notorious Peggy he gave an allowance of four shillings a week and paid her jail fees more than once.[38] Robert I. Dey Gray, Solicitor-General of Upper Canada, bought the freedom of the mulatto mother of one of his slaves in Albany for fifty dollars and brought her to live with his family; in his will he freed his woman servant and her children and left a trust fund of £1,200 for her, while giving two hundred acres of land and £50 to her two sons. Isaac Bennett, in his will of 1803, provided that his two slave boys should be educated and set free. Frederick Devoue of Annapolis left his slave one hundred acres of land. The owner of the *St. John's Royal Gazette* in Newfoundland, by his will, gave his slave her freedom and provided that her children would become free at twenty-one. The slaves of Henry Denny Denson were attended by the family doctor and received gifts at Christmas. In 1790 Joseph Fairbanks of Halifax left his Negro domestic five pounds annually for life, and Edward Barron of Cumberland County, Nova Scotia, awarded two cows, six ewes, and freedom to his slave. Joshua F. de St. Croix of

Granville bound his sons to pay his servant £10 yearly for life, while Stephen Reed of Amherst required his heirs to care for all of his slaves, freed by his will. When Henry Lewis, a slave belonging to William Jarvis, wrote to his master that he wished to purchase his freedom, he added that he had lived as well in Jarvis's house as a man could wish; Jarvis agreed to the sale.[39] In 1793 Peter Thomson, then a slave belonging to Charles McPherson of Saint John, purchased his freedom for £30, and when he died in debt from his tavern five years later, McPherson was one of two guarantors for those debts.[40] There are only two records of husband and wife being separated for sale, and but one instance of a young child being sold apart from his parents.

* * *

NOTE ON CURRENCY

Sale prices were stated in livres, Quebec pounds, Halifax pounds, Halifax dollars, American dollars, Spanish dollars, and pounds sterling. The livre preceded the franc as a French unit; six livres equalled a crown. General James Murray estimated in 1762 that a livre was worth two shillings (Shortt and Doughty, eds., *Constitutional History of Canada, 1*, 47–81), but William Renwick Riddell convincingly contests this in "Slave in Nouvelle-France," page 318, note 5, and calculates the livre at 13 1/3 pence. Two hundred Spanish dollars equalled £50 Quebec money, and both Quebec and Halifax pounds were about nine-tenths the value of pounds sterling (Riddell, p. 324, n. 19). My calculations are based on some fifty sales, all values converted to pounds sterling.

NOTES

1 Adam Shortt and Arthur G. Doughty. eds., *Documents relating to the Constitutional History of Canada, 1759–1791*, 2nd ed. (Ottawa, 1918), *1*, 22.

2 Jacques Viger, *Ma Saberdache*, M, I, and quoted in Ernest J. Lajeunesse, ed., *The Windsor Border Region, Canada's Southernmost Frontier: A Collection of Documents* (Toronto, 1960), pp. 88, 275.

3 Public Archives of Canada (hereafter PAC), Misc. Docs., *21*, no. 47: article 2, July 18, 1764.

4 Lajeunesse, *Windsor Border Region*, pp. lxvii–lxviii. Detroit Public Library, Burton Historical Collection: typescript history, "Negroes in Detroit," discusses early slave sales; see also Frederick C. Hamil, "Sally Ainse, Fur Trader,"The Algonquin Club, *Historical Bulletin, 3* (1939), 6. The Census for 1750, which shows thirty-three slaves, may be found in PAC, G 1, *461*, 28. The number of slaves in Detroit rose to 179 by 1782.

5 *Statutes at Large, Nova Scotia* (Halifax, 1805), p. 77; Public Archives of Nova Scotia (hereafter PANS), Unpassed Bills: "An Act for the Regulation of Relief of the Free Negroes within the Province of Nova Scotia."

6 The famous words credited to Mansfield, "The air of England has long been too pure for a slave and every man is free who breathes it," do not appear even in Capel Lofft's reports on the Court of King's Bench. The quotation is, in fact, from John Lord Campbell, *The Lives of the Chief Justices of England* (London, 1849), *2*, 418.

7 PAC, Misc. Docs., *16*, pt. 2: act of Aug. 1, 1790.

8 PAC, James Murray Papers, Letter Books, *2*, 15–16: to John Watts, Nov. 2, 1763.

9 In 1686 one of the settlers at Cape Sable was La Liberté, "le neigre," possibly an escaped slave from the English colonies, and as we have seen, there may have been a slave at Port Royal as early as 1606. Louisbourg's Governor Isaac, Louis Forant owned a Martinique man in 1739–40. See PANS, *2*, "French Documents relating to Acadia," vol. 1, no. 28; and Archibald M. MacMechan, *A Calendar of Two Letter-Books and One Commission-Book in the Possession of the Government of Nova Scotia, 1713–1741*, Nova Scotia Archives, publication no. 2 (Halifax, 1900), pp. 100, 102, 104–05.

10 LC, America, British Colonies, MSS: "Military Affairs at Louisburg in New England 1747," a pay and general record book.

11 PANS, *32*, Nov. 28, 1750; *Report, Board of Trustees of the Public Archives of Nova Scotia … 1941* (Halifax, 1942), pp. 23–43; Lorenzo Johnston Greene, *The Negro in Colonial New England, 1620–1776* (New York, 1942), p. 83.

12 *Halifax Royal Gazette*, May 15, 1752.

13 Quoted in T. Watson Smith, "The Slave in Canada," *Collections of the Nova Scotia Historical Society for the Years 1896–98, 10* (1899), 7.

14 *Saint John Telegraph*, May 27, 1884; Norman L. Nicholson, "Rural Settlement and Land Use in the New Glasgow Region," *Geographical Bulletin*, no. 7 (1955), p. 45; James F. More, *The History of Queens County, N.S.* (Halifax, 1873), pp. 125–26; John V. Duncanson, *Falmouth—A New England Township in Nova Scotia, 1760–1965* (Windsor, Ont., 1965), p. 32.

15 *Halifax Royal Gazette*, Nov. 1, 1760; Smith, "Slave in Canada," p. 10; Riddell, "Slave in Canada," pp. 298–99.

16 BM, Additional Manuscripts (hereafter Add. MSS), 15,485: "Exports and Imports of North America, 1768–9," pp. 28, 32; Daniel Woodley Prowse, *A History of Newfoundland, from the English, Colonial, and Foreign Records* (London, 1895), pp. 345–47, 416–18.

17 Ballston appears as Ball's Town and Bolston in several references. Neilson ("Slavery in Old Canada," p. 38) and Viger and Lafontaine, "L'esclavage" (p. 22), give Monroe as Munro; and they may be correct, although the oath of Randel Huet, in the Porteous Papers, McCord Museum, McGill University, March 9, 1761, uses Monroe. There are other variations in spelling place-names; either those most commonly accepted by contemporaries, or those now used for purposes of identification, are employed throughout this book.

18 WO61, Jeffery Amherst Papers: Thomas Hancock to Amherst, Sept. 8, Dec. 21, 1761; CO5/66, 447, and CO323/23, 79: Court of Enquiry, March 11, 1786; Brome County Historical Society, Knowlton, P.Q.: Eastern Townships Papers, Feb. 16, 1779; PAC, Misc. Docs., *16*, pt. 2: deposition, John Mittelburger vs. Patrick Langan, June 10, 1787, and statement by Monroe-Munro, July 16, 1788; PAC, Internal Correspondence, Quebec, 1788: "Grievances of the Loyalists of Sorel, Cataracoui, etc.," pp. 66, 74.

19 BM, Add. MSS 21,763, fol. 369: "Return of Negroes, brought into Canada by Scouts and sold at Montreal," n.d.

20 The British contentions are set out in the BM, Chatham MSS: bundle 343, pp. 71–72, a report endorsed September, 1819, but prepared in 1794. The British continued to insist that compensation could be paid only for "such Negroes as were not emancipated by Proclamation in the course of the War, *if any such instances can be assigned*," leaving the burden of proof to the former owners. The American version of the May meeting appears in LC, George Washington Papers, *220*, no. 71, May 6. Lord North's approval of Carleton's decision is in the PRO, Headquarters Papers of the British Army in America (commonly, Carleton Papers), *51*, North to Carleton, Aug. 8, 1783. The confusion over transporting the Negroes is discussed in Benjamin Quarles, *The Negro in the American Revolution* (Chapel Hill, N.C., 1961), pp. 163–77.

21 Carleton Papers, *46:* Alexander Leslie to Carleton, Aug. 10, and return of Loyalists at Charleston, Aug. 13, 1782; *57:* return of refugees arrived at East Florida, Dec. 23, 1782; *64:* Frederick Mackenzie to Brook Watson, March 4, 1783; *66:*

memorial, Charles Ogilvie et al. to Carleton, April 8; *77:* Henry Knipschild to Carleton, Aug. 13; *78:* Robert Morse to H. E. Fox, Aug. 23; *79:* Fox to Carleton, Aug. 26; and reply, *81,* Sept. 15; *83:* James Peters to Carleton, Oct. 5; *92:* petitioners of Norfolk and Princess Anne counties, Va., April 28, all 1783; and 55: Book of Negroes, pp. 90–104. On occasion the Carleton Papers are cited as "Royal Institute Papers," "Williamsburg Papers," or "Dorchester Papers." A copy of the Book of Negroes is in the PANS, but it contains minor errors; PAC holds a more accurate copy (American MSS, *12,* Sundry Letters). American versions of several of the returns are in the NA, Papers of the Continental Congress and Washington Papers.

22 PAC, MS Group 10, E II-1–8: list of inhabitants of Edwardsburgh (showing fifteen slaves), and Record Group 19, C35, *1,* Misc. Records: victualing lists for Ernestown and Adolphustown, provision list for Lake Township, and return of families, Cataraqui; Horace Hume van Wart, "The Loyalist Settlement of Adolphustown," *The Loyalist Gazette, 2* (1932), 2; Thomas W. Casey, "Early Slavery in Midland District," Lennox and Addington Historical Society, *Papers and Records, 4* (1912), 12–17; Thaddeus W. H. Leavitt, *History of Leeds and Grenville, Ontario, from 1749 to 1879 …* (Brockville, Ont., 1879), pp. 20–21; Mrs. W. T. Hallam, *Slave Days in Canada* [Toronto, 1919, pp. 3–4; Gerald E. Boyce, *Historic Hastings* (Belleville, Ont., 1967), pp. 34–35; Roy F. Fleming, "Negro Slaves with the United Empire Loyalists in Upper Canada," *Ontario History, 45* (1953), 27–29; William Renwick Riddell, "An Official Record of Slavery in Upper Canada," OHS, *Papers and Records, 25* (1929), 393–97.

23 A search for Russell's will in the Surrogate Office of the County of York and at Osgoode Hall, Toronto, proved fruitless. Riddell, "Slave in Canada," credits Elliott with "more than 50 slaves" on p. 326, n. 17, and on p. 333 with "some sixty."

24 One of Brant's visitors in 1797 reported much later having seen many slaves who had been taken prisoner during the war: Jeromus Johnson to William L. Stone, Dec. 1, 1837, in Stone, *Life of Joseph Brant-Thayendanegna: Including the Border Wars of the American Revolution …* (New York, 1838), *2,* xliv. One slave, Sophia Pooley, was alive in Galt in 1854. In 1801 Russell planned to sell a slave to Brant, but there is no record of whether he did or not: OPA, Russell Papers, Elliott to Russell, Oct. 8, 1801, Jan. 2, 1802, and reply to first, Oct. 31, 1801.

25 Smith, "Slave in Canada," p. 40; Richard D. Merritt, "The Davis Family of Mount Albion: A Loyalist Sketch," Head-of-the-Lake Historical Society, *Wentworth Bygones, 7* (1967), 33–38.

26 NBM, William O. Raymond Scrapbooks, F29, p. 112; "Nigger Rock—St. Armand," Missisquoi County Historical Society, *Fourth Report* (1908–09); "St. Armand Negro Burying Ground," Brome County Historical Society roneod paper (1959), pp. 1–2; text of talk, "Negro Burying Ground at St. Armand," loaned by Marion L. Phelps, Cowansville, Que.; and Archives du Palais de Justice de Montréal: William Ward, sale to P. W. Campbell, April 26, 1785.

27 *Report on Canadian Archives, 1889* (Ottawa, 1890), p. 39.

28 *Fredericton New Brunswick Royal Gazette,* July 10, 1816; *Halifax Royal Gazette,* Sept. 7, 1790, March 18, April 1, 8, 15, 1802; NBM, Scrap Book Cb.: "Negroes—In the Maritimes"; New Brunswick Legislative Library, Fredericton: file of clippings from *Saint John Telegraph Journal,* 1937, no. 86; W. Stewart MacNutt, *New Brunswick, A History: 1784–1867* (Toronto, 1963), pp. 82–84.

29 Ada Macleod, "Some Loyalists of Prince Edward Island," *Dalhousie Review, 10* (1930), 320; Smith, "Slave in Canada," 68–71, quoting bills of sale; Hallam, "Slavery," p. 7. The memorandum book referred to in Smith (p. 70) and the *Charlottetown Weekly Examiner* (Feb. 11, 1881) cannot be found in the Prince Edward Island Archives or in the Charlottetown Public Library.

30 *The Acts of the General Assembly of Prince Edward Island … 1773 … 1834* (Charlottetown, 1834), pp. 76, 372; Alexander Bannerman Warburton, *A History of Prince Edward Island* (Saint John, 1923), pp. 197, 368; William Renwick Riddell, "The Baptism of Slaves in Prince Edward Island," *JNH, 6* (1921), 307–09.

31 See William Renwick Riddell, "Additional Notes on Slavery," *JNH, 17* (1932), 368–73, and Arthur Zilversmit, *The First Emancipation: The Abolition of Slavery in the North* (Chicago, 1967).

32 Dr. Bray's Associates Minute Books, *3:* Nov. 1, 1802; NBM, Thomson Family Papers: license to Peter Thomson, Oct. 1, 1797; *Halifax Acadian Recorder,* Jan. 25, 1919; Trudel, *L'esclavage,* pp. 107, 148, 320; Neilson, "Slavery in Old Canada," pp. 31–34. See also Francis Cleary, "Notes on the Early History of the County of Essex," and A. Philippe E. Panet, "The Labadie Family in the County of Essex, Ont.," Essex Hist. Soc., *Papers and Addresses, 1* (1913), 13 and 49, respectively.

33 OPA, Crown Land Papers, General Correspondence: agreement between Mosee, Willis, and Thomas Ridout, Feb. 2, 1799, and between Parker Mills and David William Smith, Surveyor-General, Jan. 13, 1799, and Reports, *3, 5;* Ontario Department of Lands and Forests, History Branch, Survey Records, Letters Received: W. Chewett, Senior Surveyor, to Smith, Feb. 11, June 22, 1799, pp. 396, 621.

34 PANS, *49,* 25–27.

35 See, for example, Lennox and Addington Historical Society Archives, Napanee, Ont.: assignment of mulatto Tom from Eli Keeler to William Bell, pp. 11, 654–58; "Copies of Original Documents from the Collection of the Society," Lennox and Addington Historical Society, *Papers and Records, 2* (1910), 41–42; *Fredericton Royal Gazette,* Feb. 28, 1786; George MacLaren, *The Pictou Book* (New Glasgow, N.S., 1954), p. 22.

36 PAC, William Dummer Powell Papers, *1,* 606–08: Powell to Simcoe, n.d., 1795; PAC, Misc. Docs., *16,* pt. 2: Court of Common Pleas, March 18, 1788, July 19, 1793, Dec. 18, 1799, Sept. 22, 1800; NBM, Scrap Book, Cb. "Slavery," 1784, 1801; William Renwick Riddell, *La Rochefoucault-Liancourt's Travels*

in Canada, whole no., *Thirteenth Report of the Bureau of Archives for the Province of Ontario, 1916* (Toronto, 1917), p. 154.

37 *Fredericton Gleaner,* June 1, 1926; *Windsor Daily Star,* July 30, 1948; Smith, "Slave in Canada," pp. 34, 48, 76–77; Riddell, "Slave in Canada," pp. 334–35; Neilson, "Slavery in Old Canada," p. 33; Jesse Edgar Middleton and Fred Landon, *The Province of Ontario—A History* (Toronto, 1927), *1,* 101; James Edmund Jones, *Pioneer Crimes and Punishments in Toronto and the Home District* (Toronto, 1924), pp. 11–12; Henry Scadding, *Toronto of Old: Collections and Recollections* (Toronto, 1878), p. 292; Silas Farmer, *The History of Detroit and Michigan or the Metropolis Illustrated* ... (Detroit, 1884), p. 345.

38 Russell Papers: account book, Sept. 4, 11, Oct. 16, 17, Nov. 2, 19, Dec. 17, 1803, Jan. 20, Feb. 26, July 10, Nov. 6, 14, 21, 1804; Russell to Elliott, Sept. 19, 1801, and replies, Oct. 7, 1801, Jan. 2, 1802.

39 Ibid.: Russell to William Cooper, April 28, 1799; TPL: bill from Cooper to Russell, Oct. 28, 1799; Elizabeth Russell Diary, Jan. 6, 1808; TPL, William Jarvis Papers, Misc., B55: Lewis to Jarvis, May 3, 1798; PANS, F. W. Harris, "The Negro Population of the County of Annapolis," unpubl. paper (1920), pp. 7–10; J. F. Pringle, *Lunenburgh or the Old Eastern District* ... (Cornwall, Ont., 1890), pp. 318–25; Smith, "Slave in Canada," pp. 16, 48–49, 64, 66–67, 84–85, 88–89; Neilson, "Slavery in Old Canada," p. 35; Riddell, "Slave in Canada," pp. 322–33, n. 13; Duncanson, *Falmouth,* p. 33; Margaret Janet Hart, *Janet Fisher Archibald* ... (Victoria, B.C., 1934), pp. 79–82; Joseph R. Smallwood, ed., *The Book of Newfoundland* (St. John, 1937), *2,* 235–36.

40 Thomson Family Papers: certificate, March 27, 1793, and warrant, June 10, 1820.

CHAPTER 3

AMERICANS IN UPPER CANADA, 1791–1812:
"LATE LOYALISTS" OR EARLY IMMIGRANTS?

PETER MARSHALL

Historians of the first years of Upper Canada frequently, if briefly, allude to "late Loyalists" but seem reluctant to define the term.[1] Clearly, it represents a mark of distinction from an earlier or original wave of arrivals, but the dividing line is not clear. It is tempting to ignore the question and apply the assertion of James J. Talman in his introduction to *Loyalist Narratives from Upper Canada*, in which, after setting out changes in the official definition of loyalism, he adds, "The subject is further confused by the use of the absurd term 'late Loyalist,' when undoubtedly 'post-Loyalist immigrant' or 'settler' is meant. If a man was 'late' he was not a Loyalist."[2] The unfortunate fact is that this judgment, delivered in 1946, has never before or since gained general acceptance. Historians have found it nearly impossible to make a clear-cut distinction between Loyalist and immigrant, perhaps owing to decades of legal and political argument over its applicability. To this day, the "late Loyalists" can be wished, but not declared, out of existence.[3]

Such is the case despite inroads made in recent years by scholars highly skilled—if that does not sound too ungracious—in scientific guess-work. Facts, figures, and phases relating to the population growth of Upper Canada are neither substantial in quantity nor consistent in detail, but the calculations of J. David Wood and Douglas McCalla appear reconcilable. Wood posits an American influx between 1780 and 1812 that can "be legitimately separated into Loyalists, 1780 to 1787 (by which time approximately 10,000 settlers had entered Upper Canada) and the so-called Late Loyalists"—referring to those who arrived between 1788 and 1812. During this period, the 1787 population had doubled by 1794 and would reach nearly 32,000 by 1800. In the years before the war, the growth rate diminished.[4] McCalla, compiling totals for "Loyalists, 'late-loyalists,' and ordinary pioneers," notes the arrival during 1784 and 1785 of some six thousand Loyalists of European background, and a population that more than doubles by 1791 and increases fourfold between 1785 and 1796. By 1805, it is "probably over 45,000," representing an average annual growth rate of more than 10 per cent, or four times what could be expected by natural increase. By 1811, the population numbered about sixty thousand inhabitants, of whom "a large majority (which included some whose original birthplace was in Britain or Europe) came from the United States."[5]

No attempt to distinguish between the numbers of Loyalists and those who, however described, arrived later from the south has yet been undertaken. As J. K. Johnson stresses in his analysis of the Upper Canadian House of Assembly, "the important distinction has been taken to be not where someone was born, nor even necessarily when, but when, and for what motive, that person came to Upper Canada. The essential point has been to distinguish between those who belong to a Loyalist group and others who belong to a Post-Loyalist American group."[6]

Since land acquisition and ownership depended on national status, which, in turn, determined political rights, recognition of Americans as Loyalists was a matter of major concern. Can the numbers involved be estimated? If it is assumed, arbitrarily, that "late Loyalist" applies to those who arrived between 1791 and 1800, and if we apply McCalla's estimate of an excess population increase over natural growth, it would appear that the population increase of twenty thousand in that decade was fuelled by the arrival of some seventeen thousand immigrants. Their origins were diverse. Some came from elsewhere in British North America, not all from outside the British Empire, and certainly not all from the United States. If the term "Late Loyalist" is applied to some fifteen thousand of these newcomers, an inexact but not wildly improbable total can be posited.

Numbers, however, constitute a relatively simple aspect of a larger, more complex problem. The emergence of the United States disrupted an empire with little experience in defining the means by which its subjects were added or lost. No concept of a nation-state to which inhabitants pledged allegiance yet applied when loyalty was a birthright, when the ownership of property was restricted to those thus qualified, and when only entry into office required the taking of the Oaths of Allegiance, Supremacy, and Abjuration. While it is essential to bear in mind Dr. A. F. Madden's observation that "uniformity was not confused with imperial unity after the 1770s. That was the lesson of American independence,"[7] it remains equally important to remember that lessons are often long in the learning. In Upper Canadian society, the principal problem was not reconciling diversity but accepting past claims.

After coming into being in 1791, Upper Canada had an essential need for population for settlement, quite apart from the creation of a new government. After 1783, peace brought the separation of a population. If those content to inhabit the United States were to be declared Americans, what were those unwilling to accept that allegiance to be called? What case would have to be made for them? How rapid a decision was required? In Canada, put to Haldimand and to Dorchester, these questions failed to obtain answers. Members of Loyalist regiments evacuated at the end of the war did not present a problem, but of many others it had to be asked, How late did you leave? How loyal had you been? The majority could claim to be natural-born British subjects and appeal to the Common Law ruling that nationality could not be shed or lost by the action either of the subject or of the Crown. But after the signing of the Treaty of Paris in September 1783, this would no longer hold good. Henceforth, in law, Americans were aliens and accordingly not entitled to own British land.[8] How would this affect their entry into Upper Canada?

Legally, imperial statute was the only recourse, providing one certain, if restricted, qualification for admission with full rights, and another, arguable. An Act of 1740 allowed the naturalization of aliens provided that they took the oath of allegiance and completed seven years residence. But it could not have foreseen the situation of the pre-1783 American-born. In any case, land acquired by aliens before those conditions were met did not convey a valid title.[9] The second line of approach, derived from the Acts of 1731 and 1773, appeared more promising though it had not specifically come into being in anticipation of a North American problem. During the eighteenth century, British subjects living abroad, increasingly alarmed at their children's and grandchildren's potential loss of nationality, had secured legislation to prevent such a possibility. Could the same not apply to descendants of native-born subjects who had not left the United States by 1783? It was a question worth asking, but which would remain unanswered until 1824.[10]

This confusion may have resulted from unprecedented circumstances, but it was protracted by the need to populate the colony. The dilemma facing its government was so clear that any official response called for obscurity: how else could a society founded on a rejection of American government admit that its growth demanded the attracting of American immigrants, the only available and compatible source of capital, skills, and labour? If Upper Canada were to be settled, possessing a plough and knowing how to use it was altogether more desirable than was any proof of origins or of loyal activities during the Revolution. Such considerations accounted for the otherwise surprising view of the Tory Americanophobe John Graves Simcoe, the first Lieutenant Governor of Upper Canada.

Simcoe may not have led the way in encouraging recognition of late Loyalists, but he was the first to reward a migration that others had noted but could not direct. By 1788, Lillian Gates has concluded, Dorchester had been forced to prefer an increase in numbers to purity in politics: "In the end, the policy adopted seems to have been to grant land to all whom the term loyalist could be stretched to cover and to encourage the 'speedy settlement of the upper country with profitable subjects.'"[11]

On his arrival in 1792, Simcoe's "enthusiasms"—to borrow S. R. Mealing's term—distinguished him from his contemporaries and colleagues. He had assumed office determined to demonstrate that the British Empire in North America was not collapsing but would, given time and his leadership, outgrow a republican neighbour whose unwarranted aggression deserved humiliation. Mealing's most instructive essay appeared in 1958 and opened with the comment that it had been thirty-odd years since Canadians had written Simcoe's biography. Forty years later, unfortunately, the task still remains undone. Imperial Britain foisted on the world a superfluity of tedious representatives, many of whom later secured the biographers they deserved. Simcoe was not among them: his energies and personality commanded attention, though his judgments were far less assured. If he is seen only as English, it was in a fashion formed entirely in North America. Wartime service had left him with indelible memories, a grudging respect for individual Americans, and a loathing of the new nation's politics. When the Duc de La Rochefoucauld-Liancourt called at Simcoe's Niagara residence in 1795, a dinner led to an invitation to stay and extended conversations that markedly impressed a visitor to whom his qualities, both as a governor and personally, were evident: he was "actif, éclairé, juste, bon, ouvert...." But La Rochefoucauld's praise was not unbounded. Simcoe hated the United States and was still obsessed with the war's failure. His guest experienced real discomfort as Simcoe, incapable of forgetting or forgiving, boasted of the number of houses he had burned before and would burn again if war resumed. Not that he wanted this to happen, of course.

He, more than anyone, desired peace. It was just that he so hated the rebels....[12]

How did Simcoe envisage a *British* North America? By demonstrating an uncritically favourable disposition to its potential growth while remaining hostile to the land of his enemies. Outward appearances—those observed by La Rochefoucauld—were deceptive: Simcoe was something more than he seemed. As Mealing has put it, "If his Constitutional models for Upper Canada were avowedly British, his models of economic progress were basically American."[13] And, given an American working model, who better to operate it than American settlers? The only other labour force to hand was that of French Canada and, given that option, Americans were a seemingly unavoidable, but still worthwhile, risk. Nineteenth-century solutions had yet to be devised: slaves were inappropriate and too expensive, contract labour remained unknown. The days of Indians and Chinese supplied to order, destinations as required, were decades away. Simcoe really had no choice: if immigrants were required, he could have Americans—or nothing.

This held good for both Upper and Lower Canada. Identical proclamations, issued on 7 February 1792, stated the terms on which land would be made available. Grants were offered without distinction of nationality, and details were circulated through New England and the northern states. How could this be reconciled with an unrelenting mistrust of American intentions?

First, the enemy were reduced in number: this allowed them to be declared an unrepresentative group. The United States was seen to be filled with unwilling citizens desperate to escape a republican captivity and yearning for a return to old ways which, once regained, would never again be cast off. These assertions departed from reality but provided Simcoe with a necessary justification. In October 1792, he assumed responsibility, assisted by the new Council and seven land boards, for granting land certificates to incoming settlers who, taking an oath of allegiance, were advised that "tho' His Majesty's bounty is not restricted solely to his own subjects, yet it is not meant to be extended to such as have willfully resisted his Crown and Government, and who persist in principles and opinions which are hostile to the British Constitution."

How these subversive immigrants would be detected, and by whom, was not indicated. As it was, an opportunity dawned for those willing to follow, modestly, in the path of Henri IV: if Paris was worth a mass, 200 Upper Canadian acres justified an oath, "mumbled through or avoided altogether, if the settler so desired. For most immigrants it was a trivial formality that was performed in order to acquire property." Simcoe persuaded himself that, once started, population growth would come from elsewhere than the United States: he looked for sizeable arrivals from Europe, as well as many Loyalists who would seek refuge from the unbearable climate of New Brunswick.[14]

Simcoe's hopes of achieving increased numbers were partially fulfilled, though his conviction that communal unity would arise out of a mixture of newcomers proved quite unfounded. He had thought it possible to avoid too close an inquiry into the motives for American arrivals since, as Bruce G. Wilson has observed, he "believed in the centralization of political authority and in the vital role of the military in colonial government."[15] In fact, neither factor proved able to control the pattern of Upper Canadian development, a process that demanded practical deviations from conventional constitutional and legal provisions if *any* rapid and necessary growth was to be achieved.

Simcoe's grandiose ambitions, such as his vision of a Montreal that, "with the assistance of a few sluices," might dominate a waterway extending from Hudson Bay to the Gulf of Mexico, were accompanied by more modest aims: Upper Canada would control communications and commerce between the Eastern seaboard and Middle America and so link power and profit. However these prospects might be judged, their pronouncement served to distinguish the early years of Upper Canada from those of other fledgling colonies: gazing back anxiously at a mother-country from which all assistance must come, did not characterize Simcoe's outlook.

Accordingly, from these beginnings until 1812, Upper Canada remained an American community pursuing American ends. If its political structures were largely traditional, they marked an inheritance from the thirteen colonies, not the introduction of a new, imperial imposition. Partition had not transformed British North American institutions.

An estimate in 1812 of the Upper Canadian population's origins declared eight out of ten to be of American birth or descent. That this group comprised a numerical majority seems impossible to deny.[16] It is equally clear that Americans did not exercise any political influence proportionate to their numbers, though that growth served to arouse alarm. Whereas admitting new settlers to politics attracted little concern in the early 1790s, by 1795, the American presence supplied grounds for the House of Assembly to require that all non-British settlers reside seven years in the province before becoming eligible for election. Four years later, additional precautions appeared necessary after the defeat of Attorney-General Peter Russell in a by-election, allegedly by American votes. In consequence, the Assembly determined in 1800 that not only its members but also any electors who had ever lived in or sworn allegiance to the United States must have

lived in Upper Canada for seven years. The aftermath of the Revolution continued to shape the government of the province.[17]

To present the major Upper Canadian problem as a conflict between established Loyalists and an encroaching majority American population would both unduly simplify and distort the events of these early years. Certainly, constant care was taken to prevent a Loyalist loss of control: as J. K. Johnson's analysis of the Assembly Members concludes, "Post Loyalist Americans ... were largely excluded from anything more than the most basic, non-paying public offices."[18] But political power did not provide an economic living. That was seen to depend upon the securing and disposing of land. Yet legal title was not compatible with alien status. Confronted with this dilemma, as Garner concludes, "the economic self-interest of the old settlers had assuaged their misgivings as to the loyalty of the Americans."[19]

These conditions posed problems that proved as weighty for Loyalist proprietors as for recent immigrants. Fashioning a solution that would satisfy both sets of interests was not easily achieved. Development and settlement depended upon an effective use and transfer of land, but the entwined implications of legal title, alien status, and naturalization rendered the process uncertain. To remedy this situation, Loyalist recognition was bestowed long after its official September 1783 termination. This prolongation could enlist the flimsiest of excuses: as late as 1817, William Dickson, legislative councillor and owner of a Grand River township, disposed of his lands after administering, in his capacity as magistrate, the Oath of Allegiance to Americans.[20] This evaded rather than resolved an enduring legal problem. Widespread though the practice may have been, newcomers did not receive an assured property title: it was a situation that would persist and await challenge.

Before the War of 1812, Loyalists had kept a vigilant eye on the politics of American immigrants, "many of whom" were, in the July 1800 opinion of Solicitor-General Gray, "not altogether destitute of the democratical principles which prevail in that country nor is it always known whether their motives for coming into the Province are good or bad." The frequent expression of official fears of American intentions was echoed by similar alarm-raisings: shortly after his arrival, Lieutenant Governor Gore reported in 1806 that although some emigrants from the United States had "proved peaceable and Industrious settlers … there are a considerable number from that Country of a different description, who have come here adventurers, and have brought the very worst principles of their own Constitution along with them, and from what I have experienced even during my very short residence here, endeavour to oppose and perplex His Majesty's Government." Such feelings were not extinguished by the outbreak of war. It not only ensured that the residential qualification continued, but raised it to fourteen years for admission both to the House and to the franchise. It would not revert to the seven years' requirement until 1818.[21]

The significance of the War of 1812 in defining Upper Canadian allegiance seems exaggerated: the colony was not so much divided between Loyalists and Americans as trying to cope with the military demands of both sides. George Sheppard makes a convincing case in support of his assertions that "at the best of times Upper Canadians had shown themselves to be unwilling participants" and that "Upper Canadians had no strong attachment to either the United States or Great Britain."[22] It was not that the conflict remained unimportant, but rather that Upper Canadians, irrespective of their origins and attachments, were not impelled

to proclaim an allegiance to either an Imperial or an American identity. Their interests were, quite literally, far more down to earth. If Loyalists laid claim to pre-eminence in holding land, such possession was pointless in the absence of settlers. Before 1812, only the United States could furnish a supply, welcome for farming skills, essential for capital resources, and compelling Loyalists to balance economic necessity against political prejudice. If the newcomers were more concerned with the cultivation of land than the promulgation of republican doctrine—and so the great majority proved to be—then an accommodation could be reached. That this did not continue indefinitely owed not to the course or consequences of war, but to changes in the structure and composition of the colony.

After 1815, a non-American minority set to work to convert Upper Canada into a British society to be governed by truly British leaders. In 1821, the victory in a by-election of Barnabas Bidwell, who had left Massachusetts, having played a prominent part in state politics after the Revolution, provided the opportunity for resolving the American issue. Government determined to exclude Bidwell—and subsequently his son—from the political scene: the Bidwells occupied centre stage in a major confrontation, dubbed the Alien Question, that might more accurately have been entitled the American Question.

Paul Romney's excellent analysis offers an essential account of a political struggle that masqueraded as a matter of law.[23] Almost forty years after the partition of North America, it became apparent that the territorial separation, crudely undertaken as it was, had received altogether more attention than had the need to distinguish between American citizens and British subjects. What was the new order? Was residence in the United States before 1783, or subsequent birth there to British-born parents, grounds to claim to be British after a seven-year residence in Canada? If this was not so, those who found themselves in such a situation could not buy or inherit lands, vote, or sit in the Assembly. Examining these questions, Romney finds that historians have "unanimously assumed that the provincial government was correct in its view that the mass of late Loyalists were aliens."[24] Any sense of relief that one point at issue is resolved proves unfounded: this conclusion is held to proceed from excessive reliance on government documents and must be declared erroneous.

In the event, legal status was subordinated to political considerations: the decision could not be left to the courts. Its resolution would require the major step of proclaiming the Britishness of Upper Canada. If Americans were prepared to accept incorporation, ways might be found to bring this about. But if this were done, Late Loyalists would have to become precisely that, in an Upper Canadian colony of British subjects, in which true Loyalists would occupy an honoured place and the rest of the population, pending their legal acceptance, would be classified as alien. Unfortunately, so clear-cut a distinction proved impossible to maintain, even by so vigorous a proponent as John Beverley Robinson, the Attorney General: "Forced to admit that the late Loyalists possessed an equitable claim to political as well as to property rights, Robinson conceded this was so only as a political matter, a subject for legislation not a judicial right. He continued to pronounce them to be aliens, who might be admitted into the Upper Canadian community as an act of grace but could claim no right to membership."[25] As is so often the case, the law, in the absence of imperial statutes, took its stand until the outright incompatibility of contemporary conditions and legal precedents became untenable.

Many years had to pass before the "late Loyalists" were to fade from view. The terms of the Treaty of Paris waited three decades for an examination of their relevance to American rights in Upper Canada and a further ten years elapsed before the legal process was concluded. That a topic as basic as the distinction to be drawn between birthright and admitted subjects, and that the role and rights of yet another category—the Alien—should be so long undetermined, reflects not so much provincial or imperial tardiness and indifference as a situation that, for all involved, was unprecedented.

Before 1783, no body of British subjects had successfully renounced their allegiance; no means of assessing the professions of those claiming to maintain their loyalty existed. Both the emergence of the United States and the formation of British North America after 1783 involved major changes that nevertheless fell far short of revolutionary upheaval. The partition of North America brought death, suffering, and displacement in full measure but was not accompanied by the instant creation of states defined to the last national symbol. The "Americans" of Upper Canada were fortunate in their time of arrival: they did not have to follow the Texan example and experience an Alamo at Niagara. Their loyalty was limited to land and, for the great majority, expressed, in benefit or failure, a far more tangible touchstone of allegiance than would have been displayed in the mere assertion of national bonds.

If Upper Canadians eschewed patriotic commitments during the War of 1812, so too did the Americans in their midst. Who can doubt that it was the best thing to do? The relatively short casualty lists testify to the fledgling nationalisms of two peoples whose connections and similarities were still far more substantial than their rivalries.

Notes

1 For example:"Many of the loyalists … had looked with dis-favour on grants of land being made to 'late' loyalists," Lillian F. Gates, *Land Policies of Upper Canada* (Toronto: University of Toronto Press, 1968), 154; "One visitor noted that more recent arrivals, the so-called Late Loyalists," … George Sheppard, *Plunder, Profit, and Paroles* (Montreal and Kingston: McGill-Queen's University Press, 1994), 19–20.

2 James J. Talman, ed., *Loyalist Narratives from Upper Canada* (Toronto: Champlain Society, 1946), xxix–xxx.

3 Useful comment on this point is to be found in David T. Moorman, "Where are the English and the Americans in the Historiography of Upper Canada?" *Ontario History* 88 (1996): 65–49.

4 J. David Wood, "Population Change on an Agricultural Frontier: Upper Canada, 1796 to 1841," in Roger Hall, William Westfall, and Laurel Sefton MacDowell, eds., *Patterns of the Past* (Toronto: Dundurn Press, 1988), 59–61.

5 Douglas McCalla, *Planting the Province: The Economic History of Upper Canada 1784–1870* (Toronto: University of Toronto Press, 1993), 15–16, 31.

6 J. K. Johnson, *Becoming Prominent: Regional Leadership in Upper Canada, 1791–1841* (Kingston: McGill-Queens University Press, 1989), 6.

7 A. F. Madden, "1066, 1776 and All That: The Relevance of English Medieval Experience of 'Empire' to Later Imperial Constitutional Issues" in John E. Flint and Glyndwr Williams, eds., *Perspectives of Empire* (London: Longman, 1973), 19.

8 John Garner, *The Franchise and Politics in British North America 1755–1867* (Toronto: University of Toronto Press, 1969), 164.

9 Gates, *Land Policies*, 119–20.

10 Garner, *Franchise and Politics*, 164.

11 Gates. *Land Policies*, 19.

12 S. R. Mealing, "The Enthusiasms of John Grave Simcoe," in J. K. Johnson, ed., *Historical Essays on Upper Canada* (Toronto: McClelland and Stewart, 1975), 302–16; La Rochefoucauld-Liancourt, *Voyage dans les Etats-Unis d'Amérique* (Paris, 1797), vol. 2, 58–60.

13 S. R. Mealing, "John Graves Simcoe," in *Dictionary of Canadian Biography*, edited by F. G. Halpenny and J. Hamelin (Toronto: University of Toronto Press, 1983) vol. 5, 755.

14 Gates, *Land Policies*, 28–9; La Rochefoucauld, *Voyage*, 44; Sheppard, *Plunder*, 17; Garner, *Franchise and Politics*, 165.

15 Bruce G. Wilson, *The Enterprises of Robert Hamilton: A Study of Wealth and Influence in Early Upper Canada, 1776–1812* (Ottawa: Carleton University Press, 1983), 109.

16 Mealing, "Enthusiasms of John Grave Simcoe," 305; Marcus Lee Hansen, *The Mingling of the Canadian and American Peoples* (New Haven: Yale University Press, 1940), 90.

17 Garner, *Franchise and Politics*, 86–8, 165.

18 Johnson, *Becoming Prominent*, 26.

19 Garner, *Franchise and Politics*, 167.

20 Ibid., 166.

21 Ibid., 86–7; Gore to William Windham, 1 October 1806, Canadian Archives *Report*, 1892 (Ottawa, 1893), 38.

22 Sheppard, *Plunder*, 82–3.

23 Paul Romney, "Reinventing Upper Canada: American Immigrants, Upper Canadian History, English Law and the Alien Question" in Hall et al., *Patterns of the Past*, 78–107.

24 Ibid., 99

25 Patrick Brode, *Sir John Beverley Robinson: Bone and Sinew of the Compact* (Toronto: University of Toronto Press, 1984), 320.

CHAPTER 4

LAND AND SETTLEMENT IN NOVA SCOTIA

JAMES ST. G. WALKER

THE ESTABLISHMENT OF A FREE BLACK COMMUNITY, 1783–91

Most Black Loyalists were runaway slaves who deliberately sought the British and offered their services to the Loyalist cause. One further characteristic that frequently distinguished the Black Loyalist from other runaway slaves was the ideal he held of the object of his freedom: it was to become self-sufficient and secured by British justice in his rights as a subject of the Crown. The passage to Nova Scotia was therefore regarded not merely as an escape from slavery, but as an entry into a new world where the dignity and independence that came of equal citizenship were to be his.[1]

Fundamental to the realisation of the Black Loyalist ideal was the acquisition of land, for without it no true independence was believed possible. But Nova Scotia was in no position to satisfy this demand. By mid-October 1783 some 27,000 Loyalists and troops had sought refuge in the British province, and early in the following year Governor John Parr estimated the total at over 30,000.[2] All these people, of whatever colour, entered a chaotic and inefficient land-granting system, and though many officials individually attempted to see the blacks

treated with justice the priorities and prejudices of the system precluded the possibility that the blacks should find the land and independence of their ideal. Generally speaking, few blacks received any land at all, and when they did it was in smaller quantities than promised, contained some of the province's worst soil, and was often located so far from major settlements that establishing a viable farm upon it or even visiting it was extremely difficult.[3]

Definite promises of support and compensation had been given the Loyalists before their removal from the United States, and besides, the distress of 30,000 British subjects evoked feelings of kinship and humanity from the colonial administrators. Parr, Carleton and Haldimand all gave their full attention to the care and settlement of "those unfortunate Loyalists."[4] Immediate steps were taken to ensure that land was available for the incoming throng. With the exception of various reserves required for naval timber, all Crown land was eligible for distribution, and any plots previously granted but unimproved by their owners, or for which quit-rents were in arrears, were ordered escheated for redistribution to Loyalists. The usual purchase fee of ten shillings per hundred acres was remitted and there would be no quit-rents levied for the first ten years of occupation. Carleton had advocated the complete abolition of quit-rents, but was forced to accept their temporary suspension. Even the usual fees for surveying and licensing of warrants and grants were waived, the surveyor being paid his expenses and one-half his normal tariff directly from the Treasury.

According to this new policy, Loyalists were to receive lands with absolutely no charges attached. Though he warned against persons trying to monopolise tracts of land or to take grants which they had no intention of settling, Lord North authorised the Governor to distribute as much land as "the recipient shows desire and ability to cultivate" up to a maximum of 1,000 acres in excess of the regular grant. If the surveyors proved insufficient to handle this immense task, Parr was given access to the Army Engineers who would assist in laying out new home sites for the 30,000 immigrants.[5]

There was an estimated 26,000,000 acres of land in Nova Scotia, as constituted in 1783, of which 13,722,134 cultivable acres were eligible for distribution to Loyalists. In view of the pressing demand coupled with explicit orders to keep expenses to a minimum, a policy was developed according to which "such as have suffered most" in the American War, that is, those who had lost the most property, were to be served first.[6] They would be compensated with grants relative to the estates left behind in rebel hands. Thereafter ordinary refugees who had suffered less for their loyalty were to be rewarded with 100 acres for the family head plus 50 acres for every member of his family, wife, son, daughter or slave. All were eligible, under Lord North's authorisation, to apply for additional land if they could actually cultivate and improve it. The grants for disbanded troops ranged downwards from 1,000 acres for a field officer to 100 acres for a private soldier, not including allowances for family members.[7]

The procedure established for administering Loyalist grants required the initiative to come from the prospective grantee in the form of a petition to the governor. This petition might request a specific parcel of land or simply the maximum for which the petitioner was eligible, to be assigned at the governor's discretion. Since disbanded troops were settled all together only one petition, usually in the senior officer's name, would be submitted. A similar practice was followed by groups of civilian Loyalists desiring to settle in the same location. If he judged the petition worthy of his attention the governor would send a warrant to the Surveyor-General asking that a survey be made. Once made, the survey plan would be returned to the governor and a report was submitted to the Surveyor-General of the King's Woods. This latter functionary was required to determine whether timber stands on the land in question made it advisable to reserve it for the Royal Navy. If not, he issued a certificate which, with the governor's original warrant, was sent to the Provincial Secretary. He drew up a draft grant for the signature of the Attorney-General. Finally the actual grant was made out and signed by the governor. All that remained was for the grantee to take the oath of allegiance and subscribe "to the Declaration acknowledging His Majesty in Parliament to be the Supreme Legislature of this Province," and the land was legally his.[8]

Obviously there were far too many Loyalists, and the procedure was far too complicated, for new homesteads to be processed with any degree of expedition. As early as June 1783 Parr was complaining that more Loyalists were arriving than he had expected or for whom he could hope to provide. In a total population of just over 40,000, three-quarters were thrown on the responsibility of the beleaguered governor and his small coterie of officials, submitting petitions, requesting surveys, and demanding the immediate delivery of their lands. The Nova Scotian administrative structure simply could not cope with this nightmare situation.[9]

"Discontent and uneasiness have arisen in several of the New Settlements now forming in this Province," Parr admitted in a 1784 Proclamation, "because they have not hitherto received Grants for the Lands which have been assigned to them."[10] The Chief Engineer of British Forces in America, Colonel Robert Morse, wrote in his 1784 Report on the Loyalists that "a very small proportion, indeed, of these people are yet upon their lands." The reasons assigned by Morse for what he considered to be an unreasonable delay were that the Loyalists had arrived too late in the season for surveyors to operate in 1783, "delays and irregularities" in escheating cleared land, an insufficient number of surveyors, lack of suitable administrative preparations by the government and, finally, the fact that many Loyalists wasted time clearing town sites and building towns instead of expending that energy and capital on preparing farms for themselves.[11] Despite the distress and anxiety so caused, Whitehall complained of the "accumulating expenses" of settling the Loyalists and ordered a reduction in the number of deputy-surveyors, the men who were doing the actual work of laying out the grants.[12]

Even if Parr were exaggerating when he reported, in August 1784, that 4,882 grants had been finalised, it must be considered a miraculous accomplishment that so many petitions were in fact processed in so short a time. Taking the governor's estimate of four persons per family, approximately 20,000 people were settled upon their land within their first year in Nova Scotia. Still there remained a further 10,000 as yet unsatisfied, and it would be several years before the governor could spend a day at his desk without receiving a petition from some landless Loyalist. In December 1786 the total of grants issued had crept up to only 5,567, and the estimate of persons settled by these grants had actually declined to some 15,000.[13] That same year Captain Gray of the New York Rangers reminded Parr that his men had not yet been assigned lands, and in 1791 a Loyalist group at Pictou threatened to return to the United States unless their promised lands were soon forthcoming. Soldiers were frequently picked up in the streets of Halifax and confined to the Poor House, unable to support themselves without farms. John Clarkson reported to William Wilberforce in 1791 that many of the English and German troops disbanded in Nova Scotia had never received a single acre from the government.[14]

In the midst of such confusion and, at times, corruption, it is not surprising that an insignificant group of ex-slaves should be overlooked. They had lost no large estates or high positions to demand for themselves the immediate attention of Nova Scotia's harassed officials. Though Lord Sydney considered the black veterans "entitled to some protection and favour,"[15] by every rule of priority laid down in Whitehall and in Halifax the blacks fell rather low in the list. One of the officials partly responsible for Loyalist settlement, though well aware of a generally bad situation, later was moved to admit that there had been "an injudicious and unjust Mode of assigning [the blacks] their Lands," and that they had "laboured under some disagreeable Circumstances with respect to their Lands."[16]

The largest single group of free blacks coming to Nova Scotia was settled at Port Roseway, a new Loyalist centre expected to become "the most flourishing Town for Trade of any part of the World," and spiteful proof to the southern Republic that citizens loyal to the Crown could successfully transplant the best elements of colonial society. Agents representing some of the most prominent Loyalists visited Nova Scotia in the final days of the war and decided upon Port Roseway as their future home, largely on the basis of its location which appeared most advantageous for shipping and fisheries. The surrounding countryside, however, with its swamps and forests, was quite unsuited for agriculture.[17] On 21 April 1783 the survey for the proposed town site was begun at Port Roseway, and two weeks later the first Loyalists arrived. By the time Governor Parr visited there in late July, to initiate a municipal government and to name the settlement Shelburne, after the Secretary of State, there was already a population of 7,400. But the site was as yet far from cleared of its forest, and the survey was two years from completion.[18]

Among the first arrivals at Shelburne was a group of Black Pioneers who had been enlisted by the Chief Engineer, Colonel Robert Morse, to help with the clearing and subsequent construction of the town itself. Lieutenant Lawson, the engineer in charge of Shelburne's public buildings, was authorised to use the black labourers in any way he saw fit, "but in His Majesty's service only."[19] In immediate charge of the black corps was Colonel Stephen Blucke, "a mulatto of good reputation,"[20] who organised his people for the construction of Shelburne and also of a town for themselves. Located by the governor's orders on the northwestern outskirts of the white town, the new black settlement was named Birchtown after their old friend and protector, General Birch. On 28 August 1783 Benjamin Marston, the deputy-surveyor for Shelburne and district, recorded that he "went up the North West Arm ashore with Colonel Bluck to show him the

ground allotted for his people. They are well satisfied with it." Two days later Marston was at work "laying out lands for Colonel Bluck's black gentry."[21] When in the summer of 1784 a muster was held in Shelburne County, the roll included 1,521 free blacks then living at Birchtown, 649 men, 485 women and 387 children. The blacks were organised in 21 companies, each one under the command of a black "captain," for their continuing work on the barracks, jails and jetties of Shelburne.[22]

While the blacks were thus employed, Surveyor Marston was attempting to lay out plots of land for the 6,401 white Loyalists then living in temporary shacks and tents in the town. The inevitable delays occurred, followed by the equally inevitable complaints of the Loyalists. Not only were the surveyors taking too long, according to Loyalist agent James Dole, but the best lands were being reserved for government use and the farm lots were virtually inaccessible. They refused to be assuaged by the argument that the delay was caused by the region's being "a Wilderness covered with deep Swamps and almost impenetrable Woods." People began selling their assigned lands, even before they received grants for them, and moved to greener pastures. The complaints of their purchasers added another complication to the unhappy situation. Others gave up hope and simply left without waiting for the survey to be completed.[23] One "piece of villainy," in Marston's terms, that resulted from the confusion, was an attempt by a surveyor to include Birchtown in the grants to whites. This would "shift the niggers at least two lots," so the fairminded Marston devoted a day to extracting a promise "to overhaul that business" and preserve Birchtown's integrity as a black community. Finally a special board was established in Shelburne to process applications for land. When the board was dissolved two years later, in November 1786, all the Loyalists were settled and the lands laid out "except those for the Negroes at Birch Town."[24] Despite Marston's best efforts, only small town lots had been given to some of the Birchtowners. Their promised farms still lay unsurveyed beneath the district's "deep Swamps" and "impenetrable Woods."

The delays and public disturbances at Shelburne meant that some white settlers had to wait up to three years before receiving their lands. According to the governor's orders all Shelburne County Loyalists were to receive a town lot, big enough for a house, and 50 acres of country land suitable for farming. In fact, for 119 whites who received lands near Birchtown, farm lots ranged from 5 to 350 acres in size, and the average farm measured 74 acres.[25] Of the 649 black men at Birchtown only 184 received any farms at all. This fortunate third had to wait two more years after their white colleagues were satisfied, and when their grants were finalised in 1788 they averaged only 34 acres.[26] Colonel Blucke himself was located on 200 acres in April 1786, but he was apparently tardy in submitting a plan for his brethren.[27] Eventually a survey was done for 184 Black Loyalists, in the name of Joseph Raven, on 8 December 1787. Attorney-General S. S. Blowers signed the warrant the following week and on 28 February 1788, the governor authorised the grant.[28]

Those who had town lots often earned their livelihood in Shelburne, applying their savings toward the purchase of a farm. Blucke reported that 300 were in possession of farms, which would mean that over 100 must have bought them. When 151 men applied for passage to Sierra Leone in 1791, 67 claimed to have received government-granted farms and 10 others to have purchased theirs privately. Eighteen had paid for their town lots.[29] The majority, however, remained landless. Even taking the desperate situation of the white Loyalists and their

land into consideration, it appears quite evident that the blacks of Birchtown fared much worse than their white neighbours in Shelburne.

Annapolis County offered better prospects for agriculture. Good sandy soil was present around the town itself and along the banks of the Annapolis River. This proved highly attractive to Loyalist immigrants: over 2,000 arrived in the first wave during the autumn of 1783 and one year later the population was given as 4,000. Over 1,200 of these newcomers settled at Conway, renamed Digby in February 1784, among them a significant proportion of free blacks. In June 1784 a muster listed 211 then living around Digby, 69 of whom were former Black Pioneers and their families. Two months later 65 families of free blacks were reported to be living in their own community of Brindley Town, about one mile from Digby itself.[30] Next to Birchtown, Brindley Town was the second largest settlement of Black Loyalists in Nova Scotia.

John Robinson, the man responsible for the 1784 Annapolis County muster, reported to General Campbell that

> many of the Loyalists who have come to this part of the Province are still unsettled....This was owing to the Negligence and diletary Conduct of the persons who have been appointed to lay out the Lands for them.[31]

The persons so described were four agents appointed by Governor Parr to assign Loyalist grants, and they seem to have been at least careless and probably corrupt in their parcelling out of the 20,000 acres available in Digby Township. In May and June 1785 some impatient Loyalists took matters into their own hands and moved onto vacant lots, common and glebe lands, refusing to leave until their legitimate allotments were assigned. An enquiry instituted by the governor and council into "the Disorders and unhappy dissentions at Digby" found a scapegoat, Major Robert Tempany, who was removed as a justice of the peace.[32]

The problems continued, however, and it was not until 1800 that most Digby Loyalists received secure title to their lands. A commission of enquiry set up by Governor John Wentworth reported that "no accurate plan of the surveys of [Digby Township] had been made." The commission reprimanded the four original agents for "the improvident and in some cases surreptitious obtaining of special grants," and pointed out that most Digby Loyalists had been forced to pay for their grants "owing to their distance from the place of application at Halifax, and to their want of ability to break thro' the scene of confusion attending the first forming and settlement by the Agents." To correct this situation the House of Assembly authorised the payment of £200 to re-survey the lands of the 200 Loyalists still in Digby.[33]

Stumbling directly into this stormy situation two sergeants of the Black Pioneers, Thomas Peters and Murphy Still, submitted a petition to the governor on 21 August 1784 in the name of their fellow veterans at Digby. Citing the promise of Sir Henry Clinton, made at the time of their enlistment, that black troops would receive the same allowances of land and provisions as "the Rest of the Disbanded Soldiers of His Majesty's Army," they asked that Clinton's promise now be fulfilled.[34] Surveyor-General Morris added a note to their petition to the effect that if the governor would grant a warrant he would issue immediate orders to his deputy at Digby to begin the survey. After a second petition had been received from the Digby area blacks, Parr wrote to deputy surveyor Thomas Millidge asking him to place the petitioners "in the most advantageous Situation" and to "comply with their wishes, as far as lies in your power."

Unfortunately Millidge was prevented by the snow then on the ground from surveying farm lots, and so contented himself with laying out one-acre town lots in Brindley Town for 76 Pioneers and other Black Loyalists.[35]

A third petition for the complete allotment was received in Halifax at the time of the disturbances in Digby. Despite his other preoccupations Charles Morris repeated Parr's earlier desire and wrote to his deputy asking that "you will pay all due attention, to the Inclosed Memorial, and Accomodate these Black people According to their Wishes, in the best Manner You can." In the meantime a number of the blacks had moved on to some land belonging to an absentee named McKenney, where they cleared lots, built houses and prepared small gardens for themselves. Millidge was of the opinion that they should be allowed grants to remain on this land, rather than that they be moved to new lands. Despite this suggestion a new location was selected and a survey completed in June 1785 for 467 acres, giving 23 black men farm lots of about 20 acres each, located on a peninsula across the Annapolis River from Brindley Town. No sooner had this been done than Charles Morris was informed by an irate "Secretary to the Society for Propogateing of the Gospel" that the land in question had been reserved for a glebe and school. He had to tell Millidge to remove the blacks once again.[36]

Before another survey could be begun, the pay of deputy surveyors was discontinued by the government, and Millidge was informed that if he wanted to proceed with a survey for the Digby blacks he must "endeavour to procure Satisfaction from them for his labour." It was not until October 1788 that anything further was done, when Joseph Leonard approached the governor with yet another request for lands for himself and the other blacks then subsisting on their one-acre town lots. Again Parr proved sympathetic and asked Morris to order one of the surveyors for the district, John Greben, to seek out some available land for them "that these Poor People may be accomodated, and set to work, or they will soon become a Burthen to the Community." Greben, however, misinterpreted this order and rather than simply reporting on whether any land was available he went ahead with an actual survey, laying out 147 lots of 50 acres each and one, for Leonard, of 100 acres. Morris wrote to his unfortunate deputy that "no order for any Survey was implyed or intended … and I am in doubt whether you will get any thing for your worke." His only hope for payment would be if "Joseph Leonard signifys to the Govr that the worke is done to the satisfaction of his People." To Millidge, Morris wrote, "I think [Greben] will in Justice be entitled to pay, but it must appear to the Governor that the Negroes are satisfied, and to me, that all these Lots are vacant before we can proceed any Further."[37]

Greben's superior in the district, Thomas Millidge, assisted in the completion of the survey. The new grant, which was located in Clements Township, was shown to have been granted previously but some of the original grantees had never arrived to take possession of their lands and others had returned to the United States. It was, therefore, available to be granted again. Millidge then took Joseph Leonard, "the Head and Supreme Representative of his Ethiopian Brethren from Digby," to show him the 7,500-acre tract surveyed by Greben. Asked if he approved of the land, Leonard answered in the affirmative, and signed a certificate stating that he and all the blacks were now satisfied. The official warrant was signed on 11 September 1789 for Joseph Leonard and 148 others, and the Surveyor-General of the King's Woods issued a certificate to allow the grant to proceed.[38]

Though Millidge, with undoubted sincerity, wrote: "I now hope an end will be put to a piece of business which [we] have had much trouble about," a sentiment surely shared by the Black Loyalists who had now waited over six years for their lands, no final grant was in fact authorised. The last document in this frustrating episode is the warrant to survey of September 1789. Evidently a road was cleared to their tract by the blacks themselves, but no further improvements were made and the land was never cleared or occupied. Whether the blacks, their suspicions alerted from two previous displacements, declined to move onto their lands until a final grant was in their hands, or whether the grant was withheld by the authorities because the blacks had not occupied the land, the result was the same: the Black Loyalists of Digby were never put in possession of their farms. The seventy-six acres in Brindley Town remained the only land legally deeded to any of Digby's free black settlers.[39]

Into the rough and isolated regions of Sydney County moved another 2,000 Loyalists. Though the land here was barren, at least their experience in acquiring it was more favourable than those of their compatriots in Shelburne and Annapolis Counties. The 1,200 settled around Chedabucto, for example, were all placed on their farms in early 1785. On a tract of 45,650 acres, 201 white Loyalists received an average grant of almost 200 acres each, and at Guysborough another 104 whites received an average farm of over 200 acres each. At the end of the Chedabucto list appears an anonymous mass of "One hundred and Eighteen Negroes at 50 Acres p. Family—5900 Acres." Since they were not listed by name it has been impossible to verify this mention as constituting an authentic grant, though it is certain that they did not appear in the final grant for the Chedabucto tract mentioned here.[40]

It is known that there were some Black Pioneers in Chedabucto in 1788 who had never received lands at all. Even if these 118 were placed on farm lots, the amounts were much smaller than those given to whites, and in a district where virtually all the white Loyalists received some land there remained a body of landless blacks.

Other free blacks were located at Tracadie Harbour on the eastern end of the peninsula, and it has been reported that local authorities planned to move the county's black people to one large settlement there. Thomas Brownspriggs, an educated Black Loyalist, was appointed agent by Governor Parr with responsibility for forming the settlement. In the event, however, it was for only 74 black families that Brownspriggs petitioned for land in September 1787. The survey was duly completed and certified the same day, granting a tract of 3,000 acres at Little Tracadie bordering the Tracadie River. Each family received a farm of forty acres.[41] When in 1788 another 16 former Black Pioneers then landless in Chedabucto petitioned for land at Little Tracadie, a warrant to survey 800 acres for them was cancelled and the grant refused.[42] It is only possible to state with any degree of confidence that those 74 families led by Brownspriggs, containing 172 individuals, were actually put in possession of their lands. At least some of this Tracadie grant was reallocated to white Acadians in April 1799, when 2,720 acres of the total of 3,000 were distributed among 28 "Acadians and Negroes."[43] Possibly the original grantees found that a 40-acre farm was uneconomical, and hence some of them moved away to seek a livelihood elsewhere. What began as one of the most promising experiences for Black Loyalists in Nova Scotia, therefore, ended eventually in a situation little different from that of others of their colour across the province.

Those three communities, Birchtown, Brindley Town and Little Tracadie, were the only all-black settlements in Loyalist Nova Scotia and the only grants of land made directly to free black people. There were, however, other large concentrations of Black Loyalists contained within general Loyalist communities, the most important being Preston on the eastern side of the harbour near Halifax.

Loyalist refugee Theophilus Chamberlain was appointed deputy-surveyor and agent for laying out and settling Preston Township on his arrival in Nova Scotia in 1783. He seems to have attracted to his settlement a particularly hard-working group of people, both black and white, perhaps reflecting the large proportion of disbanded troops among them who, because of a possible younger average age and less affluent background than many Loyalists, might be expected to perform well as pioneers in a new land. In the opinion of one member of the Legislative Assembly, "there are not better working men, or more honest and sober, than those of the town of Preston," and he was referring particularly to the Black Loyalists then in the settlement.[44] It is possible that this type of Loyalist was attracted by Preston's location. Though unsuited for ocean trade, as Shelburne was, and lacking good quality soil for large agricultural undertakings, as Annapolis had, Preston was close to the Halifax market for small-farm produce such as vegetables and poultry, the lakes, rivers and coasts nearby offered excellent opportunities for fishing, and the timber stands would find an ideal outlet in the Halifax shipbuilding and construction industries.[45]

Chamberlain's original settlement consisted of 85 people, 56 of them white and 29 black. The agent-surveyor recommended grants to them averaging 160.7 acres for each of the whites and 50 acres for each of the blacks. When the actual grant was made in December 1784 the settlement was larger and the discrepancy between white and black wider than anticipated in Chamberlain's earlier plan. Thirty-two thousand acres were eventually divided among 164 grantees, the whites receiving an average of 204 acres each, the blacks remaining at 50. Furthermore there were only 10 blacks included in the final grant, none of whom had been among the original 29. Two of the 10, British Freedom and John Smith, were also given one and a half acre town lots in Preston in addition to their farms.[46] For some reason the other 29 had to wait, completely landless, for a further two years.

A survey was made in Preston in July 1785 for Ensign Joshua Garratt and 34 others, 22 of whom were from Chamberlain's initial group of Black Loyalists, the other 12 and Garratt himself being white. Though a final grant was issued for this land, in the confusion of the times it appears that the grantees were not informed of it, for they never occupied the land. All of Garratt's people were included in grants a year later, the whites receiving lands in Dartmouth and the blacks, this time all 29 of them, finally acquiring their 50-acre farms as part of a grant to Patrick Byrns in March 1786. The 1785 Garratt survey in Preston remained on the books and was escheated for non-occupation in 1810.[47]

In the meantime more blacks were moving to Preston from Halifax, unable to find decent employment in the capital city and probably encouraged by the success of some 39 of their brethren in winning farms and independence. One unofficial estimate put the latecomers at "50 or 60 Families."[48] Twelve of these received 50 acres each included in a grant to white Loyalist Thomas Young in December 1787. One of this group, Sam Elliott, was also assigned a town lot in Preston, as were two more of Chamberlain's black grantees, Cuff Preston and Brutus Jones. Of 48 original town lots, five went to blacks, though the size of their lots was less than half that granted to the 43 white pioneers in Preston.[49]

Though no grant was made directly to Black Loyalists in Preston Township, 51 of them received farms as part of three grants to whites. As was the practice in Shelburne and Sydney Counties, the grants when made were considerably smaller than those for whites in the same district. This situation was particularly stark in Preston, where black and white were part of the same grants, yet the portion allotted to the blacks was less than a quarter of the average assigned to their white neighbours. There was also a large body of free blacks living there who received no lands at all. There may have been as many as 100 Black Loyalists and their families in Preston during the 1780s. Of 39 black Prestonians signing a petition in 1791, 16 of them were landless.[50] When called upon for an explanation, surveyor Chamberlain placed the blame directly on the blacks themselves. By the time most of them arrived in Preston, he claimed, his pay from the government had been discontinued and he was forced to extract his fees and expenses from the grantees themselves. He therefore made a general survey for the Black Loyalists but refused to divide it into individual lots until his money was forthcoming. The blacks, in their turn, either could not or would not pay the fees. Chamberlain even offered to take them out to show them their proposed lands, "but for this they have been too negligent, and every one knows that Acres of Land are not like a Flock of Sheep that may be drove by Thousands before Peoples Door for them to look on."[51] For about half of Preston's black population, therefore, the position was similar to that taking place in Digby

Township at the same time: the people were kept from their promised lands not so much by any deliberate attempt to deprive them but by the inefficiencies and misplaced priorities inherent in Loyalist land distribution.

Halifax was often the landing place for Black Loyalists arriving in Nova Scotia, and many of them decided to remain there, as servants, labourers, or tradesmen, rather than face the risks of pioneer life in uncertain country. About a hundred free blacks, while still in New York, accepted an opportunity to enlist for one year in a Black Pioneer labour corps to be employed in the Engineer's Department in Halifax. Theoretically this one year of government service was intended as a stop-gap until proper land grants should be laid out.[52] It is likely, however, that there was little movement from Halifax out to the black communities, except for those who went to Preston. Indeed there was a gradual movement into Halifax by those frustrated by the difficulties in obtaining lands elsewhere, and a consequent increase in Halifax's black population. Later arrivals in the province, for example a group of 194 from St Augustine in April 1785, also frequently chose to stay in the capital city where they hoped that their familiar occupations could find them employment. The 1791 Halifax census showed 422 blacks in a total population of 4,897.[53] There is no record that any of these people received any lands.

In late September 1783 a party of black "Guides and Pioneers" landed at the St John River, there, as in Halifax and Shelburne, to be employed in labour and construction of the public works. When the general Loyalist muster was taken exactly one year later, the returns submitted by Deputy Commissary Thomas Knox listed 182 persons in "Black Companies" that had been "Mustered on the River St John."[54] Others arrived in the area, named New

Brunswick in 1784, from other settlements in Nova Scotia. Thomas Peters, in his continuing search for land, left Annapolis County for New Brunswick where he petitioned for a "small lot in the rear of Fredericton." This was discovered to be part of a tract already granted to someone else, so Peters remained landless. Three black veterans were given allotments along with the rest of their disbanded corps. Others were granted town lots in St John, but when it became obvious that they could not support themselves on such tiny pieces of land the local government suggested in 1785 that they form themselves into companies and apply for tracts of farmland.[55]

Eventually three such companies were formed, of 47, 50, and 24 families respectively, and surveys were conducted to lay out a corresponding number of 50-acre lots in three separate tracts. According to Thomas Peters, however, this land was "so far distant from their Town Lots (being 16 or 18 Miles back) as to be entirely useless to them and indeed worthless in itself from its remote situation." Only five families actually occupied and improved their farms and the other 116 lots were escheated and reassigned to whites. In 1791 there remained "about 100 Families or more" around St John, without land or with only small town lots.[56]

The 184 Black Loyalists in Joseph Raven's Birchtown grant were not the only ones in Shelburne County to receive land. David George reported that he was given a one-quarter acre town lot in Shelburne and he later purchased four more town lots and a 50-acre farm. The other 70 black families living in the North Division of Shelburne city, however, had no government allotments, though it is possible that they too were able to purchase some land. Four black pilots shared one 50-acre lot on McNutt's Island as part of a 2,000-acre grant to white Loyalists. Characteristically, all the whites received 50 acres each except Benjamin McNutt, whose share was 250 acres.[57]

Other blacks went to Windsor, where they remained landless while a neighbouring group of South Carolina whites won farms averaging 418 acres each. In May 1787 Simeon Perkins enumerated 50 blacks in Queens County, 20 men, 11 women and 19 children, all but two of them in the town of Liverpool. None had any land. Scattered families of Black Loyalists were reported to be in Lunenburg, Wilmot, Cornwallis, St Margaret's Bay, Granville and Port d'Hebert. All of them had their land promises unfulfilled. Besides the residents of Brindley Town there were blacks living in Digby and over 100 in Annapolis. Though none of them had official grants some occupied lands belonging to others, and one, Liberty Legree, gave his name to the small black settlement of Liberty Road.[58]

Nova Scotia offered refuge to at least 3,000 Black Loyalists from New York, undetermined numbers from Boston, Charleston and Savannah, and at least 194 from St Augustine. A conservative estimate of those whose whereabouts were known in Nova Scotia would place their number at about 3,550.[59] Of these it is certain that 184 received 6,382 acres at Birchtown, 76 received one acre each at Brindley Town, 74 received 3,000 acres at Little Tracadie, and 51 received 2557 1/2 acres at Preston. Placing the average family membership at three persons, this would mean that 1,155 Black Loyalists were actually settled on a total acreage of 12,015 1/2. The grant at Chedabucto, if one were indeed made, would add about 350 people and 5,900 acres to the total. The size of the farms occupied by the three black families near St John is not known, but judging from experience elsewhere they would probably not have been larger than 50 acres each.

If many whites suffered delays, were assigned poor land, or had no land at all, it is obvious that the Black Loyalists experienced an even less favourable fate. Their disappointment, and the discrimination with which they were met, indicated that they were not to be treated as equal citizens after all, and encouraged many of them to believe that they would have to look beyond the governor and his surveyors to complete their escape from slavery and to achieve the independence they sought.

Notes

[1] This sentiment was acknowledged by John Clarkson as being a fundamental motivation driving the blacks to the British and, later, to the Sierra Leone Company (Clarkson Papers, II, fols. 8–9, "Reasons given by the Free Blacks for wishing to leave Nova Scotia"). Frequent expressions of the Black Loyalists' faith in British justice can be found in the Book of Negroes (PANS vol. 423) and in the Loyalist Claims (AO 12 and 13). Both these pieces of evidence are confirmed by the pattern of Black Loyalist activities in Nova Scotia and in Sierra Leone, and in particular by their continual search for land and independence and for their rights as British freemen.

[2] PANS vol. 369, doc. 198, "Return of Loyalists gone from New York to Nova Scotia," 12 October 1783. The exact numbers and destinations were noted as being:

Port Roseway	8,896 including	1,312	black servants
Annapolis Royal	2,530	397	
Halifax	928	73	
River St John's	14,162	1,578	

Though the total shown in the Return is 27,009, these figures indicate a total of 26,516, being 23,156 whites and 3,360 blacks. For the 1784 estimate see PANS vol. 367 1/2, doc. 31, Parr to Haldimand, 14 June 1784.

[3] PANS, Family Papers, Clarkson, Clarkson's Mission to America, pp. 51–3, 99–100, 188–9; Clarkson Papers, II, fols. 1–3, 8, 21, and III. fols. 157, 164; C. H. Fyfe, "Thomas Peters: History and Legend," SLS (ns), no. 1, December 1953, p. 6; George A. Rawlyk, "The Guysborough Negroes: A Study in Isolation," Dalhousie Review, Spring 1968, p. 25; The Philanthropist, vol. IV, 1814, pp. 101, 104, "History of the Colony of Sierra Leone." See also the specific references to Black Loyalist land grants throughout this chapter.

[4] PANS vol. 367 1/2, Haldimand to Lord North, 14 June 1784; vol. 286, doc. 149, John Parr to Thomas Townshend, 26 October 1782.

5 PANS vol. 349, doc. 33, 10 June 1783; vol. 369, doc. 6, Additional Royal Instructions to Governor Parr, 10 June 1783; Carleton Papers, doc. 9299, Carleton to Lord North, 5 October 1783; CO 217/56, Lord North to Parr, 7 August 1783; PANS vol. 32, doc. 78, North to Parr, 24 June 1783; vol. 33, doc. 3, Lord Sydney to Parr, 12 March 1784.

6 CO 217/56, Parr to North, 23 April 1783; PANS vol. 394, doc. 31, Morris to Ruggles, 19 July 1783.

7 CO 217/56, North to Parr, 7 August 1783. Military grants were to be assigned as follows:

field officer	1,000 acres
captain	700
subaltern	500
non-commissioned officer	200
private	100

8 PANS vol. 346, doc. 91, 1 March 1784; vol. 369, doc. 6, 10 June 1783; Margaret Ells, Settling the Loyalists in Nova Scotia, Ottawa, 1933, p. 105.

9 PANS vol. 47, doc. 11, Parr to Townshend, 6 June 1783, and doc. 15, Parr to North, 20 November 1783; James S. MacDonald, "Memoir of Governor John Parr," Collections of the Nova Scotia Historical Society, vol. XIV, 1910, p. 57; W. Ross Livingston, Responsible Government in Nova Scotia, Iowa City, 1930, p. 25; Allison, History of Nova Scotia, II, Appendix D, pp. 893–5, "Report of Colonel Morse," 1784.

10 PANS vol. 346, doc. 88, 22 January 1784.

11 Allison, History of Nova Scotia, II, Appendix D, pp. 893–5, "Report of Colonel Morse," 1784; J. Plimsoll Edwards, "Vicissitudes of a Loyalist City," Dalhousie Review, October 1922, pp. 328–9.

12 PANS vol. 137, Richard Bulkeley, circular letter to district surveyors, 20 May 1785.

13 PANS vol. 47, doc. 27, Parr to Sydney, 13 August 1784; vol. 223, doc. 146, "Farm Lots laid out for the Loyal Emigrants and Disbanded Corps, between 1 May 1783 and 31 December 1786."

14 PANS vol. 137, Parr to Thomas Carleton, 6 April 1786; CO 217/63, Parr to Henry Dundas, 13 August 1791; PANS vol. 301, doc. 57, "Representation of the Overseers of the Poor," Halifax, 1784; Clarkson's Mission, p. 187, John Clarkson to William Wilberforce, 27 November 1791, and p. 202, diary entry for 1 December 1791.

15 PANS vol. 33, doc. 12, Sydney to Parr, 5 October 1784.

16 CO 217/68, Alexander Howe to W. D. Quarrel, 9 August 1797.

17 PANS vol. 369, doc. 66, Parr to Carleton, 25 July 1783, doc. 138, "Petition on behalf of Associated Loyalists," n.d. (1782); J. Plimsoll Edwards, "The Shelburne that Was and is Not," Dalhousie Review, April 1922, p. 180; PANS vol. 380, p. 129.

18 W. O. Raymond (ed.) "The Founding of Shelburne and Early Miramichi. Marston's Diary," Collections of the New Brunswick Historical Society, vol. III, no. 8, 1908, pp. 205, 210, 222; PANS vol. 47, doc. 13, Parr to North, 30 September 1783; vol. 368,

doc. 45, "Return of the Number of Loyalists gone to Port Roseway"; David George, "Life," p. 478.

19 Edwards, "The Shelburne that Was," Appendix A, pp. 194–5, "Robert Morse, Chief Engineer, Instructions to Lieut. Lawson, Engineer going to Port Roseway in Nova Scotia," 19 April 1783; Carleton Papers, doc. 8800, Proposals submitted by Lt. Col. Morse to Brig. Gen. Fox, 23 August 1783, doc. 8886, Fox to Carleton, 26 August 1783, doc. 9130, Carleton to Fox, 15 September 1783.

20 Edwards, "The Shelburne that Was," p. 187. The "Book of Negroes" described Blucke as a free-born black from Barbados.

21 Raymond, "Marston's Diary," pp. 227, 228, 230.

22 PANS, Shelburne Records, "A List of those Mustered at Shelburne in the summer of 1784," and General Sessions, 15 September 1784; PANS, White Collection, III, doc. 340, "Mustered at Shelburne, 1784."

23 CO 217/56, Parr to Carleton, 3 February 1784; PANS vol. 369, doc. 109, James Dole to Carleton, 19 September 1783; CO 217/57, Isaac Wilkins to Parr, 26 June 1785; PANS vol. 346, doc. 90, 10 January 1784; SPG Journal, vol. 24, p. 63, report of Rev. Walter, 3 January 1784.

24 Raymond, "Marston's Diary," p. 234; PANS vol. 213, Council Minutes, 5 August 1784; vol. 137, Richard Bulkeley to Isaac Wilkins and Members of the Board of Agents for Locating the Loyalists on Lands at Shelburne, 20 November 1786.

25 PANS vol. 394, docs. 135, 162, 164, Morris to Benjamin Marston, 24 January, 9 March and 14 April 1784; Land Papers, passim.

26 PANS vol. 371, Joseph Raven and 183 others, n.d., Shelburne, 6,382 acres. See footnote 28 below.

27 PANS, Land Papers, Morris Robert, and 38 others, including Stephen Blucke with 200 acres, 28 April 1786; Shelburne Records, "Loyalist Land Grants," Stephen Blucke, 200 acres; vol. 396, memo dated 11 September 1789.

28 PANS vol. 394A, J. Raven and 183 others, 12 December 1787; Land Papers, Raven, Joseph and 182 others, Shelburne, 8 December 1787, 6,382 acres; vol. 459, No. 596, Joseph Raven and 183 others; vol. 213, 28 February 1788, "Granted to Joseph Raven and 183 others, 6382 acres at Shelburne." It will be noted that there is a discrepancy in the above sources with respect to the number of grantees included with Raven in the Shelburne grant. The actual grant, despite the title, listed 184 people by name, including Raven himself.

29 An Account of the Designs of the Associates of the late Dr Bray, with an Abstract of their Proceedings, Abstract for 1787, pp. 34–5, Stephen Blucke to Associates, 22 December 1787; CO 217/63, "List of the Blacks of Birch Town who gave in their names for Sierra Leone in November 1791."

30 PANS vol. 380, pp. 142–3; vol. 368, doc. 46, "Return of the number of Loyalists gone to Annapolis Royal," 1783; vol. 47, doc. 39, Parr to Sydney, 27 December 1784; Isaiah W. Wilson, A Geography and History of the County of Digby, Nova Scotia, Halifax, 1900, pp. 50–1; PANS vol. 376, "Return of Negroes

and their families mustered in Annapolis County between 28 May and 30 June 1784"; C.W.Vernon, *Bicentenary Sketches*, Halifax, 1910, p. 166; PANS vol. 367 1/2, doc. 50, John Monro to Haldimand, n.d. (1784).

31 PANS vol. 376, John Robinson to Ed.Winslow, 16 September 1784.

32 Wilson, *County of Digby*, pp. 52, 77; PANS vol. 394, doc. 159, Morris to Amos Botsford, 6 April 1784; vol. 213, Council Minutes, 16 June 1785.

33 PANS vol. 287, doc. 107, "Report of the Committee to investigate Digby," 21 April 1800, doc. 104, "Message of Governor Wentworth to His Majesty's Council," 14 April 1800; vol. 302, doc. 75, "Report of the House Committee on the Governor's Message of 14 April 1800."

34 PANS vol. 359, doc. 65, "The Humble Petition of the Black Pioneers," 21 August 1784, Thomas Peters and Murphy Still to Parr.

35 Ibid., note signed by Charles Morris written on petition cover; CO 217/63, Bulkeley to Dundas, 19 March 1792, enclosing a petition signed by Solomon Hamilton and Joseph Leonard on behalf of 31 Black Loyalists, n.d. (before April 1785), also enclosing Millidge to Parr, March 1785 and Parr to Millidge, 9 April 1785; PANS, Index to Land Grants, 1730–1958, 1785, Leonard, Joseph and others, 76 acres, Digby Township; Crown Land Grants, Old Book 16, p. 35, notice of payment of quit-rents, Joseph Leonard and others, 76 acres, town lots, Digby Township.

36 PANS vol. 395, Morris to Millidge, 16 July 1785; CO 217/63, Bulkeley to Dundas, 19 March 1792, enclosing Millidge to Parr, March 1785 and Morris to Millidge, 26 July 1785; Land Papers, Leonard, Joseph, and 148 others, including a "Plan of Negro Farm Lots at Digby," surveyed June 1785. Written on a margin of the survey plan is the note: "This land was reserved for School and Common and ought not to be granted."

37 PANS vol. 395, doc. 201, Morris to Parr, 19 April 1787; vol. 396, Morris to John Greben, 29 October 1788 and 4 February 1789, and Morris to Millidge, 4 February 1789.

38 PANS, Box of Annapolis County Land Grants, 1732–1827, doc. 57, Millidge to Morris, 18 May 1789; vol. 394A, Joseph Leonard and 148 others, Clements Township, Annapolis County, 7,500 acres, 19 September 1789; Land Papers, Leonard, Joseph, and 148 others, 7,500 acres, Clements Township, 11 September 1789; vol. 459, no. 720, Joseph Leonard.

39 PANS, Box of Annapolis County Land Grants, 1732–1827, doc. 57, Millidge to Morris, 18 May 1789; Land Papers, Jordan, Abedingo, and others; vol. 224, doc. 103, Petition of James Hughston, 17 March 1796. Margaret Ells, *Settling the Loyalists in Nova Scotia*, p. 108, lists 149 "Loyalist Negro grantees" in Annapolis County. Evidently she is referring to the warrant to survey for Joseph Leonard and 148 others noted in footnote 38 above. Though a warrant was usually taken as being final, and the actual grant a mere formality, it would seem from the other evidence that in this case, at least, the warrant was an untrustworthy indication of what really happened.

40 PANS vol. 380, p. 15; vol. 47, doc. 39, Parr to Sydney, 27 December 1784; vol. 223, doc. 107, "List of People at Chedabucto," 6 April 1785, and doc. 146, "Farm Lots laid out for Loyal Emigrants and Disbanded Corps, between 21 May 1783 and 31 December 1786;" vol. 359, doc. 66, "A List of the British Legion and other Loyalists at Guysborough," 8 September 1784; Allison, *History of Nova Scotia*, p. 895; Land Papers, Hubbill, Nathen, and 277 others, 53,850 acres, Chedabucto Bay, Guysborough Township, Sydney County, 1785. This grant contained the names of all those listed on 6 April 1785 plus another 76 names. None of the plots was for 50 acres. It is possible that some of the 118 blacks could have received lands as part of another grant somewhere in the district, but there is no record of any group that size receiving 50-acre farms.

41 Rawlyk, "The Guysborough Negroes," p. 29; PANS, Box of Guysboro County Land Grants, Folder I, 1781–1833, doc. 17, Thomas Brown Spriggs and 73 others, 3,000 acres, Tracadie Harbour, 29 September 1787; Land Papers, Brownspriggs, Thomas, and 73 others, 28 September 1787; vol. 371, Thomas Brownspriggs and 73 others, 20 December 1787; vol. 394A, T. B. Spriggs and 73 others, 29 September 1787; vol. 459, no. 579, T. Brownspriggs.

42 PANS, Land Papers, Gilchrist, Cornelius, and others, warrant approved for 800 acres, 9 December 1788, not granted.

43 PANS, Box of Guysboro County Land Grants, Folder 1, docs. 29 and 30, 9 April 1799, "part of 3000 acres formerly Granted to the Black People of Tracadie."

44 Clarkson's Mission, p. 54, quoting Mr Putman, MLA for Sydney County.

45 See Chamberlain's accounts in PANS vol. 359, doc. 56, 25 May 1784 to 15 September 1785, and vol. 224, docs. 91 and 123, 6 June and 5 October 1785.

46 PANS vol. 359, doc. 57, "Disbanded Soldiers and other Loyalists Recommended for Lands on the Dartmouth Side," signed by Theophilus Chamberlain, n.d. (before December 1784); Land Papers, Chamberlain, Theophilus, and 163 others, 32,000 acres, Preston Township, 3 September 1784 (survey date); vol. 370, "Names of Original Grantees," 14 December 1784, 32,000 acres to Chamberlain and 163 others, and "Original Entrey of the Survey of the Town Lotts in Preston." British Freedom's grant dated 12 February 1784, 1 1/2 acres, John Smith's dated 20 February 1784, 1 1/2 acres.

47 PANS, Land Papers, Garratt, Joshua, and 34 others, 3,850 acres, Preston Township, 25 July 1785 (escheated 1810). By this grant the whites were to receive over 200 acres each, the blacks their usual 50. Vol. 370, grants made 23 March 1786, 10,450 acres to Patrick Byrns and others.

48 *Bray Abstract, 1787*, p. 32.

49 PANS, Land Papers, Young, Thomas, and 34 others, 4,700 acres, Preston, 5 December 1787; vol. 370, grants made 20 December 1786, 4,700 acres, to Thomas Young and 34 others. The date in the Preston Township book is evidently incorrect, since according to the Land Papers the survey was

not even ordered until 29 May 1787. "Original Entrey of the Survey of the Town Lotts in Preston," Cuff Preston, Brutus Jones and Sam Elliott, 1 1/2 acres each, 20, 21, and 24 February 1787.

50 Clarkson's Mission, pp. 293–4, petition dated 26 December 1791.

51 Clarkson Papers, I, Chamberlain to Lawrence Hartshorne, 26 December 1791.

52 Carleton Papers, doc. 8800, Morse to Fox, 23 August 1783, doc. 8886, Fox to Carleton, 26 August 1783, doc. 9130, Carleton to Fox, 15 September 1783.

53 SPG, Dr Bray's Associates' Minute Books, vol. III, 1768–1808, minutes for 1 December 1808, Stanser to Associates, 24 October 1808; PANS vol. 47, doc. 43, Parr to Sydney, 29 April 1785; Akins, "History of Halifax," p. 103.

54 PANS vol. 369, doc. 97, Hewlett to Carleton, 29 September 1783; PANB, Raymond Collection, "Return of the Total Number of Men, Women and children of the Disbanded Loyalists Mustered on the River St. John," 25 September 1784.

55 PANB, RNA Series 2, Thomas Peters to Thomas Carleton, 25 October 1785; RNA Bundle Series, Peters to Carleton, 18 March 1789; Colonial Correspondence, New Brunswick, vol. III, 1791–95, Carleton to Dundas, 13 December 1791.

56 CO 217/63, "The Humble Memorial and Petition of Thomas Peters a free Negro"; PANB, Colonial Correspondence, New Brunswick, III, Carleton to Dundas, 13 December 1791; Letter Book, George Sproule, 1785–89, Sproule to Thomas Harper, 9 July 1785.

57 David George, "Life," p. 478; CO 217/63, "List of the Blacks of Birch Town"; Bray Abstract, 1787, pp. 34–5; PANS, Land Papers, Pitcher, Moses, and 35 others, 2,000 acres, McNutts Island, 17 June 1785.

58 Clarkson's Mission, pp. 66–7 and 160–1, diary entries for 22 October and 24 November 1791; PANS vol. 359, doc. 63, "Return of the Loyalists from So. Carolina settled near Windsor," n.d.; D. C. Harvey (ed.), The Diary of Simeon Perkins, vol. II, 1780–89, Toronto, 1958, p. 369; PANS vol. 443, "Poll Tax and Census Rolls," Queens County, 30 April 1787; SPG Journal, vol. 25, pp. 60–2, 71, 157, 308–9, 340, 358; CO 217/63, "Petition of Thomas Peters"; PANS vol. 376, "Muster Rolls of Loyalists"; Wilson, County of Digby, p. 62.

59 The estimate is based on the following figures:

Birchtown, 1784	1,521 individuals
Brindley Town, 1784	211 individuals
Chedabucto, 1785	118 families or about 350 individuals
Little Tracadie, 1787	172 individuals
1788	16 families or about 50 individuals
Preston, 1780s	100 families or about 300 individuals
Halifax, 1780s	400 individuals
St John, 1784	182 individuals
Shelburne, 1787	70 families or about 200 individuals
McNutt's Island, 1787	4 families or about 12 individuals
Liverpool, 1787	50 individuals
Annapolis, 1780s	100 individuals
Small centres, 1780s	unknown
	3,548 individuals

BIBLIOGRAPHY

Reports

An Account of the Designs of the Associates of the late Dr Bray, with an Abstract of their Proceedings, nos. 11–19, 1785–99.

Collected and Edited Documents

Perkins, Simeon, The Diary of Simeon Perkins, eds. H. A. Innis, D. C. Harvey and C. B. Fergusson, 4 vols., Toronto, 1942–67.

Raymond, W. O., "The Founding of Shelburne and Early Miramichi, Marston's Diary," Collections of the New Brunswick Historical Society, vol. III, 1907, pp. 204–97.

Primary Sources: Manuscripts

British Museum, Manuscript Room (London)

Add. Ms. 41262A. Clarkson Papers, vol. I.

Public Record Office (London)

CO 217. Colonial Correspondence, Nova Scotia and Cape Breton, vols. 56–74, 1783–1800.

PRO 30/55. Carleton Papers, vols. 46–92 (selected), 1782–83.

Society for the Propagation of the Gospel, London

Dr Bray's Associates Minute Books, vols. III–VII, 1768–1858.

Society for the Propagation of the Gospel. Journal, vols. 23–43, 1782–1832.

Public Archives of New Brunswick (Fredericton)

Raymond Collection.

Public Archives of Nova Scotia (Halifax)

Manuscript Volumes

Vol. 32. Whitehall Dispatches, 1770–83.

Vol. 33. Whitehall Dispatches, 1784–99.

Vol. 47. Letters to the Secretary of State and Board of Trade, 1783–89.

Vol. 137. Inland Letter Book, Governor Parr and Secretary Bulkeley, 1784–91.

Vol. 213. Minutes of His Majesty's Council, 1783–98.

Vol. 224. Miscellaneous Papers, 1788–1806.

Vol. 286. Legislative Council Papers, 1760–90.

Vol. 287. Legislative Council Papers, 1791–1809.

Vol. 301. House of Assembly Papers, 1758–87.

Vol. 302. House of Assembly Papers, 1788–1800.

Vol. 346. Proclamations, Province of Nova Scotia, 1748–1807.

Vol. 349. Royal Instructions to Governors, 1756–90.

Vol. 359. Old Townships and Loyalist Settlements.

Vol. 367–1/2. Military and Loyalist Documents, Haldimand Collection, 1761–83, vol. III.

Vol. 368. Military Correspondence, Dorchester Papers, vol. I, 1776–84.

Vol. 369. Military Correspondence, Dorchester Papers, vol. II, 1772–84.

Vol. 371. A List of Grantees of Land in Nova Scotia between 1763 and 1811.

Vol. 376. Muster Rolls of Loyalists and Military Settlers, Annapolis, Digby, and Adjacent Places, 1784.

Vol. 380. Titus Smith's Survey, 1801–2.

Vol. 394. Letter Book, Surveyor General Charles Morris, 1783–84.

Vol. 394A. Abstracts of Surveys, Reports for Grants of Land, 1784 to 1807.

Vol. 395. Letter Book, Surveyor General Charles Morris, 1784–88.

Vol. 396. Letter Book, Surveyor General Charles Morris, 1788–1800.

Vol. 423. Book of Negroes.

Vol. 443. Poll Tax and Census Rolls, 1791–96.

Vol. 459. Docket of Land Grants made out for which Certificates from Surveyor of King's Woods have been given, September 1783–about 1845.

Boxes and Folders

Annapolis County Land Grants, 1732–1827.

Family Papers. Clarkson, Clarkson's Mission to America.

Guysborough County Land Grants, 1781–1833.

Land Papers.

Shelburne Records, 1769–1868.

White Collection, vol. II, 1780–82; vol. III, 1783–84; vol. IV, 1785–86; vol. VI, 1790s.

Secondary Sources: Books

Allison, David, *History of Nova Scotia*, 3 vols., Halifax, 1916.

Ells, Margaret, *Settling the Loyalists in Nova Scotia*, Ottawa, 1933.

George, M. D., *London Life in the Eighteenth Century*, London, 1825.

Livingston, W. Ross, *Responsible Government in Nova Scotia*, Iowa City, 1930.

Wilson, Isaiah W., *A Geography and History of the County of Digby, Nova Scotia*, Halifax, 1900.

Secondary Sources: Articles

Edwards, J. Plimsoll, "The Shelburne That Was and Is Not," *Dalhousie Review*, April 1922, pp. 179–97.

———, "Vicissitudes of a Loyalist City," *Dalhousie Review*, October 1922, pp. 313–28.

Macdonald, James S., "Memoir of Governor John Parr," *Collections of the Nova Scotia Historical Society*, vol. XIV, 1910, pp. 41–78.

Rawlyk, George A., "The Guysborough Negroes: A Study in Isolation," *Dalhousie Review*, Spring 1968, pp. 24–36.

FURTHER READING

Cooper, Afua. *The Hanging of Angelique: The Untold Story of Canadian Slavery and the Burning of Old Montreal.* Toronto: Harper Collins Canada, 2006.

This is the story of a young female slave who was convicted of starting a fire that destroyed a major section of Montreal in 1734. Her punishment of death by hanging was modified to a brutal leg-crushing. The author brings an unknown chapter in Canadian history to life with this narrative of a rebellious Portuguese-born black woman. Cooper sheds light on what might have compelled a young woman to commit such a crime, and, at the same time, she demolishes the myth of a benign, slave-free Canada, revealing a damning centuries-old record of legally and culturally endorsed slavery.

Errington, Jane. *The Lion, the Eagle, and Upper Canada: A Developing Colonial Ideology*. Montreal and Kingston: McGill-Queen's University Press, 2003.

Errington's examination of the attitudes and beliefs of the Upper Canadian elite between 1784 and 1828, as seen through their private papers, public records, and the newspapers of the time. Errington argues that in order to appreciate the evolution of Upper Canadian beliefs, it is necessary to first understand the various and changing perceptions of the United States and Great Britain held by different groups of colonial leaders. The author's description of these early attempts to establish a unique Upper Canadian identity reveals the historical background of a dilemma that has yet to be resolved.

Knowles, Norman. *Inventing the Loyalists: The Ontario Loyalist Tradition and the Creation of Usable Pasts*. Toronto: University of Toronto Press, 1997.

The Loyalists have often been credited with planting a coherent and unified tradition that has been passed on virtually unchanged to subsequent generations and that continues to define Ontario's political culture. Challenging past scholarship, Norman Knowles argues that there never has been consensus on the defining characteristics of the Loyalist tradition. He suggests that the very concept of tradition has constantly been subject to appropriation by various constituencies who wish to legitimize their point of view, and their claim to status, by creating a usable past. The picture of the Loyalist tradition that emerges from this study is not of an inherited artifact but of a contested and dynamic phenomenon that has undergone continuous change. By exploring the ways in which the Loyalist past was, and still is, being negotiated, *Inventing the Loyalists* revises our understanding of the Loyalist tradition and provides insight into the politics of commemoration.

Maaka, Roger C.A., and Chris Andersen. *The Indigenous Experience: Global Perspectives*. Toronto: Canadian Scholars' Press, 2006.

The Indigenous Experience is the first book of its kind. In attempting to present the reader with some of the richness and heterogeneity of indigenous people's colonial experiences, the articles featured in this provocative volume constitute a broad survey of indigenous people from around the globe. Examples are drawn from the North American nations of Canada and the United States; the Hispanic nations of Latin America; Australia; New Zealand; Hawaii and Rapanui from Oceania; from Northern Europe and the circumpolar region, Norway; and from the continent of Africa, an example from Nigeria.

The readings focus on the broader issues of indigenousness in globalization, as the book is organized by four universal themes stretching across national and geographic boundaries: (1) the processes of colonization, including conquest, slavery, and dependence; (2) colonialism, genocide, and the problem of intention; (3) social constructs, myths, and criminalization; and (4) the ongoing struggle to attain social justice, self-determination, and equity.

MacKinnon, Neil. *This Unfriendly Soil: The Loyalist Experience in Nova Scotia*. Montreal and Kingston: McGill-Queen's University Press, 1986.

Following the American Revolution, more than 20,000 loyalists fled to Nova Scotia, doubling the population in a single year. Neil MacKinnon provides the first detailed account of this great wave of immigrants, their exodus and settlement, their adjustment to the new land, and their effect upon its people and institutions.

Prosperity was elusive. The Loyalists were disappointed not only by their treatment at the hands of the British government, but also by the apparent unwillingness of the government and the people of Nova Scotia to recognize their sacrifice and encourage their advancement.

Miller, J.R. *Skyscrapers Hide the Heavens: A History of Indian-White Relations in Canada*, 3rd Edition. Toronto: University of Toronto Press, 2000.

First published in 1989, *Skyscrapers Hide the Heavens* was the first comprehensive account of Indian-white relations throughout Canada's history. Miller charts the deterioration of the relationship from the initial, mutually beneficial contact in the fur trade to the current impasse in which Indians are resisting displacement and marginalization.

Pulis, John W., ed. *Moving On: Black Loyalists in the Afro-Atlantic World*. New York: Routledge, 1999.

During the American Revolution, thousands of colonists loyal to Britain left the colonies and resettled in Canada, Britain, and the Caribbean. Among them were a substantial number of Black Loyalists. This book explores the lives, struggles, and politics of Black Loyalists who dispersed throughout the Atlantic world, including Canada, Britain, Sierra Leone, and Jamaica. The struggles of these populations for political and economic independence under various British colonial regimes highlight the variety of challenges that faced Black Loyalists.

PART II

SPACE AND RACIALIZED COMMUNITIES

*T*he term *racialization*, which is closely linked to the concepts of "race" and racism (see Introduction), is defined as "the process by which attributes such as skin colour, language, birthplace and cultural practices are given social significance as markers of distinction."[1] Geographical space is yet another mark of difference through which groups experience the historical social process of racialization. Over the 19th and early 20th centuries, as Canada became inhabited by various populations (both "desirable" and "undesirable"), certain regions and neighbourhoods in Canada became identified with particular (often marginal) populations. Aboriginal reserves, Chinatowns, black and Jewish ghettos, and the planned ethnic agricultural communities that flourished in the Canadian West during the turn of the 20th century are well-known examples. All serve as powerful descriptive shortcuts that allow us to locate and tie certain populations to geographical areas. Defining the relationship between racialization and space, however, is a more complicated exercise than mere description can manage.

Many scholars who work on the role of space in forming social relations (often but not exclusively geographers who specialize in spatial theory) caution us that it is important to think about spaces as products of society, rather than only empty pockets of land that happen to fill with people who choose to congregate in certain areas based on the proximity of others who look or speak like they do. Rather, we must think about space as something that is socially produced, both in a material sense (lower-class people live in slums as a result of class bias) and a symbolic sense (certain spaces come to represent people who are diseased, poor, filthy, dangerous, or prone to vice).[2]

This chapter explores the material and symbolic ways in which the Chinese and blacks in Canada experienced racialization through the creation of space. Kristen McLaren's excellent chapter takes up the issue of the forced segregation of public schools in Canada West in the 1850s. This was a struggle that had both material and symbolic importance. Many blacks in Canada West who were former slaves or freeborn immigrants from the United States who sought refuge from prejudice wanted their children to have access to school facilities and teachers, which they supported through their taxes. This right was actively denied to black citizens through legally sanctioned segregation. The schools question also had important symbolic weight because the schools represented blacks' aspirations for full civic equality in Canada.

The next two chapters take up the Chinese experience in turn-of-the-century British Columbia. Patricia Roy's foundational work explores the very early arrival of the Chinese on this colonial frontier and the settlement of the Chinese into communities that came to be known as "Chinatowns." Roy explores how and why white settlers' perceptions and reception of the Chinese and their communities in British Columbia changed over time, from grudging acceptance to vilification. Kay Anderson's chapter builds on these themes and more pointedly analyzes the dynamic relationships that developed among dominant ideas about "race," public policy, and their roles in creating racialized spaces in Vancouver.

NOTES

[1] Constance Backhouse, *Colour-Coded: A Legal History of Racism in Canada, 1900–1950* (Toronto: University of Toronto Press, 1999), 148.

[2] Sherene Razack, *Race, Space, and the Law: Unmapping a White Settler Society* (Toronto: Between the Lines, 2002), 8–15.

CHAPTER 5

"We had no desire to be set apart":

Forced Segregation of Black Students in Canada West

Public Schools and Myths of British Egalitarianism

Kristin McLaren

The legend of the Underground Railroad and the image of Canada as a promised land for American slaves have been pervasive in the Canadian imagination. From children's stories to television vignettes, Canada's proud heritage as a refuge for fugitive slaves, culminating in the arrival of up to 40,000 fugitives in Canada, is often told.[1] Little in this popular lore discusses the experiences of these people once they arrived in Canada. The discrimination they faced in their daily lives and their exclusion from social institutions such as churches and schools is for the most part ignored or misrepresented.

One facet of black Canadian history[2] that has not been well understood is education. When black education is discussed, the emergence of segregated schools is often presented as a response to requests by blacks to be separate. Although contemporary work in the area of African-Canadian history tends to emphasize the racist attitudes that allowed segregation in education, much of the scholarship still points to segregationist tendencies in the black community with very little evidence to support this assumption.[3] A re-examination is warranted of historical evidence surrounding the introduction of the segregated racial schools clause in the *School Act* of 1850 and of historical interpretations regarding separate black education in Canada West. In addressing this question, this study thus speaks directly to the myth of Canada as a haven from racism.

In the mid-nineteenth century, Canada West saw itself as a proud province of the British Empire, in which the rights and privileges of all were guaranteed under the British constitution. Early colonists of British descent strove to recreate Upper Canada's government structures, institutions, and landscape in Britain's image. This rigid adherence to an established sense of identity in the face of a changing environment, combined with a language about cultural purity, has had a significant impact upon relations between British-Canadians and others who were not seen to be of the British race.[4]

British settlers believed that Canada, as part of the British Empire, was a moral example to all nations on earth.[5] The abolition of slavery was seen as a moral victory for the Empire over the United States, and the fact that thousands of fugitive slaves fled to Canada via the Underground Railroad to live in freedom reinforced a sense of superiority among white citizens whose myths presented Canada as a land of freedom and equal opportunity by virtue of its British character. These stories of our origins continue to influence Canadians' image of ourselves. Popular histories of Ontario have tended to highlight the accomplishments of the British in the formation of this province with little recognition of the indispensable efforts of a diversity of immigrants from around the world. Until only recently, published histories of Ontario began with the settlement of Loyalists in the territory, with few references to Native peoples who made European exploration possible, or to French Canadians who entered the territory almost a century before the arrival of the British.[6]

These popular histories articulate what it means to be a Canadian for a certain segment of the population. They function as myths in that they describe how contemporary reality has come into being and provide a sense of meaning, orientation, and identity for a people.[7] As Canadian historian and self-proclaimed myth-maker Arthur Lower suggests, "[H]istory begins in myth."[8] Myths in this sense are not fictional tales but stories of origins formulated in relation to reality. Historical narratives claim to have a purely spatial and temporal basis; however, any understanding of human origins is often legitimated by some sense of transcendent power or sacred structure. In nineteenth-century Ontario, for example, the British Empire took on a sacred significance for many who derived their identity from their British heritage. English-Canadian leaders such as John Strachan saw the Empire as an instrument of God and believed that, as part of the Empire, Canada had a significant role to play in making the earth "the garden of the Lord."[9] Symbols of Britain such as the monarchy, British law, and British institutions were manifestations of a timeless, transcendent, sacred

reality in relation to which many Canadians formulated a sense of who they were.

* * *

Many African-American immigrants originally looked to Canada as a refuge from the discrimination they faced in the United States. Samuel Ringgold Ward, black leader and proud British gentleman, suggested that "there is no country in the world so much hated by slaveholders, as Canada; nor is there any country so much beloved and sought for, by the slaves … [because] it is a free country."[10] According to the North American Convention of Colored Freedmen held September 10, 1851, "[T]he British government was the most favourable in the civilized world to the people of colour and was thereby entitled to the entire confidence of the Convention."[11] In her plea to American fugitive slaves to immigrate to Canada West, the young Mary Ann Shadd praised the British Empire and asserted, "[T]here is no legal discrimination whatever affecting coloured immigrants in Canada, nor from any cause whatever are their privileges sought to be abridged."[12]

By mid-century, between 20,000 and 40,000 black people had settled among British and French Canadian colonists, primarily in the rural areas of the southwestern and Niagara peninsulas of Canada West.[13] Significant concentrations of African Canadians lived in municipalities along the Detroit River and Lake Erie shores such as Amherstburg, Fort Malden, Sandwich, Anderdon, Maidstone, Mersea, Gosfield Colchester, Harrow, and New Canaan from the early nineteenth century. The southwestern shore of Lake Ontario, including the Niagara region, St. Catharines, and Hamilton, was another important area of settlement for black immigrants. Large numbers of African

Canadians had also settled further inland in towns such as London and Brantford, in and around Chatham, and as far north as Oro, on the northern shore of Lake Simcoe. By 1861 an estimated 40 per cent of Canada West's black population had been born in the province,[14] and, like other Canadians, many African Canadians believed strongly in the egalitarian potential of British law. They thus fought for their rights to equal participation in British-Canadian institutions. The Committee for the Colored People of Windsor asserted in 1859 that, as "Her Majesty's subjects," we "desire to share the common blessings of a Free Government in the education of our rising generation ... according to the established Laws of the country of our adoption and choice."[15]

* * *

Many Chatham citizens were able to maintain a claim to egalitarian values in the face of their racist practices because black people were presented as morally inferior and thus not subject to the same laws as white people. Across Canada West, white Canadians articulated fears that black children would prove to be a bad moral influence upon their own children if both were allowed to attend the same schools. Giving his opinion on the reasons behind the introduction of the law allowing segregated schools, Chief Justice Beverly Robinson suggested in 1854 that white parents felt "an apprehension that the children of the coloured people, many of whom have but lately escaped from a state of slavery may be, in respect to morals and habits, unfortunately worse trained than the white children are in general, and that their children might suffer from the effects of bad example."[16] White people expressed fears that "African barbarism" might "triumph over Anglo-Saxon civilization" if black children

were allowed to attend schools with white children.[17] In a similar fashion, white citizens of London expressed their concern in 1861 that blacks were "rude in speech, uncouth in manners and address and untidy in attire." It was feared that they could have a negative influence upon other children, especially adolescent white girls, if they were to be admitted into the senior classes at London's Central School.[18]

Toronto was perhaps the one place where segregation in public education was never the norm. Black doctors graduated from the city's medical schools and Emaline Shadd, Mary Ann's sister, received top honours from the Toronto Normal School in 1855.[19] Egerton Ryerson attributes this inclusive spirit to the "good sense and Christian and British feeling" of the citizens of Toronto,[20] but the reasons for integration in Toronto are perhaps better understood in more practical terms.

According to Daniel G. Hill, author of one of the few studies on Toronto's black community prior to the late nineteenth century, an affluent population of African Canadians in the city had immigrated over a long period of time and had established a strong infrastructure to support new immigrants. Black immigrants from the United States arrived in a slow and steady migration by mid-century, never by sudden influx, and found work easily in the city's growing economy.[21] Some of Canada's most vocal anti-slavery activists lived in Toronto and were opposed to racial segregation. George Brown, editor of the *Globe*, ironically a vehement anti-Catholic as well, had an important influence on preventing the introduction of segregation into the city's institutions.

In spite of Toronto's good record on school integration, racism was not completely absent. As one man reported to the American abolitionist S. G. Howe, "I must say that, leaving the law out of the question, I find that prejudice here is equally strong as on the other side [in the United States]."[22] The vast majority of black settlers lived in one section of the city, St. John's Ward.[23] As a result, policies of school segregation may not have seemed necessary if large numbers of black students were together in the same school section, already separated from white students by virtue of district boundaries. In addition, African Canadians made up only 2 per cent of Toronto's total population in 1854, compared with between 20 to 30 per cent of some towns in the southwestern regions of Canada West;[24] it is thus not surprising that issues of segregated schooling were less pronounced in Toronto and more of an issue in communities with larger concentrations of African Canadians.

In most Canada West towns, the majority of white parents as well as school trustees were opposed to integration. If black children were allowed into the schools, they were usually forced to sit on separate benches.[25] More often than not, however, black children were not admitted into publicly funded elementary schools (known as common schools) at all, and little concern was shown for their education. In Amherstburg, it was said the parents of white children would "sooner ... cut their children's heads off and throw them into the road side ditch" than send their children to school with "niggers."[26] In 1847 the London Auxiliary Bible Society reported that, in spite of the fact that blacks in London paid the school tax, "[I]f any Coloured child enters a school, the white children are withdrawn, the teachers are painfully obliged to decline, and the Coloured people ... yield to an injustice which they are too weak to redress."[27] In towns such as Colchester and Sandwich, trustees divided school districts to avoid contact between the races.[28]

These efforts to segregate black students were blatantly against the laws in force prior to 1850. The *School Act* of 1843 clearly states: "it

shall not be lawful for such Trustees, or for the Chief, or other, Superintendent of Common Schools, or for any Teacher to exclude from any Common School or from the benefit of education therein, the children of any class or description of persons resident within the School district to which such common school may belong."[29] The Department of Education received several appeals to intervene against segregation, and in response superintendent Egerton Ryerson admitted that exclusion was "at variance with the letter and spirit of the law, and with the principles and spirit of British Institutions, which deprive no human being of any benefit ... on account of the colour of his skin."[30] However, Ryerson continued to tolerate illegal discrimination in the schools, claiming there was nothing he could do to stop it.

* * *

Admission to common schools was an important goal among African Canadians in Canada West. An 1841 report to Lord Sydenham suggested that "the cause of first complaint of our coloured men is the difficulty they experience in procuring admission for their children into common schools."[31] Faced with exclusion from the common school in Amherstburg, a group of African Canadians worked with the missionary Isaac Rice to start their own public school, open to students of all backgrounds, in 1846, and the school trustees made numerous appeals for their share of the government grant. African and French Canadian populations of Amherstburg lived in close proximity and were forced to compete for a school in the same district; it would seem that the municipality would not allow for more than one public school aside from the institution already established for white, English-speaking citizens of the town.[32]

Where black children were excluded from public education, black teachers often took the initiative to start their own schools. In Sandwich and Windsor, Mary Bibb and Mary Ann Shadd opened schools for children who did not have access to public education.[33] While some received a small amount of assistance from American philanthropists, most black teachers in Canada West were poorly paid; their schools were largely under-funded and most were short-lived.[34]

* * *

The Buxton mission school, a private institution established at the Elgin settlement for black people at Raleigh by Rev. William King, was open to all children regardless of race. Because the quality of instruction, given by graduates of Knox Presbyterian College in Toronto, was far superior to that of schools in neighbouring Chatham, by 1851 almost all the white students from the common school, run by King's nemesis Edwin Larwill, had joined the black students in Buxton.[35]

Indeed, the vast majority of private schools established by or for African Canadians were open to black, white, and aboriginal students who wanted to attend. These schools were often opened as an alternative to the strict segregation imposed in government schools. Mary Bibb, who worked for a government school in Sandwich for a short time, opened a private school in Windsor that was to be "free to all, irrespective of color."[36] By 1855, 7 of her 46 students were white.[37] According to Mary Ann Shadd, "[T]he colored common schools have more of a complexional character than the private, which, with no exception I have heard of, are open to all."[38] Schools managed by African Canadians were rarely, if ever, exclusive. Instead, the vast majority of black educators in Canada West looked to promote integration.

At the same time as African Canadians sought integrated education, public education officials imposed segregation upon an unwilling black population. By 1850 the Council of Public Instruction had introduced education laws that accommodated racist tendencies. The *School Act* of 1850 added a provision to the already established separate schools clause allowing for separate schools based on race. Section XIX reads: "It shall be the duty of the Municipal Council of any Township, and of the Board of School Trustees of any City, Town or incorporated Village, on the application, in writing, of twelve, or more, resident heads of families, to authorize the establishment of one, or more, Separate schools for Protestants, Roman Catholics, or Coloured people."[39]

* * *

When first confronted with opposition to integration in public schools, Ryerson suggested that a law acknowledging the racist tendencies of Upper Canadians would be "a disgrace to our Legislature." In his draft of the 1847 School Bill for cities and towns, he allowed trustees a broad base of power to "establish any kind or description of schools they may please." This vague directive was deliberately left open to interpretation, so that trustees could "establish one or more schools for coloured children. Thus the best interests as well as the rights of the coloured people can be respected and promoted, and nothing insidious be admitted into the Statute book."[40]

After his tour of the Western District in 1848, Ryerson came to the conclusion that this newly introduced provision did not allow for the education of black children, and so he drafted another "authorizing each District council to establish one or more Schools for the children of Coloured people."[41] This proposal became law in the 1850 *School Act*. Ryerson submitted this proposal "with extreme pain and regret." He claimed to "have exerted all the power that I possessed, and employed all the persuasion I could command, but the prejudices and feelings of the people are stronger than law."[42] As evidenced by his responses to appeals by African Canadians against exclusion and his correspondence with local school officials, however, Ryerson, unlike his predecessor Robert Murray, was more inclined to tolerate discrimination than to exert any pressure to resolve the issue. As Chief Justice Beverly Robinson remarked in a later Supreme Court ruling regarding the exclusion of black children from common schools, "separate schools for coloured people were authorized … out of deference to the prejudices of the white population."[43]

The new *School Act* proved controversial. Many groups, both black and white, expressed their opposition to separate racial education. A petition from Toronto argued that the introduction of the "coloured school" provision would "not only be detrimental to our elevation, but … the first step toward taking away that equality which the British law guarantees to all Her Majesty's subjects."[44] Citizens of Canada West's westernmost county, Essex, complained that the separate school provision was an unjust infringement upon their rights and that it was unfair to put the control of black education into the hands of municipalities.[45] Certain teachers' associations also expressed their disapproval.[46]

During the 1850s, black parents sent over 20 petitions to the Canada West Education Department complaining of exclusion and requesting admission for their children into common schools.[47] A petition from black parents at Simcoe claimed that they had been "deprived of the privilege for many years of sending children to common schools." Yet they were compelled to pay school taxes.

We have tried every lawful and civil means to get our children into the common schools … we have applied to the trustees time after time and year after year and failed in it. We have taken our children into the schools and desired the teachers to receive and teach them which thing has also been refused…. [We] voted for the School Trustees together with other persons, and expected our children educated with the white children … we had no desire to be set apart, nor never had….[48]

* * *

In the Hill case of 1854 the Supreme Court ruled that, if a separate racial school had been established, black students had to attend it, no matter the quality of the school or its distance from home. In 1852 Dennis Hill of Camden Township, northeast of Chatham, wrote to Egerton Ryerson complaining that, although he had paid taxes, his son was excluded from the common school in his section because his "skin is a few shades darker than some of my neighbours."[49] In reply, Ryerson remarked, "I cannot express any opinion upon the case which you submit," but suggested that, if there was no separate school for his son to attend, Hill should prosecute for damages.[50] Hill did prosecute and his case was heard in the Supreme Court of Upper Canada in 1854.

In 1852 the trustees of Camden had designated the British American Institute, located in the Dawn settlement, a common school "for the exclusive benefit of the coloured population."[51] The limits of this school section encompassed the entire township and gore of Camden as well as the adjacent township of Zone, a region over 15 miles across. Although the Dawn school was a full four and a half miles away from Dennis Hill's property, the court ruled that his children must attend there or be denied access to education. In 1856 citizens of Camden complained that their taxes went to common schools in their section while the segregated school was inaccessible at a distance of up to 15 miles away.[52] Most of the black children of Camden township were effectively denied access to education because the segregated school was too far for them to attend.

Public schools for black children were sorely lacking in public funding, as local trustees were not always forthcoming with their share of government grants. In 1852 the Anti-Slavery Society of Canada reported that teachers at black separate schools were poorly paid and poorly qualified and that the quality of education at these schools was decidedly inferior to that at other common schools.[53] On his tour through Canada West in 1855, Benjamin Drew noted the poor quality of black separate schools in the province.[54]

In Windsor no public education was available to African Canadians until 1859, although trustees had passed a by-law in 1854 claiming they would establish a "coloured school." The construction of this school was delayed, however, until 1862. The temporary accommodation made available in 1858 measured 16 by 24 feet and was intended to accommodate up to 80 school-aged children. Parents likened the school to a "coop."[55] In 1856 African Canadians in St. Catharines boycotted their separate school because they felt they were at a disadvantage and intended to claim "their lawful right to ... [send] our children to whatever public school is established in our ward."[56]

When the town of Amherstburg introduced free common schools in 1851, the public school trustees appealed to the people of the town "to take the responsibility of keeping the coloured children from entering any of the schools." A committee of four trustees was appointed to set up a separate school for black children.[57]

Drew remarked in 1856 that the separate school in Amherstburg was "comfortless and repulsive." It had no blackboard or chairs, the two inkstands in use yielded "a little bad ink," and the readers were "miserably tattered and worn-out."[58] In declaring his judgement in the Hill case, Chief Justice Robinson observed, "[I]t can hardly be supposed that the Legislature authorized such separate schools under the idea that it would be more beneficial or agreeable to the coloured people to have their children taught separately from whites."[59]

Trustees in other regions altered the boundaries of school districts according to the presence or absence of blacks. According to Rev. David Hotchkiss, working for the AMA in Amherstburg, "the whites will not let the coloured children attend their schools. They [draw] their lines around their districts in a zig zag course so as to throw all the coloured families out."[60] In Norwich, north of Charlotteville, the black population was denied access to the school they were using in their area after one white moved in nearby and the school was annexed to a white school section.[61] This gerrymandering of school districts was declared illegal by the Supreme Court in the 1854 case of *Washington v. the Trustees of Charlotteville*. In this case, George Washington paid the school fees and was assessed for repairs of the common school in his section. In 1849 trustees had instructed the local teacher not to admit Washington's son Solomon. Washington appealed to the district superintendent, who in turn appealed to Ryerson. The district and provincial superintendents informed the trustees that their conduct was illegal, but the school administrators of Charlotteville were determined to exclude Mr. Washington's children from the common school whatever the consequences. In 1850 the Municipal Council of Charlotteville redrew the school section boundaries so as to exclude Washington's land from any school district; however, he continued to be assessed for school taxes. Ryerson did not directly intervene, claiming he "never supposed the trustees would resist the law" and suggesting that Washington take his grievances to court.[62] The Supreme Court heard Washington's case in 1854; by this time, his eldest son Solomon had reached the age of 12. The court ruled in Washington's favour, outlawing the gerrymandering of school districts for the sole purpose of excluding black students.[63]

This victory was bittersweet for Washington because he received no assistance with his legal expenses and lost his farm in payment of the fees incurred.[64] The precedent set by this case was only a qualified victory for black education rights because the ruling did not prevent school trustees from creating segregated school sections. It became common practice for trustees to open three different kinds of schools in their districts: one for Protestants, one for Roman Catholics, and one for African Canadians. Schools opened for African Canadians were usually set up and managed by the central board of white trustees and not requested by the parents of black students.[65]

Although much contemporary historical work points out that school segregation was enforced by the white population of Canada West, several established historians have argued that African Canadians favoured segregation out of a desire for "comfort" and "security,"[66] a "sense of inadequacy,"[67] or "lack of confidence to compete"[68] or because they were "unable to do the regular work set by the Education Department."[69] These claims regarding black support for segregation fly in the face of all evidence. As countless appeals against separate education illustrate, large numbers of African Canadians found little comfort in segregation. Robin Winks acknowledges that, in

most instances, the same texts were used in black separate schools and "examination papers were also creditable."[70] Thus black students were capable of and did the same work as whites, and assumptions that they could not attain the same standards of education are without foundation.

In addition to unsubstantiated claims about general segregationist tendencies, some historians have made more specific claims regarding the strategic support for separate schools among black leaders. In his influential works on African-Canadian history, James W. St. G. Walker asserts that segregation was most certainly not a "black idea," although several African Canadians accepted segregation in the face of harsh discrimination by white Canadian society, which they had "no inspiration to enter."[71] While African-Canadian history has undoubtedly, and understandably, not been devoid of advocates for racial separation, the historical record shows that the overwhelming trend among blacks in mid-nineteenth-century Canada West favoured integration. In spite of assertions by Walker and others that, in towns such as Windsor, Colchester, and Chatham, "several black communities took immediate advantage of the 1850 *School Act*] to establish separate school districts,"[72] segregated schools in these regions were set up by white trustees in the face of vocal opposition by the black community.[73]

* * *

Like Walker and Winks, Donald Simpson and Jason Silverman make important contributions to an understanding of black education in Canada West, and they point to several examples of enforced segregation and discrimination against black students in Canada West schools. However, Simpson and Silverman also make some unsupported claims regarding black parents' requests for separate schools in certain regions. After having referred to numerous petitions against school segregation in Amherstburg, Simpson claims that there is no way of knowing whether the black citizens of this town wanted separate schools.[74] In spite of the assertion by African Canadians in Simcoe that "we had no desire to be set apart nor never had"[75] and the refusal of black parents in Windsor to "yield to prejudice" and establish a separate school,[76] Silverman assumes that the black population of these towns desired separate schools.[77]

While there is little doubt that some elements of the black population in Canada West had little choice but to accept school segregation, there is no evidence that any blacks in Canada West ever endorsed segregated education. On the contrary, African Canadians in Canada West worked toward integration and were determined to claim their rights to equal access to schooling. A CCSS missionary to Dawn Mills, northeast of Chatham, suggested that black people in his town would "rather be without schools than excluded."[78] In 1859 the Committee for the Colored People of Windsor asserted, "[W]e as a people … love British Law and will ever defend it, but we shall equally stand up for all the rights that the law provides us."[79] Numerous petitions appealed to education administrators' "sense of justice and judgment,"[80] demanding that they live up to their British-Canadian egalitarian ideals and allow for equal access to education.[81] As Dr. A. T. Jones of London declared to S. G. Howe in reaction to the school board's proposal to open separate schools for black children:

I have eight children, who were all born in this town—British subjects, as much as the whitest among you; and they don't believe in anything else but the Queen. Now, instead of leaving these children to grow up with

that love of country and the Queen, you are trying to plant within them a hatred for the country; and the day may come when you will hear them saying, "This is the country that disenfranchises us, and deprives us of our rights."[82]

As much as black leaders pushed for integration, white trustees proved equally adamant in their opposition to integration. Letters from local trustees to the Council of Public Instruction complained that black parents must not be allowed to "force their children" into classes with the white children because "schools have been broken up"[83] and "the harmony … in school matters … [has been] lost [due to the] demands of a few of the coloured inhabitants."[84] This "harmony" was ensured through a policy of forced segregation that was sanctioned by the Supreme Court of Canada West in 1854.

The majority of black-run schools welcomed a diversity of Canadian children, regardless of heritage and in spite of their meagre funding. Schools established by or for black communities in several towns opened their doors to white children who had no other option for education themselves or whose parents recognized the better calibre of education provided in a few cases by well-educated missionary teachers. The segregated schools imposed by Colchester trustees accepted white students, and eventually many of them served a majority of white children.[85] Robin Winks points to a similar situation in Brantford, where the level of instruction at the black school was superior to that at the white school. White students began to enrol here until the two schools were eventually integrated.[86] The government-imposed separate school in Chatham also accepted the occasional white student.[87]

The fact that African Canadians accepted people of all backgrounds into their schools demonstrates an acceptance of the heterogeneous nature of Canada West society. Those who ran black schools appear to have accepted the refashioning of human identity that becoming Canadian entailed. In contrast, the powers controlling schools in the province showed a strong propensity toward segregation and thus a reluctance to adapt to their newly plural Canadian surroundings. During the mid-nineteenth century, many Canadians did not perceive the contradiction between their British ideals and the lived reality of racial exclusion in the education system, the "powerful instrument of British Constitutional Government." Education administrators espoused a deep desire to refashion Canada West as the British province described in Canadian foundational myths, and the equal participation of black students in the public education system could have been seen as a threat to the maintenance of this religiously secured notion of British purity. At the same time, the ideal of British morality was so pervasive in the consciousness of nineteenth-century Canadians that the discrimination inherent in Canada West's education system was not confronted by its proponents and was allowed to continue virtually undetected.

Although Canadian conceptions of identity have changed significantly since the mid-nineteenth century, contemporary myths continue to perpetuate some of the dominant nineteenth-century perceptions of Canada West as a bastion of morality, freedom, and equality. Popular Canadian mythology emphasizes this country's role as an Underground Railroad destination; yet its history of racism is often ignored. Perhaps the omission of this history of exclusion from popular historical accounts reflects fears that our society's foundational cultural myths might collapse under threat.

Some modern historians seem to reflect the dominant myths of nineteenth-century British Canada West when, contrary to historical evidence, they assert that African Canadians advocated segregated schools and underemphasize the integrated nature of black-run institutions of the period. Historical evidence confirms that the vast majority of black parents and community leaders worked toward an integrated society in Canada West as they asserted their rights to equal treatment under purportedly egalitarian and morally upright British-Canadian laws and institutions.

NOTES

1   See, for example, *The CRB Foundation Heritage Project: 60th Minute commemorative Video: The Underground Railroad*, CRB Foundation, 1998, videocassette; *Canada: A People's History*, episode 8, videocassette A, *The Great Enterprise*, prod. and dir. John Williamson, Canadian Broadcasting corporation, 2001. The black population in the mid-nineteenth century was considerably more diverse than popular estimations suggest, consisting of a mix of fugitive slaves and free immigrants, as well as former Upper Canadian slaves and long-established loyalists who had lived in the province since the late eighteenth century. In 1852 the Anti-Slavery Society of Canada estimated that the black population of Canada West was 30,000. Cited in Benjamin Drew, *A Northside View of Slavery. The Refugee: or the Narrative of Fugitive Slaves in Canada. Related by Themselves, with an Account of the History and Condition of the Colored Population of Upper Canada* (1856;

Toronto: Coles, 1972), p. v. in 1855 Samuel Ringgold Ward suggested that there were between 35,000 and 40,000 blacks in the province; see Ward, *Autobiography of a Fugitive Negro* (London: John Snow, 1855), p. 154. Recently, Michael Wayne has argued that the population has been overestimated and was likely between 22,500 and 23,000 in 1861; see Wayne, "The Black Population of Canada West on the Eve of the American Civil War: A Reassessment Based on the Manuscript Census of 1861," *Histoire sociale/Social History*, vol. 28, no. 56 (November 1995), p. 470.

2   Following current practice, I use the terms "African Canadian" and "black" interchangeably to refer to the historic community of immigrants of African heritage (the vast majority of whom came from the United States) and their descendants in Canada. See James W. St. G. Walker, "African Canadians," in Paul Robert Magocsi, ed., *Encyclopedia of Canada's Peoples*

(Toronto: University of Toronto Press, 1999), pp. 139–176. Many of these people were of mixed descent and were identified as "Negroes," "coloured" people, "blacks," or "Africans" in nineteenth-century Canada West. I examine the relationships between these people and the dominant British-Canadian population in Canada West. The term "British Canadian" refers to Canadians of British descent, who arrived directly from the British Isles or who were descended from these emigrants and came to the Quebec colony (and later Upper Canada) via the Thirteen Colonies (later the United States). These people were racialized as "white." On racialization, see Timothy J. Stanley, "Why I Killed Canadian History: Towards an Anti-Racist History in Canada," *Histoire sociale / Social History*, vol. 33, no. 65 (May 2000), pp. 95–103.

3   Robin Winks, *The Blacks in Canada: A History*, 2nd ed. (Montreal and Kingston: McGill-Queen's University Press, 1997); Walker, "African Canadians," p. 159; Claudette Knight, "Black Parents Speak: Education in Mid-Nineteenth-Century Canada West," *Ontario History*, vol. 89 (December 1997), p. 275; Susan E. Houston and Alison Prentice, *Schooling and Scholars in Nineteenth-Century Ontario* (Toronto: University of Toronto Press, 1988); J. Donald Wilson, "The Ryerson Years in Canada West," in J. Donald Wilson, Robert M. Stamp, and Louis Philippe Audet, eds., *Canadian Education: A History* (Scarborough, Ont.: Prentice-Hall, 1970), pp. 232–233; Donald G. Simpson, "Negroes in Ontario from Early Times to 1870" (PhD dissertation, University of Western Ontario, 1971).

4   On notions of cultural purity in Canada, see Jennifer Reid, "'A Society Made by History': The Mythic Source of Identity in Canada," *Canadian Review of American Studies*, vol. 27 (1997), pp. 1–19.

5   William Westfall suggests that a shared attachment to a British Protestant moral code was the main basis for social stability in Victorian Canada West. Westfall, *Two Worlds: The Protestant Culture of Nineteenth-Century Ontario* (Montreal and Kingston: McGill-Queen's University Press, 1989), p. 201.

6   See Gerald M. Craig, *Upper Canada: The Formative Years, 1784–1841* (Toronto: McClelland & Stewart, 1963); Ontario Historical Society, *Profiles of a Province: Studies in the History of Ontario. A Collection of Essays Commissioned by the Ontario Historical Society to Commemorate the Centennial of Ontario* (Toronto: Ontario Historical Society, 1967). Several histories romanticize the Loyalist heritage of the province. See *Loyal She Remains: A Pictorial History of Ontario* (Toronto: United Empire Loyalists' Association of Canada, 1984); Charles J. Humber, ed., *Allegiance: The Ontario Story* (Mississauga, Ont.: Heirloom, 1991).

7   Mircea Eliade, *Myth and Reality*, trans. Willard R. Trask (New York: Harper Torchbooks, 1963), p. 5.

8   Arthur R. M. Lower, cited in Welf H. Heick, ed., *History and Myth: Arthur Lower and the Making of Canadian Nationalism* (Vancouver: University of British Columbia Press, 1975), p. 1.

9   Westfall, *Two Worlds*, p. 5. According to British missionary Samuel Wilberforce, the British Empire was a gift of God destined to spread across the earth: "what works of God

might not be worked through it!" Wilberforce also described the Empire as timeless, in that it would live eternally through the Christian nations it founded and nurtured. See "Sermon by William Wilberforce, 'The Conditions of Missionary Success', 1850," in John Wolffe, ed., *Religion in Victorian Britain*, vol. 5: *Culture and Empire* (Manchester: Manchester University Press, 1997), pp. 306–307.

10   Ward. *Autobiography of a Fugitive Negro*, p. 158.

11   *Provincial Freeman*, September 10, 1851.

12   Mary Ann Shadd, *A Plea for Emigration Or, Notes of Canada West*, ed. Richard Almonte (1852; Toronto: Mercury, 1998), pp. 29, 74.

13   See note 1 for population estimates.

14   For an analysis of 1861 census data, see Wayne, "The Black Population of Canada West," p. 473.

15   Archives of Ontario [hereafter AO], Ontario Department of Education, Incoming Correspondence [hereafter Incoming Education Correspondence], RG 2–12, vol. 26, Committee for the Colored People of Windsor to Ryerson, March 2, 1859.

16   "Re: *Dennis Hill v. the School Trustees of Camden and Zone*," *Upper Canada Queen's Bench Reports*, vol. 11, p. 578 [hereafter *Hill v. Camden and Zone*].

17   AO, Incoming Education Correspondence, RG 2–12, vol. 18. Philip Smith to Ryerson, August 1, 1854.

18   *London Free Press*, July 22, 1861.

19   Daniel G. Hill, *The Freedom Seekers: Blacks in Early Canada* (Agincourt, Ont,: Book Society of Canada, 1981), p. 158.

20   AO, Outgoing Education Correspondence, RG 2–8, vol. 7, Ryerson to Dennis Hill, November 30, 1852.

21   Daniel G. Hill, "Negroes in Toronto, 1793–1865," *Ontario History*, vol. 55, no. 2 (June 1963), pp. 76–84.

22   S. G. Howe, *The Refugees from Slavery in Canada West: Report to the Freedmen's Inquiry Commission* (1864; New York: Arno Press and the *New York Times*, 1969), p. 45.

23   Adrienne Shadd, Afua Cooper, and Karolyn Smardz Frost, *The Underground Railroad: Next Stop, Toronto!* (Toronto: Natural Heritage Books, 2002), p. 33.

24   According to Benjamin Drew, the peak population of blacks in Toronto was 1,000 out of a total population of 47,000 in 1854. In Amherstburg there were approximately 400 to 500 blacks out of a total population of 2,000; in Colchester, 450 blacks out of a total population of 1,500; and in Chatham, 800 blacks out of a total population of 4,000. Drew, *A Northside View of Slavery*, pp. 94, 234, 348, 367.

25   This was common practice in Hamilton and in West Flamboro before black children were excluded from the town's common schools altogether. AO, Incoming Education Correspondence, RG 2–12, vol. 4, Patrick Thornton to Alexander McNab, November 26, 1844; vol. 20, James Douglas to Ryerson, February 3, 1856; vol. 25, Jefferson Lightfoot to Ryerson, October 5, 1858.

26 Isaac Rice et al. to Egerton Ryerson, cited in Hodgins, *Documentary History, Volume VI: 1846*, p. 294,

27 AO, J. George Hodgins Fonds, F1207, London Auxiliary Bible Society to William H. Draper, March 27, 1847.

28 AO, Incoming Education Correspondence, RG 2–12, vol. 4, John Cowan (Sandwich) to Alexander McNab, October 15, 1845; Harrow and Colchester South Township School Area Board, *A Story of Public Schools in Colchester South Township* (Harrow: School Board, 1966), p. 8.

29 *An Act for the Establishment and Maintenance of Common Schools in Upper Canada*, section 44, clause 7, in Hodgins, *Documentary History, Volume IV: 1841–1843* (1897), p. 258.

30 AO, Outgoing Education Correspondence, RG 2–8, vol. 3, Ryerson to Isaac Rice et al., March 5, 1846.

31 National Archives of Canada, Colonial Office 42/478, Original Correspondence, Secretary of State, Upper Canada: Dispatches, E. de St-Remy to Lord Sydenham, April 5, 1841,

32 AO, Incoming Education Correspondence, RG 2–12, vol. 5, Rice et al. to Ryerson, January 23, 1846; Peden to Ryerson, February 23, 1846; Outgoing Education Correspondence, RG 2–8, vol. 3, Ryerson to Peden, March 5, 1846.

33 Afua Cooper, "Black Teachers in Canada West, 1850–1870: A History" (MA thesis, University of Toronto, 1991), pp. 29–45, and "Black Women and Work in Nineteenth Century Canada West: Black Woman Teacher Mary Bibb," in Peggy Bristow, ed., *"We're Rooted Here and They Can't Pull Us Up": Essays in African Canadian Women's History* (Toronto: University of Toronto Press, 1994), pp. 143–170.

34 Cooper, "Black Teachers," pp. 64–92.

35 "Schools in Canada," *Voice of the Fugitive*, July 18, 1852; Victor Ullman, *Look to the North Star: A Life of William King* (Boston: Beacon Press, 1969), pp. 148–149.

36 Mary Bibb to Horace Mann, January 20, 1853, cited in Cooper, "Black Teachers," p. 38.

37 Drew, *A Northside View of Slavery*, pp. 321–322.

38 Shadd, *A Plea for Immigration*, p. 66. Several white students attended the schools at which Shadd taught. Hill, *The Freedom Seekers*, p. 156.

39 J. George Hodgins, *Historical and Other Papers and Documents Illustrative of the Educational System of Ontario, 1853–1868* (Toronto: L. K. Cameron, 1911), p. 213.

40 AO, J. George Hodgins Fonds, F1207, p. 12, Ryerson to W. H. Draper, April 12, 1847.

41 Egerton Ryerson, "Explanation of the Provisions of a Proposed School Bill of 1849," in Hodgins, *Documentary History, Vol. VIII: 1848–49*, (1901), p. 91.

42 Ibid.

43 *Hill v. Camden and Zone*, p. 578.

44 Toronto *Globe*, June 25, 1850.

45 "Objections to the Provision for Separate Schools for Coloured Children," in Hodgins, *Documentary History, Volume IX: 1850–51* (1902), p. 26.

46 Dumfries Teachers' Association remarks, in Hodgins, *Documentary History, Volume IX: 1850–51*, p. 64.

47 AO, Incoming Education Correspondence, RG 2–12.

48 AO, Incoming Education Correspondence, RG 2–12, vol. 11, Petition of colored inhabitants of Simcoe, December 12, 1851.

49 AO, Incoming Education Correspondence, RG 2–12, vol. 14, Dennis Hill to Egerton Ryerson, November 22, 1852.

50 AO, Outgoing Education Correspondence, RG 2–8, vol. 7. Ryerson to Hill, November 30, 1852.

51 *Hill v. Camden and Zone*, p. 575.

52 AO, Incoming Education Correspondence, RG 2–12, vol. 20, William P. Newman to Ryerson, January 13, 1856; Peter B. Smith et al. to Ryerson, June 29, 1856.

53 Anti-Slavery Society of Canada, *First Annual Report of the Anti-Slavery Society of Canada* (Toronto, March 24, 1852).

54 Drew, *A Northside View of Slavery*.

55 AO, Incoming Education Correspondence, RG 2–12, vol. 26, Clayborn Harris to William Horton, February 16, 1859.

56 *Provincial Freeman*, May 24, 1856; AO, Incoming Education Correspondence, RG 2–12, vol. 23, Daniel Jones et al. to Ryerson, January 24, 1853.

57 AO, Alvin D. McCurdy Papers, F 2076-11-0-1, container 53, Public School Trustees Minutes with reference to King St. School and Coloured School Teachers, April 1, 1851.

58 Drew, *A Northside View of Slavery*, p. 348. As further testament to their destitute situation, schools for blacks in Amherstburg and Colchester received grants from the Education Department's Poor School Fund after petitions to Ryerson. AO, Outgoing Education Correspondence, RG 2–8, vol. 19, Ryerson to James Kevill, March 13, 1857; vol. 21, Ryerson to F. G. Elliot, December 3, 1857.

59 *Hill v. Camden and Zone*, p. 578.

60 AO, AMA manuscripts, F19–F1 S42, 1846–1860. Hotchkiss to Whipple, March 4, 1851.

61 AO, Incoming Education Correspondence, RG 2–12, vol. 11, Charles Joiner to Ryerson, January 8, 1852.

62 AO, Outgoing Education Correspondence, RG 2–8, vol. 12, Ryerson to J. G. Henton, May 20, 1855.

63 *Washington v. Charlotteville*.

64 AO, Incoming Education Correspondence, RG 2–12, vol. 6, William Clarke to Ryerson, June 2, 1849; vol. 18. Philip Smith to Ryerson, August 1, 1854; vol. 19, J. G. Henton to Ryerson, May 25, 1855; Outgoing Education Correspondence, RG 2–8, vol. 4. Ryerson to William Clarke, n.d., 1849; vol. 10, Ryerson to Henton, May 20, 1855.

65 In 1854 the school trustees of Windsor voted to erect three such schools (Simpson, "Negroes in Ontario," p. 641). Colchester had a similar system in place since 1846 (Harrow and Colchester South Township School Area Board, *A Story of Public Schools*, p. 11).

66 Walker, "African Canadians," p. 159.

67 Jason H. Silverman, *Unwelcome Guests: Canada West's Response to American Fugitive Slaves, 1800–1865* (Millwood, N.Y.: Associated Faculty Press, 1985), p. 132.

68 Simpson, "Negroes in Ontario," p. 493.

69 Winks, *The Blacks in Canada*, p. 365.

70 Ibid., n. 5.

71 James W. St. G. Walker, *A History of Blacks in Canada: A Study Guide for Teachers and Students* (Hull: Minister of Supply and Services Canada, 1980), pp. 135, 151.

72 Walker, "African Canadians," p. 159; see also Claudette Knight, "Black Parents Speak: Education in Mid-Nineteenth-Century Canada West," *Ontario History*, vol. 89 (December 1997), p. 275.

73 No public education was available to blacks in Windsor until 1859, and petitions to Ryerson expressed strong opposition to the establishment of a segregated school. In letters to blacks and whites in Windsor, Ryerson suggested that white trustees should establish separate schools in spite of black opposition. AO, Incoming Education Correspondence, RG 2–12, vol. 26, Clayborn Harris to William Horton, February 15, 1859; "Re: Colored Inhabitants of Windsor," February 16, 1859; Outgoing Education Correspondence, RG 2–9, vol. 12, Ryerson to W. Horton, February 21, 1859; Ryerson to Rev. A. R. Green, March 10, 1859. White trustees in Colchester had set up segregated schools in the 1840s (Harrow and Colchester South Township School Area Board, *A Story of Public Schools*, pp. 8–11); blacks in Chatham wrote Ryerson in 1852 claiming that they had never requested a separate school and appealing for admission into a common school (AO, Incoming Education Correspondence, RG 2–12, vol. 12, Committee of the Colored Citizens of Chatham to Ryerson, March 7, 1852).

74 Simpson, "Negroes in Ontario," p. 576. Simpson refers to Levi Foster's petition that his children be included in the white-run common school, and cites assertions by both Isaac Rice and district superintendent Robert Peden that black people in Amherstburg were opposed to the establishment of separate schools. See AO, Incoming Education Correspondence, RG 2–12, vol. 5, Isaac Rice et al. to Ryerson, January 23, 1846; Robert Peden to Ryerson, February 23, 1846.

75 AO, Incoming Education Correspondence, RG 2–12. vol. 11, Inhabitants of color now residing in Simcoe and surrounding county to Ryerson, December 12, 1851.

76 AO, Incoming Education Correspondence. RG 2–12, vol. 26, "Re. Colored Inhabitants of Windsor," Clayborn Harris to William Horton, February 15, 1859; Thomas Jones et al. Committee for the Colored People, Windsor, to Ryerson, March 2, 1859.

77 Silverman, *Unwelcome Guests*, pp. 134, 138.

78 Colonial Church and School Society, Mission to the Fugitive Slaves, *Annual Report* (1863–1864), pp. 11–12.

79 AO, Incoming Education Correspondence, RG 2–12, vol. 26, Jones et al. to Ryerson, March 2, 1859.

80 AO, Incoming Education Correspondence, RG 2–12, vol. 23, Henry Brent et al. (Sandwich) to Ryerson, March 9, 1858.

81 AO, Incoming Education Correspondence, RG 2–12, vol. 26, Jones et al. to Ryerson, March 2, 1859; vol. 20, Peter B. Smith (Dresden) to Hodgins, June 29, 1856; vol. 23, Henry Brent et al. to Ryerson, March 9, 1858; vol. 25, Jefferson Lightfoot (West Flamboro) to Ryerson, October 5, 1858; vol. 26, Clayborn Harris (Windsor) to William Horton, February 16, 1859.

82 Howe, *The Refugees from Slavery*, p. 51–52.

83 AO, Incoming Education Correspondence, RG 2–12, vol. 4, John Cowan (Sandwich) to Rev. McNab, October 15, 1845; vol. 20, James Douglas (West Flamboro) to Ryerson, February 3, 1856.

84 AO, Incoming Education Correspondence, RG 2–12, vol. 12, George Duck (Chatham) to Ryerson, March 7, 1852.

85 Harrow and Colchester South Township School Area Board, *A Story of Public Schools*, p. 12.

86 Winks, *The Blacks in Canada*, p. 367.

87 Victor Lauriston, "Chatham Vetoed Co-education in 1856," *London Free Press*, June 3, 1950.

CHAPTER 6

THE COLONIAL SOJOURNERS, 1858–1871

PATRICIA E. ROY

The Chinese immigration, which was expected, is beginning to set in. About 800 Chinamen have arrived within the last fortnight, some of them in two vessels from China direct, others from San Francisco. They have nearly all gone up to the mines.

Accounts from China say that a large immigration may be expected if the Chinese are well treated.

There are no distinctions made against them in these colonies. They have the same protection as all other persons, and in the mines they are allowed the same rights, liberties, and privileges as all other miners, and the great bulk of the population is very glad to see them coming into the country. Fears for the result are the phantoms of a few nervous and ill-informed persons.[1]

*T*hese observations, made in May 1860 by the Victoria correspondent of the London *Times*, remained reasonably correct throughout the colonial period. By the early 1870s, however, Chinese in British Columbia were not "well treated," they did not have the "same rights, liberties, and privileges" as others, the "great bulk of the population" strongly opposed any more of them "coming into the country," and certainly the fears of Chinese were more than "phantoms" felt by "a few nervous" persons.

Created in 1858 after the discovery of gold in the Fraser River, British Columbia was an instant colony. Its economy, like that of Victoria, the capital of the colony of Vancouver Island and chief commercial centre for both colonies, was volatile. As one mining area petered out, the population and economic activity declined. When a new field was discovered, boom conditions recurred. Although gold was the principal staple, other industries, notably agriculture and lumbering, expanded to meet local needs. The lumber industry, like coal-mining, also developed an export trade, and by the 1870s it was replacing gold as the economic base of British Columbia.[2]

As the *Times* correspondent noted, racial conflict was not present at the creation of British Columbia. Colonial British Columbians were initially remarkably tolerant of the thousands of Chinese who came. British officials refused to countenance any discrimination, and whites, rather than pressing for hostile action, boasted of the British justice enjoyed by the

Chinese. Few whites in the 1850s or 1860s perceived the Chinese as a direct threat to their well-being; some regarded them as "useful" or "valuable" members of the communities, especially since whites and Chinese shared the goal of making as much money as they could. The Chinese, however, set themselves apart in the Chinatowns that became a part of many British Columbia communities. This separation reduced opportunities for conflict and competition, but it also suggested that the Chinese were sojourners who did not want to mingle with the whites, settle permanently in British Columbia, or invest their earnings in its economy. Once the gold fever faded and the colony had to develop other resources to restore prosperity, there was little room for sojourners, especially ones whose presence might discourage more desirable settlers.

Such a shift from acceptance to hostility was not confined to British Columbia. European diggers in the Australian colonies of Victoria and New South Wales initially expressed a "measure of toleration for the Chinese on the gold fields." After a decline in mining activity and a continuation of Chinese immigration, they complained of the differing habits of the "inferior" Chinese and their alienation from the rest of the community as their California counterparts had done.[3] Many Californians had also welcomed the Chinese as cheap and reliable labour, but after a large influx in 1852, they had adopted the negative image of the Chinese previously spread by traders, missionaries, and diplomats and the popular pseudo-scientific idea that coloured races were inferior. They particularly objected to Chinese morals, to their lack of attention to sanitation, to the alleged involuntary servitude of "coolie" labour, to their lower standard of living, to their sojourning habits, and to their failure to contribute to the development of the community.

In some Australian colonies and on the American Pacific Coast, the Chinese met violence, had to pay special taxes, and were denied certain civil rights.[4]

Variations of these complaints appeared in Vancouver Island and in British Columbia, but the argument that sojourners failed to contribute a "fair share" to colonial revenues was most important. Nevertheless, the Chinese posed little threat to white society. Despite the presence of some ex-Australians and many ex-Californians, the Chinese encountered little violence and suffered no economic or political penalties in the colonies of Vancouver Island and British Columbia.

The Chinese first came to Victoria in 1858 along with thousands of other gold seekers who then crossed the Straits of Georgia to the Fraser River gold fields. At first, most came from California; others later arrived directly from Hong Kong and China. Only a few, such as Lee Chong, a prosperous merchant who stayed in Victoria, sent for their wives and children. By the summer of 1860 there were approximately 4,000 Chinese on the Mainland, but their numbers fluctuated according to the prosperity of the gold industry. In 1866, the governor estimated there were 3,070 whites and 1,705 Chinese in the mainland colony, but no one was sure of the exact figures. One fact was clear; both groups were minorities; the Mainland was also home to over 30,000 native Indians.[5]

In both British Columbia and Vancouver Island, as in Britain's Australian colonies, the Chinese enjoyed equal protection before the law. In a book promoting immigration, J.D. Pemberton, the colonies' surveyor-general, observed that the Chinese, "in common with all foreigners," were certain "to meet with protection as well as toleration."[6] On one of the few occasions of violence reported, the Hudson's Bay Company compensated six Chinese for property lost when would-be white miners forced them off a Hudson's Bay Company ship preparing to embark for new gold fields.[7] During an 1869 visit to Barkerville, then the largest Chinese community in British Columbia, Governor Anthony Musgrave assured Chinese residents that the Queen earnestly desired "that the denizens of whatever nationality residing under our flag should possess ... equality and protection."[8] Such proclamations were not merely for show; the "best friend in high places" of the Chinese was Chief Justice Matthew Baillie Begbie.[9] Since every male inhabitant of British Columbia was allowed to vote for the five elected legislative councillors, the Chinese occasionally availed themselves of the privilege.[10] Indeed, certain politicians dragged them up to the polling booth and "taught them to lisp the name of the ambitious candidate for legislative honours."[11]

The corollary of protection from the law was liability for violation of it. Priding themselves on obeying the law, a delegation of Victoria Chinese told Governor Arthur Kennedy of Vancouver Island: "Us believe success will come in obeying rules."[12] Though Chinese were charged with crimes ranging from petty theft to murder, proportionately they probably appeared in court less often than their white contemporaries. In any event, since both parties in such cases were usually Chinese, the press reported the court proceedings without comment.

Except at a formal level, the Chinese showed little desire to mingle with white society. Probably because of their experiences with hostile whites elsewhere and their desire to establish their own social life, the Chinese established distinctive neighbourhoods or Chinatowns wherever they settled. Yet Chinatowns were not completely isolated. White residents of both Victoria and Barkerville complained of the unsanitary conditions, but they freely admitted that the problem was not

unique to the Chinese section and was partly the result of the government's failure to install adequate drains.[13]

Whereas some of their "strange" customs contributed to sinophobia in California. in British Columbia and Vancouver Island the Chinese initially aroused more curiosity than scorn. The press reported Chinese funerals and the very rare Chinese weddings as exotic ceremonies. Complaints about the noise of Chinese New Year's celebrations were overshadowed by the opportunity for conviviality as white men visited Chinatown to enjoy free delicacies and drink. No one seems to have objected seriously to Chinese gambling. Indeed, at Williams Creek white miners enjoyed playing "whiskey pool" with "John Chinaman" since they were almost certain to win![14]

Many white miners brought anti-Chinese prejudices from California, but in British Columbia they had little reason to perceive the Chinese as economic competitors. Nevertheless, some tried to intimidate the Chinese to prevent them from going to the Cariboo. Until at least 1865, the Chinese, many of whom had experienced segregation in California, seemed to have "entertained a wholesome fear of encroaching further on the white man's assumed prerogative." Although, like the whites, they were transients who moved about British Columbia as they heard of new finds, they confined themselves chiefly to placer diggings "deserted by white miners, under the excitement of new discoveries," purchased the rights to worked over bars from white men, and, rarely, ventured into distant areas such as Omineca where few white men sought to go.[15] Some feared the winters and returned to the warmer climes of California; a few made fortunes and went back to China. Every spring, new Chinese came.

Few white men objected to Chinese willingness to work for lower wages since labour shortages were more common than unemployment. During a temporary lull in the gold fields, the New Westminster *British Columbian* complained that the government allowed public works contractors to employ Chinese at fifty cents or a dollar a day less then white men. The Chinese, however, were as anxious to earn good wages as anyone else. Three months later, during the Big Bend excitement of 1865, Edgar Dewdney, a government surveyor, had trouble finding any labourers to construct a trail from Princeton to Wild Horse Creek on the Columbia River and was only able to persuade seventy-five Chinese to work by offering them the high wage of $75 per month, all found.[16] As an early observer noted, "John Chinaman was keen to have better and more varied fare than rice if he could afford it." When demand for vegetables increased at Barkerville, the Chinese, who monopolized local production, doubled the price of potatoes. On at least two occasions, Chinese miners in the Cariboo struck unsuccessfully for higher wages, but in Nanaimo, where "John caught the 'striking fever' from the white colliers," they apparently got the $1.50 per day they demanded. As long as the Chinese did not descend to the "bottomless pits" of the coal mines, their presence, though "distasteful" to white miners, did not cause ill-feeling. But in 1867 when the Vancouver Coal Mining and Land Company reduced the wages of its Chinese employees below the level paid to white workers, the white miners, fearing for their jobs, struck. Two months later, the company ended the strike by granting concessions in wages and working conditions to the whites and agreeing to dismiss the Chinese. However, it turned the work of "running," that is, taking empty cars to the miners, over to private contractors, who were free to hire Chinese. This strike marked the beginning of a long controversy over the use of Chinese labour in the coal mines.[17]

Whether or not the Chinese were economic assets was warmly debated; rivalry between Victoria, the Island capital, and New Westminster, the Mainland capital, intensified the dispute. Victorians, aware of Californian and Australian arguments, did not regard the Chinese as the most desirable immigrants, but they did not wholly oppose their entry. After outlining the evils of Chinese immigration in California, the degradation of labour, gross immorality, and poor sanitation, the Victoria *Gazette* suggested setting aside certain inferior diggings for the Chinese, who were the only people who could make remunerative wages from them. Indeed, Victoria interests welcomed Chinese merchants as pioneers in a trans-Pacific trade that would be profitable to all. Most of the trade of the gold fields passed through the city, and Victorians were reluctant to discourage Chinese from going to the gold fields, providing cheap labour in other industries, or generally, by sheer numbers, contributing to the colonial economy. When some Victoria residents suggested the Mainland impose a special poll tax on Chinese instead of taxing mules carrying goods into the interior, the *Colonist* reminded them that a heavy poll tax would discourage consumers and repel

> a class of immigrants that we cannot at present afford to dispense with. They may be inferior to Europeans and Americans in energy and ability, hostile to us in race, language and habits, and may remain among us a Pariah race; still they are patient, easily governed, and invariably industrious, and their presence at this juncture would benefit trade everywhere in the two colonies. We are disposed to accept them as a choice between two evils—no white immigration or a Chinese immigration. That they do not eat, wear, and otherwise use merchandise is untrue....

Large fortunes have been amassed supplying them, which fully disproves the charge that they spend nothing....There is ample room in British Columbia for some thousands without greatly interfering with the white miners. Hereafter, when the time arrives that we can dispense with them, we will heartily second a check to their immigration—treaty obligations to the contrary.

This belief that the Chinese, though not the most desirable of immigrants, were "useful and inoffensive members of society" persisted on Vancouver Island, where it found, for example, full expression in Matthew Macfie's 1865 guide book and in the speeches of members of the Legislative Assembly, who overwhelmingly rejected a proposal to impose special taxes on the Chinese. Of course, few Chinese resided in Victoria. In 1870, when the white population of the city was 2,842, there were only 211 Chinese there.[18]

Residents of the Mainland, where most of the Chinese lived, were much less sympathetic to the Chinese, whom they regarded as being "of no use as members of society." White miners may not have feared being driven out by the Chinese, but they clearly resented them. Placer-mining required little capital investment; it was an example of almost pure exploitation of a natural resource. By 1865, however, the gold rush seemed to be over.[19]

Economic distress stimulated complaints about the failure of the Chinese to contribute to the local economy. What little they did buy in North America was purchased from Victoria merchants rather than on the Mainland. White miners spent at least part of their earning's locally, but the Chinese, "mere slaves" under the control of wealthy merchants, were likened to "a swarm of locusts" who exhausted the mines and left the country "impoverished and desolate." Though the Chinese who came to British Columbia were not coolie labourers in the sense of being indentured, many of them owed their passage money to labour contractors who advanced it on the "credit-ticket" system. Given the opportunities the gold rush provided to make money quickly, most Chinese soon repaid their fares and became completely independent.[20] Nevertheless, since the majority of the Chinese were engaged in the most menial forms of work, the white community, which made little effort to understand them or their customs, tended to think of them as indentured coolies or virtual slaves.

As far as white British Columbians were concerned, the root problem was the Chinese custom of sojourning, of working hard, living frugally, and always planning to return home. "It is undeniable that Chinamen, as a class, are the smallest consumers, the least producers, and the most unprofitable of all who resort to these shores," complained the Columbian. "Economical in their diet and nomadic in their habits, all we have in return for the really large quantities of gold they carry away is the paltry revenue derived from rice and opium." Moreover, they were neither colonists nor permanent settlers since, the Columbian concluded, "Dead or alive, 'John' is always homeward bound."[21] The Chinese, in sum, did not contribute to building up a British colony.

Some rhetoric emanating from New Westminster can be attributed to jealousy of Victoria businessmen even after the union of the colonies in 1866 ended Victoria's advantage as a free port. Yet, the Columbian's views represented a common mainland feeling. One of the most comprehensive attacks on Chinese appeared in the Cariboo Sentinel of Barkerville. It listed six reasons, all more or less relating to sojourning, for opposing the introduction of Chinese labour:

First, because they the Chinese are aliens not merely in nationality, but in habits, religion, (and to such a degree that Christianity is deemed barbarism by them,) allegiance, and even to the extent of believing that the remains of their dead would be desecrated by resting in the country where they had gained their money. Second, because they never become good citizens, they never serve on juries or on fire companies, or in any way in which the citizens of any other country would lend a hand in cases of emergency. They never marry or settle in any country but their own, and are more apt to create immorality than otherwise hence they are a bad example, and their presence injurious. Third, they deal entirely with their own countrymen and consume few articles of the production of the country in which they reside; their consumption in all cases is confined to articles of the first necessity, and they do little to assist in the accumulation of wealth in any country where they may be located. Fourth, they hoard their money with the intention of sending it away to the country whence they came, so that its accumulation and exploitation is an absolute loss to the people amongst whom it is amassed. Large sums are in this way yearly sent away from British Columbia that would otherwise, if circulated in the colony, add vastly to its prosperity. Fifth, they evade payment of the taxes to which the citizens of the colony are subjected, and thus are the most privileged class, while they are at the same time the most unprofitable. Sixth, they are inimical to immigration; they fill every position that could be occupied by a good colonist, and from their peculiar mode of living can afford to do it for much lower remuneration than any Europeans or Americans.

The fallacy that all men are free in a free country in relation to Chinese, is as erroneous as it is destructive to the country that they inhabit. If they adopted the country as a home, and fulfilled all the duties of a good citizen, then we should have no reason to object to them but when we know that they are filling the position of those who would bring wealth and population to the country, and at the same time carrying off our very life's blood in the shape of our gold, it is quite another affair.[22]

The essence of the problem was presented in economic terms. British Columbians estimated that the Chinese spent only a third to half as much as white men. As well, the Chinese lived mainly on rice, which was charged no duty, and they neither drank wine nor smoked cigars, two important sources of tax revenue. Since most Chinese worked abandoned claims, they had little incentive to purchase mining licences, a voluntary action by those who wanted to protect themselves from claim jumpers. Their refusal to buy licences may also have been a form of passive resistance against informal attempts to limit their access to the mines.[23]

Imposing special taxes and licence fees seemed the obvious way to force the Chinese to contribute a "fair share" to declining colonial revenues and help to relieve the immediate problem caused by sojourning. The gold commissioner at Barkerville posted a notice in Chinese instructing all Chinese working at the mines to take out a licence. By sending out a collector to nearby creeks, the commissioner violated a decision of the Legislative Council that many Chinese were too poor to pay and that a compulsory fee would only fill the jails. Above all, the British government forbade the governor to permit any tax which appeared to be on racial grounds. Thus, Chinese could not be compelled to buy mining licences unless the regulation was universal. Similarly, early in

1871, Arthur Bunster, the member of the Legislative Council for Nanaimo, had to withdraw his suggestion that a fifty-dollar poll tax be imposed on all Chinese "engaged in any occupation in this colony" when the attorney-general reminded him that the governor was forbidden to sign any bill imposing taxes on a special class. The debate itself revealed the division of opinion on the Chinese. Some members agreed with Bunster that the Chinese should be regulated, but others contended that the Chinese were "industrious and frugal and in some respects valuable." Interestingly, in contrast to the situation a few years earlier, the members from the Mainland tended to be sympathetic to the Chinese; the members from the Island, to oppose them. In withdrawing his motion, Bunster predicted that the Chinese question would be an issue at a future election.[24] Although no one mentioned the Chinese during the Confederation debates of 1870 or in the negotiation of the Terms of Union with Canada, Bunster was soon able to help fulfil his own prophecy. As long as British Columbia was a British colony, the tradition that all men were equal before the law protected the Chinese from legal discrimination. With Confederation in 1871 British Columbia became a Canadian province with responsible government and ample opportunity to legislate or attempt to legislate against the Chinese. In the new circumstances created by Confederation, an increasing number of whites were to become hostile to the Chinese.

Notes

1   *The Times* (London), 26 June 1860.

2   Vancouver Island was created a British colony in 1849. The mainland area became the colony of British Columbia on 19 November 1858. Six years later, the colonies were united under the name of the latter. For convenience of expression, the term British Columbia will be used to refer both to the mainland colony and to both colonies.

   A useful survey of the colonial economy may be found in Paul A. Phillips, "Confederation and the Economy of British Columbia," in W. George Shelton, ed. *British Columbia & Confederation* (Victoria: University of Victoria, 1967), pp. 43–66.

3   Andrew Markus, *Fear and Hatred: Purifying Australia and California, 1850–1901* (Sydney: Hale and Iremonger, 1979), pp. 19–21 and pp. 237–41.

4   Kil Young Zo, *Chinese Immigration into the United States, 1850–1880* (New York: Arno Press, 1978), pp. 117–18; see also Elmer Clarence Sandmeyer, *The Anti-Chinese Movement in California* (Urbana: University of Illinois Press, 1973) [first published, 1939, ch. 3; Stuart Creighton Miller, *The Unwelcome Immigrant* (Berkeley: University of California Press, 1969).

5   British Columbia, Governor, Blue Book, 1866. In 1865, estimates ranged from fifteen hundred to six thousand Chinese; from eight to ten thousand whites; and about fifty thousand native Indians (*Colonist*, 5 April 1865; *Columbian*, 15 June and 20 September 1865).

6   J.D. Pemberton, *Facts and Figures Relating to Vancouver Island and British Columbia* (London, 1860), p. 133.

7   *Colonist*, 15 and 17 August 1865.

8   *Cariboo Sentinel*, 22 September 1869.

9   David R. Williams, *"… The Man for a New Country": Sir Matthew Baillie Begbie* (Sidney, B.C.: Gray's, 1977), p. 128.

10 British Columbia, Governor, Blue Book, 1864, p. 67. British Columbia had an extremely limited form of representative government. Only five of the fifteen legislative councillors were elected, and the governor reserved the right to reject any of the elected candidates. When British Columbia and Vancouver Island were united, the British Columbia franchise and limited self-government prevailed.

11 *Columbian*, 11 November 1865.

12 *Colonist*, 5 April 1865.

13 *Cariboo Sentinel*, 7 August 1869; *Colonist*, 25 March 1869.

14 *Colonist*, 30 January 1862 and 6 January 1865. On the various epithets applied to Chinese, see W. Peter Ward, *White Canada Forever: Popular Attitudes and Public Policy towards Orientals in British Columbia* (Montreal: McGill-Queen's University Press, 1978), p. 3.

15 *Columbian*, 23 February 1865 and 24 November 1866; *Colonist*, 10 July 1860, 15 November 1866, 29 June 1865, 18 January 1870, 13 October 1870; *Cariboo Sentinel*, 25 December 1869; Jin Tan, "Chinese Labour and the Reconstituted Social Order of British Columbia," *Chinese Ethnic Studies* 19 (1987), p. 79.

16 *Columbian*, 6 May and 17 August 1865.

17 *Colonist*, 26 April and 24 July 1861, 24 July 1867, 21 May 1869, 7 May 1871; *Cariboo Sentinel*, 11 and 18 June 1870;

Lynne Bowen, *Three Dollar Dreams* (Lantzville: Oolichan, 1987), pp. 125–26.

18 Victoria *Gazette*, 31 March 1859; *Colonist*, 10 May and 1 July 1861, 8 March 1860, 19 May 1865; *Columbian*, 11 April 1861; Matthew Macfie, *Vancouver Island and British Columbia* (London, 1865), pp. 381–87; British Columbia, Governor, Blue Book, 1870.

19 *Columbian*, 9 May 1865.

20 Tan, "Chinese Labour," p. 72.

21 *Columbian*, 11 April and 14 March 1861, 23 February, 2 March, and 6 May 1865.

22 *Cariboo Sentinel*, 16 May 1867.

23 Tan, "Chinese Labour," pp. 82–83.

24 *Mainland Guardian*, 9 February 1871; *Colonist*, 27 January 1871.

CHAPTER 7

Creating Outsiders, 1875–1903

Kay J. Anderson

Pioneers from China

At the time of its creation as a British colony in 1849, Vancouver Island was little more than a fur trade preserve, scattered with settlements of indigenous people and a few trading forts. By 1854, just 450 settlers had made their home in the colony, and no more than 500 acres of land had been developed. By the end of that decade, however, the discovery of placer gold on the Fraser, Thompson, and Columbia rivers attracted thousands of prospectors, miners, and adventurers to the region, and in 1858 the imperial authorities proclaimed a mainland colony of British Columbia to govern the influx of people. The island and mainland colonies merged in 1866, but many of the new residents were no more permanent than the placer camps, and within one year of the merger the total "white" population had fallen below 10,000. The number was, however, sufficient to boost the growth of the main townships of Victoria, New Westminster, and Nanaimo, and the province's early staple industries of mining, agriculture, manufacturing, and fishing.

* * *

Most of the work in canneries and mining, and later in railway construction, was organized on a contract basis. Chinese bosses recruited "gangs" of labourers and then made contracts with industrial managers for the workers' services. In other industries, Chinese sold their labour as part of the normal market for unskilled work at the time. Either way, the labour of immigrants from China was critical to the establishment of British Columbia's economic base at a time when most production work was labour-intensive and white labour was in short supply. Chinese were paid one-half to two-thirds the wage rates of other workers, and they accepted long hours and seasonal work—often in places distant from their homes.[1]

Given the part they played in opening up the BC frontiers, early Chinese settlers won praise from certain quarters of white society. A royal commissioner and judge on the BC Supreme Court, Dr John Hamilton Gray, heard evidence on the "Chinese Question" from a number of entrepreneurs in 1885 and declared in his report: "It may safely be said that there are several industries that would not have succeeded—perhaps it might be said undertaken—if it had not been for the opportunity of obtaining their labour." After describing Chinese as "living machines," Dr Justice Gray went on to say that there was "preponderating testimony as to the sobriety, industry and frugality of the Chinese as manual labourers ... and up to this time their presence in the province has been most useful if not indispensable."[2]

* * *

For white workers of British Columbia then, just as for entrepreneurs, Chinese immigrants were somehow irremediably beyond the body of eligible citizenry from the time they entered the province. According to a complex ideological matrix, the Chinese in this New World society were an undifferentiated category of outsiders, fundamentally and constitutively "different" from those immigrants for whom British Columbia became home automatically. The different classes of European immigrants had different (economic) reasons for embracing the idea of an essential "John Chinaman." There may also have been significant gender variations in the European response to immigrants from China. It is clear, however, that belief in "John's" existence, and his alien status in the new community, transcended sectional interests. In March 1859, the first colonial newspaper, the *Gazette*, captured such overriding sentiments as it editorialized on the theme of Chinese immigration: "They are, with few exceptions, not desirable as permanent settlers in a country peopled by the Caucasian race and governed by civilized enactments. No greater obstacle to the coming of the class of immigrants needed in British Columbia could be devised, than the presence of Chinamen in large numbers."[3]

* * *

VICTORIA FORMALIZES OUTSIDER STATUS

The late-nineteenth-century legislatures of British Columbia were unreservedly opposed to the inflow of cheap labour from China, despite their commitment to economic growth and their deference toward private companies in the province.[4] There was division in the house from year to year over whether Chinese labour should be regulated by government intervention, but there was unanimity that further Chinese immigration should be restricted, if not excluded. In that conviction, the legislative body ran uncharacteristically but resolutely against its own frontier-acquisitive mentality. Only one form of labour was to develop the province, it was urged, and in 1883 a unanimously carried resolution under the Smithe government requested the dominion government to inaugurate a "liberal scheme of white immigration to British Columbia."[5] An address on the Chinese question at the same time declared that with a "white population alone, we can hope to build up our country and render it fit for the Anglo-Saxon race."[6]

The Walkem, Beaven, and Smithe governments also went to considerable lengths in the late 1870s and early 1880s to try to avert the threat that had been pending since British Columbia joined Confederation—the employment of Chinese labour on the transnational rail link. Walkem actually visited Ottawa in 1880 to request that Chinese labour be prohibited from railway construction. By 1882, however, when a resolution was passed by Robert Beaven's government "to induce the contractors on the Canadian Pacific Railway to import and employ white labour on their works, instead of Chinese,"[7] contractor Andrew Onderdonk had already secured the co-operation of Chinese labour recruitment companies in San Francisco. Between them, the companies found approximately 15,000 Chinese to build the mountainous section of the transnational connection.[8]

The proportion of the province's population of Chinese origin thus increased to 9 per cent by the mid-1880s, a development that so perturbed the Smithe government that in 1884 it decided to take matters completely into its own hands. While submitting to Prime Minister John A. Macdonald that "the hordes of Chinese … surge in upon the country and carry with them the elements of disease, pestilence and degradation over the face of the fair land," William Smithe presented to his own legislature an Act to Prevent the Immigration of Chinese, carried in February 1884.[9] According to this bill, entry to the province was denied to "any native of China or its dependencies not born of British parents, or any person born of Chinese parents." Another bill, the Act to Regulate the Chinese Population of British Columbia, insisted that "any person of Chinese race" over fourteen years of age pay an annual tax of ten dollars for a licence to work.[10] The tax was warranted, according to the act's preamble, because "the incoming of Chinese to British Columbia largely exceeds that of any other class of immigrant, and the population so introduced are fast becoming superior in number to our own race; [they] are not disposed to be governed by our laws; are dissimilar in habits and occupation from our people; evade the payment of taxes justly due to the Government; are governed by pestilential habits; are useless in instances of emergency; habitually desecrate grave yards by the removal of bodies therein; and generally … Chinese are inclined to habits subversive of the comfort and well-being of the community."

Within six weeks, the Act to Prevent the Immigration of Chinese was disallowed by the governor-general-in-council, possibly as much in the interests of completing the railway as ensuring conformity with the British North America Act. The Regulation Act was eventually declared unconstitutional by the BC Supreme Court, but a third act passed in the 1884 session was allowed to stand. According to clause 122 of the Land Act, it was deemed unlawful "for a Commissioner to issue a preemption record of any Crown land, or sell any portion thereof, to any Chinese, nor grant authority to any Chinese to record or divert any water from any natural channel of any stream, lake or river of the province."[11]

Such a measure was hardly enough to halt the animosity that swelled in British Columbia when, with the rail track completed in Vancouver in 1885, thousands of relatively underpaid Chinese labourers were discharged onto the regular labour market. As theorists of the "split labour market" in the province have argued, the market of cheap, racialized labour bred an independent economic grievance that compounded conflict between the European and Chinese-origin population.[12] Ottawa's failure to "abate the evil" therefore grew increasingly provocative, and in 1885 a stronger appeal was made by the Smithe government to the dominion to act on behalf of the province. A resolution drafted for transmission to Ottawa in 1885 said:

> The Chinese are alien in sentiment and habits. They do not become settlers in any sense of that word … The Chinese population chiefly consists of male adults, and thus they come into unfair competition with white labour … Their presence exerts a baneful influence in restricting the immigration of white labour, especially house-servants, who will not be brought into contact with this race. They have a system of secret societies which encourages crime amongst themselves … The use of opium has extended throughout the Province to the demoralization of the native races …

This House urgently requests that some restrictive legislation be passed to prevent our Province from becoming completely overrun by Chinese.[13]

And in case Ottawa did not register the sincerity of this plea, the Smithe government re-enacted the disallowed act of 1884 by levying a fifty-dollar tax on all Chinese immigrants to Canada—only to have it overruled again.[14]

Thoroughly hampered in its attempts to control the entry of immigrants from China, the Smithe government turned again to residents. In 1890, the legislature forbade the employment of Chinese in underground work at coal mines. Perhaps more significant, a standard anti-Chinese employment clause was prepared by a select committee in 1886 for inclusion in private bills. However, the relentless member for Victoria, Robert Beaven, found it difficult to muster the necessary support for his clause when decisions over incorporation bills for private companies were presented to the assembly. As mentioned earlier, the legislature was split on the issue of restricting so docile, sober, and industrious a work-force as Chinese were perceived to be, especially at a time when rail networks were opening up the seemingly infinite resources of the province. Some members did not want Chinese at any price; others felt the inherently cheap nature of their alien labour sufficient justification to use it. Both groups, however, shared the view that Chinese labour should be managed in the "public interest" of establishing a European society. Beaven's day of glory did arrive in fact, in 1891, when the house set a precedent by carrying his motion to include a Chinese-exclusion clause in the Act to Incorporate the British Columbia Dyking and Improvement Co.[15]

In 1897, the government of Premier John Turner, facing a year of economic recession and labour unrest, attempted a more decisive stand on Chinese employment with the passage of an ambitious Act to Regulate the Employment of Chinese (and Japanese) Persons on Works Carried on under Franchises granted by Private Acts.[16] The legislature once again ran into constitutional problems, however. The lieutenant-governor reserved assent of the bill, and, when the act was renamed and recarried in 1898 as the Labour Regulation Act, it suffered at the hands of the dominion minister of justice the same fate as other measures involving the rights of aliens.

One significant, unanimously carried anti-Chinese clause that did remain on the statute books in this period (through insertion in contracts rather than as blanket legislation) determined that "if any Provincial aid be granted in the way of contributions of public funds of the province, or a grant of Crown lands in aid of public works undertaken, [it shall] be conditional upon a contract being entered into … that no Chinese or Japanese be employed upon any such undertaking."[17] In this way the legislature set an example of discriminatory action; it could not enforce such action across the private sector by law, but it could provide it with de facto legitimacy through the spirit of its own employment practices.

In the last years of the century, the legislative assembly intensified its efforts to transmit local definitions of the "Chinese" to legislators and officials in Ottawa, who at the time did not have first-hand experience of "them." Successive governments carried resolutions in 1893, 1894, 1897, and 1899 calling for more stringent restrictions on Chinese immigration than had eventually been introduced by the House of Commons in 1885. That dominion measure (discussed in the next section of this chapter) had proved effective in limiting Chinese immigration to less than 300 for several years until 1892, when over 3,000

Chinese entered Canada. The provincial resolution of 1899 declared that, without more effective measures, "the destructive incursion of Asiatics" would drive "workingmen of British race and blood out of many of the fields of labour" and threatened "to leave very little occupation remaining for the white labourer." In 1900, another provincial government (under Premier Joseph Martin) attempted to cater to its anti-Chinese electorate with yet another Act to Regulate Chinese Immigration. It was promptly disallowed.

In the mean time, provincial régimes of the late 1890s did what they could to curtail the public-health risk which was assumed to accompany increasing numbers of Chinese in the province. With Charles Semlin's government in power in 1899, the assembly unanimously carried a motion "that the attention of the government be directed to the urgency of enforcing the sanitary regulations laid down in the provincial Health Act where ever Chinese congregate," while in 1894 and 1897, motions had been carried asking the dominion for more strict quarantine inspections of incoming Chinese or "Mongolians."[18]

Another request to Ottawa in 1900 revealed the strength of the provincial government's belief in some essential Chineseness, independent of citizenship, birthplace, and adopted country of residence. The assembly unanimously carried a motion "that this House views with alarm the admission of Mongolians to the rights of citizenship, and that the Dominion Government be requested so to change the naturalization laws that it will be impossible for any Mongolian, or person belonging to the native races of Asia, to become British subjects."[19] Within British Columbia, some movement toward this goal had been achieved five years earlier, under the Turner government. The Provincial Elections Act of 1895 denied the franchise to naturalized and Canadian-born subjects of Chinese (and Japanese) origin. "Chinese" had been legally labelled as alien in 1875, and in turn this had been used to justify denying them further access to insider status. Commissioner Gray put it this way in his 1885 report: "By provincial legislation in British Columbia and the general hostility towards them, the Chinese are practically prohibited from becoming attached to the country. They are made so far as provincial legislation can go, perpetual aliens."[20]

* * *

THE VIEW FROM OTTAWA

Consistent with economic theorizing of the day, many members of Canada's House of Commons appeared uncomfortable with the requests of BC representatives for dominion intervention in the free flow of labour. When Arthur Bunster (Vancouver) moved in 1878 that an anti-Chinese clause be inserted in Canadian Pacific Railway (CPR) contracts, Alexander Mackenzie, leader of the opposition, protested: "It [the motion] is one unprecedented in its character and spirit, and at variance with those tolerant laws which afford asylum to all who come into our country, irrespective of colour, hair or anything else."[21] The following year, Mackenzie informed the restless BC members that "the principle that some classes of the human family were not fit to be residents of this Dominion, would be dangerous and contrary to the Law of Nations ... however unpleasant the neighbourhood of the Chinese might be."[22]

Ideological support for open immigration came easily to a government that had construction of a transnational railway as a primary mandate. Prime Minister John A. Macdonald, more explicit than most, made a blunt statement of the race-development dilemma to BC member Amor de Cosmos in 1882. Just like many BC entrepreneurs and labourers, Macdonald assumed an intrinsic quality to Chinese labour that made it automatically cheaper than other labour and eminently suited to the menial and onerous tasks of an expanding economy, such as railway construction. He told de Cosmos: "I share very much the feeling of the people of the United States and the Australian colonies against a Mongolian or Chinese population in our country as permanent settlers. I believe that it is an alien race in every sense, that would not and could not be expected to assimilate with our Aryan population. [But] … it is simply a question of alternatives—either you must have this labour or you cannot have the railway."[23] One year later, Macdonald deflected another appeal from British Columbia: "I am sufficient of a physiologist to believe that the two races cannot combine, and that no great middle race can arise from the mixture of the Mongolian and the Aryan. I believe it would tend to the degradation of the people of the Pacific; and that no permanent immigration of the Chinese people into Canada is to be encouraged, but under the present system there is no fear of that … They are not permanent settlers … and therefore there is no fear of a permanent degradation of the country by a mongrel race."[24]

The idea of a Chinese race clearly lent itself to all manner of politically convenient twists. It was used to argue against immigration restriction at the same time as it could be used to argue in favour of it. For Canadian and foreign entrepreneurs and the dominion government in the early 1880s, it was precisely the (putatively) inherent nature of Chinese labour—docile, industrious, and alien—that entitled the country to use it and dismiss it; for others, the competition created by the uniquely Chinese living standard was sufficient reason to reject Chinese labour altogether.

Linking these apparently alternative voices was the force of the race idea itself in Canadian culture and the political utility of such a cross-class belief. The class divisions of Canada's emerging industrial base ensured that owners of capital had good reasons for using Chinese labour—reasons that when translated into employment practices entrenched occupational segregation along colour lines and boosted profits to owners. But it was the prevailing racial frame of reference that justified the recruitment and exploitation of labour from China during a labour-intensive stage of Canadian economic development. This view more adequately explains the co-operation between the dominion and the CPR on the use of Chinese labour than the arguments of Warburton and others. These scholars have seen it in terms of "the class relations, which [as] the essential mechanism of the system of production, required these workers."[25] Aside from its silence on the question of why "these workers" were chosen or why they were cheap, that view overlooks the fact that Ottawa had its own reasons for contracting Chinese in the early 1880s—namely, to promote colonization of Canada's territories, unite a nation, and render it European. As long as the mutually beneficial arrangement with the railway company existed, then, the protests of BC members in Ottawa, against the "worse than worthless element," "the greatest pagans on earth," and the like, were simply deflected.[26]

But the voices of the west were not forgotten entirely. With the end of the railway in sight in 1884, Macdonald set up the Royal Commission into the Chinese Question in British Columbia, "to obtain proof that the principle of restricting Chinese immigration is proper and in the interest of the Province and the Dominion." The commissioners, Dr Justice Gray of the BC Supreme Court, and Dr Joseph Adolphe Chapleau, dominion secretary of state, entered the investigation with relatively open minds. Their commitment to laissez-faire political philosophy seems to have predisposed them against government intervention in the issue. But laissez-faire thinking lent itself easily to Darwinist arguments about the "fit" and "unfit" races, and both commissioners were well versed in evolutionary theory.

Dr Justice Gray argued, for example, that "it is something strange to hear the strong, broad-shouldered superior race, superior physically and mentally, sprung from the highest types of the old and new world, expressing a fear of competition with a small, inferior and comparatively speaking, feminine race."[27] He believed that society, like nature, was a harmonious hierarchical structure, with each element set in its appointed place. Trading heavily in the language of the "great chain of being," he said in the commission's 1885 report: "How derogatory to the French, English and American races in Canada to assert that the presence of a few labouring ignorant Chinese will cause the Canadian people to abandon the religion of their fathers, the morals, education and higher Christian civilization of their institutions, to adopt the idol worship and debasing morals and habits of the heathen … In moral and social habits, beyond a very limited circle, the influence of the foreigner in a debasing direction will be extremely small, and upon the great masses of the people absolutely imperceptible when the country into which they come is of a higher organization in morals and civilization."[28]

Applying this version of race logic to dominion concerns of the day, the commissioners recommended a cautious policy of "limited restraint" on Chinese immigration. This accommodated laissez-faire views, while accepting the "objection that there is no homogeneity of race between them and ourselves, nor can they comprehend or assimilate themselves to our institutions." To bring about this limited restraint, the commissioners suggested a ten-dollar duty on each entrant from China. Dr Justice Gray argued that such a tax would be "judicious," because "sound policy will regulate the coming of the Chinese, not stop it, any more than a clear-headed farmer would dry up a river because it may sometimes overflow its banks and perchance create temporary derangement in the lands through which it flows, but which when properly restrained, its waters irrigate and enrich." The politics of race could assume poetic heights indeed.

Soon after the commission reported, Chapleau himself introduced in the House of Commons a Bill to Restrict and Regulate Chinese Immigration into the Dominion of Canada. While observing his fellow commissioner's fears about stemming the "flow," it conceded more to BC pressure by raising the tax on Chinese immigrants to fifty dollars. Chapleau was well aware of the significance of this first act of intervention by the Canadian government in the free flow of labour to the country's shores. He sought to defend it, therefore, in a way that struck a chord with mounting public opinion about race. He asked the house: "Is it not a natural and well-founded desire of British subjects, of the white population of the Dominion, who come from either British or other European States and settle in this country, that their country should be inhabited by a vigorous, energetic and white race of people?"[29]

On 2 July 1885, parliament approved Chapleau's poll tax, and henceforth the dominion government became more united in its mode of implementing the concept of a Chinese race. The government also became a chief mediator of the composition and idea of "Canada." The new act, for example, divided potential immigrants to Canada into two classes. One comprised people of Chinese origin; the other, all people not of Chinese origin, who were covered by the general Immigration Act. The new law also led to the appointment of officials whose task was to execute the spirit and the letter of a law strictly for "Chinese." A chief controller of Chinese immigration at the ports of Victoria and Vancouver was entrusted to enforce the act, and special records of Chinese entry, exit, occupation, and other statistics began to be compiled. In such ways, the act gave the category "Chinese" an administrative existence and a reality in Canadian official life that did not need to acknowledge the criteria immigrants from China might have used to define themselves and each other. This system of racial classification had major ramifications for those who were defined in its terms, and also for dominion politics in Canada, as the following analysis of the act and its administration and amendment to the turn of the century will demonstrate.

The 1885 Act to Restrict and Regulate Chinese Immigration was cumbersome compared with the simpler, 1882 Exclusion Act of the United States. It demanded fifty dollars from any person of Chinese origin entering Canada and not entitled to exemption.[30] Those exempt from the tax were diplomatic and consular representatives, tourists, merchants, and students. Merchants, it was believed, would contribute capital and trade arrangements to Canada's development, and state officials were reluctant to deter their entry. Such merchants were not on equal terms with white immigrants of commerce, however; their racialization still set them administratively apart.

A further barrier to Chinese entry was the imposition by a section of the act of a maximum ratio of one immigrant for every fifty tons of ship's weight. Another section recognized the right of an immigrant to visit China and return to Canada without paying the tax again on presentation of a certificate of entry. The provision proved exceedingly troublesome to port officials, however, because certificates were routinely sold in China. The act was therefore amended in 1887 to make the registration of all Chinese in Canada compulsory. The amendment did not stop fraudulent practices surrounding return certificates—a fact that encouraged accusations about the untrustworthiness of the "Chinese" character—and by 1892 return certificates were replaced by a system in which returning Chinese were obliged to prove their identity to the satisfaction of the controller.

The 1887 amendment also refined the official definition of "Chinese," which became "a person born of a Chinese father irrespective of the nationality of the mother" and extended exemption from the tax to women of Chinese origin married to "British and Christian subjects." These changes flowed directly from a controversy surrounding the entry of a Mr Moore, "an Englishman of standing," who arrived in Canada to find that he was required to pay a tax for his Chinese wife and their children.[31] According to the revised act of 1887 such women and children were no longer officially "Chinese."

The Moore incident was seized on by those in the house who considered the tax on women from China an ultimate menace to the community. The member for Bothwell, seeing the double standard of the amendment, requested that all women of Chinese origin be relieved of the tax so as to encourage family settlement. However, John A. Macdonald saw his own opportunity in the suggestion: "The whole point of this measure is to restrict the immigration of the Chinese into British Columbia and into Canada … If wives are allowed, not a single immigrant would come over without a wife, and the immorality existing to a very great extent along the Pacific coast would be greatly aggravated … I do not think that it would be to the advantage of Canada or any other country occupied by Aryans for members of the Mongolian race to become permanent inhabitants of the country."[32] Chapleau similarly subscribed to the logic that allowing Chinese wives to come in would promote not morality but greater immorality. As he had noted in the royal commission report of 1885: "If they came with their women they would come to settle and what with immigration and their extraordinary fecundity, would soon overrun the country."[33] Limited family settlement was an important effect of the official recognition of the category "Chinese." Like the head tax itself, it further realized the alien and non-settler status of residents of Chinese origin.

Public debate about the merits of the tax continued from its implementation into the next century. Questions concerning trade and commerce, diplomacy, and even basic justice were recognized as militating against the law. Sir Richard Cartwright, minister for trade and commerce, felt moved to excuse the act in this way: "It appears to me, although it may be said that this practice of taxing Chinamen is opposed to British practice … to a very considerable extent the instinctive feeling which prevails in British Columbia has its origin in a wholesome feeling of self-preservation."[34]

*　*　*

The nineteenth century closed with the idea of race well entrenched in North American public opinion and science. Despite the nagging difficulties being encountered by scientists and anthropologists in their attempts to typify the globe's populations, few white people—including intellectuals and governing élites—questioned the belief that the mental, moral, and physical differences between "the races" were profound. Monogenist beliefs in the unity of the globe's people had been solidly overturned, not least in white Canada, by deterministic thinking about racial difference.

The nature and strength of the consensus about race were amply demonstrated in the proceedings of the new royal commission, conducted by Roger Chute, Daniel Munn, and Christopher Foley. During 1901, they received more than 300 submissions from British Columbia, and virtually none expressed opposition to the proposal that immigration from China be prohibited completely. This despite the fact that the province's Chinese population, numbering 16,000 in 1900, was solidly outnumbered by the 129,000 "whites."[35]

While in 1900 Chinese labourers were still regarded favourably by employers in the province for "their sobriety, machine-like regularity, economy and their disposition to remain with one employer,"[36] the majority of large entrepreneurs interviewed by the commissioners claimed that Chinese immigrants of all classes had outgrown their usefulness. Sufficient white labour had been available since the rail link was completed, they suggested, and the major economic activities of the province (except for the canneries) would not suffer from greater restriction of their labour. The changed mood among employers was highlighted in the testimony of Samuel Robins, of the New Vancouver Coal Co. In the 1885 royal commission, Robins had on balance favoured the continued employment of Chinese labour. In 1901, he told the commissioners that

Chinese immigration was an evil that "should be stopped before it grows to unmanageable dimensions." White self-employed businessmen had also joined the cry against Chinese immigration, as more Chinese immigrants turned to the urban trades. In its 1902 report, the royal commission described the "under-consumption" of the Chinese and their predisposition to "live under conditions insufferable to a white man." The white working class had for decades charged that this amounted to "unfair competition"; by 1901 royal commissioners agreed that such competition was no less than "deadly … because it strikes at home life."[37]

Chute, Foley, and Munn also invoked a "numerously signed petition from the residents of British Columbia" to the governor-general-in-council in May 1900. The petition protested: "The province is flooded with an undesirable class of people non-assimilative and most detrimental to the wage-earning classes of the people of the province." It also urged that "it is in the interest of the Empire that the Pacific Province of the Dominion should be occupied by a large and thoroughly British population rather than one in which the number of aliens forms a large proportion."[38] The commissioners concluded that further immigration from China would indeed be injurious and unanimously recommended that the head tax on Chinese immigrants be raised to $500.

Given a report so lacking in equivocation, the Laurier government wasted no time in implementing its recommendations. The 1903 session of parliament amended the immigration act of 1885 to raise the entry tax to a hefty $500, with the dissent of only a few "free traders," as the member for Russell called himself.[39]

Such dominion endorsement of the racial category was not an uncomplicated or automatic response to beliefs about race, as we have seen. But clearly the twin ideas of a Chinese race and

of Chinese inferiority had grown in force and political utility, so that by 1903 most members of parliament—the large majority of whom were yet to have local experience with "Chinese"—were prepared to overcome whatever moral, economic, and diplomatic reservations remained about legally imposed discrimination.

The prime minister defended the outcome in 1903, when he said that "the difference between the two races" bred an antagonism that even the state needed to respect. "It seems impossible to reconcile them [the differences]," Laurier said, "and the conclusion of all who have considered the matter seems to be that the amalgamation of the two is neither possible [nor] desirable. There are so many differences of character that it is supposed to be impossible to overcome them. At all events in the province of British Columbia, this feeling is very strong."[40]

Even with immigrants from Japan, Laurier continued, "the ethnical differences are of such a character as to make it very doubtful whether assimilation of the two races could ever take place."[41] The marginality of the "Oriental" in Canada had been divinely ordained, or so Laurier wanted to believe, and his government's responsibility was to respect and facilitate the unfolding of that higher will. Thenceforth, immigration from China to Canada fell to a trickle.

* * *

THE GEOGRAPHY OF RACE IN VANCOUVER

The staking of a new town and citizenry was—like the defining of a new province—a territorial process, and by 1886, with anti-Chinese measures in place at both senior levels of government, Vancouver's "white" pioneers were as accepting as other British

Columbians of officially sanctioned definitions of "us" and "them." Many saw the primary challenge facing the new town to be the prevention of permanent Chinese settlement. The reported sale to Chinese of two lots in the business section of town in April 1886 certainly sparked indignation throughout the white community. It was, for the *Vancouver World*, no less than "a violent wrench to the public sentiment," a danger, the *Herald* warned, to property values in the emerging commercial section.[42] When a "small horde of unemployed Chinamen" tried to locate a new business in the section, the *Vancouver News* said: "Let their efforts, however little we know them, be promptly discouraged … The thin edge of the wedge, in this case, had better be obstructed."[43]

In the mean time, white residents did what they could to discourage Chinese settlement. At the first municipal election, of May 1886, the cultural and political bounds of the new community were quickly asserted when sixty men of Chinese origin were chased from the polls back to the Hastings Mill, from which they had been brought by manager and mayoral candidate Mr R.H. Alexander.[44] It had been inscribed in the statute to incorporate the city of Vancouver that no "Chinese" or "Indian" was entitled to the municipal franchise—and this closure was vigilantly enforced with clubs and fists at the first opportunity.

Driving the Chinese back as far as the Hastings Mill was not far enough for many Vancouver citizens. They saw a better opportunity in the great fire of 13 June 1886, which levelled the new city and with it the residences and businesses of Chinese. In the week after the fire, three street meetings, held with the support of the new Scottish-born mayor, Alderman M.A. MacLean, and fellow Scots-born Alderman L.A. Hamilton, passed resolutions aimed at preventing Chinese from re-establishing themselves. But

by July, the *News* lamented: "They seem to have recovered from the fire scare which drove them out," and a "number are coming into the city taking up their locations principally on the outskirts."[45] From the outskirts, which included a 160-acre tract that "a colony of Mongolians" had leased for cultivation on the road to New Westminster, Chinese supplied private residences, hotels, and boarding-houses which depended almost entirely on them for their vegetable products. Hamilton found the threat so serious as to take the matter to council in November of that year, when he pressed for the city to "take some action in trying as far as possible to prevent Chinese from locating within the City limits."[46]

Local assemblies of the Knights of Labor, also mounted a campaign to "avert the evil effects which are sure to follow wherever those miserly rice eaters locate."[47] In November 1886, they passed a resolution declaring that "the employment of Chinese not only lowers the dignity of labour but is exceedingly injurious and detrimental to the best interests of the working classes," and for this reason, they resolved "to do [their] utmost … to lessen the grievance by an active and persistent action against all persons who continue to employ Chinese."[48] True to their word, the Knights organized a boycott of all Vancouver businessmen who employed, sold food to, or in any way patronized Chinese residents; they painted a cross in front of any store that broke with white solidarity. Hotel-keepers agreed to discharge Chinese help. The city also respected the initiative by refusing to hire Chinese and by prohibiting the employment of "any person of Chinese race" on municipal contracts or city-assisted projects—an exclusion the Vancouver Trades and Labour Council scrupulously monitored.

The fear that Chinese labourers would undercut white workers was not without foundation.

As stated earlier,BC employers exploited the race concept to their own advantage and paid Chinese workers a wage in proportion to their perceived worth.Thus in late 1886, when John McDougall recruited "batches of Mongolians" from Victoria for his 350-acre clearing contract in Vancouver's West End, he quickly came under attack from the local white labouring class. At $1.25 to $1.50 per day, Chinese labour would halve his costs, the contractor explained. It was a defence that few accepted, and McDougall's action bristled workers and also community-minded citizens, businessmen, and officials who were trying hard "to stop the growing evil while yet it is in its infancy."[49]

In early January 1887, a citizens' meeting at City Hall appointed a committee, which included Mayor MacLean and Alderman Joseph Humphries, to establish a fund for defraying the expense of returning Chinese "to the place from whence they came." A second committee, also including the mayor, was chosen "to wait upon all employers of Chinese labour for the purpose of inducing them to replace it with white help." Within two days, the committee had convinced twenty or so West End workers to decamp and sail away to Victoria, to the "hearty cheers" of "fully 600 citizens."[50] Others were escorted to the road to New Westminster, while substitute Chinese workers from Victoria quickly sensed the reception they would get in Vancouver and sailed on to Port Moody.

The intimidation strategy was quickly strengthened and diversified. A joint-stock company was formed to buy out Chinese-owned laundries in the Old Granville Townsite; a vegetable ranch at False Creek was said to have been vacated, and it was rumoured that some of the more eager citizens raided Alderman Hamilton's house and packed off his two houseboys on the steamer to Victoria.[51]

One Chinese "boss," Lew Shew, refused to be harassed in this fashion, and in late January he retained a lawyer to bring action against Mayor MacLean, Alderman Humphries, and others on the new citizens' committees, for molestation he allegedly suffered in an attempt to expel him from the city limits.Although the defendants were exonerated, Lew Shew and "McDougall Chinee," as the clearance contractor became dubbed, won an injunction from the BC Supreme Court discouraging similar acts of expulsion in the future.[52] Armed with this injunction, and determined to complete his contract to clear the Brighouse Estate, McDougall brought back the necessary labour in February 1887, only to find that an anti-Chinese league had been formed with the specific intention of preventing Chinese from relocating within the city limits. Popular support for anti-Chinese activities had grown extensively in the weeks since the citizens' committees were formed. During four well-attended January meetings at City Hall, various means of soliciting pledges from the community had been devised to prevent Chinese securing another foothold.When it was rumoured that Chinese were en route from Victoria, some 300 people had sped to the wharf.[53] Citizens had also continued to paint crosses on establishments that were said to deal with Chinese.

It was into this atmosphere of anxiety and growing antagonism that the Brighouse Estate workers returned, with the defiant "McDougall Chinee" no doubt preparing for strong reaction, but not quite for what transpired on 24 February 1887. On that evening, the frustration of residents came to a head at a crammed public meeting at City Hall. Unimpeded by local police, approximately 300 angry men surged from the meeting to the camps of sleeping workers at Coal Harbour, with their own solution to the Chinese presence in mind.

Shanties were pulled down, bedding, clothing, and provisions thrown into a fire, and some twenty-five workers, it was said by the press, "kicked and knocked about." Around midnight a smaller mob completed the deed at Carrall Street, where the homes of some ninety Chinese residents were burnt or damaged.

The following day, Chinese living in the vicinity of Carrall Street were notified to leave the city. They agreed to do so peaceably on condition that one person could be left in charge of each store. With those terms met, the settlers were carried off to New Westminster. Three rioters (a logger, a milkman, and a clerk) were arrested, given bail by Magistrate J. Blake (a member of the original citizens' committee), and later discharged for what was said to be lack of evidence.

The riot marked the first act of concerted physical violence against the Chinese in Canada. In Victoria, the events of 24 February drew official disapproval, despite the obvious sympathy of the legislature and the province's difficulty in translating its own political will into legal action. Even anti-Chinese champion John Robson said that while Vancouver's civic authorities possessed ample powers, they had "strangely and persistently refrained from exercising them in upholding the law."[54]

Attorney-General Davie immediately drafted urgent legislation. A Bill to Preserve the Peace in Vancouver passed through all three readings in the house in one day, effectively suspending the city's charter and annulling its judicial powers.[55] Much to the resentment of Vancouver's mayor and council, some forty special constables were also sent from Victoria to take charge of what the attorney-general described as a decline into "mob rule."

Ironically, then, the protection of a reluctant provincial government allowed the immigrants from China to return to Vancouver and re-

establish residence. Most returned to the vicinity of Carrall and Dupont streets on district lot 196, the land some had been expelled from. Many of the Brighouse labourers also gravitated there after they finally completed the clearing contract in 1888. By 1889, according to Henderson's *British Columbia Directory* published in Victoria in that year, the settlers of Chinese origin had become concentrated in the vicinity of Dupont and Carrall streets. While nine of fourteen Chinese laundries were scattered through the Old Granville Townsite and district lot 196, the twenty-nine Chinese companies and merchant premises were confined almost entirely to Dupont and Carrall streets. Of the merchants, five were grocers, three owned general stores, one was a shoemaker, one was a labour contractor, one owned a store, and the trades of the others were not specified. A Chinese school was located at 115 Hastings Street. No mention was made in the directory of the sundry shacks of labourers, but many were located on the tidal flat on block 14 with good access to industrial and commercial wharfs, industrial shops, the gas works, and the Royal City Planing Mill, built in 1886. By 1892, this spatial pattern was consolidated, as was the relative concentration of Chinese in Vancouver.

The area of concentrated settlement was a depressed, swampy district, covered at high tide by the waters of False Creek, which flowed closest to Burrard Inlet between Carrall and Columbia streets. At Hastings and Carrall streets, a rocky outcrop further enclosed and protected the area, the adverse physical character of which paralleled its residents' marginal cultural, legal, and economic status. The spatial referent of the category "Chinese" was not a legislated one, however; settlers from China did not locate in a concentrated pattern through formal civic suasion or restrictive covenant. When the city attempted to rid Stanley Park of some Chinese squatters by such direct means in the years 1888–90, Attorney-General Davie was quick to query its jurisdictional competence. (City council in turn advised the board of health to indict the squatters as a public nuisance to facilitate their removal.)[56]

* * *

CONCLUSION

This chapter has examined the roles of the different levels of Canadian government in shaping the definition and status of immigrants from China in British Columbia in the late nineteenth century. For governing élites, no less than other members of Canadian society, "John Chinaman" stood as the image of all men and women from China. This typification can be traced to the modern idea of race which collapsed class and gender divisions among Chinese and assimilated an ancient and medieval baggage of distinctions between "West" and "East," civilized and barbarian, master and slave, Christian and heathen, white and non-white into a doctrine of discrete and immutable types. By the mid-nineteenth century, with British power straddling the globe, the oppositions had congealed into an ideological structure of formidable rigidity. Darwinism was adapted to lend scientific status to the views that there existed such things as races; that there were lower and higher races, progressive and non-progressive races ("John" being a prime example of the latter); and that a natural antipathy engendered conflict between the races.

This influential ideology of "difference" informed the outlook of white British Columbians from the 1870s, when settlers from China began arriving there. Thirty years later, despite the fact that people of Chinese origin constituted less than half of one per cent of Canada's population, it was entrenched in the ethos and institutions of the province, and a whole epistemology of separation had been built between "Chinese" and "whites."

The state played a crucial role in sponsoring and enforcing this arbitrary distinction of race as a line of division around which both rhetoric and practice were directed. After the province joined a confederated Canada, the social cleavage was etched firmly as politicians began to stake out a *British* British Columbia. One of the means by which they marked the limits of, and boosted collective legitimacy for, their staked claim was by imposing disabilities on the out-group labelled "Chinese." They did so not out of irrational prejudice, nor as blind agents of capital, but as active propagators of a legally bound cultural hegemony. Greater caution was exercised in Ottawa, but eventually dominion politicians were content to forfeit an open immigration policy in the interests of control over Chinese entry. At the local level, Vancouver's city council gave moral force to racial categorization through its support for strategies, including violence, to rid the city of Chinese. Its leadership was an important factor in setting the context for a settlement that [...] gave concrete form to the concept of a "Chinese race."

The Canadian state's institutional authority carried a stamp of legitimacy that collective opinion of the time lacked. Through a combination of "proactive" and reactive measures, the levels of government rendered the idea of a Chinese race a social fact of considerable material consequence, both for those so defined and for white society. By the close of the nineteenth century, "John's" perceived threat to this British settler society had achieved a magnitude that prompted the intervention of all three levels of government, the momentum of which was to resound through the decades to come.

NOTES

1. In cannery work, Chinese were paid $25 to $35 per month, and "whites" $40. Road building earned Chinese $15 to $20 per month, and "whites" $40. Canada, *Sessional Papers*, 1885, No. 54a, "Royal Commission on Chinese Immigration" (hereafter cited as Canada, *Report*, 1885), 26 and 11.

2. Ibid., 14, 70, 49.

3. Cited in P. Ward, *White Canada Forever*, 25.

4. See Robin, *The Rush for the Spoils*, chap. 2.

5. *JLABC*, 1883, 12, 17.

6. Ibid., 83.

7. *JLABC*, 1882, 11, 10.

8. Berton, *The Last Spike*, chap. 2.

9. British Columbia, *Sessional Papers*, 1885, "Correspondence in connection with the mission of Hon. W. Smithe to Ottawa relating to Chinese immigration and other questions," 2. British Columbia, *Statutes*, 1884, 47 Vict., chap. 3.

10. British Columbia, *Statutes*, 1884, 47 Vict., chap. 4.

11. Ibid., chap. 16.

12. See Bonacich, "Theory." On the BC context see Creese, "Immigration Policies."

13. *JLABC*, 1885, 14, 46. See also British Columbia, *Sessional Papers*, 1886, "Destitute Condition of Chinese Recently Discharged from the CPR Works, 1885."

14. British Columbia, *Statutes*, 1885, 48 Vict., chap. 13.

15. *JLABC*, 1891, 20, 145. Without access to the debates, it is not possible to establish why that motion was carried, nor the numerous others involving what became called "the usual Chinese clause."

16. British Columbia, *Statutes*, 1897, 60 Vict., chap. 1.

17. *JLABC*, 1900, 28, 99.

18. Ibid., 1894, 23, 117; 1897, 28, 57.

19. Ibid., 1900, 24, 58–9.

20. Canada, *Report*, 1885, 11.

21. Canada, House of Commons, *Debates* (hereafter *DHC*) 18 March 1878, 1209.

22. *DHC*, 16 April 1879, 1262.

23. Ibid., 12 May 1882, 1477.

24. Ibid., 30 April 1883, 905.

25. Warburton, "Race and Class," 82. Basran also argues that Canadian immigration practices can be explained by "the general role of the Canadian state," which has been "to help capitalists in the accumulation process and to assist them to increase their profits"; "Canadian Immigration Policy," 11.

26. *DHC*, 18 March 1878, 1208; 16 April 1879, 1253.

27. Canada, *Report*, 1885, 69.

28. Ibid., 94.

29. *DHC*, 2 July 1885, 3002–11.

30. Canada, *Statutes*, 1885, 48–49 Vict., chap. 71. In the same session, Macdonald introduced an amendment to the Franchise Act that prevented any "person of Mongolian or Chinese race" from the dominion franchise; ibid., chap. 40, s. 2. Macdonald was one of the most ardent supporters of the amendment. He said "The Chinaman ... has no British instincts or British feelings or aspirations, and therefore ought not to have the vote"; *DHC*, 4 May 1885, 1589.

31. *DHC*, 4 May 1887, 277.

32. Ibid., 31 May 1887, 643.

33. Canada, *Report*, 1885, 98.

34. *DHC*, 4 September 1891, 5059.

35. Canada, *Report*, 1902, 273. Chinese immigration and Japanese immigration were investigated separately in the report.

36. Ibid., 274.

37. Ibid., 277.

38. Cited in *Report*, 1902, 13.

39. The amendment passed its third reading on 5 May 1903; *DHC*, 5 May 1903, 2399. The amendment was passed despite the protest of the president of the Canadian Pacific Railway, Mr T. Shaughnessy, who claimed that "legislation by Canada would deprive us of the revenue from the carriage of Chinamen back and forth between this country and their own and would so seriously affect the revenue of our Pacific steamships that we could not afford to keep them running"; Canada, *Report*, 1902, 201.

40. *DHC*, 27 March 1903, 597–8.

41. Ibid., 599.

42. The two newspaper references are taken from Roy, "Preservation," 45.

43. *Vancouver News*, 2 June 1886.

44. Morley, *Vancouver*, 73.

45. *Vancouver News*, 27 July 1886.

46. City of Vancouver Archives (hereafter CVA), Vancouver City (hereafter Van. City), *Council Minutes*, Vol. 1, 8 November 1886, 164.

47. *Vancouver News*, 30 December 1886.

48. Ibid., 9 November 1886.

49. See *Vancouver News*, 8, 9, 14, January 1887, on local response to McDougall.

50. Ibid., 9, 11 January 1887.

51. Morton, *In the Sea*, 148.

52. *British Columbia Federationist*, 9 December 1911.

53. Morton, *In the Sea*, 148.

54. Robson to Vancouver City Council, cited in *Vancouver News*, 15 March 1887.

[55] British Columbia, *Statutes*, 1887, 50 Vict., chap. 33.

[56] On the squatters, see CVA, Van. City, Council Minutes, Vol. 3, 3 June 1889, 33; ibid., Vol. 3, 30 June 1890; ibid., Clerk's Incoming Correspondence (hereafter In Corresp.), Vol. 3, 27 June 1890, 2103.

BIBLIOGRAPHY

Government Documents

British Columbia. *Journals of the Legislative Assembly of British Columbia (JLABC)*, various dates, 1872–1950.

———— *Reports*. 1878, 1885, 1888.

———— *Sessional Papers*, 1880, 1885, 1886, 1894.

———— *Statutes*, 1872, 1875, 1878, 1883, 1884, 1885, 1886, 1897, 1900, 1919.

Canada. *Debates of the House of Commons (DHC)*, various dates, 1879–1980.

Books, Articles, and Theses

Berton, P. *The Last Spike*. Toronto: McClelland and Stewart 1971.

Bonacich, E. "A Theory of Ethnic Antagonisms: The Split Labor Market." *American Sociological Review*, 37 (1972): 547–59.

Robin, M. *The Rush for Spoils: The Company Province 1871–1933*. Toronto: McClelland and Stewart 1972.

Warburton, R. "Race and Class in British Columbia: A Comment." *B.C. Studies*, 49 (1981): 79–85.

Ward, P. *White Canada Forever: Popular Attitudes and Public Policy toward Orientals in British Columbia*. Montreal: McGill-Queen's University Press 1978.

FURTHER READING

Das Gupta, Tania, Carl E. James, Roger C.A. Maaka, Grace-Edward Galabuzi, and Chris Andersen, eds. *Race and Racialization: Essential Readings*. Toronto: Canadian Scholars' Press, 2007.

Edited as a theoretically strong, cohesive whole, this provocative volume examines the history of race and racialization and unites a remarkable ensemble of academic thinkers and writers from a diversity of backgrounds. Themes of ethnocentrism, cultural genocide, conquest and colonization, disease and pandemics, slavery, and the social construction of racism run throughout.

Race and Racialization profiles the work of international thinkers such as Edward W. Said, Stuart Hall, Paul Gilroy, Robert Miles, Rudy Torres, Franz Fanon, Audrey Smedley, and Linda Tuhiwai Smith. It showcases the work of Canadian scholars, writers, and social critics such as Sherene H. Razack, Celia Haig-Brown, George J. Sefa Dei, and Vijay Agnew. It highlights institutional racism alongside the failures in an ideology of integration, the politics of multiculturalism, and the many paradoxes of diversity. It explores the intersections of racism with other forms of oppression marked by gender, class, indigenousness, and sexuality.

Razack, Sherene, ed. *Race, Space, and the Law: Unmapping a White Settler Society*. Toronto: Between the Lines Press, 2002

Racial categories can be spatial categories. The writers in this collection reject the idea that spaces, and the arrangement of bodies within them, emerge naturally over time. Do Native reservations, Chinatowns, or slums simply emerge naturally? Or are they products of more active, often violent, resettlements? The contributors ask critical questions such as "How did such places come to exist?" and "What is the future of the ideas that formed these places?" This book belongs to a growing field of exploration that spans critical geography, sociology, law, education, as well as critical race and feminist studies.

Ward, Peter. *White Canada Forever: Popular Attitudes and Public Policy Toward Orientals in British Columbia.*
Montreal and Kingston: McGill-Queen's University Press, 2003.

Between the mid-19th and mid-20th centuries, white British Columbians directed recurring outbursts of prejudice against the Chinese, Japanese, and East Indians who lived among them. This book reveals the full extent of
West Coast racism. Ward draws upon a rich record of events and opinion in the provincial press, manuscript collections, and successive federal inquiries and royal commissions on Asian immigration. He locates the origins of
West Coast racism in the frustrated vision of a white British Columbia and an unshakeable belief in the "unassimilability" of the Asian immigrant. Canadian attitudes were dominated by a series of interlocking, hostile stereotypes derived from western perceptions of Asia and modified by the encounter between whites and Asians on the
north Pacific coast. Public pressure on local, provincial, and federal governments led to discriminatory policies in
the fields of immigration and employment, and culminated in the forced relocation of West Coast Japanese residents during World War II.

PART III

DANGEROUS OTHERS: NON-CITIZENS AND THE STATE

*T*he next two parts take up the issue of dangerous non-citizens in Canada's midst at the turn of the century until the Great Depression. After the Canadian government quashed the Metis Rebellion of 1885, it began a renewed effort to assimilate First Nations peoples. The Indian Act of 1876 contained an array of measures to both centralize and facilitate the process of assimilation; however, by the 1880s the government "became increasingly impatient about the slow pace of Indians 'civilization' and 'assimilation'."[1] To meet its objective, the government implemented a range of "protective" and coercive measures, such as the pass system, the prohibition of liquor and Native ceremonies, and the residential school system. The government also attempted to turn the First Nations peoples of Western Canada into farmers, but within certain strict parameters. Aboriginal peoples became a threat when they sought to go beyond the strict limits placed upon them by the Department of Indian Affairs.

While the government was ratcheting up its program of Aboriginal governance, it was also opening its borders to unprecedented levels of immigration from the British Isles and non-traditional sources. This was also a time of economic expansion in Canada. The young Canadian government pushed for agricultural settlers in Western Canada. While the government supported the increasingly quaint ideal of agricultural settlement, the economy was rapidly changing in this era and so emerged the need for workers created by the upsurge in heavy industry such as mining, forestry, and railway construction. When these new settlers arrived, they brought their ideas with them. Socialism and Communism, in particular, were considered dangerous and foreign by various constituencies within Canada. Largely as a result of this, the "dangerous foreigner" weighed heavily on the minds of the country's economic and cultural elites. At the same time, these "radical" ideologies lubricated the often difficult processes of adjustment, community building, and social protest.

Sarah Carter's work on the government's Indian agricultural policy—perhaps the most influential written on this subject—recounts how the government attempted to make peasant farmers out of Aboriginal people. The article makes some surprising arguments and conclusions.

Donald Avery's chapter nicely fleshes out the social, economic, and cultural dimensions of the "world of the immigrant worker" at the turn of the century and the state's response to the labour militancy that was often a product of this world. The last two chapters tighten Avery's broad lens to focus in on the stories of two particular groups of immigrant workers: Jews and Hungarians. In both populations, radical political leaders fought for the hearts and minds of their community members, while seeking to help the immigrant worker survive the challenges of a new country.

NOTE

[1] J.R. Miller, *Skyscrapers Hide the Heavens: A History of Indian-White Relations in Canada, Third Edition* (Toronto: University of Toronto Press, 2000), 254.

CHAPTER 8

Two Acres and a Cow: "Peasant" Farming for the Indians of the Northwest, 1889–97

Sarah A. Carter

*I*ndian Commissioner Hayter Reed announced in 1889 that a new "approved system of farming" was to be adopted on western Indian reserves.[1] Indian farmers were to emulate "peasants of various countries" who kept their operations small and their implements rudimentary. In Reed's opinion a single acre of wheat, a portion of a second acre of roots and vegetables, and a cow or two could provide sufficiently for an Indian farmer and his family. He argued that it was better for Indians to cultivate a small acreage properly than to attempt to extend the area under cultivation. Moreover, this restricted acreage eliminated any need for labour-saving machinery. Peasants of other countries, Reed contended, farmed successfully with no better implements than the hoe, the rake, cradle, sickle, and flail, and he believed that Indians had to be taught to handle these simple tools. They were to broadcast seed by hand, harvest with scythes, bind by hand with straw, and thresh with flails. In some districts Indians were discouraged from growing wheat altogether in favour of root crops, and this further reduced the need for any machinery. As part of the program, Indians were required to manufacture at home, from materials readily available, many of the items they needed such as harrows, hay forks, hay racks, carts, and ox yokes.

Indian farmers were compelled to comply with the peasant farming policy until 1897, when Reed's career with the department abruptly ended. This policy, along with the permit system and the subdivision survey of portions of reserves into forty-acre plots, had a stultifying effect on Indian farming, nipping reserve agricultural development in the bud.

Agriculture was not well-established on western Indian reserves by the turn of the century. It has generally been argued that Indians, because they were hunters and warriors, were unable to adapt to farming, and that they could not be transformed into sedentary farmers.[2] The story is far more complex, however. There was an initial positive response to agriculture on the part of many reserve residents which has been overlooked in the literature to date. There were also many difficulties. Some of these problems were those experienced by all early settlers—drought, frost, hail, and prairie fire, an absence of markets, and uncertainties about what to sow, when to sow, and how to sow. There were other problems that were not unique to the Indians but were likely magnified in their case. For example, reserve land often proved to be unsuitable for agriculture. Indian farmers also had limited numbers of oxen, implements, and seed: the treaty provisions for these items were immediately found to be inadequate. Indians were greatly hampered in their work because they lacked apparel, particularly footwear. They were undernourished, resulting in poor physical stamina and vulnerability to infectious diseases.

Indian farmers were also subject to a host of government policies and regulations which hampered agricultural development. If an Indian farmer sought better railway, market, or soil advantages he was not able to pull up stakes and try his luck elsewhere, since an Indian could not take out a homestead under the 1876 Indian Act. Nor could Indians raise outside investment capital; reserve land could not be mortgaged and Indians had difficulty obtaining credit. Freedom to sell their produce and stock and to purchase goods was strictly regulated through a permit system, just as movements off the reserves were rigidly monitored through a pass system.

* * *

The peasant farming policy emerged during an era when the stated priorities of the Department of Indian Affairs were to dismantle what was called the "tribal" or "communist" system and to promote "individualism." After 1885 in particular these goals were undertaken with great vigour and commitment, along with an increased emphasis on the supervision, control, and restriction of the activities and movements of the Indians. Hayter Reed, a major architect of Indian policy in the Northwest in the decade following the 1885 resistance, fully endorsed these goals. Appointed

commissioner in 1888 and deputy superintendent general in 1893, Reed was in a position to articulate and compel obedience to his views. He boasted that under his administration "the policy of destroying the tribal or communist system is assailed in every possible way, and every effort made to implant a spirit of individual responsibility instead."[3] Although Reed's ultimate goal was to see the reserves broken up, he claimed that in the meantime his department was teaching the Indians step by step to provide for themselves through their own industry, and inculcating in them a spirit of "self-reliance and independence."

One way to undermine the tribal system was to subdivide reserves into separate farms. Large fields worked in common fostered the tribal system; according to Reed they did not encourage pride and industry. The individual farmer did not feel it worth his while to improve land significantly when other members of the band also claimed it as their own.[4] With a certificate of ownership, it was believed, the enterprising Indian would be induced to make permanent improvements such as superior cultivation, improved housing, and better fencing, all of which would have the effect of tying the owner to the locality. Reed was also convinced that private property created law-abiding citizens. Property would render the Indians averse to disturbing the existing order of things, as "among them as among white communities, the lawless and revolutionary element is to be found among those who have nothing to lose but may perhaps gain by upsetting law and order."[5]

Severalty was not a new idea in Canadian Indian policy, nor was Reed the first official to promote the scheme for the Indians of western Canada, but under his administration the program began in earnest. In his annual report for 1888 Reed announced that reserves in the

Northwest were to be subdivided into forty-acre plots or quarter quarter sections.[6] Survey work, which began the following spring, was done on reserves where farming had met with some success—that is, where the capacity of the land for agriculture had been proven.[7] Reserves with poorer land—such as the File Hills and Touchwood Hills—were not subdivided. The forty-acre plots were located well back of the main-line Canadian Pacific Railway and the new towns along its route, well back of the fine agricultural reserve land that new settlers and townspeople were beginning to covet—the land that was eventually surrendered.

It is clear that what was in the best interests of the agricultural future of these bands was not in the minds of those who devised this policy. When the subdivision surveys were proposed, government and Indian Affairs officials had objectives in mind beyond the establishment of agriculture on an individual model. John A. Macdonald was enthusiastic about severalty, not as a method of promoting individual initiative and private ownership, but as means of defining "surplus" land on reserves that might be sold.[8] If each Indian were allotted the land he would likely require for cultivation, the amount of surplus land available for surrender and sale could be ascertained.

*   *   *

The peasant farming policy, introduced at the same time as severalty, was also presented as a means of destroying the system of community ownership on reserves and enhancing individualism and self-support. The central rationale advanced in support of the policy was that it was "the manner best calculated to render [the Indians] self-supporting when left to their own resources."[9] Reed repeated many times in his correspondence and public pro-

nouncements that he believed the time was not far distant when the Indians would have to depend entirely upon their own resources. "Our policy," he stated, "is to make each family cultivate such quantity of land as they can manage with such implements as they can alone hope to possess for long enough after being thrown upon their own resources."[10]

*   *   *

According to Reed, labour-saving machinery was not required by Indians. They should cultivate root crops rather than concentrate upon extensive grain growing.[11] In Reed's view, root and not cereal crops taught Indian farmers to be diligent and attentive: "I've always advocated growing as many root crops as possible but Indians have to be humoured a good deal in such matters; and as soon as they begin to make some little progress they become fired with an ambition to grow larger quantities of wheat and other cereals [rather than] roots which require working and weeding at the very time they like to be off hunting while the former only require to have cattle kept away by means of a good fence."[12]

*   *   *

Reed drew on aspects of an evolutionary argument to support his peasant farming policy. In the late nineteenth century, those who took an evolutionary view of the North American Indian and other "primitive" people believed that there were immutable laws of social evolution.[13] It was thought that man developed progressively through prescribed stages from savagery through barbarism to civilization. These stages could not be skipped, nor could a race or culture be expected to progress at an accelerated rate. The Indians were perceived to be many stages removed from nineteenth-century civilization, and while they could take the next step forward, they could not miss the steps in between.

* * *

What accounts for the sudden introduction and enforcement of a ban on machinery? Immigrant settlers resented Indian competition for the limited markets of the Northwest. The 1880s saw increasingly strained relations between Indian and white farmers, a situation that was aggravated by the lean times. Local department officials generally came to the defence of the Indians' interests, while more distant officials appeared willing to please the more politically powerful settlers, at the Indians' expense. The recent arrivals believed that everything should be done to encourage their enterprise. They considered themselves the "actual" settlers, the true discoverers and developers of the country's resources. They believed that the government had bought the land from the Indians, and it was now the government's "right and duty to look after the interests of the settlers, both present and future, for whom the land was bought, and out of whose earnings it is expected ultimately to be paid for."[14]

By the late 1880s, farmers in some areas of the Northwest were complaining loudly about "unfair" competition from Indians in obtaining a share of the markets for farm produce, and a share of contracts for the supply of hay, wood, and other products. They believed that government assistance gave the Indians an unfair advantage, allowing them to undersell the white farmer. Complaints from the Battleford district were particularly strident as the markets there were strictly limited and local, and competition was intense. In 1888 the residents of that town petitioned their member of parliament, stating that "the Indians are raising so much grain and

farm produce that they are taking away the market from the white settlers."[15]

A visit to Battleford that year appears to have had an important impact on Hayter Reed. There he was "assailed" by complaints about the effects of Indian competition.[16] As a Department of the Interior "chief land guide" in Manitoba in 1880–1, Reed had urged settlers to consider points as far west as Battleford.[17] He had given his assurance that despite the absence of a railway, farmers could be guaranteed a market for their produce as the government's demands alone for the Indians, the Mounted Police, surveyors, and other crews would absorb all of a farmer's surplus.[18] If the Indians were able to provide for themselves as well as sell a surplus, the already limited markets were further restricted.

Following his 1888 visit to Battleford, Reed decided that until a railway extended the settlers' opportunities, his department must do what it could to prevent jealous competition.[19] Competition for markets, he claimed, was disastrous to the Indians in any case, as they were so anxious to find purchasers that they would part with their products for a "trifling consideration."[20] Reed arranged with the Battleford citizens to divide up the limited markets in the district. Much of the trade in cordwood was left to the Métis, as this was their mainstay over the winter. The Indians were allowed to supply wood to the agency and, for one more year, to the industrial school. The sale of grain in the district was left exclusively to the white settlers.

The peasant farming policy, introduced a year after Reed's visit to Battleford, helped eliminate the Indians from effective competition. The permit system was another means of regulating the Indians' participation in the market economy. Under the Indian Act the department could regulate the sale, barter, exchange, or gift of any grain, roots, or other produce grown on reserves.[21] The official rationale for the permit system was that Indians had to be taught to husband their resources. John A. Macdonald stated that "if the Indians had the power of unrestricted sale, they would dispose of their products to the first trader or whiskey dealer who came along, and the consequence would be that the Indians would be pensioners on the Government during the next winter."[22] The permit system, however, further precluded the Indians from participation in the market economy as they could not buy, sell, or transact business.

While the peasant policy excluded Indians from effective competition with white farmers, Hayter Reed may have hoped that it might, nonetheless, provide a secure means of subsistence for the Indians. In nineteenth-century liberal economic thought the peasant proprietor gained a new respectability.[23] Among others, John Stuart Mill opposed the concentration of landed property in the hands of a few great estate owners and favoured the creation of a class of peasant proprietors. This it was believed would raise agricultural productivity, lower prices, and reduce urban unemployment. Peasant proprietorship would have social as well as economic consequences as the owner would take a permanent interest in the soil. He would be "thrifty, sober, honest and independent."[24] With a stake in the country, former day labourers would be less inclined to "wanton aggressions," or "mischief," and instead would be interested in preserving tranquility and order. These were exactly the qualities Reed attributed to his peasant proprietors.

In the 1880s these ideas had wide public support in England and America. "Three acres and a cow" was promoted by individuals and charitable organizations as a means of reforming and controlling the behaviour of the working classes, veterans, immigrants, and criminals.[25] In 1890

the Salvation Army's founder, William Booth, published *In Darkest England and the Way Out*, in which he advocated the settlement of the poor on three- to five-acre allotments with a cottage and a cow.[26] Reed's plan bears some resemblances to Joseph Chamberlain's 1885 election cry, "Three Acres and a Cow."[27] Chamberlain's loosely sketched agrarian reform policy involved the compulsory purchase of land by local authorities in order to repopulate the country with independent English yeoman. A visit to Canada in 1887 may have generated interest in Chamberlain's ideas on land reform.[28]

The peasant farming policy and subdivision of reserves into forty-acre plots were probably also inspired by the general allotment policy in the United States, codified in the Dawes Act of 1887. The rhetoric was precisely the same—that individual lots and ownership would create stable, sedentary farmers. In the United States those who supported allotment in severalty argued that the policy of concentration and isolation upon reservations had failed to resolve the Indian "problem."[29] Private property was the key to transforming the Indians into "civilized" agriculturalists. Pride of ownership generated individual initiative and taught the Indians self-support. Private property destroyed the tribal relationship, breaking the yoke of authoritarian chiefs and allowing "progressive" Indians to accumulate wealth and property. Supporters of the Dawes Act felt that an end to the isolation of the reservation would enhance Indian farming as Indians would reap the benefit of close association with enlightened white farmers. Tardy progress had resulted from this isolation as the Indians' environment was closed to all progressive influences. Assimilation, through allotment in severalty, seemed to offer a permanent solution. Isolation was condemned as an obstacle to national unity, and as a means of keeping alive racial distinctions.[30] Reservations seemed to have no place in a country which championed the concept of equal rights for all.

The Dawes Act was a major triumph for humanitarian reformers who were convinced that individual ownership was the key to the "civilization" of the Indians, but it also appealed to those with overt self-interest in mind. It was obvious from the outset that allotment would open much reserve land for settlement. By granting land to individual Indians, "surplus" lands could be defined and made accessible. After a stipulated acreage went to each Indian family, the remaining land would be thrown open to white settlement, and sizeable portions of reservations would be sold. Many of those who supported the measure were interested in securing Indian land at a time when farm land was becoming increasingly scarce.[31]

Reed was convinced that the independent, subsistence farm could exist on the Canadian prairie, and he was not alone in cherishing the ideal of the self-sufficient farm where the family produced its own food, manufactured at home necessary non-agricultural goods such as clothing and furniture, and did not buy or sell. The notion that this was a superior way of life was widespread and persistent, and was reflected in the suspicion of labour-saving machinery and concern about the use of debt and credit. The ideal of the self-sufficient farmer continued to appeal to the general public whereas the concept of agriculture as a market and profit-focused business met with considerable criticism.[32]

Commercial agriculture required new ideas, attitudes, and knowledge. What and how much should be produced on the farm were determined by external market conditions rather than by the family's needs and desires. Under market conditions the farmer made a business decision and had to take into consideration the nature of the soil, the characteristics of commodities, access to markets, and world prices. Commercial farming involved a "rational" approach to technology. Potential profit rather than immediate need led the commercial farmer to purchase expensive implements on credit; payment would in part come from the increased productivity contributed by the new implement. The efficient, profitable management of the farm enterprise thus required new attitudes towards technology, credit, and debt, for immigrant settlers and Indians alike. Hayter Reed felt that Indians were incapable of understanding these concepts, and could not operate farms as business enterprises. His belief in the inability of Indians to manage their own financial affairs, and to handle debt, credit, or the new technology thus precluded commercial farming.

In the United States the ideal of the self-sufficient farm was never more than "a nice dream of a golden age"; nor was Canadian pioneer agriculture ever self-sufficient.[33] Pioneer farmers, economist Vernon Fowke has argued, were "from the beginning tied in with the price system and the urban economy on a national and international basis."[34] The farmer had to purchase his transportation and to outfit himself with the necessary provisions and implements. Although the farmer may not have produced a marketable staple for some years, he had products such as hay and wood to sell locally. Exchanges might be made through barter rather than cash, but these nonetheless constituted commercial transactions. Homesteaders were in need of cash and could rarely acquire enough to finance their operations. They could not borrow against their land until title was acquired, which involved a minimum three-year's wait. The farmer required credit to secure his provisions, implements, and other supplies. The standard practice was to have credit advanced at the beginning of the crop season for seed, tools, and consumable goods, with payment made at harvest time.

Subsistence farming was not characteristic of the pioneer farms of the prairie west. From the beginning these farms were connected to the local, national, and international economy. Nor did the difficulties of the 1880s imply a need for self-sufficient farms. Large-scale, single-crop farming and the introduction of the techniques and technology of dry farming would be more likely to encourage agricultural prosperity on the plains. Like other western farmers, Indian farmers tended more towards commercial than subsistence farming, focusing on wheat culture, acquiring machinery to accommodate large acreages, and adopting techniques such as summer-fallowing. In their need to acquire cash, make purchases, and sell products, Indian farmers were just as linked to the larger economy as white settlers. Yet the peasant farming policy required Indian farmers to function in isolation from the rest of western Canadian society.

This attitude was unrealistic. Subsistence farming remained at best a questionable model for the arid Canadian plains, and it may even have been impossible.[35] Western farmers were independent neither of the markets, nor of each other. Settlement of the prairies required mutual assistance and co-operation among neighbours and relatives. Working bees, pooled purchasing, and beef rings were characteristic of the pioneer years. Indians were denounced, however, when they undertook such co-operative action. Indian farmers were expected to conform to the nostalgic ideal of the independent, self-sufficient yeoman.

It soon became clear that peasant farming was a dubious model for reserve agriculture. Farm instructors, Indian agents, inspectors, and Indian farmers all protested the system. Despite this advice, Reed rigidly enforced the policy.

As commissioner, he kept a vigilant eye on every kettle and lamp ordered, and he maintained close surveillance as deputy superintendent general. Agents were not allowed to spend a "single copper" without the authority of the commissioner.[36] Reed's replacement as commissioner, Amédée Forget, had very limited powers of expenditure; even the most minute expense had to be sanctioned by Reed. Forget could under no circumstances authorize the purchase, hire, or use of machinery. When Forget requested greater powers of expenditure in 1894 in order to be able to respond to requests requiring immediate action during critical seasons, Reed replied: "I would say that I am only too desirous that you take upon your shoulders this part of the work, and thus relieve me of it. The fear I have had—to be candid—is that my policy might not be strictly carried out, and I forsee that if it is slackened in the slightest, it will lead us not only to a largely increased expenditure but upset what I have in view, and this is, causing our Indians to work upwards by learning how to cut and sow their grain in the most crude manner possible, and not beginning at the large-end of the norm, with self-binders and reapers."[37]

During haying and harvest time the full weight of the policy was felt. Agents and instructors were to see that the Indian farmers accomplished these tasks without the aid of any machinery. Even when bands had reapers and self-binders purchased before the policy was adopted, the farmers were to use hand implements. Larger farmers were expected to purchase the labour of others rather than revert to the use of machinery, or were to restrict their acreages to what they could handle with hand implements. "The general principle," Reed explained in 1893, "is not to allow them machinery to save them work which they should with hands available on Reserves, do by help of such implements as are alone likely for long enough, to be within their reach."[38]

Department officials in the field protested the peasant farming policy from its inception. They were dismayed by a policy which appeared to rob the Indians of any potential source of revenue. Their main objection was that the use of hand implements involved much loss in yield at harvest time. Harvesting coincided with haying, and both had to be secured with haste. As the Edmonton agent wrote in 1896: "Personally, I do not see how any band of Indians in this district can ever raise sufficient grain or cattle to become self-supporting as long as they have to work with sickles and scythes only, as the seasons are so very short, haying and harvesting coming together. Perhaps in the south where the seasons are longer the system would work successfully, but up here no whiteman attempts to do so."[39]

Agents throughout the Northwest—even those much further south than Edmonton—agreed that the seasons were too short for the use of hand implements. Once ready to cut, it was vital that grain remain standing for as brief a time as possible. The Carlton agent advised that because the climate brooked no delay with regard to securing grain, conditions in the Northwest could not be equated with the early days of farming in the eastern provinces when hand implements were used.[40] If not harvested as quickly as possible, grain could be lost to frost, hail, dry hot winds, or an excess of moisture. Agent Grant, of the Assiniboine reserve, protested that "the seasons in this country are too short to harvest any quantity of grain, without much waste with only old-fashioned, and hand-implements to do the work with."[41] In his view it was not possible to harvest the 240 acres of grain on his reserve with hand implements without a great loss in yield. The grain had to be cut as soon as it was ready to avoid

loss, since the harvest weather was generally hot, windy, and very dry. Grant estimated that the amount of grain lost in his agency would be of sufficient quantity in two years to pay for a binder. Loss occurred, not only through the grain being too ripe, but in the gathering and binding by hand as well. Grant informed Reed that the prairie straw was dry and brittle, and would not tie the grain without breaking, which caused considerable loss. While the farmers on his reserve used the long slough grass to bind grain, collecting it took up much time, leaving the grain in danger of over-ripening.

Agents also complained that the cradles broke constantly during harvest, which caused delays for repairs. The policy of employing labour to help take off a crop seldom proved feasible. Workers had their own fields to harvest. One agent reported that farmers who hired others spent more for labour than their crop was worth.[42] He tried to get neighbours to exchange work in each others' fields, but those available to help were usually those without crops who required pay for their labour.

Inspector Alex McGibbon was also critical of the peasant farming policy. He informed Reed in 1891 that it was contrary to common sense to ban universally the use of machinery.[43] Exceptions had to be made and flexibility shown. McGibbon gave the example of the Onion Lake band which had 500 acres under crop, much of which would be lost if the department insisted it be cut with cradles. Then there was a farmer with about fifteen acres "of as pretty wheat as could be seen anywhere."[44] The man was in frail health, however, and could not secure the help of others who had their own fields to look after. McGibbon observed the man cradling and his wife binding but was certain that "the waste on that field alone would be nearly half the crop."[45]

Agents and instructors reported difficulty

enforcing the peasant policy. It was almost impossible to get the Indians to cut with cradles or sickles, especially those who had implements already.[46] Agents provided Reed with numerous examples of farmers who attempted the work and gave up, refusing to return, and of others who would not even attempt it.[47] It was reported that the Indians became discouraged, and lost all interest in their crops.[48] These were not "lazy" Indians. Agent Campbell of the Moose Mountain agency, for example, cited the case of an Indian farmer whom he considered to be the most "progressive" in the agency.[49] He began to cradle his grain but quit, declaring that he would let his grain stand and never plough another acre. By no means averse to hard work, the man chose to work on the straw pile of a threshing machine, a job "not usually considered pleasant." Agent Grant described the reaction of "Black Mane," who had fifteen acres of very good wheat and, "when told that he would have to cut and bind it by hand, gave up his oxen, and left both his wheat and *reserve*. I gave his wheat to his brother. I have been told that he is now at Wolf Point, in the States. This will show how hard it is to compel an Indian to harvest his grain by hand."[50] It was also the case that some Indian farmers were not strong enough, either because of age or sickness, to harvest their grain by hand. In August 1890 the Pelly agent reported that "the Indians here, from scrofulitic [sic] effects have not enough strength to mow [hay] with a scythe and put up any quantity."[51] If they had only two or three head they could manage to put up enough hay but any more was beyond their ability with scythes and rakes.

The Indians often became discouraged when they saw white farmers using machinery. Agent Grant reported that the Indians on his reserve worked for white settlers, used binders when they stooked for them, and not surprisingly were discouraged when asked to cut and bind their own crops by hand.[52] Indian farmers were also keenly aware of what methods were used on reserves throughout the Northwest. McGibbon reported in 1891 that "the Indians know all that is going on at the various agencies."[53] The Carlton agency Indians knew precisely how many binders the Crooked Lakes Indians had and how many seeders were in another agency. Chief Mistawasis demanded to know in 1891 why the Battleford Indians, and John Smith's band, had reapers when his farmers were not allowed them.[54] McGibbon informed the chief that these were purchased before the policy was adopted, that such sales were now being cancelled, and that he and his men should be out in the fields cutting and stacking grain rather than wasting valuable time talking.

Restrictions on the use of machinery were not the only aspects of the peasant policy that agents disliked. The home manufactures program, which called for the use of Indian-made implements, also proved unrealistic. Indian-made wooden forks, for example, could not be used for loading hay, grain, or manure.[55] Iron forks were required and even these frequently broke or wore out and had to be replaced. In some districts, moreover, appropriate materials such as hides and lumber were not available to manufacture ox-plough harness, wagon tongues, or neck yokes. Poorly made or faulty neck yokes could break going down a hill, and cattle could be injured if not killed. Other items struck from agents' estimates included lanterns and tea kettles. Agents protested that Indians could not look after their cattle at night without lanterns and that not having proper kettles resulted in the waste of much time.[56]

Hayter Reed was not the slightest bit sympathetic to nor moved by the objections and complaints of his agents, inspectors, and commissioner. His response was to dismiss their claims. Reed was aware of a "lack of sympathy" among agents and employees, but he was convinced that they were inclined to be too lenient with the Indians.[57] "Naturally," he wrote to McGibbon, "Indians and their overseers prefer to take the method easiest for themselves, and it is only after a hard and long continued fight, that I am beginning to get the policy carried into effect."[58] Officials in the field, Reed believed, desired to make things as easy as possible for the Indians and consequently for themselves.[59] Indians "naturally" preferred to have machinery do their work for them.

Reed refused to give in to the "whims of Farmers and Indians," and advised that growing less grain or losing some of the crop was preferable to the use of machinery.[60] He did not believe, however, that any grain need be lost by harvesting with hand implements, but that the loss in yield was due entirely to the "half-heartedness" of instructors and agents.[61] With greater firmness they could manage to save their crop. If grain was being lost, the solution was for the farmers to confine their acreage to what they could handle. Reed informed one official that "any loss suffered in the course of enforcing the policy will prove in the long run true economy."[62] Supplementary hay, Reed naïvely assumed, could be acquired after harvesting, and he saw no conflict between the two operations.

Farm instructors were told not to meddle in the issue of machinery but simply to obey orders. Agents explained to all employees working in the fields with the Indians "that it was their duty to set aside completely any opinions they might hold regarding the feasibility, etc., of carrying out this policy, and to act and speak always as if they had full confidence in the wisdom of getting the Indians to cut their grain by hand, and in the possibility of succeeding in doing so."[63] Inspectors were instructed neither to convene nor be present at meetings

with Indian farmers, as this would give an "exaggerated importance" to their requests for machinery.[64] Instead, they were to defend vigorously the department's policy and severely discourage labour-saving machinery. Political opposition to the peasant policy was also dismissed by Reed: "It may distress one in opposition to the Government to see what he does not understand the reasons of, but I fancy if we were to pamper up Indians in idleness while we supply machinery to do their work, the opposition would soon give tongue to the distress occasioned by such a course."[65]

Department employees risked dismissal if they refused to comply with the peasant farming policy. Agent Finlayson of the Touchwood Hills agency was fired because he would not "make his Indians provide hay and harvest their crop without the use of labour saving implements as the department is opposed to for Indian use."[66] Despite this powerful lever to enforce policy, Reed's peasant program showed signs of crumbling by the season of 1896. That year many disgruntled and angry agents defied orders and used machinery. At his Regina office, Forget was harangued by officials requesting permission to use machinery.[67] That season was subject to severe hailstorms. Seventy thousand acres of crop were destroyed in western Manitoba in one storm, and many settlers were hailed out near Regina.[68] It was of vital importance that the crop be cut as soon as it was ready. Forget granted permission to several agents to borrow or hire binders from settlers. He informed Reed that authority was granted only on the understanding that the agent "make a bona fide effort to secure the whole crop, or as much of it as possible, by hand appliances and it is understood that only upon all such efforts failing to secure the crop with sufficient rapidity either on account of the state of the weather or the inadequacy of the workers, is the authority to employ machinery to be made use of."[69]

During the harvest of 1896 some agents openly defied the peasant policy or complied only half-heartedly. Agent McDonald of Crooked Lakes stated that he and his staff made no efforts that season to force the Indians to harvest their grain without the aid of labour-saving machinery.[70] He noted that earlier attempts to do so had failed, and that the Indians became discouraged and would not work. The agent claimed to have done his honest best to carry out the department's policy, but the Indians were "so far advanced" with such large acres of grain that he could make no headway. He had tried to get those with smaller crops to harvest by hand, but even they had someone with a binder cut their crop for them. Had he expressed "violent opposition to the Indians, I should only have achieved the result of making the smaller farmers so sullen, that they would have put in no crop at all, had they the prospect to cut it with a sickle, and the large farmers would have met me with contempt, and gone their own way, with a wide breach between us."[71] McDonald noted that the harvest of 1896, amounting to over 9000 bushels of wheat and 3500 bushels of oats, "would have been impossible without implements."[72]

J.P. Wright, the Touchwood Hills agent, also admitted that the harvest in his agency was accomplished with the aid of labour-saving machinery.[73] Gordon and Poor Man's bands each owned a self-binder, and it was useless, the agent claimed, to ask them to cut their grain with sickles and cradles because they would not do it. Wright reminded Reed, as all the agents did, that the Indians were busy with their haying at harvest time and the grain had to be cut with as little delay as possible. Other agents in the Northwest in 1896 claimed to have accomplished one-half or less of the harvest by

hand methods before they were obliged to save the balance of the crop with machinery.[74] Reed remained adamant, demanding that the peasant policy be rigorously pursued.[75] Although he admitted that machinery might be necessary where Indians had large crops, he nonetheless expected that a strong effort be made to carry out the policy for all others.

The agents' reports reveal some glimpses of how Indian farmers reacted to the peasant farming policy. Many became angry and discouraged, while some refused to work and gave up farming altogether. The outlets for Indian protest during the 1890s were few. Grievances related to instructors and agents generally went no further. Inspectors were not allowed to hold audiences with the Indians. The published reports of agents and inspectors were to divulge only that "which it was desired the public should believe."[76] Visiting officials, journalists, or other observers were taken to a few select agencies. When the governor general planned a visit to the west in 1895, Reed arranged to have him visit only the most "advanced" reserves, such as the Crooked Lakes.[77] The August visit was to be hastily diverted elsewhere, however, if the crops failed on the reserves.

An 1893 petition from the head men of the Pasquah and Muscowpetung bands, addressed to the House of Commons, succeeded in gaining the attention of officials in Ottawa.[78] The Indians resented the restrictions on their freedom, and the interference of the agent in all of their affairs. Among other things they protested the permit system: "Whenever we have a chance to sell anything and make some money the Agent or Instructor steps in between us and the party who wants to buy, and says we have no power to sell: if this is to continue how will we be able to make a living and support ourselves? We are not even allowed to sell cattle that we raise ourselves."[79] The petitioners wished to purchase a binder, noting that taking off the grain with a cradle was too slow, but "the Commissioner objected to us buying a Binder as he said it would make the young men lazy."[80] The Indians claimed that "when we ask the Agent for farm implements he sends us to the Commissioner, and he in turn sends us back to the Agent. This has completely discouraged us, as our old implements are worn out," and "many of the fields we used to farm are now all grown over with grass."[81]

This petition received no action; the allegations were dismissed and the document filed away and forgotten. Hayter Reed denied the legitimacy of and refuted the charges and grievances. In a memo dealing with the petition, Reed vigorously defended his department. The permit systems he argued, was a necessity. Without it, "Indians would be defrauded, and would part with hay while their cattle was left to starve—grain and roots which they require for sustenance, etc. etc., squander the proceeds, and then come on the Government for support. Our object is to make them acquire the limit of stock to afford them an annual surplus to dispose of, meanwhile when they have a steer or other animal which can not be profitably kept longer they are allowed to sell. If left to their own discretion there would not be a head of stock left."[82]

The 1893 petition from the Pasquah and Muscowpetung Indians was dismissed, but in the 1890s this kind of protest was not unusual. Discontent over the peasant policy, permit system, and other restrictions was widespread. In 1893 the Dakota of the Oak River reserve in southwestern Manitoba protested the same issues, but even though they succeeded in receiving considerable attention through their petitions, letters, a visit to Ottawa, and their defiance of regulations, their actions did not occasion a reconsideration or revamping of policy.[83] By this time a formula response to all Indian grievances was well entrenched. Indians were dismissed as chronic complainers and lazy idlers willing to go to any lengths to avoid work. At the same time, nefarious "outside agitators"—usually unnamed—were blamed for any discontent.

Official pronouncements of the Department of Indian Affairs emphasized that Indian interests were paramount and that such measures as the peasant policy and the permit system were undertaken out of concern for their welfare and development. In this period and well into the twentieth century, however, Indian interests were consistently sacrificed to those of the new settlers, and there was little concern to develop independent Indian production. Organized interests were able to influence the course of Indian policy by petitioning and lobbying their members of parliament. Agents on the spot and visiting officials were pressured from neighbouring whites. The Indian's interests were easily sacrificed as they had no vote and no economic power. This pattern continued into the twentieth century when effective pressure was mounted to have the Indians surrender reserve land that was suitable for agriculture. White settlers proved loath to see the Indians establish any enterprise that might compete with or draw business away from them. Government policy reflected the economic interests of the new settlers, not the Indians.

* * *

[In] western Canada, measures like the permit system, severalty, and peasant farming combined to undermine and atrophy agricultural development on reserves. The administration acted not to promote the agriculture of the indigenous population but to provide an optimum environment for the immigrant settler. Comparisons between the situation in colonial

FIGURE 8.1: **Saskatchewan Indian Agencies (acres under cultivation)**

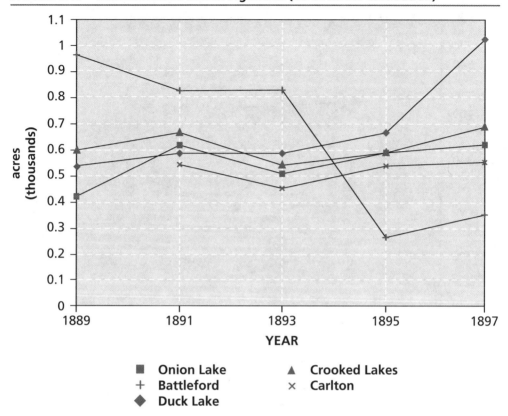

Africa and western Canada, however, remain dubious as the Africans were always in the majority. Yet in the 1880s and 1890s the west was sparsely settled by non-Indians, and there was a similar anxiety to see an immigrant farming class established. After 1885 immigration to the west was at a virtual standstill and the drought years of the 1880s did little to attract settlers. Consideration was not given to the possibility of enhancing Indian production as a means of creating an export sector, although it was grumbled in an 1892 item in the Regina *Leader* that it would be preferable to make farmers of Indians and have them settle on empty lands than to bring in "Russians and Jews."[84] Instead, new settlers were to be attracted, and policies were determined by the need to maintain the viability of this community.

Large-scale settler agriculture in Africa required access to cheap labour. Policies that were aimed at suppressing African production were also intended to force Africans into the labour market. This situation did not prevail in western Canada, where the single-family homestead became the principal economic unit. It is worth noting, however, that in the 1890s Reed promoted the Indians of the Northwest, particularly the graduates of industrial schools, as a cheap labour supply for farm or domestic work.[85] This was a clear message broadcast at national and international fairs, exhibitions, and displays aimed at prospective settlers.

In the United States, government policy of the 1880s led to a marked decline in Indian farming.[86] Before general allotment was enacted in 1887 there was a steady growth of

FIGURE 8.2:   **Saskatchewan Indian Agencies (acres under cultivation)**

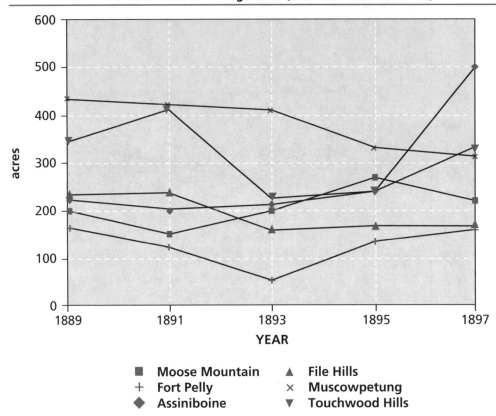

reservation agriculture, but this was followed by stagnation and regression. American Indian policy, though distinct from Canadian in many ways, was similarly shaped by non-Indian economic interests.

Not surprisingly, there had been very little progress made in reserve farming during the 1890s. There was a modest increase in acreage on some reserves, while on others acreage stayed at about the same level or even decreased (see figures 8.1 and 8.2). The likelihood of agriculture forming the basis of a stable reserve economy faded even further after 1896, as the new administrators of Indian Affairs promoted land surrender and so further limited the agricultural capacity of reserves. Because much Indian land appeared to be "idle," "unused," or

"surplus," the hand of those who clamoured for land surrender was strengthened. Indians were living in some cases in the midst of fine farm land that was not cultivated at all, or was worked with obsolete methods and technology. Indians appeared to cling stubbornly to the past and remain impervious to "progressive" influences. People concluded that Indians lacked industry and were not natural farmers. These observations, reflected in the histories that have been written until very recently, obscure or overlook the Indians' positive response to agriculture in earlier years. Equally obscured and forgotten has been the role of Canadian government policy in restricting and undermining reserve agriculture in a critical period of agricultural development.

NOTES

[1] Canada, *Sessional Papers*, 1889, no 10, 162. Hayter Reed was born in 1849 in L'Original, Prescott County, Ontario. His early training and career interests were military. In 1871 he served with the Provincial Battalion of Rifles when they were dispatched to Fort Garry as reinforcements during the Fenian scare. Reed was called to the bar of Manitoba in 1872. He retired from military service with the rank of major in 1881. In 1880 he worked out of Winnipeg as "chief land guide" with the Department of the Interior. He was appointed to the position of Indian agent in Battleford in 1881. He had little direct experience with or knowledge of Indians before his first posting. Yet he quickly rose through the ranks of assistant commissioner in 1884, commissioner in 1888, and in 1893 he assumed the position of deputy superintendent general of Indian Affairs. In 1897 he was dismissed by Clifford Sifton, minister of the interior. Reed found employment in 1905 as manager-in-chief of the Canadian Pacific Railway's hotel department.

[2] G.F.G. Stanley. *The Birth of Western Canada: A History of the Riel Rebellions* (1936; Toronto 1975), 218

[3] *Sessional Papers*, 1889, no 12, 165

[4] Ibid., 166

[5] McCord Museum, McGill University, Hayter Reed Papers, address on the aims of the government in its dealings with the Indians, nd, 29

[6] *Sessional Papers*, 1888, no 16, 28

[7] On Pasquah's reserve, for example, 164 forty-acre plots were surveyed. Sixteen of these were divided by deep ravines, leaving 148 lots. The population of the reserve was 124, so there was little room for future expansion. This 6560 acres was only a fraction of the 38,496 acres of the reserve. See NA, National Map Collection, 0011553, Pasquah no 179, 1889.

[8] Kenneth J. Tyler, "A Tax-eating Proposition: The History of the Passpasschase Indian Reserve" (MA thesis, University of Alberta, 1979), 114

[9] *Sessional Papers*, 1889, no 10, 162

[10] McCord Museum, Reed Papers, "Address," 28

[11] Ibid., vol. 3793, file 46,062, Reed to Dewdney, 11 April 1888

[12] Ibid., vol. 3746, file 29,690–3, Reed to superintendent general, 30 Sept. 1886

[13] Brian Dippie, *The Vanishing Indian: White Attitudes to U.S. Indian Policy* (Middletown 1982), 164–71. See also Robert E. Bieder, *Science Encounters the Indian, 1820–1880: The Early Years of American Ethnology* (Norman 1986).

[14] Edmonton *Bulletin*, 17 Jan. 1881

[15] House of Commons, *Debates*, 19 May 1880, 1610. See also Walter Hildebrandt, "From Dominion to Hegemony: A Cultural History of Fort Battleford," unpublished manuscript, 1988, Department of Environment, Parks, Prairie Region.

[16] *Sessional Papers*, 1888, no 16, 127

[17] NA, RG 15, records of the Department of the Interior, vol. 245, file 23, 563, part 1

[18] Ibid., Hayter Reed, "Canadian and United States Immigration," May 1880

[19] NA, RG 10, vol. 3806, file 52,332, Reed to Vankoughnet, 27 Oct. 1888

[20] Ibid.

[21] *The Historical Development of the Indian Act* (Ottawa 1978), 93

[22] Canada, House of Commons, *Debates*, 24 March 1884, 1063

[23] Clive J. Dewey, "The Rehabilitation of the Peasant Proprietor in Nineteenth-Century Economic Thought." *History of Political Economy* 6 (1) (1974): 17–47

[24] Ibid., 32–47

[25] See Clark C. Spence, *The Salvation Army Farm Colonies* (Tucson 1985), 2–7, and Frederic Impey, *Three Acres and a Cow* (London 1885).

[26] William Booth, *In Darkest England and the Way Out* (London 1890)

[27] Richard Jay, *Joseph Chamberlain: A Political Study* (Oxtord 1981), 99

[28] Willoughby Maycock, *With Mr. Chamberlain in the United States and Canada, 1877–88* (London 1914)

[29] Dippie, *Vanishing Indian*, 160

[30] Loring B. Priest, *Uncle Sam's Stepchildren: The Reformation of United States Indian Policy, 1865–1887* (New York 1969), 126

[31] Ibid., 232

[32] Rodney C. Loehr, "Self-sufficiency on the Farm," *Agricultural History* 26, (2) (1952): 37, and Clarence Danhof, *Change in Agriculture: The Northern United States, 1820–1870* (Cambridge 1969), 15

[33] Loehr, "Self-sufficiency," 41

[34] Vernon Fowke, *The National Policy and the Wheat Economy* (Toronto 1957), 12

[35] Irene M. Spry, "The Tragedy of the Loss of the Commons in Western Canada," in Ian A.C. Getty and Antoine S. Lussier, eds., *As Long as the Sun Shines and Water Flows: A Reader in Canadian Native Studies* (Vancouver 1983), 221

[36] NA, RG 10, deputy superintendent general letterbooks, vol. 1115, p. 220, Reed to Forget, 12 June 1894

[37] Ibid.

[38] NA, Hayter Reed Papers, vol. 14, Reed to T.M. Daly, 10 March 1893

[39] NA, RG 10, vol. 3964, file 148,285, Chas. De Cases to Reed, 19 Nov. 1896

[40] Ibid.

[41] Ibid., W.S. Grant to Reed, 1 Oct. 1896

42 Ibid., W.E. Jones to Reed, 1 Nov. 1896

43 NA, Reed Papers, vol. 13, no 869, McGibbon to Reed, 16 March 1891

44 Ibid.

45 Ibid.

46 Ibid., vol. 14, no 989, R.S. McKenzie to Reed, 16 Dec. 1890

47 NA, RG 10, vol. 3964, file 148,285

48 Ibid., Grant to Reed, 1 Oct. 1896

49 Ibid., J.J. Campbell to Reed, 8 Oct. 1896

50 Ibid., Grant to Reed, 1 Oct. 1896

51 Ibid., vol. 3812, file 55,895, W.E. Jones to Reed

52 Ibid., vol. 3964, file 148,285, Grant to Reed, 1 Oct. 1896

53 NA, Reed Papers, vol. 13, no 869, McGibbon to Reed, 16 March 1891

54 Ibid.

55 Ibid., vol. 14, no 989, McKenzie to Reed, 16 Dec. 1890

56 Ibid.

57 Ibid., vol. 14, no 1206, Reed to McGibbon, 7 Nov. 1891

58 Ibid.

59 NA, RG 10, vol. 3964, file 14,285, Reed to Forget, 24 Aug. 1896

60 Ibid., deputy superintendent general letterbooks, vol. 115, 220, Reed to Forget, 12 June 1894

61 NA, Reed Papers, vol. 14, Reed to Daly, 10 March 1893

62 Ibid.

63 NA, RG 10, vol. 3964, file 14,285, Campbell to Reed, 8 Oct, 1896

64 NA, Reed Papers, vol. 14, no 1206, Reed to McGibbon, 7 Nov. 1891

65 Ibid., vol. 14, Reed to Daly, 10 March 1893

66 NA, RG 10, deputy superintendent general letterbooks, vol. 115, 382, memorandum relative to Mr Agent Finlayson

67 Ibid., vol. 3964, file 148,285, Forget to Reed, 20 Aug. 1896

68 Ibid.

69 Ibid.

70 Ibid., McDonald to Reed, 16 Feb. 1897

71 Ibid.

72 Ibid.

73 Ibid., J.P. Wright to Reed, 16 Feb. 1897

74 Ibid., Grant to Reed, 1 Oct. 1896; Jones to Reed, 1 Nov. 1896: de Cases to Reed, 19 Nov. 1896

75 Ibid., Reed to Forget, 25 Feb. 1897

76 Ibid., deputy superintendent general letterbooks, vol. 1115, Reed to J. Wilson, 3 Aug. 1894

77 Ibid., vol. 1117, p. 319, Reed to Forget, 20 July 1895

78 NA, Reed Papers, vol. 13, no 960, McGirr to Reed, 8 March 1893

79 Ibid.

80 Ibid.

81 Ibid.

82 Ibid.

83 See Sarah Carter, "Agriculture and Agitation on the Oak River Reserve, 1875–1895," *Manitoba History* 6 (1893): 2–9.

84 Regina *Leader*, 10 Oct. 1892

85 Jacqueline Judith Kennedy, "Qu'Appelle Industrial School: White 'Rites' for the Indians of the Old North-West" (MA thesis, Carleton University, 1970), 116–23

86 Leonard A. Carlson, *Indians, Bureaucrats and Land: The Dawes Act and the Decline of Indian Farming* (Westport 1981)

CHAPTER 9

European Immigrant Workers and Labour Protest in Peace and War, 1896–1919

Donald Avery

The transatlantic migration of thousands of immigrant workers between 1896 and 1914 greatly altered the social and economic fabric of Canada and the United States. In both countries much of the rapid economic progress in railway construction, mining, lumbering, and secondary manufacturing during this time can be attributed to immigrant manpower. Yet the immigrants themselves paid a high price for North American economic gains.[1] In *Men in Sheepskin Coats*, Vera Lysenko graphically described the plight of these foreign workers: "they were systematically underpaid ... tortured by physical labour, torn by nostalgia for the old country, crushed by loneliness in a strange land, and by the fear of death which [they] often looked in the face." This theme of exploitation and alienation has fascinated many historians of immigration.[2]

"A Sort of Anthropological Garden"

The inferior occupational positions and the low social status afforded European immigrant workers in Canada prior to the Great War were essentially functions of Anglo-Canadian immigration

priorities. As John Porter persuasively argued in *The Vertical Mosaic*, the most important factor in determining entrance status for immigrant groups was "the evaluations of the 'charter' members of the society of the jobs to be filled and the 'right' kind of immigrants to fill them."[3] Quite clearly, in this period most Anglo-Canadians recognized the importance of having an available source of cheap unskilled labour for use in both the agricultural and industrial sectors of the economy. Combined with this, however, were a number of reservations about the movement of immigrant workers within Canadian society. Throughout the latter part of the nineteenth century Canadian politicians and immigration officials had assured the public that Canada's recruitment of immigrants would be confined to Great Britain and to northwestern Europe, a selective policy that would be greatly superior to the American open door.[4] In 1890 Sir John A. Macdonald had deplored the influx of millions of Slavic and southern European immigrants into the United States: "It is a great country, but it will have its vicissitudes and revolutions. Look at that mass of foreign ignorance and vice which has flooded that country with socialism, atheism, and all other isms."[5] In contrast, Canada would seek only those vigorous northern races who were culturally sound and who could quickly conform to the norms of Anglo-Canadian life.

The employment boom at the turn of the century, with its insistent demand for Slavic and Italian workers, shattered this vision of a culturally harmonious Canada. Not surprisingly, the Anglo-Canadian response to these new immigrants from central and southern Europe was initially hostile. The Toronto *Mail and Empire* set the tone in 1899 when it branded Clifford Sifton's immigration policy as "an attempt to make of the North-West a sort of anthropological garden … to pick up the waifs and strays of Europe, the lost tribes of mankind, and the freaks of creation."[6] Organized labour had particular fears; as the guardian of the rights of Canadian workingmen it stood squarely against the importation of cheap labour. The fears, prejudices, and emotions of Canadian trade unionists were epitomized in a 1904 article of *The Independent*, a Vancouver labour newspaper: "This question of alien immigration … strikes at the foundation of every labour organization in the Country…. This labour is generally garnered from the slums of Europe and Asia, and thus thrown into direct competition with all kinds of Canadian labour. The immigrants having been brought up under conditions which no Canadian … [would] tolerate—work for wages upon which no Canadian could … exist."[7]

Many Anglo-Canadians were also disturbed by evidence of social deviance among immigrant workers. The ethnic ghettos, which quickly sprang up in the major Canadian cities and almost all single-enterprise communities west of the Ottawa River, were increasingly thought of as a breeding ground for "filth, immorality and crime."[8] The reports of the Royal North-West Mounted Police (RNWMP) from western Canada frequently stressed the tendency of foreign workers to take the law into their own hands; according to these accounts the prevalence of knives and guns could turn even minor disagreements into violent confrontations. When the foreign worker was brought into contact with liquor, especially at festive occasions, social anarchy ensued.[9] This situation was vividly described by the Reverend C.W. Gordon (Ralph Connor) in his famous novel, *The Foreigner*:

> In the main room dance and song reeled on in uproarious hilarity. In the basement below, foul and fetid, men stood packed close drinking while they could…. In the dim light of a smoky lantern, the swaying crowd, here singing in maudlin chorus, there fighting savagely to pay off old scores or to avenge new insults, presented a nauseating spectacle.[10]

Outraged by these conditions, Gordon and other Anglo-Canadian reformers such as J.S. Woodsworth sought to alleviate the lot of the immigrant workers. Their vision of immigrant life accords well with the notions of the historian Oscar Handlin, who has written of the period: "Immigration had transformed the entire … world within which the peasants had formerly lived. From surface forms to inmost functioning, the change was complete…. In the process, they became, in their own eyes, less worthy as men. They felt a sense of degradation that raised a most insistent question: Why had this happened?"[11] That the lives of immigrant workers had been seriously disrupted cannot be doubted, but was the transformation as complete as reformers such as Gordon and Woodsworth and historians such as Handlin would have it? Any attempt to answer this question in the Canadian context must of necessity take account of the reasons why emigrants left

Europe for Canada, and of the social and economic adaptations they made on Canadian soil.

The World of the
Immigrant Worker

The majority of European immigrant workers who came to Canada between 1896 and 1914 were of peasant background. Generally speaking, they came from regions where agricultural technology was primitive, crop productivity was low, and peasant landholdings were very small; for many, emigration was "an alternative to the restrictive opportunities of [their] traditional agrarian societies." In the case of immigrants from the Austro-Hungarian Empire, about 60 per cent were Slavs from the provinces of Galicia and Bukovina, regions where most of the landholdings were below the five hectares necessary for subsistence. A similar situation prevailed in other areas of high emigration, most notably in southern Italy, Slavonia, and the coastal regions of Sicily.[12]

The peasant face of all these societies belies the true nature of their employment patterns. Thus, while the traditional life of the land was the focus of work, economic circumstances forced many peasants to become migratory industrial workers for at least part of the year. The produce of the land and the industrial wage had for some formed the economic package by which they and their families were sustained. Modernization had intruded on these societies, and rural proletarians could "feed themselves from their own soil for only a few months, and for the rest of the year ... worked as hired labour for 'others'."[13] In their search for casual employment these peasant workers had considerable geographical mobility both within their own and neighbouring countries. In 1908 alone some 300,000 Slavic workers from the Austro-Hungarian Empire crossed into Germany seeking short-term employment in the Junker farms of East Prussia and in the coal-mining and steel-producing regions of the Ruhr and Saar. Such labour mobility had transformed traditional peasant life in many parts of central and southern Europe. By 1900 the closed nucleated village of the nineteenth century had been replaced by a relatively open community whose residents "continuously interacted with the outside world and tied their future to its demands." In time, this "outside world" became transatlantic as well as continental.[14]

Returned sojourners acted as a source of information about economic conditions in North America and were of great importance in chain migrations whereby prospective migrants learned of job opportunities, were provided with transportation, and had initial accommodation in North America arranged for them. This adaptation of "familial and dyadic patronage" significantly influenced immigrant behaviour across the Atlantic. One familiar aspect of this was the creation of a series of "Little Italies" and "Slavtowns" in the towns and cities of the United States and Canada; another less well explored aspect was the carving out of ethnic niches within the North American job market.[15] *The Social Survey of Ukrainian Rural Settlement in Western Canada* (1917) showed that the kinship and village patterns of the Old World clearly influenced settlement patterns in the New. Similarly, Reino Kero's study of Finnish immigrants from the commune of Karvia has revealed that the majority gravitated toward three communities: Port Arthur and Nipigon in Ontario and Covington in Minnesota. Close familial and fraternal ties persisted among these immigrants, the international boundary notwithstanding.

* * *

Prior to 1914 the most spectacular attempts to organize European immigrant workers in Canada were undoubtedly those made by the Industrial Workers of the World (IWW), the famous American-based syndicalist movement. In this work the "Wobblies" had a number of advantages. In the first place, their approach was entirely class-oriented; unlike the situation in most Canadian craft unions, there was little Anglo-Saxon hostility toward ethnic workers. As one Prince Rupert Wobbly exclaimed, "when the factory whistle blows it does not call us to work as Irishmen, Germans, Americans, Russians, Greeks, Poles, Negroes or Mexicans. It calls us to work as wage workers, regardless of the country in which we were born or colour of our skins."The second great advantage of the IWW was the extent to which its organization was geared to the migratory work patterns of the foreign worker: its initiation fees and dues were low, the membership cards were transferable, and the camp delegate system of union democracy made it possible for an immigrant worker to become "a full time organizer while he wandered." Nor did the IWW waste time in sterile ideological controversy; despite its syndicalist underpinnings the IWW concentrated on specific grievances. Moreover, IWW organizers usually waited until a labour disturbance erupted before launching a recruiting drive.[16]

The IWW entered the hard-rock mining regions of the Kootenays in 1907, but it was their involvement in the spectacular Canadian Northern railway strike of March, 1912, that put them on the front lines of Canadian labour. Worker protest against low pay and harsh working and living conditions resulted in a bitter dispute involving over 7,000 workers. This massive confrontation was to test severely the IWW's ability to organize unskilled labour in western Canada. Initially they seemed to stand a reasonable chance of victory, thanks to the remarkable degree of labour solidarity. An article in the *British Columbia Federationist* of April 5, 1912, hailed the walkout as "an object lesson as to what a movement animated by an uncompromising spirit of revolt … can accomplish among the most heterogeneous army of slaves that any system of production ever assembled together." On the other hand, these workers were responding to specific grievances and few had any real knowledge of unionism; they were also vulnerable to the threat of destitution and displacement by strike-breakers. Ultimately, a hostile British Columbia government helped crush the strike by arresting more than 250 IWW activists.[17] Although the IWW had failed, the memory of its involvement and the syndicalist creed of industrial unionism cast a long shadow over future industrial relations in western Canada.[18]

Beyond the unions were the various socialist parties that actively operated among European immigrant workers, especially in western Canada and northern Ontario. The most successful of these organizations were usually located in single-enterprise communities or major urban centres, drawing much of their support from the ethnic enclaves.[19] This was particularly true of regions with large numbers of Ukrainian and Finnish immigrants.[20] In both cases, emphasis on cultural and ethnic values enabled the socialists to secure considerable popular support throughout western Canada and northern Ontario; thus, the socialist hall was not only a political but a social institution.[21]

Finnish women were also involved in the various socialist parties. As early as 1907 a female branch of the SPC had been organized in Toronto and campaigned for both economic and political reform in the city. Other Finnish women were active in SPC locals in Sudbury and Port Arthur, as well as in western Canada. The extent that women were afforded equal rights with the Finnish left greatly impressed the SPC, especially the editors of its newspaper, *The Western Clarion*. "The Finnish comrades have taken a high stand in the matter of discouraging smoking and drinking, and in making their socialist gatherings a meeting place for both sexes of all ages."[22]

Eastern European Jewish women garment workers demonstrated considerable militancy in the needle trades of Toronto, Montreal, and Winnipeg and organized themselves into a variety of trade unions. This was not an easy task, given an industry characterized by economic instability and intransigent management, as well as problems with ethnic rivalries, anti-Semitism, and the difficulty of overcoming the timidity of women garment workers, the poorest paid and most vulnerable segment of the labour force. According to Ruth Frager, one of the major reasons why so many Jewish women were involved in socialist organizations was because so many of them had been radicalized in the European ghettos, "not only in response to class consciousness, but also in response to the oppression they faced as Jews." On the other hand, she points out that Canadian Jewish labour organizers recognized the danger of concentrating on Jewish rights "precisely because it would weaken the working class by dividing Jewish workers and non-Jewish workers." Women union organizers also had another problem: how to carry their struggle "against class oppression and anti-semitism," while having to cope with the onerous "triple day of labour" (job, home, union). In addition, there was the reality that many of Toronto's Jewish women unionists allowed themselves to be "incorporated into the Jewish labour movement on the basis of an implicit acceptance of their own subordination."[23] Notable exceptions to this pattern were Becky Buhay and Annie Buller of Montreal, both of whom later became prominent members of the Communist Party of Canada.[24]

In 1908 Winnipeg gained notoriety when Emma Goldman, one of North America's most famous anarchists, visited the city. What was notable about this was not her lecture, but rather the frantic attempts by Winnipeg civic officials to have her barred from the country. Mayor J.H. Ashdown, a prominent local businessman, articulated the views of the city's Anglo-Canadian elite when he criticized the Immigration Branch for not excluding such "professional agitators":

> … we have a large foreign population in this City, it consists approximately of 15,000 Galicians, 11,000 Germans, 10,000 Jews, 2,000 Hungarians and 5,000 Russians and other Slavs and Bohemians. Many of these people have had trouble in their own country with their Governments and have come to the new land to get away from it but have all the undesirable elements in their character that created the trouble for them before. They are just the right crowd for Emma Goldman or persons of her character to sow seeds which are bound to cause most undesirable growths in the future.[25]

Emma Goldman was eventually allowed into Winnipeg, but this incident cleared the way for a 1910 amendment to the Immigration Act, which provided for the exclusion and deportation of those professing anarchist views. The amendment was a portent of what was to follow in 1919.[26]

THE WAR YEARS

The economic status of immigrant workers on the eve of World War One was not favourable. By 1912 the unsettled state of European affairs had helped produce a prolonged economic slump in the transatlantic economy. This recession was particularly felt in western Canada, a region very dependent on foreign capital for its continued prosperity. By the summer of 1914 there was widespread unemployment in the area, the more so since over 400,000 immigrants had arrived in the previous year.[27] Before long many Prairie and west coast communities were providing relief to unemployed workers.[28] But worse was to follow—especially for those immigrants unlucky enough to have been born in those countries that took up arms against the British Empire.

The outbreak of war in August, 1914, forced the Dominion government to adopt a comprehensive set of guidelines for dealing with the enemy alien residents of the country. Of those classified as enemy aliens, there were 393,320 of German origin, 129,103 from the Austro-Hungarian Empire, 3,880 from the Turkish Empire, and several thousands from Bulgaria.[29] The government's position was set forth in a series of acts and proclamations, the most important being the War Measures Act of August, 1914. This measure specified that during a "state of war, invasion, or insurrection ... the Governor in Council may do and authorize such acts ... orders and regulations, as he may ... deem necessary or advisable for the security, defence, order and welfare of Canada." Specific reference was made to the following powers: censorship on all forms of communication and the arrest, detention, and deportation of dangerous enemy aliens. Subsequent orders-in-council in October, 1914, and September, 1916, prohibited enemy aliens from possessing firearms and instituted a system of police and military registration. By the end of the war over 80,000 enemy aliens had been registered, though only 8,579 of these were actually interned. This number included: 2,009

Germans, 5,954 Austro-Hungarians, 205 Turks, 99 Bulgarians, and 312 classified as miscellaneous. These prisoners of war were located in twenty-four different camps, although most were placed in either Kapuskasing, Ontario, or Vernon, B.C.[30]

There were very few incidents of sabotage or espionage on the home front during the war, but enemy aliens soon became the object of intense Anglo-Canadian hostility.[31] This was particularly true of those enemy aliens categorized as Austrians since most of them were immigrants of military age who retained the status of reservists in their homeland.[32] Throughout the fall of 1914 there were also alarming reports about what was afoot in the German-American communities of several American cities; one agent reported from Chicago that "should the Germans achieve a single success I believe that we in Canada are in danger of a repetition of the invasion of 1866 on a larger scale." What made the threat from the United States even more ominous was the steady flow of migrant labourers across a virtually unpatrolled border; many of those on the move were either enemy aliens or members of alleged pro-German groups, such as Finns.[33]

The fear of a fifth column among unemployed and impoverished enemy alien workers was also widespread.[34] Conversely, strong support existed in the country for enemy aliens who had jobs to be turned out of them; in 1915 there were many dismissals for "patriotic" reasons. This policy was popular among both Anglo-Canadian workers and immigrants from countries, such as Italy and Russia, now allied with the British Empire.[35] Some labour-intensive corporations, however, held a different point of view.[36] The Dominion Iron and Steel Company, for example, resisted the pressure to dismiss their enemy alien employees on the grounds that Nova Scotia workers "would not undertake the rough, dirty jobs."[37] It was only when the company obtained an understanding from the Immigration Branch that it could import even more pliable workers from Newfoundland that it agreed to join temporarily in the patriotic crusade.[38] Elsewhere, corporate resistance was even stronger. In June, 1915, English-speaking and allied miners threatened strike action at Fernie, B.C., and Hillcrest, Alberta, unless all enemy alien miners were dismissed. The situation was particularly tense at Fernie, where the giant Crow's Nest Coal Company initially balked at this demand. Eventually a compromise was achieved: all naturalized married enemy alien miners were retained; naturalized unmarried enemy aliens were promised work when it was available; the remainder of the enemy alien work force, some 300 in number, were temporarily interned. Within two months, however, all but the "most dangerous" had been released.[39]

This action indicated that, despite severe local and provincial pressure, the Borden government was not prepared to implement a mass internment policy. The enormous expense in operating the camps and an antipathy to adopting police-state tactics partly explain the government's reluctance. There was also a suspicion in Ottawa that many municipalities wanted to take advantage of internment camps to get rid of their unemployed. Arthur Meighen articulated the view of the majority of the cabinet when he argued that instead of being interned, unemployed aliens should each be granted forty acres of land that could be cultivated under government supervision; he concluded his case with the observation that "these Austrians … can live on very little."[40] By the spring of 1916 even the British Columbia authorities had come around to this point of view. One provincial police report gave this account of how much things had quieted down: "From a police

point of view, there has been less trouble amongst them [aliens] since the beginning of the war than previously, the fact that several of them were sent to internment camps at the beginning of the war seemed to have a good effect on the remainder…. In my opinion, if there is ever any trouble over the employment of enemy aliens, it will be after the war is over and our people have returned."[41]

But the changed attitude in British Columbia also reflected a dramatically altered labour market. As the war progressed serious labour shortages developed in the province and throughout the country. In the summer of 1915 there was a demand for about 10,000 harvest labourers in the Prairie provinces. Many of those who came to do the harvesting were unemployed enemy alien workers from the slums of Vancouver and Winnipeg who had their transportation subsidized by the federal and western provincial governments.[42] Government involvement in the recruitment of such workers was increased in 1916 when it became apparent that the supply of labour available on the Prairies would again be insufficient to meet the harvest demands. The Immigration Branch now began placing advertisements in United States newspapers urging Americans to look northward for employment. Instructions were also issued to the agents of the branch that the money qualifications of the Immigration Act were to be relaxed. By the end of September 1916, over 5,000 harvesters, attracted by generous wages ($3.50 a day) and cheap (one cent a mile) rail fares from border points, had crossed the international border.[43]

Increasingly, the practice of securing industrial workers from the United States was also regarded as essential to the maintenance of the Canadian war economy. By an order-in-council of August, 1916, the Alien Labour Act was temporarily shelved to facilitate the movement of industrial labour northward. Thousands of American residents were soon streaming into Canadian industrial communities.[44] But with the entry of the United States into the war in 1917 this source of labour supply was abruptly cut off. Of necessity, the focus of Canadian recruitment efforts now shifted overseas, most notably toward Asia and the West Indies. The most ambitious proposal called for the importation of thousands of Chinese workers on a temporary basis. But this solution met with the same violent objections it had always encountered from organized labour and nativist opinion, and was ultimately rejected by the Dominion government.[45]

With an overseas solution seeming impossible, the new labour situation put a premium on the surplus manpower available in the country. This made the alien worker, whether of enemy extraction or not, a very desirable quantity indeed. The implementation of conscription in the summer of 1917 only aggravated an already difficult situation; by the end of the year the country faced an estimated shortage of 100,000 workers. From the spring of 1917 on, foreign workers found themselves not only wanted by Canadian employers, but actually being "drafted" into the industrial labour force by the government.[46] As of August, 1916, all men and women over the age of sixteen were required to register with the Canadian Registration Board, and in April, 1918, the so-called "Anti-Loafing Law" provided that "every male person residing in the Dominion of Canada should be regularly engaged in some useful occupation."[47]

As early as 1916, the government had adopted the practice of releasing non-dangerous interned prisoners of war under contract to selected mining and railway companies, both to minimize the costs of operating the camps and to cope with labour shortages. Not surprisingly, this policy was welcomed by Canadian industrialists since these enemy alien workers received only $1.10 a day and were not susceptible to trade union influence.[48] One of the mining companies most enthusiastic about securing large numbers of the POW workers was the Dominion Iron and Steel Corporation. In the fall of 1917 the president of the company, Mark Workman, suggested that his operation be allocated both interned and "troublesome" aliens since "there is no better way of handling aliens than to keep them employed in productive labour." In December, 1917, Workman approached Borden, before the latter left for England, with the proposal that the POWs interned in Great Britain be transferred to the mines of Cape Breton. Unfortunately for the Dominion Steel Company, the scheme was rejected by British officials.[49]

The railway companies, particularly the Canadian Pacific, also received large numbers of POW workers. The reception of these workers harked back to some of the worst aspects of the immigrant navvy tradition of these companies. During 1916 and 1917 a series of complaints were lodged by POW workers, and on one occasion thirty-two Austrian workers went on strike in the North Bay district to protest dangerous working conditions and unsanitary living conditions. Neither the civil nor military authorities gave any countenance to these complaints; the ultimate fate of these workers was to be sentenced to six months' imprisonment at the Burwash prison farm "for breach of contract."[50]

This coercion was symptomatic of a growing concern among both Anglo-Canadian businessmen and federal security officials about alien labour radicalism. Not surprisingly, a 65 per cent increase in food prices between August, 1914, and December, 1917, created considerable industrial unrest, and the labour shortages that began in 1916 provided the trade unions with a superb opportunity to strike back. In 1917 there was a record number of strikes and more than one million man days were lost. Immigrant workers were caught up in the general labour unrest, and in numerous industrial centres in northern Ontario and western Canada they demonstrated a capacity for effective collective action and a willingness to defy the power of both management and the state. The coming of the Russian Revolution in 1917 added to the tension in Canada by breathing new life into a number of ethnic socialist organizations.[51]

By the spring of 1918 the Dominion government was under great pressure to place all foreign workers under supervision, and, if necessary, to make them "work at the point of a bayonet." The large-scale internment of radical aliens and the suppression of seditious foreign-language newspapers were also now widely advocated.[52] In June, 1918, C.H. Cahan, a wealthy Montreal lawyer, was appointed to conduct a special investigation of alien radicalism. In the course of his inquiry Cahan solicited information from businessmen, "respectable" labour leaders, police officials in both Canada and the United States, and various members of the anti-socialist immigrant community in Canada. The report Cahan submitted to cabinet in September, 1918, was the basis of a series of coercive measures: by two orders-in-council (PC 2381 and PC 2384) the foreign-language press was suppressed and a number of socialist and anarchist organizations were outlawed. Penalties for possession of prohibited literature and continued membership in any of these outlawed organizations were extremely severe: fines of up to $5,000 or a maximum prison term of five years could be imposed.[53]

THE RED SCARE

The hatreds and fear stirred up by World War One did not end with the armistice of 1918;

instead, social tension spread in ever-widening circles. Anglo-Canadians who had learned to despise the Germans and Austro-Hungarians had little difficulty transferring their aroused passions to the Bolsheviks. Though the guns were silent on the Western Front, Canadian troops were now being sent to Siberia "to strangle the infant Bolshevism in its cradle."[54] Within Canada, there was widespread agitation against potentially disloyal aliens and those involved in socialist organizations. An editorial in the *Winnipeg Telegram* summed up these sentiments: "Let every hostile alien be deported from this country, the privileges of which … he does not appreciate."[55]

In the early months of 1919 the Borden government was deluged by a great wave of petitions demanding the mass deportation of enemy aliens. Inquiries were actually made by the government concerning the possible implementation of a policy of mass expulsion. Surveys by the Department of Justice revealed that there were over 80,000 enemy aliens registered, 2,222 of whom were located in internment camps. There were also 63,784 Russian subjects in Canada, many of whom officials in Ottawa believed to be potentially hostile.[56] The policy of mass deportation was rejected, however, both because of its likely international repercussions and because of the demands it would make on the country's transportation facilities at a time when the troops were returning from Europe.[57]

The need to find jobs quickly for the returning soldier also affected the situation of the foreign worker. Both politicians and businessmen faced a powerful argument in the claim that all enemy aliens should be turned out of their jobs to make way for Canada's "heroes"; but their actions were also motivated by the fear that the veterans would be radicalized and lured into socialist organizations if their economic needs were not immediately satisfied. By February, 1919, the British Columbia Employers' Association, the British Columbia Manufacturers' Association, and the British Columbia Loggers' Association had all announced that their memberships were prepared to offer employment to returned soldiers by dismissing alien enemies. This pattern was repeated in the mining region of northern Ontario, where in the early months of 1919 the International Nickel Company, for instance, dismissed 2,200 of its 3,200 employees, the vast majority of whom were foreigners.[58] Even the CPR joined the "patriotic crusade" of dismissals. As vice-president D.C. Coleman put it, "The aliens who had been on the land when the war broke out and who went to work in the cities and towns, taking the jobs of the men who went to the front ... [should] go back to their old jobs on the land."[59]

But not even the land of the "men in sheepskin coats" was now safe for the immigrant worker; rumours were abroad that the government intended to cancel large numbers of homestead patents, and assaults on aliens by returned soldiers were commonplace.[60] Even the usually passive *Canadian Ruthenian* denounced the harsh treatment that Ukrainians and other foreigners were receiving from the Anglo-Canadian community and the government:

> The Ukrainians were invited to Canada and promised liberty, and a kind of paradise. Instead of the latter they found woods and rocks, which had to be cut down to make the land fit to work on. They were given farms far from the railroads, which they so much helped in building—but still they worked hard ... and came to love Canada. But ... liberty did not last long. First, they were called "Galicians" in mockery. Secondly, preachers were sent amongst them, as if they were savages, to preach Protestantism. And thirdly, they were deprived of the right to elect their representatives in Parliament. They are now uncertain about their future in Canada. Probably, their [property] so bitterly earned in the sweat of their brow will be confiscated.[61]

By the spring of 1919 the Borden government had received a number of petitions from ethnic organizations demanding either British justice or the right to leave Canada. The *Toronto Telegram* estimated that as many as 150,000 Europeans were preparing to leave the country. Some Anglo-Canadian observers warned, however, that mass emigration might relieve the employment problems of the moment but in the long run leave "a hopeless dearth of labour for certain kinds of work which Anglo-Saxon will not undertake."

Concern about the status of the alien worker led directly to the appointment of the Royal Commission on Industrial Relations on April 4, 1919. The members of the Commission travelled from Sydney to Victoria and held hearings in some twenty-eight industrial centres. The testimony of industrialists who appeared before the Commission reveals an ambivalent attitude toward the alien worker. Some industrialists argued that the alien was usually doing work "that white men don't want" and that it would "be a shame to make the returned soldier work at that job." But in those regions with high unemployment among returned soldiers and where alien workers had been organized by radical trade unions, management took a strikingly different view. William Henderson, a coal-mine operator at Drumheller, Alberta, informed the Commission that the unstable industrial climate of that region could only be reversed by hiring more Anglo-Canadian workers, "men that we could talk to ... men that would come in with us and co-operate with us...." Many mining representatives also indicated that their companies had released large numbers of aliens who had shown radical tendencies; there were numerous suggestions that these aliens should not only be removed from the mining districts, but actually deported from Canada.[62]

In the spring of 1919 Winnipeg was a city of many solitudes. Within its boundaries rich and poor, Anglo-Saxon and foreigner lived in isolation. The vast majority of the white-collar Anglo-Saxon population was to be found in the south and west of the city; the continental Europeans were hived in the North End. This ethno-class division was also reflected in the disparity between the distribution of social services and the incidence of disease. Infant mortality in the North End, for example, was usually twice the rate in the Anglo-Saxon South End. The disastrous influenza epidemic that struck the city during the winter of 1918–19 further demonstrated the high cost of being poor and foreign.[63]

During January and February, 1919, there were a series of anti-alien incidents in the city. One of the worst occurred on January 28 when a mob of returned soldiers attacked scores of foreigners and wrecked the German club, the offices of the Socialist Party of Canada, and the business establishment of Sam Blumenberg, a prominent Jewish socialist.[64] Reports of the event in the *Winnipeg Telegram* illustrate the attitude adopted by many Anglo-Canadian residents of the city toward the aliens. The *Telegram* made no apologies for the violence; instead, the newspaper contrasted the manly traits of the Anglo-Canadian veterans to the cowardly and furtive behaviour of the aliens:"It was typical of all who were assaulted, that they hit out for home or the nearest hiding place after the battle."[65] Clearly, many Anglo-Canadians in the city were prepared to accept mob justice. R.B.

Russell reported that the rioting veterans had committed their worst excesses when "smartly dressed officers ... [and] prominent members of the Board of Trade" had urged them on. Nor had the local police or military security officials made any attempt to protect the foreigners from the mob.[66]

At the provincial level Premier Norris's response to the violence was not to punish the rioters, but to establish an Alien Investigation Board that issued registration cards only to "loyal" aliens. Without these cards foreign workers were not only denied employment but were actually scheduled for deportation. Indeed, the local pressure for more extensive deportation of radical aliens increased during the spring of 1919, especially after D.A. Ross, the provincial member for Springfield, publicly charged that both Ukrainian socialists and religious nationalists were armed with "machine guns, rifles and ammunition to start a revolution in May."[67] The stage was now set for the Red Scare of 1919.

The Winnipeg General Strike of May 15 to June 28, 1919, brought the elements of class and ethnic conflict together in a massive confrontation. The growing hysteria in the city brought with it renewed propaganda against aliens, a close co-operation between security forces and the local political and economic elite, and finally, attempts to use the immigration machinery to deport not only alien agitators but also British-born radicals. The sequence of events associated with the Winnipeg Strike has been well documented: the breakdown of negotiations between management and labour in the metal trades was followed by the decision of the Winnipeg Trades and Labour Council to call a general strike for May 15. The response was dramatic; between 25,000 and 30,000 workers left their jobs. Overnight the city was divided into two camps.[68]

On one side stood the Citizens' Committee of One Thousand, a group of Anglo-Canadian businessmen and professionals who viewed themselves as the defenders of the Canadian way of life on the Prairies. Their purpose was clear: to crush the radical labour movement in Winnipeg. In their pursuit of this goal the Citizens' Committee engaged in a ferocious propaganda campaign against the opposing Central Strike Committee, both through its own newspaper *The Citizen* and through the enthusiastic support it received from the *Telegram* and the *Manitoba Free Press*. The committee's propaganda was aimed specifically at veterans, and the strike was portrayed as the work of enemy aliens and a few irresponsible Anglo-Saxon agitators.[69] John W. Dafoe, the influential editor of the *Free Press*, informed his readers that the five members of the Central Strike Committee—Russell, Ivens, Veitch, Robinson, and Winning—had been rejected by the intelligent and skilled Anglo-Saxon workers and had gained power only through "the fanatical allegiance of the Germans, Austrians, Huns and Russians." Dafoe advised that the best way of undermining the control the "Red Five" exercised over the Winnipeg labour movement was "to clean the aliens out of this community and ship them back to their happy homes in Europe which vomited them forth a decade ago."[70]

The Borden government was quick to comply. On June 15, the commissioner of the RNWMP indicated that 100 aliens had been marked for deportation under the recently enacted section 41 of the Immigration Act, and that thirty-six were in Winnipeg. In the early hours of June 17 officers of the force descended on the residences of ten Winnipegers: six Anglo-Saxon labour leaders and four "foreigners" were arrested.[71] Ultimately none of these men were summarily deported, as

planned. In the case of the Anglo-Saxon strike leaders, an immediate protest was registered by numerous labour organizations across the country. Alarmed by this uproar, the Borden government announced that it did not intend to use section 41 against British-born agitators either in Winnipeg or in any other centre.[72]

The aliens arrested were not so fortunate. The violent confrontation of June 21 between the strikers and the RNWMP, in which scores were injured and two killed, encouraged the hard-liners in the Borden government. On July 1 raids were carried out across the country on the homes of known alien agitators and the offices of radical organizations. Many of those arrested were moved to the internment camp at Kapuskasing, Ontario, and subsequently deported in secret.[73] In its attempts to deport the approximately 200 "anarchists and revolutionaries" rounded up in the summer raids of 1919, the Immigration Branch worked very closely with United States immigration authorities. This co-operation was indicative of a link being forged between Canadian and American security agencies; the formation of the Communist Labour Party of America and the Communist Party of America in the fall of 1919 further strengthened this connection.[74] This RNWMP and military intelligence also maintained close contact with the British Secret Service. Lists of undesirable immigrants and known Communists were transmitted from London to Ottawa. Indeed, the Immigration Branch had now evolved from a recruitment agency to a security service.[75]

IMMIGRATION "REFORM"
The events of 1919 produced a spirited national debate on whether Canada should continue to maintain an open-door immigration policy. Since many Anglo-Canadians equated

Bolshevism with the recent immigration from eastern Europe, support grew for policies similar to the quota system under discussion in the United States.[76] The Winnipeg Strike, the surplus of labour, and a short but sharp dip in the stock market removed some of the incentive for industrialists to lobby for the continued importation of alien workers. Even the Canadian Manufacturers' Association, a long-time advocate of an open-door policy, sounded a cautious note: "Canada should not encourage the immigration of those whose political and social beliefs unfit them for assimilation with Canadians. While a great country such as Canada possessing millions of vacant acres needs population, it is wiser to go slowly and secure the right sort of citizens."[77] Ethnic, cultural, and ideological acceptability had temporarily triumphed over economic considerations. Whether Canada was prepared to accept a slower rate of economic growth to ensure its survival as a predominantly Anglo nation now became a matter of pressing importance.

Among the European workers themselves the enemy alien hysteria and the Red Scare produced great bitterness. This was especially true for Ukrainian, Finnish, and Russian immigrants, many of whom had considered returning to Europe in the spring of 1919. The unsettled economic and political conditions in their homelands had, however, ultimately prevented their exodus. But their future prospects in Canada looked anything but promising. Certainly there seemed little reason to believe that they could ever become part of the mainstream of Canadian life. In these circumstances, some of their ethnic organizations offered an alternative to the "Canadian Way of Life"—an alternative that found sustenance in the achievements of Soviet communism.[78] The distinctive outlook of Slavic and Finnish socialists in Canada was described as follows in a 1921 RCMP intelligence report:

> If in earlier years they came sick of Europe, ready to turn their back on their homelands, and full of admiration for the native Canadian and Canadian civilization, they have changed their point of view. The war and revolution have roused their intense interest in Central Europe. They belong almost wholly to the poorest element in the community, and it is highly exciting to them to see the class from which they come, composed in effect of their own relatives, seize control of all power and acquire all property.[79]

Such was the legacy of 1919—the floodtide of radical labour politics in Canada.

NOTES

[1] Oscar Handlin, *The Uprooted* (Boston, 1951), 90–105; John Higham, *Strangers in the Land* (New York, 1966), 50–165; John Brodar, *The Transplanted: A History of Immigrants in Urban America* (Bloomington, Ind., 1987), 104–16; Gad Horowitz, *Canadian Labour in Politics* (Toronto, 1968); Martin Robin, *Radical Politics and Canadian Labour 1880–1930* (Kingston, 1968); Gerald Rosenblum, *Immigrant Workers: Their Impact on American Labour Radicalism* (New York, 1973), 60–82, 124–39, 146–75.

[2] Vera Lysenko, *Men in Sheepskin Coats: A Study in Assimilation* (Toronto, 1947), 101.

[3] John Porter, *The Vertical Mosaic: An Analysis of Social Class and Power in Canada* (Toronto, 1965), 60.

[4] See the annual reports of the Immigration Branch, *Sessional Papers*, 1890–1905; Dafoe, *Sifton*, 132–44, 318–23; Macdonald, *Immigration and Colonization*, 240–80.

[5] Toronto *Empire*, 2 October 1890.

[6] Toronto *Mail and Empire*, 10 April 1899. The author has examined some twenty-two daily newspapers that commented negatively on the influx of Ukrainian immigrants between March and May, 1899. See IB, 60868, No. 1.

7   *The Independent* (Vancouver), 23 July 1904.

8   C.A. Magrath, *Canada's Growth and Some Problems Affecting It* (Ottawa, 1910), 53, 71–74; Henry Vivian, "City Planning," Address to the Ottawa Canadian Club, 22 October 1910, *Addresses Delivered before The Canadian Club of Ottawa, 1910* (Ottawa, 1911), 1; Dr. Charles Hodgetts, "Unsanitary Housing," Quebec City, 17 January 1911, *Addresses to the Second Annual Meeting of the Commission on Conservation* (Ottawa), 32–42; J.S. Woodsworth, *My Neighbour* (Toronto, 1911), 28–156.

9   Annual Report of the Commissioner of the RNWMP, A. Bowen Perry, *Sessional Papers*, 1904–14. This viewpoint was confirmed by the municipal police chiefs, especially at the 1913 annual convention. *Chief Constables Association, Ninth Annual Convention*, Halifax, 25-27 June 1913, IB, 813739, No. 11.

10 Ralph Connor, *The Foreigner* (Toronto, 1909), 34.

11 Woodsworth, *Strangers Within Our Gates*, 136, 195, 226; *The Christian Guardian*, 8 September 1909; ibid., 16 July 1913; Handlin, *The Uprooted*, 94.

12 Joseph Barton, *Peasants and Strangers: Italians, Rumanians and Slovaks in an American City, 1890–1950* (Cambridge, Mass., 1975), 9–77; Brodar, *The Transplanted*; M.H. Marunchak, *The Ukrainian Canadians: A History* (Winnipeg, 1970), 99–114; Peter Stearnes and Daniel Walkowitz, eds., *Workers in the Industrial Revolution* (New Brunswick, N.J., 1914), 25–34, 72–82; Thomas Childers, "The Austrian Emigration: 1900–1914," in Donald Fleming and Bernard Bailyn, eds., *Dislocation and Emigration: The Social Background of American Immigration*, Perspectives in American History, vol. VII (Cambridge, Mass., 1973), 275–375.

13 Childers, "Austrian Emigration," 325.

14 Ibid., 321; Vladimir Kaye, *Early Ukrainian Settlement in Canada* (Toronto, 1964), 5–27, 34, 47–50, 126–33.

15 John S. Macdonald and Leatrice D. Macdonald, "Chain Migration, Ethnic Neighbourhood Formation and Social Networks," *Milbank Memorial Fund Quarterly*, 52 (January, 1964), 82–97; Charles Tilly and C. Harold Brown, "On Uprooting Kinship, and the Auspices of Migration," *International Journal of Comparative Sociology* (1967), 138–64; Bruno Ramirez, *On the Move: French-Canadian and Italian Migrants in the North Atlantic Economy, 1860–1914* (Toronto, 1991).

16 Melvyn Dubofsky, *We Shall Be All: A History of the Industrial Workers of the World* (Chicago, 1969), 4–35.

17 A.R. McCormack, "The Industrial Workers of the World in Western Canada: 1905–1914," Canadian Historical Association, *Historical Papers* (1975), 167–91; *British Columbia Federationist*, 5 April 1912.

18 One of the most successful attempts to organize immigrant workers into lasting industrial unions was made by the United Mine Workers of America, most notably in District 18, which encompassed the Rocky Mountain coal-mining region. By 1912 most of the miners in the region were foreign-born, and the membership of the UMWA realized that unless they successfully appealed to the immigrant workers they would "go out of existence."

19 Most lumber companies operating in northern Ontario tended to regard French Canadians as the best woodworkers "on account of their skills and docility." Finns were equally prized because of their industriousness and consistency. By 1914, however, many companies began to regard their Finnish workers as being "very susceptible to all labour movements and untrustworthy where they are in a majority." This concern became even more pronounced when Finnish IWW organizers began to organize the bush camps and working-class communities of northern Ontario. Radforth, *Bushworkers and Bosses*, 33–34.

20 Robin, *Radical Politics and Canadian Labour*; Norman Penner, *The Canadian Left: A Critical Analysis* (Toronto, 1977), 1–124.

21 Mauri Jalava, "The Finnish-Canadian Cooperative Movement in Ontario," Douglas Ollila, Jr., "From Socialism to Industrial Unionism (I.W.W.): Social Factors in the Emergence of Left-Labor Radicalism among Finnish Workers of the Mesabi, 1911–1919," both in Michael Karni et al., eds., *Finnish Experience in the Western Great Lakes Region: New Perspectives* (Turku, 1975).

22 *Western Clarion*, 16 November 1907, cited in Varpu Lindstrom-Best, "The Socialist Party of Canada and the Finnish Connection, 1905–1911," in Dahlie and Fernando, eds., *Ethnicity Power and Politics in Canada*, 113–22. Varpu Lindstrom-Best, "'Defiant Sisters': A Social History of Finnish Women in Canada, 1890–1930" (Ph.D. thesis, York University, 1986). By 1911 most Finnish socialists had parted company with the SPC and were instrumental in creating the Social Democratic Party of Canada.

23 Ruth A. Frager, *Sweatshop Strife: Class, Ethnicity and Gender in the Labour Movement of Toronto, 1900–1939* (Toronto, 1992), 149, 212–14.

24 Rebecca (Becky) Buhay came to Canada in 1912 and became active in the Amalgamated Clothing Workers of America and the Ladies' Garment Workers prior to 1922, when she joined the CPC. Annie Buller also came out of Montreal's Jewish socialist movement; during the 1920s she was an important organizer for the CPC-dominated Industrial Union of Needle Trades Workers. Ibid., 130–34, 177; William Rodney, *Soldiers of the International: A History of the Communist Party of Canada, 1919–1929* (Toronto, 1968), 164; Joan Sangster, *Dreams of Equality: Women on the Canadian Left, 1920–1950* (Toronto, 1989).

25 IB, 800111, J.H. Ashdown to Frank Oliver, 9 April 1908.

26 During the 1910 session of the House of Commons the member for West Huron, E.L. Lewis, introduced a private member's bill calling for the restriction of immigration from the area of Europe south of 44° north latitude and east of 20° east longitude in order to prevent Canada from becoming "a nation of organ grinders and banana sellers." *Debates*, 1909–10, 3134; ibid., 1914, 140.

27 *Labour Gazette*, 1914, 286–332, 820–21.

28 *Robotchny Narod*, 14 March 1914. On November 12, 1913, the *Guardian* reported that over 3,000 Bulgarian navvies had returned to Europe during the fall of that year.

29 *Census of Canada*, 1911 (Ottawa, 1913), vol. II, 367; *CAR*, 1915, 353.

30 Revised Statutes of Canada, 1927, Chapter 206, vol. IV, 1–3; *Canadian Gazette*, 15 August 1914; Borden Papers, 56666, C.H. Cahan to C.J. Coherty, 14 September 1918.

31 Canadian citizens of African, Chinese, Japanese, East Indian, and Aboriginal background also encountered discrimination during the war years. One of the most blatant was how volunteers from these groups were treated by the Canadian military establishment. Although about 5,000 Native Canadians, 1,000 blacks, and several hundred Chinese and Japanese enlisted in the Canadian forces, they were predominantly assigned to low-status jobs in the construction or forestry units overseas. Most blacks and Aboriginals were assigned to their own segregated battalions, with white officers. An offer by Japanese Canadians to form a separate battalion was rejected. In addition to their racial bias, Canadian politicians were reluctant to encourage large-scale military participation of these groups because it might lead to renewed demands for full civil rights. In contrast, the persistence of these groups "in volunteering, their insistence upon the right 'to serve', their urgent demand to know the reasons for their rejection, all suggest that 'visible' minorities had not been defeated by the racism of white society.... " James Walker, "Race and Recruitment in World War I: Enlistment of Visible Minorities in the Canadian Expeditionary Force," *Canadian Historical Review*, LXX, 1 (March, 1989), 26.

32 Major-General W.D. Otter, Internment Operations, 1914–20 (Ottawa, 30 September 1920), 2, 6, 12; *CAR*, 1916, 433.

33 *CAR*, 1916, 433; Joseph Boudreau, "The Enemy Alien Problem in Canada, 1914–1921" (Ph.D. thesis, University of California, 1964), 50–103.

34 *Canadian Ruthenian*, 1 August 1914.

35 NAC, Department of Militia and Defence Headquarters (hereafter DND), file C-965 #2, Report, Agent J.D. Sisler, 9 August 1914. There were numerous other reports in this file.

36 Some of the strongest support for internment camps came from prominent citizens in heterogeneous communities. In Winnipeg, for example, J.A.M. Aikins, a prominent Conservative, warned that the city's enemy aliens might take advantage of the war "for the destruction of property, public and private." Borden Papers, 106322, Aikins to Borden, 12 November 1914.

37 *Canadian Mining Journal*, 15 August 1914.

38 IB, 775789, T.D. Willans, travelling immigration inspector, to W.D. Scott, 9 June 1915; Borden Papers, 106499, H. McInnes, Solicitor, D.H. McDougall, Dominion Iron and Steel Corporation, to Borden, 17 May 1915.

39 *The Northern Miner* (Cobalt), 9 October 1915; *CAR*, 1915, 355; DND, file 965, No.9, Major E.J. May to Colonel E.A. Cruickshank, district officer in command of military district #13, 28 June 1915.

40 Otter, Internment Operations, 6-12; NAC, Arthur Meighen Papers, 106995, Meighen to Borden, 4 September 1914. The European dependants of these alien workers obviously had to live on even less because after August, 1914, it was unlawful to send remittances of money out of the country. Chief Press Censor, 196, Livesay to Chambers, 4 December 1915.

41 British Columbia Provincial Police (BCPP), file 1355-7, John Simpson, Chief Constable of Greenwood, to Colin Campbell, supt. of the BCPP, 26 January 1916.

42 IB, 29490, No.4, W. Banford, Dominion immigration officer, to W.D. Scott, 13 May 1915; McBride Papers, McBride to Premier Sifton (Alta.), 30 June 1915. About 20,000 Canadian troops had also been used in gathering the harvest during 1915.

43 IB, 29490, No. 6, W.D. Scott, "Circular Letter to Canadian Immigration Agents in the United States," 2 August 1916.

44 NAC, Sir Joseph Flavelle Papers, 74, Scott to Flavelle, director of imperial munitions, 11 August 1916; IB, 29490, No. 6, J. Frater Taylor, president of Algoma Steel, to Flavelle, 17 August 1917. The number of American immigrants entering the country was 41,779 in 1916 and 65,739 in 1917.

45 China provided over 50,000 labourers to the Allied cause. They were transported from Vancouver to Halifax in 1917 for service in France. *British Columbia Federationist*, 18 January 1918; Vancouver *Sun*, 7 February 1918; Wickberg, ed., *From China to Canada*, 119.

46 IB, 75789, A. Macdonald, Employment Agent, Dominion Coal Company, to Scott, 25 July 1916.

47 *CAR*, 1918, 330; ibid., 1916, 325–28; Statutes of Canada, 9-10 Geo. V, xciii. The reaction of the Trades and Labour Congress to the treatment of enemy alien workers varied. On one hand they endorsed the "patriotic" dismissals in 1915 and supported the scheme to relocate enemy aliens on homesteads on the uncultivated lands of "New" Ontario. In June, 1916, however, the Congress executive, concerned over the possibility that the government intended to use large numbers of enemy aliens in the mines of northern Ontario, strongly protested the practice of forced labour. *Proceedings of the Thirty-First Annual Session of the Trades and Labour Congress of Canada* (1915), 16–17; ibid. (1916), 43.

48 Otter, Internment Operations, 9-14; NAC, Secretary of State Papers, Internment Operation Section, file 5330, No. 7, Major Dales, Commandant Kapuskasing, to Otter, 14 November 1918; Desmond Morton, "Sir William Otter and Internment Operations in Canada During the First World War," *Canadian Historical Review* (March, 1974), 32–58.

49 Borden Papers, 43110, Mark Workman to Borden, 19 December 1918; ibid., 43097, Borden to A.E. Blount, 1 July 1918.

50 *CAR*, 1915, 354; Internment Operation Papers, Otter to F.L. Wanklyn, CPR, 12 June 1916.

51 Robin, *Radical Politics*, 138–39; McCormack, *Rebels, Reformers and Revolutionaries*, 143–216; Francis Swyripa and John Herd Thompson, eds., *Loyalties in Conflict: Ukrainians in Canada During the Great War* (Edmonton, 1983).

52 DND, C-2665, Major-General Ketchen, officer commanding Military District 10, to secretary of the Militia Council,

7 July 1917; NAC, Department of Justice Papers, 1919, file 2059, Registrar of Alien Enemies, Winnipeg, to Colonel Sherwood, Dominion Police, 17 August 1918; NAC, Chief Press Censor Branch, 144-A-2, Chambers to secretary of state, 20 September 1918.

53 Borden Papers, 56656, C.H. Cahan to Borden, 20 July 1918; ibid., 56668, Cahan to Borden, 14–20 September 1918. The fourteen illegal organizations also included the IWW, the Group of Social Democrats and Anarchists, the Chinese Nationalist League, and the Social Democratic Party; the latter organization was removed from the list in November, 1918. Ibid., 56698, Cahan to Borden, 21 October 1918; Statutes of Canada, 1919, 9-10 Geo.V, lxxi-lxxiii.

54 James Eayrs, In Defence of Canada: From the Great War to the Great Depression (Toronto, 1967), 30.

55 Winnipeg Telegram, 28 January 1919.

56 Internment Operations, file 6712, Major-General Otter to Acting Minister of Justice, 19 December 1918; Justice Records, 1919, vol. 227. Report, chief commissioner, Dominion Police, for director of public safety, 27 November 1918.

57 Borden Papers, 83163, Sir Thomas White to Borden, February 21, 1919. On February 28, 1919, the German government lodged an official complaint with British authorities over "the reported plan of the Canadian government to deport all Germans from Canada." IB, 912971, Swiss ambassador, London, England, to Lord Curzon, 28 February 1919.

58 Vancouver Sun, 26 March 1919; Mathers Royal Commission on Industrial Relations, "Evidence," Sudbury hearings, 27 May 1919, testimony of J.L. Fortin, 1923, Department of Labour Library.

59 Montreal Gazette, 14 June 1919.

60 In April, 1918, an amendment to the Dominion Land Act denied homestead patents to non-naturalized residents; the subsequent amendments to the Naturalization Act in June, 1919, also made it extremely difficult for enemy aliens to become naturalized. Justice Papers, 1919, file 2266, Albert Dawdron, acting commissioner of the Dominion Police, to the Minister of Justice, 28 July 1919. Statutes of Canada, 1918, 9-10 Geo.V, c. 19, s. 7; Debates, 1919, 4118-33.

61 Chief Press Censor, 196-1, E. Tarak to Chambers, 11 January 1918 (translation), 91. IB, 963419, W.D. Scott to James A. Calder, Minister of Immigration and Colonization, 11 December 1919; Toronto Telegram, 1 April 1920; Meighen Papers, 000256, J.A. Stevenson to Meighen, 24 February 1919; Canadian Ruthenian, 5 February 1919.

62 IB, 963419, W.D. Scott to James A. Calder, Minister of Immigration and Colonization, 11 December 1919; Toronto Telegram, 1 April 1920; Meighen Papers, 000256, J.A. Stevenson to Meighen, 24 February 1919; Canadian Ruthenian, 5 February 1919.

63 Mathers Royal Commission, "Evidence," Victoria hearings, testimony of J.O. Cameron, president of the Victoria Board of Trade; ibid., Calgary hearings, testimony of W. Henderson;

ibid., testimony of Mortimer Morrow, manager of Canmore Coal Mines.

64 Alan Artibise, Winnipeg: A Social History of Urban Growth 1874–1914 (Montreal, 1975), 223–45; Manitoba Free Press, 3 November 1918.

65 DND, C-2665, Secret Agent No. 47, Report (Wpg.), to Supt. Starnes, RNWMP, 24 March 1919.

66 Winnipeg Telegram, 29 January 1919.

67 PAM, OBU Collection, R.B. Russell to Victor Midgley, 29 January 1919.

68 Manitoba Free Press, 7 May 1919; Western Labor News, 4 April 1919. The Alien Investigation Board was legitimized by the passage of PC 56 in January, 1919, which transferred authority to investigate enemy aliens and to enforce PC 2381 and PC 2384 from the Dominion Department of Justice to the provincial attorney general. Between February and May the board processed approximately 3,000 cases; of these, 500 were denied certificates. RCMP Records, Comptroller to Commissioner Perry, 20 March 1919; Manitoba Free Press, 7 May 1919; Meighen Papers, 000279, D.A. Ross to Meighen, 9 April 1919.

69 D.C. Masters, The Winnipeg General Strike (Toronto, 1959), 40–50; David Bercuson, Confrontation at Winnipeg (Montreal, 1974), 103–95.

70 Murray Donnelly, Dafoe of the Free Press (Toronto, 1968), 104; RCMP Records, 1919, vol. 1, Major-General Ketchen to secretary of the Militia Council, 21 May 1919; The Citizen (Wpg.) 5–20 June 1919.

71 Manitoba Free Press, 22 May 1919.

72 Borden Papers, 61913, Robertson to Borden, 14 June 1919; Diary of Sir Robert Borden, 13–17 June 1919; RCMP, CIB, vol. 70, J.A. Calder to Commissioner Perry, 16 June 1919; IB, 961162, Calder to Perry, 17 June 1919.

73 Tom Moore to E. Robinson, 24 June 1919, cited by Manitoba Free Press, 21 November 1919; Borden Diary, 20 June 1919; Borden Papers, 61936, Robertson to Acland, 14 June 1919; Manitoba Free Press, 18 June 1919.

74 Ukrainian Labor News, 16 July 1919; Norman Penner, ed., Winnipeg 1919: The Strikers' Own History of the Winnipeg General Strike (Toronto, 1973), 175–81; IB, 912971, No. 3, T.J. Murray, telegram to J.A. Calder, 30 October 1919; Justice Records, 1919, file 1960, deputy minister of justice to Murray and Noble, 5 November 1919.

75 In October, 1918, the United States Congress had passed an amendment to the "Act to Exclude and Expel from the United States Aliens Who Are Members of the Anarchist and Similar Classes"; Emma Goldman, Alexander Berkman, and 247 other "Reds" were deported to Russia under this measure in December, 1919. John Higham, Strangers in the Land (New York, 1966), 308–24; IB, 961162, No. 1, F.C. Blair, secretary of immigration and colonization, memorandum to J.A. Calder, 24 November 1919; ibid., John Clark, American consul-general, Montreal, to F.C. Blair, 19 June 1920.

76 Ibid., A.J. Cawdron to supt. of immigration, 24 June 1919; ibid., assistant director, CIB, RCMP, to F.C. Blair, 4 August 1920.

77 In addition to the pressure to exclude enemy aliens and pacifists, there was considerable support for the suggestion that Canada should not accept immigrants from certain regions because of their alleged racial deficiencies. Hume Conyn, MP for London, Ontario, cited the writings of eugenicist Madison Grant as justifying the exclusion of "strange people who cannot be assimilated." Higham, *Strangers in the Land*, 308–24; *Debates*, 30 April 1919; 1 May 1916; 9 May 1919, 2280–90.

78 *Industrial Canada* (July, 1919), 120–22.

79 After the merger in 1919 of the RNWMP and the Dominion Police, the joint force was renamed the Royal Canadian Mounted Police in 1920. Surveillance of Communist infiltrators continued throughout the 1920s. NAC, Department of Justice, 1926, file 293, C. Starnes to deputy minister of justice, 27 October 1926. Ivan Avakumovic, *The Communist Party in Canada: A History* (Toronto, 1975), 1–53; Barbara Roberts, *Whence They Came: Deportation from Canada 1900–1935* (Ottawa, 1988), 71–97, 125–58.

"MIXING WITH PEOPLE ON SPADINA": THE TENSE RELATIONS BETWEEN NON-JEWISH WORKERS AND JEWISH WORKERS

RUTH A. FRAGER

"God Protect Us from Gentile Hands and Jewish Wits."

—YIDDISH FOLK SAYING[1]

*A*rmed with knuckledusters, two unemployed Toronto ILGWU members assaulted two of the Union's leaders in October 1936, beating them badly. The victims were both Jews, the assailants were not. "The attackers, in a statement to the police, which the press featured, attempted to create anti-Semitic feeling, by the contention that they were being discriminated against, because of being Gentiles," reported another local Jewish union leader. "This is without foundation, of course," the official declared, explaining that "we countered with a statement in the press by the Gentile Local repudiating this, stating that discrimination does not exist in our Union." He was so concerned about the incident that he immediately called the union members together in a mass meeting and also made a point of visiting each shop "to pull out as much poison as possible." Although he believed the base instincts of some elements among the membership have been put to flight," he felt that "generally speaking the incident was rather injurious [to the union]."[2] When David Dubinsky, president of the ILGWU, learned "the startling news," he, too, stressed that this was an explosive issue, adding: "This, in my

judgment, is the effect of the propaganda being disseminated by Father Coughlin and other groups, who are interested in stirring up racial prejudice."[3]

This assault was only one of the more dramatic manifestations of the serious divisions between Jewish workers and non-Jewish workers in Toronto's needle trades. Although, initially, the vast majority of the city's garment workers were Anglo-Celtic, the proportion of Jews in this sector had increased to slightly less than half by 1931. Among the male garment workers in particular, the proportion of Jews had risen to a little under two-thirds by that year.[4]

The language barrier was only one of the many ways in which Jewish workers stood apart from their non-Jewish counterparts, but the language problem itself was no minor matter. Yiddish-speaking immigrants had seldom learned any English before emigrating, and, once here, they found that learning English involved mastering a whole new alphabet as well as the different syntax and vocabulary. Beyond the language issue, the separateness of Jewish workers reflected, in part, the legacy of relative isolation Jews had experienced for centuries in Eastern Europe in the context of vicious anti-Semitism. Even though prejudice against Jews was less severe in Toronto, the city's immigrant Jews still experienced significant discrimination. Contrary to a common present-day misconception, anti-Semitism in Toronto (as well as in Canada as a whole) constituted a serious problem not only during the rise of Fascism in the 1930s but during the preceding three decades as well. Jewish experiences of persecution in Eastern Europe, combined with the very real presence of anti-Semitism in Canada, made Jewish workers wary of their non-Jewish co-workers.[5]

* * *

The leaders of the needle trades unions did, however, try to overcome the relative separateness of the two groups of workers by appealing to the ideal of working-class solidarity. The need for class solidarity was, of course, very real, particularly since Jews and non-Jews often toiled beside each other on the shop floor in this sector. Within a particular union, separate locals may have eliminated some problems, but representatives from each local had to work together on their union's joint board. More broadly, of course, union members needed to function smoothly together at many levels.

In some cases, there were leftist political links between some of the Jews and some of the non-Jews, who might have been connected through the CCF, the Communist party, the Socialist party, the Social Democratic party, the Trotskyist movement, or the Anarchist movement. Partly because there were relatively few non-Jewish garment workers involved in these political groups, however, ethnic divisions among the city's needle trades workers were difficult to bridge.[6]

* * *

The friction between Jewish workers and non-Jewish workers was, in part, related to issues arising out of the differences in the skills involved in their work. In Toronto, such issues became particularly important for male workers in the men's clothing industry in the 1910s. In this particular period, the conflict between Jews and non-Jews was also heightened by interunion rivalry in this section of the industry. A detailed examination of the development of the Amalgamated Clothing Workers highlights not only the conflicts of the 1910s but demonstrates also the problems of ethnic conflict that continued into the 1920s and 1930s, resulting in further interunion rivalry in the midst of the Great Depression.

In the 1910s the three rival unions were the Journeymen Tailors' Union of America (JTUA), the United Garment Workers (UGW), and the Amalgamated Clothing Workers (ACW). The JTUA had been established for those involved in custom tailoring (a process whereby clothing was made up according to the specifications of the individual customer). The other two unions competed sharply in the ready-made branch of the men's clothing industry, for the ACW had been formed by a group of secessionists from the UGW in 1914. In Toronto, as in many of the other clothing centres in Canada and the United States, the ACW was composed mostly of Jews from the beginning of its formation. In contrast, the members of the JTUA tended to be non-immigrants, as did the members of the UGW.[7]

Shortly after the formation of the ACW, the JTUA worked out an agreement with it, merging the two organizations into one industrial union. This merger led, in fact, to a lot of friction between the two groups, both in Toronto and elsewhere. As a result, the merger was liquidated not long after it had been established. During the period of the merger, the Toronto members of the JTUA had been involved in attempts to organize the ready-made men's clothing workers, together with the ACW.

Much of the friction between the two groups stemmed from the ways in which employers used the Jewish immigrants as part of the deskilling process in this period. The traditional custom tailor was highly skilled and made the whole garment either by himself or with the help of an apprentice. This craft was being seriously undermined, however, by the increasing popularity of ready-made clothing as well as by the dramatic increases in the division of labour in the remaining custom tailoring establishments. Many of the skilled custom tailors resented those workers who made clothing according to these newer—and cheaper—systems of production. The custom tailors looked down on those whom they viewed as far less skilled than themselves, and they saw these newcomers as a threat to their own positions. In Toronto, as elsewhere, many of the workers who did these less skilled jobs were Jewish immigrants. Ironically, a considerable number of these Jews were themselves victims of deskilling, for they had done skilled tailoring before emigration and then found themselves relegated to less skilled roles in the newer production processes on this side of the ocean.[8]

* * *

In Toronto, James Watt, a key JTUA official, experienced serious difficulties during the brief JTUA–ACW merger, when he tried to help his organization unionize the less skilled men's clothing workers. "The section worker [the person who puts together only one section of the garment] finds it as difficult to understand the journeyman tailor as it is for the journey-

man tailor to understand the section worker," declared the frustrated Watt in 1915.[9] The difficulties were compounded by the fact that Toronto's journeymen tailors were usually Anglo-Celtic, while many of the section workers were Jewish.[10] Ethnic tensions were directly related to the specific role many Jewish workers played in the labour process.

* * *

In the meantime, both during and after the short-lived merger with the JTUA, Toronto's Amalgamated Clothing Workers concentrated on recruiting all the ready-made clothing workers in the city's men's clothing industry. This involved trying to persuade workers they were better off in the ACW than in the United Garment Workers. At the international level, the founders of the ACW had seceded from the UGW largely because of the anti-immigrant attitudes of the UGW's head office.[11] Indeed, Jewish readers of the UGW's newspaper might well have been offended by the occasional anti-Semitic jokes it contained.[12]

In Toronto, as well, there is evidence of the UGW's insensitivity to the Jewish garment workers. Sam Landers, the union's organizer for Toronto and its most important Canadian organizer in this period, was hardly in a position to inspire confidence in Jewish workers. Originally a Jew, Landers had joined the Salvation Army, and he publicly referred to Jews as "Kikes" in the pages of the UGW's newspaper. Other indications of the UGW's insensitivity include the fact that, in 1915, the Toronto branch of the UGW held an important organizing meeting at the same time that the city's Jews had scheduled a mass meeting to organize relief for their persecuted co-religionists in Poland.[13]

In the contest between the ACW and the UGW in Toronto, ethnic differences were sometimes reinforced by skill differences. In 1917, at a time when the city's ACW had seven hundred dues-paying members, not even one cutter had joined this union. The ACW's organizer reported that the cutters had their own UGW local and that it would be a "mighty hard job" to organize the members of this highly skilled occupation into the ACW. In this branch of the city's needle trades, almost all of the cutters were non-Jews. Thus the ACW organizer suggested that the union renew its efforts to organize them by hiring a local non-Jew, someone who would be "well known amongst the Gentile element in Toronto" and well known among the cutters in particular.[14]

Although some of the cutters had joined the ACW by the following year, there was friction between them and the other ACW members. More broadly, it was still difficult for the ACW to "make any progress at all among the English speaking element." The union strove to remedy the situation by setting up a separate office for the non-Jews.[15]

In addition to the cutters, other non-Jews eventually began to join Toronto's ACW, partly to work in the shops where the employers had signed contracts with this union. This ethnic mix led to further tensions within the union itself. In 1920, for example, certain English-speaking union members reportedly had a constant "feeling of irritation" that they did not yet have their own separate local. These anglophones had temporarily been placed in a sublocal of the Jewish coatmakers' local, and their Jewish co-workers did not object to their request for their own local. When the manager of Toronto's ACW wrote to the union's head office to emphasize the need for a separate local, he explained that the new local's "designation cannot be properly placed for any particular branch of the industry, and the only distinction seemingly can be made that they

cannot under any circumstances meet with the Jewish Speaking element; to them it's a matter of a moral prestige."[16]

Several years later, after the new English-speaking local had been established, the anglophone members of Toronto's ACW continued to press for more separation from the Jewish ACW members. The executive board of this English-speaking local, together with the executive board of the English-speaking cutters' local, protested to the ACW's Toronto Joint Board "against the disorderly conduct of some members at the mass meeting in the Standard Theatre. [They] recommend[ed] that in the future separate meetings shall be arranged for the Jewish and English speaking members."[17] Although the union's records do not indicate the nature of this "disorderly conduct," the non-Jews' call for separate meetings highlights the serious ethnic tensions within the union.

Relations between these two groups of ACW workers remained strained. In the context of a 1927 joint board decision to ensure that all union members were up to date with their dues payments, for example, the ACW's English-speaking local pointedly asked the board "why the English membership is being checked up more on the dues than the others." Although the board replied there was no evidence of discrimination, the anglophones clearly felt they were being discriminated against.[18] Another incident in the same year illustrates that Jews, too, were concerned they were being discriminated against within the union. In this case, "Brother Beckerman," an executive member of local 233, expressly asked the joint board to clarify whether this particular local was "a Gentile Local or an English-speaking Local." Beckerman decided to push for this clarification after attending one of the local's executive meetings where "an English-speaking woman who was Jewish by nationality applied for membership [in local 233 and some of the members of [the local's] Executive tried to refer her to the Jewish Locals." When he objected to her treatment, "stating that every English-speaking person has a right to belong to the Local," "he was denounced, even by Brother Tovey," the union's anglophone business agent. "By what right did Brother Tovey tell him that he would expel him from the Organization?" Beckerman indignantly inquired.[19]

Further problems developed. Several years later, for example, an ACW official reported that, in Toronto, "an attempt has been made to disrupt loyalty [to the union] by bringing in the element of antisemitism." "That is being checked, however," he optimistically declared.[20]

While Toronto's ILGWU experienced its own difficulties with "the Jew Gentile problem,"[21] tensions between Jews and non-Jews in the men's clothing industry continued to plague the ACW, leading directly to the establishment of the rival National Clothing Workers of Canada (NCWC). The NCWC was the product of the All-Canadian Congress of Labour (ACCL), a central labour body founded in 1927 in explicit opposition to the international unions that were based in the United States and included Canadian locals. While advocates of the ACCL maintained they were fighting to free the Canadian labour movement from American domination, much of the motivation for the formation of the NCWC was far less noble.[22] (Characteristics of the ACW and the NCWC are outlined in table 7 of the appendix.)

Although the ACCL had made some efforts to organize Toronto garment workers in 1931, it did not gain a significant foothold in this sector until the NCWC was launched in early 1934, arising out of a struggle with the ACW at Ontario Boys' Wear. This struggle began in late 1933 when more than one hundred workers struck this Toronto shop for recognition of the

Amalgamated Clothing Workers and for a substantial wage increase. After the strike had dragged on for several months, the employer turned around and signed a closed-shop agreement with the ACCL's newly formed National Clothing Workers of Canada. The NCWC supplied the firm with workers, while the ACW continued to picket for a time.[23]

The owner of Ontario Boys' Wear himself had been a key initiator of the formation of the NCWC at this shop. In the midst of the strike, Mezza Finch (soon to become president of the NCWC) contacted the ACCL's head office to explore the possibility of forming an ACCL affiliate at this firm. She explained that "the firm [is] determined against the amalgamated [the ACW] and ap[p]ealed to me as a worker against them."[24] Since Finch was already associated with the ACCL at this time, the employer was apparently turning to her in the hopes that an ACCL local could be formed in his shop to enable him to avoid having to settle with the ACW.

The collusion between management and the pro-ACCL workers at this shop was based on ethnic prejudice. The ACCL's newspaper pointedly asserted that Ontario Boys' Wear was "almost the only non-Hebrew shop in Toronto."[25] In the letter to the ACCL's head office in which Finch first explored the possibility of forming an ACCL affiliate at this firm, Finch explained that "the employees [of Ontario Boys' Wear] are all gentiles and they are a gentile firm." "The firm," she continued, "does not wish to employ any but gentiles."[26] Neither Finch nor her correspondent, the secretary-treasurer of the ACCL, objected to management's plans for continued discrimination. This employer apparently preferred the ACCL over the ACW partly because the ACCL was liable to go along with his discrimination against Jewish workers.[27] The ACCL's NCWC was formed out of this collusion.

This incident raises crucial questions about the nature of the Canadian nationalism of the ACCL. Finch, who became a member of the national executive board of the ACCL, saw herself as British and appears to have been highly ethnocentric. Her brand of Canadian nationalism was not a multicultural brand, and her belief in Canadian unionism seems to have been rooted in a more xenophobic form of nationalism. Finch's opposition to what she saw as the foreign domination of Canadian labour implied not only opposition to American control but also opposition to control by immigrants inside Canada—and Jews were considered to be foreigners by definition.[28] Moreover, Finch was not the only such nationalist labour leader opposed to Jews. Ernest Smith was another nationalist who played a leading role in the ACCL's work in the Toronto needle trades. In an attempt to discredit the ACW, Smith wrote to Ontario's attorney-general, describing the ACW as "an American union controlled by Russian Jews."[29]

The NCWC's ethnically based collusion with the boss at Ontario Boys' Wear led to significant collusion around low wages as well, for the NCWC attempted to block government officials from investigating low pay at the firm. In the late 1930s these government officials were attempting to ascertain whether this shop was violating the legal minimum wage rates, but the NCWC, which still had a closed-shop agreement with Ontario Boys' Wear, refused to allow the officials to question union members. Finch, leader of the NCWC, believed that the ACW was determined to put both Ontario Boys' Wear and the NCWC itself out of business. She apparently feared this could be done by forcing the firm to increase wages to meet the minimum wage rates stipulated in the Industrial Standards Act. Thus she wound up fighting the act as well

as the ACW.[30] Meanwhile, it was the boss himself who had profited from exploiting the divisions between Jewish and non-Jewish workers in Toronto's needle trades.

Tensions between these two groups of Toronto garment workers were pronounced not only among the men's clothing workers but also among the furriers. A detailed examination of the development of the city's International Fur Workers' Union (IFWU) further illuminates the nature and sources of these interethnic tensions from the 1910s through the 1930s. In the early years the IFWU was weak, consisting of only a handful of non-Jewish cutters in local 35 and a handful of Jewish operators in local 40. As a result, Toronto's IFWU leader suggested to the head office in 1915 that they dissolve local 40 "until times improve" and that the Jews from that local join local 35.[31] He soon realized, however, that the non-Jews found this unacceptable. He wrote to the head office: "I am given to understand that local #35 does not want Jews as members, and that bringing them in would most likely cause a decrease in the already small membership of local 35. Local 35 committees have [repeatedly] declined to invite Jews [in] local #40 to partake in the social gatherings of local 35. Hence I don't believe local 35 will accept them. Further local #40 prefers its own Charter [and] Union."[32]

By the late 1920s there were three IFWU locals, all of which were in the fur-coat branch of the industry. Local 40 was a Yiddish-speaking local for all the Jewish workers, regardless of skill and gender. Local 35 was for the non-Jewish cutters mainly, although it also included some non-Jewish men who were blockers and operators. There was also local 65, which was mainly for non-Jewish women. Ed Hammerstein, an IFWU activist, recalled there was a great deal of tension between the non-Jewish locals and the Jewish local: "The Joint

Board consisted of the three locals, and, as you can well see, that [the Jewish] local 40 was a ... minority group. And there were some very heated arguments and battles that took place at [the Joint Board] meetings, so much so that the Labour Council of Toronto had to appoint a person to act as chairman, to sort of mediate between these groups. Otherwise, they would've never been able to come to any [agreement]." Hammerstein explained: "The decision there arrived at was that, in order to bring some equality and balance, [they should] organize the [fur] collar and cuff workers. So, aside from it being an organizing drive to help workers who were terribly exploited, it also served sort of a political purpose insofar as the union was concerned in order to equalize the strength of the two [groups]." The union succeeded in organizing the collar and cuff trade and set up local 100 for these workers, who were mostly Jewish men. However, according to Hammerstein, "the problem wasn't resolved when local 100 was formed because then you had a balance. And because you had that balance, they could very seldom come to terms on issues." As a result, the IFWU again turned to the Toronto Labour Council, which assigned a person to chair the IFWU joint board meetings "so this sort of broke the constant tie votes that took place."[33]

By 1931 "the difficulties and misunderstandings" between the Jews and non-Jews had assumed such a "serious character" that the local IFWU leaders were appealing to the union's president to come to Toronto to help them straighten out the situation. As the IFWU minutes reveal, the local officials warned the union's head office that the two non-Jewish locals were "threatening to engage their own business agent and also to hire an office for themselves."[34]

The tensions between the Jewish and non-Jewish members of Toronto's IFWU exploded a year later during a general strike in the city's fur industry. As the union prepared for the strike, some of the bosses succeeded in influencing around two dozen members of the non-Jewish local 35, the cutters' local, to break away from the IFWU and form their own union. A key Jewish IFWU leader denounced this breakaway union as a tool of the manufacturers and declared it was being used against the other workers.[35]

The *Yiddisher Zhurnal* was nonetheless optimistic about developments in the IFWU. A week before the strike began, the newspaper reported that the union's head office had succeeded in uniting the four Toronto IFWU locals under one joint board that would take over negotiations with the manufacturers. Locals 35 and 65 had apparently agreed to give up their own office and work closely with the two Jewish locals, but it soon became clear that the non-Jews were not honouring this agreement. At that point, the leaders of the two Jewish locals announced that if the manufacturers signed a contract with locals 35 and 65, the Jewish locals would not honour it. The Jewish unionists felt that a strike was becoming necessary not only to win better wages but also to force the manufacturers to recognize the joint board, of locals 40 and 100.[36]

When the 1932 general strike began in Toronto's fur industry, hundreds of Jews walked off the job while most of the non-Jewish workers refused to join the strike. The local Jewish IFWU leaders enlisted the support of the union's head office to try to solve the problem of "the two locals which didn't join the strike and [which], with their deeds, hindered the organization of the fur workers."[37] The local IFWU strike leaders had even tried, to no apparent avail, to appeal to the Trades and Labour Council of Toronto to pressure the strikebreakers into cooperating. Although the Jewish workers eventually won the month-long strike anyway, this general strike provides one of the most graphic examples of the conflict between Jewish workers and non-Jewish workers in Toronto's garment industry.[38]

Recalling the clashes between these two groups in Toronto's IFWU, Ed Hammerstein indicated that the hostility stemmed from the fact that "the Jews who were coming into the industry were, in the eyes of the Gentiles, threatening their position." He felt that much of the friction arose because the non-Jewish fur workers were less militant than the Jews:

Well, basically the Jewish worker[s], who had come over here with a tradition of fighting for issues and demands ... were occupying lesser positions in the industry. They were newcomers in the industry; they were working for lower wages than the others who had been here a long time, the cutters and the people in locals 35 and 65. And the position of the Jewish worker[s] was that they should be entitled to some of the same type of wages that the others are getting. And the only way to achieve that would be by strike action. And the others were quite happy with their lot, and they could get increases in wages as a result of their experience and expertise. And this created the conflict.

Employed in the better section of the industry and "secure in their jobs," the non-Jews "didn't cotton to this militancy that was developing" among the Jews.

When Hammerstein was asked if he had experienced anti-Semitism within the union, his reply emphasized the way in which ethnic differences were reinforced by skill differences (at least as far as the male workers were concerned): "You'd find there might be some latent, incipient type of anti-Semitism on the part of individual fellow workers, particularly,

as I said, people who were in local 35, your cutters, who would sort of look down upon you not only as a result of a racial approach but also denigrate your type of work and everything else. So you found that. But it wasn't *overt*; it may have been *latent* and covert. But certainly you didn't feel it in the sense that you'd have to take up arms and fight them."

As Hammerstein explained, the Jewish workers and the non-Jewish workers had two very different conceptions of trade unionism. The Jewish IFWU leaders, who were themselves divided into rival Communist and CCF camps in the 1930s, felt that unions should be seriously involved in progressive political action. In contrast, the non-Jewish members, who, in any case, often voted Liberal or Conservative, did not think the union should be involved in any political activity. The fact that the non-Jewish IFWU leaders were generally opposed to socialism added to the friction between them and their Jewish counterparts.[39]

Jacob Black, another Jewish activist in the furriers' union, similarly emphasized that the non-Jewish IFWU leaders were less militant than the Jewish leaders. As an illustration, he described an incident that took place when the joint board was discussing calling a particular strike. During this discussion, an Anglo-Saxon woman expressed concern that it would not be "nice" to call a strike at a time when the employers had to make their samples. Moreover, Black, who was himself a supporter of the CCF, also stressed that the non-Jewish IFWU leaders were politically conservative. Very few of them would have supported the CCF. According to Black, these non-Jewish leaders were "the old-timers ... mainly the Anglo-Saxon types,' who were 'old Orange people."[40]

Differences between Jewish furriers and non-Jewish furriers were also heightened by the fact that Jacob Black, along with many of the other Jewish IFWU leaders, worked to involve the union in political actions that had special significance for Jews. The non-Jews, for example, tended to be relatively indifferent to the fight against world Fascism, whereas the Jews were highly concerned about this issue. Some of the Jewish IFWU leaders were also involved in support work for the Jewish labour movement in Palestine, which did not generally interest non-Jewish workers.[41]

In the context of ethnic tensions within the various needle trades unions, many of Toronto's garment manufacturers employed a "divide and conquer" strategy, attempting to pit non-Jewish workers and Jewish workers against each other, particularly during strikes. In so doing, these garment manufacturers were acting like many other employers in Canadian industry who strove to manipulate ethnic divisions within the workforce to their own advantage. Indeed, early twentieth-century Canadian immigration policy had been strongly shaped by key Canadian entrepreneurs whose insistence on the open-door policy stemmed partly from their plans to benefit from an ethnically diverse labour force. Within Toronto's garment industry, even some of the Jewish manufacturers tried to capitalize on ethnic divisions on the shop floor. Many of the non-Jewish employers, in particular, did not hesitate to try to discredit the Jewish unions through appeals to anti-Semitism.[42]

These issues surfaced, for example, during two key Toronto strikes in 1912. In the midst of the JTUA's lengthy general strike in that year, the union's newspaper emphasized—and denounced—the bosses' "shallow schemes" to create "dissension in our ranks by appeals to race prejudice."[43] Appeals to prejudice were even more pronounced during the large Eaton strike of the same year. As the ILGWU's newspaper reported: "Those affected [by the dispute at Eaton's] are almost entirely Jewish: and the

chief slogan by which it was hoped to cut off public sympathy was the report ... that this is 'only a strike of Jews.' The appeal to race and creed prejudice has succeeded, too, in so far as it has prevented the Gentile Cloak Makers from joining in the sympathetic strike."[44] In fact, the non-Jewish cloakmakers' failure to join the strike, together with the firm's recruitment of additional non-Jewish strike-breakers, were key factors contributing to the union's defeat.[45]

Toronto's garment manufacturers used various tactics to inflame ethnic divisions in the workforce. During a shop strike in 1920, for example, one of the bosses apparently reported to the police and the magistrate that the strike was caused by the strikers' refusal to work with Christian workers. The unionists denied this was the case, and the *Zhurnal* interpreted this charge as yet another slur against Jewish workers. "Racial denunciations have already been dragged in," explained the *Zhurnal*, because "the bosses realized that they cannot fight the workers with the usual [economic] methods."[46]

"The bosses have plainly become anti-Semites," reported a Toronto ILGWU official a few years later. "They incite the English workers against the Jewish workers using such expressions as 'we want to get rid of the damned Jews.'"[47] As the employers continued to stir up racial hatred among the garment workers, Toronto's ILGWU prepared for a cloakmakers' general strike, appealing in the *Zhurnal* to the Jewish cloakmakers to support the union. This appeal explained: "At each strike ... such ugly deeds of the bosses are noted, when they try, through racial hatred between Jews and non-Jews, to incite one against the other. On you, union members, lies the obligation to enlighten the non-Jewish workers that a fight for the union means only an economic, not a racial fight ... Explain to [the non-Jewish workers] also the significance of strike-breakers [and the importance of unity]."[48] Toronto's garment manufacturers also sometimes threatened Jewish union members that if any of them protested too much, they would replace them with non-Jewish women.[49]

The manufacturers' attempts to exploit ethnic divisions were particularly apparent during the 1934 strike in a dress department of Eaton's garment factory. The employees of this department were non-Jews, and several of the women strikers testified that when they became interested in the ILGWU, "[management] would try to bring in [the] racial question, about the Jewish people, telling us we should not belong to the union at all that was controlled by Jews."[50] The women were allegedly "out of [their] class" because, in seeking the help of ILGWU officials, "they were mixing with people on Spadina."[51]

The manufacturers' interest in trying to keep the non-Jewish workers from "mixing with people on Spadina" stemmed partly from the fact that, by the interwar period, Toronto's Jewish garment workers were generally more militant than the others. In the earlier years, however, the pattern of militancy was more complex. In the early to mid 1910s, in particular, the JTUA found it difficult to organize Jews, while Jewish unions such as the ILGWU found it difficult to organize the non-Jews in Toronto's needle trades. More specifically, although there was not a simple pattern of non-Jewish strikers pitted against Jewish strike-breakers during the JTUA's large, lengthy strike in 1912, some of the strike-breakers were drawn from "the scab Jewish element."[52]

Jewish garment workers tended to be less militant in the early part of the twentieth century than they were to become in the interwar years. Indeed, this increase in Jewish militancy took place despite the fact that the proportion of clothing manufacturers who were Jews was significantly higher in the interwar period. In the earlier period, when the percentage of Jews

in Toronto was much smaller, Jewish working-class culture was just beginning to put down roots in this city. By the 1920s, as organizations such as the Arbeiter Ring became more firmly established, Jewish militancy was strengthened by a more solid cultural base. As Jewish workers increased in numbers and became organized in unions that were predominantly Jewish, their union activities tended to increase.

Yet even in the early 1910s there were situations where Jewish workers—mobilized by the Jewish unions—were significantly more militant than their non-Jewish counterparts. Not only the Eaton strike of 1912 but also the Puritan strike of 1911 presented a pronounced pattern of Jewish strikers and non-Jewish strike-breakers. The strike of cloakmakers and skirtmakers at the Puritan factory began when forty-five males and females walked out in protest against wage cuts and the employer's discrimination against ILGWU members. "Who takes the place of the workers in this factory?" asked *Cotton's Weekly*, the newspaper of the Social Democratic Party of Canada. Dramatically, the newspaper exclaimed:

> In British Columbia, when miners rise up in rebellion against the shameful conditions, Chinese are brought into the mines. In this and other Western provinces, Japs, Hindoos, and Indians fill the places of the white toilers because they live on cheaper food and under such intolerable conditions no white people can stand it. Half-castes, ignorant, poverty-stricken and oppressed, slave in Southern mill-yards, plantation fields and swamps.
>
> No nation is supposed to be so advanced as the British nation, no race so progressive as the white. BUT HERE IN TORONTO NO CHINESE, NO HINDOOS, NO JAPS, NO INDIANS, NO BLACKS, NO FOREIGNERS NEED BE IMPORTED, WHITE GIRLS AND MEN OF BRITISH BIRTH

BREAK THE STRIKES. Capitalists need not take the trouble to send to other lands for scabs. WE HAVE THEM ALWAYS READY IN TORONTO. LOYAL, PATRIOTIC CANADIANS, ANXIOUS TO KEEP THEIR JOBS, REFUSE TO GO OUT with strikers who are brave enough to struggle for human treatment. CANADIAN GIRLS ARE HANDED WORK THAT JEWISH GIRLS REFUSE TO DO.[53]

Puritan's non-Jewish cutters apparently refused to join this strike, and *Cotton's Weekly* concluded that "Craft Unionism was shown up as selfish and incompetent, for men of other unions refused to even attempt persuading the English speaking cutters to go out, when asked to do so by the Jewish, who cannot speak English very well."[54]

This newspaper's account of the strike focused particularly on the non-Jewish women who were doing work that formerly had been done by the Jewish strikers. According to this account, "this union realizes that as they are Jewish, racial and religious prejudices are animating the girls to take their places and to decline to go out on strike with Jews."[55] The newspaper declared:

> We are disgusted to find that our Canadian girls are not unwilling to slave "faithfully" and "diligently" at the very work our Jewish comrades who are in the overwhelming majority in this Union would scorn to touch....
>
> But this is no unusual feature in our strikes. The girls and women who have been taught to sing "Britons never never shall be slaves," put to shame the worst of lackeys in their endeavor to "keep in with the boss" and "have nothing to do with Unions or strikes."

"In every strike it is the same," declared *Cotton's Weekly*. "Gentile girls break them. English speaking workers are unwilling to struggle for better conditions, shorter hours or higher pay for fear of losing 'my job.'"[56]

Here, ethnic and gender concerns intertwined significantly: the newspaper's indignation against the female strike-breakers was heightened by "the injustice of [the girls'] act in taking the places of these family men who cannot live on ten dollars per week, a wage that is considered exceptionally good by a single girl." "OH TORONTO WORKING WOMEN, WHY BE SO BLIND, SO SELFISH SO HEARTLESS? SHAME ON THE VAUNTED WARMTH OF WOMANLY HEARTS IF JEWISH WORKINGMEN CAN BE REPLACED BY CHEAP FEMALE LABOR!" exclaimed *Cotton's Weekly*.[57]

ILGWU activists continued to find that Toronto's non-Jewish garment workers tended to respond less favourably to their appeals than did the Jews. In 1916, for example, the *Industrial Banner*, an Ontario labour newspaper, reported that this union had experienced difficulties in trying to capture the interests of the non-Jewish workers. Although the newspaper optimistically declared that the ILGWU's new Gentile organizer was stimulating the non-Jews to become enthusiastic about the union,[58] the problem was by no means solved. In 1917 Toronto's ILGWU was carrying out an ambitious organizing campaign, when some of the employers, including Eaton's, responded by making concessions to try to keep the workers away from the union. Eaton's reduced the work week, increased wages, and instructed its supervisors to be more polite. According to the ILGWU's newspaper, "these concessions, instead of keeping the Jewish workers away from joining the union, enthused them all the more, but [the concessions] influenced a certain number of the gentile women workers in the trade, mainly in the T. Eaton shops." In response, the ILGWU's leaders were relying on the aid of two new non-Jewish organizers, one female and one male, to try to recruit more of Toronto's non-Jewish garment workers.[59] However, these workers remained a problem for the ILGWU.[60]

Toronto's Amalgamated Clothing Workers experienced similar difficulties. In 1918, for example, the *Yiddisher Zhurnal* reported that the city's ACW was hiring non-Jewish organizers "for the non-Jewish [workers] in the trade, whom no one had ever been able to organize."[61] A while later, the ACW and the manufacturers' association signed a new contract that stipulated non-union workers in the association's shops had to join the union. The signing of this agreement "brought into the ranks of the Amalgamated about 1000 members English speaking, the majority of whom had never previously belonged to a trade union." The ACW was faced with the need for a massive internal educational campaign. Although the ACW's anglophone business agent felt that the union was succeeding in instilling "the principles for which we are organised into [the] hearts and minds" of these non-Jewish workers,[62] the non-Jews continued to lag behind.

In 1925, for example, when Toronto's ACW was in the midst of an organizing campaign, the non-Jewish locals were apparently less involved in the campaign and had to be specially urged to participate.[63] Similarly, a year later, when the ACW was involved in two important shop strikes, a union official reporting on strike-support work declared: "What is really wanted now is a little more co-operation from the English speaking members and a special committee will have to be organized for that purpose."[64]

The Jewish needle trades unions continued to experience these kinds of difficulties in the 1930s as well. During the ILGWU's 1931 general strike in Toronto's dress trade, for example, the *Canadian Forum* reported that "the shops employing mostly gentile help" did not join the strike.[65] Non-Jewish workers apparently also posed a problem for the Communist union that was organizing Toronto's dressmakers. In 1935, for example, at a time when the Industrial Union of Needle Trades Workers had contracts with most of the city's dress shops, "nearly everyone of the workers employed in [the] open shops are Anglo-Saxon."[66]

The Jewish unions' difficulties with the non-Jewish garment workers thus took a number of different forms. In some cases, particularly in the early period when these unions were weaker, many of the non-Jews stayed away from the Jewish unions altogether. In other cases, these workers were members of the unions but were significantly less active than their Jewish counterparts. At certain times, such as during the Eaton strike of 1912 and the ILGWU's dress strike of 1931, non-Jewish workers even served as strike-breakers while Jews went out on strike. The deep divisions between the two groups emerged particularly sharply during the large 1932 fur strike, when non-Jews acted as strike-breakers against their Jewish fellow unionists.

Although Jews still constituted less than half of Toronto's garment workers in 1931, they clearly predominated in the labour movement in the city's needle trades in the interwar years. The non-Jewish garment unions, particularly the JTUA and the UGW, were dwarfed by the Jewish unions in this period. Jewish workers tended to be more militant than non-Jews, partly because the activism of the Jewish workers was deeply rooted in a vibrant Jewish working-class culture. The Jewish workers' loyalty to their unions was further reinforced by the ways in which the Jewish unions served a number of special functions for them, over and above the function of collective bargaining. These unions addressed specifically Jewish concerns, such as relief work for Jewish refugees in Eastern Europe and protests against the rise of world Fascism. The unions also served as social and cultural centres for the Jewish immigrants in the strange New World.

While these factors bound the Jewish workers more closely to their unions, however, they probably alienated the non-Jewish workers to a certain extent, thereby deepening the rift between the two groups. The more the unions addressed specifically Jewish concerns, the more the non-Jewish union members may have felt themselves to be outsiders. As a consequence, the non-Jews tended to be less active in the Jewish unions.

The lower level of militancy of the non-Jewish garment workers was also partly a product of language problems. In the 1920s and 1930s, many of the Jewish workers could speak Yiddish in the shop and at the meetings of their locals. In contrast, most of the various non-Jewish, non-English-speaking workers were lumped together in a local that conducted its business in English. Since their command of English was often not good, members of these different ethnic groups had trouble understanding what was going on at union meetings. It is not surprising that this kind of a miscellaneous local, within both the ACW and the ILGWU, had a reputation for being weak.[67] Although most of the non-Jewish garment workers were Anglo-Celtic, this particular aspect of the language problem was significant.

The leaders of Toronto's Jewish unions made some efforts to eliminate the friction between the Jewish and non-Jewish garment workers. These efforts included carefully recruiting non-Jewish organizers and business agents, appealing to union members for understanding, and sometimes even entreating officers of the Toronto Trades and Labour Council to help mediate. However, the Toronto leaders of these garment unions did not make the kinds of

major efforts that historian Steven Fraser claims to have found in his study of Jewish-Italian relations in the ACW's major centres. Fraser argues that the ACW leaders worked hard to reconcile Jews and Italians in the men's clothing centres of North America, contending that these efforts were critical because of the predominance of these two ethnic groups in this branch of the needle trades. Even if he were right about the extent—and success—of the ACW's efforts to unite these particular ethnic groups in New York City (and he would need more evidence to prove his case), clearly these extensive efforts were not being made in Toronto.

This was perhaps partly due to limited local resources and perhaps also to the different ethnic composition of the workforce in Toronto's men's clothing industry, where Italians were a small minority. It may have been an easier task to bring Jewish and Italian immigrants together in early twentieth-century polyglot New York than to unite Jewish and Anglo-Celtic workers in the predominantly Anglo-Celtic city of Toronto. Particularly important is the absence of strong, class-conscious anglophone leadership within the Toronto branches of the "Jewish unions." Although there was an assortment of Anglo-Celtic organizers, business agents, and members of the various unions' joint boards, the Toronto branches of these unions lacked strong, dynamic non-Jewish leaders who might have made major efforts to bring the non-Jews and the Jews closer together.[68]

Throughout the period under consideration, Jewish workers and non-Jewish workers in Toronto's needle trades continued to constitute two fairly separate groups, customarily speaking different languages and organized in separate union locals. Despite the ideal of—and the real need for—working-class solidarity, serious ethnic tensions persisted within the garment unions and often emerged as key factors in the rivalries between particular unions in this sector. In some cases, these tensions were reinforced by the different roles the two groups played in the labour process. The manufacturers often attempted to heighten these tensions, particularly by using anti-Semitic appeals to try to keep the non-Jews from uniting with more militant Jewish workers in the interwar years. Although the anti-Semitism of non-Jewish garment workers did not usually lead to assaults with knuckledusters, this prejudice was an important factor not only during the 1930s but during the earlier part of the twentieth century as well. The ethnocentrism of both the Jewish and the non-Jewish workers also constituted an important factor. Consequently, it was extremely difficult to overcome the deep ethnic divisions within the workforce.

NOTES

[1] Kumove, *Words like Arrows*, 141. The translation from the Yiddish is Kumove's.

[2] H.D. Langer to D. Dubinsky, 12 Oct. 1936, box 74, file 4A, DDP. See also TG and TS, 9 Oct. 1936.

[3] D. Dubinsky to H.D. Langer, 15 Oct. 1936, box 74, file 4A, DDP. Several right-wing populist, anti-Semitic movements arose in the United States during the 1930s. One of the most notorious and influential was headed by Charles E. Coughlin, the Canadian-born "Radio Priest" who broadcast his sensationalist appeals from Detroit.

[4] Calculations based on unpublished disaggregated census data available from Statistics Canada.

[5] On anti-Semitism in Eastern Europe see, for example, Baron, *The Russian Jew under Tsars and Soviets*, 52–75; and Antonovsky, ed., *The Early Jewish Labor Movement*, 18–26. The interviews with Joe Salsberg are especially useful for providing information on anti-Semitism in Toronto.

[6] The interview with Ed Hammerstein, for example, provides useful information.

[7] See, for example, Stowell, *The Journeymen Tailors' Union of America*. 86; Hardy, *The Clothing Workers*, 75, 78–84; and Foner, *Women and the American Labor Movement*, 376–8.

[8] See, for example, Stowell, *The Journeymen Tailors' Union of America*, 38, 51–2, 113–30, 135; T, 15 June 1915. Useful information is also available in the interviews with Ida and Sol Abel and Ed Tannenbaum.

[9] T, 24 Aug. 1915

[10] See, for example, Belkin, *Di Poale Zion Bavegung in Kanade*, 84.

[11] See, for example, Foner, *Women and the American Labor Movement*, 376–8.

[12] See, for example, GW, 7 Jan. and 19 May 1916.

[13] See, for example, *Western Clarion*, 27 Oct. 1906; GW, 10 Jan. 1919; and J. Watt to E.J. Brais, 7 March 1915, box 55, file 14, AC.

[14] H. Madanick to J. Schlossberg, 18 and 25 July, 18 Aug., and 13 Oct. 1917, box 12, file 34, AC. See also Ontario Department of Labour, *Vocational Opportunities*, 5.

[15] J. Blugerman to J. Schlossberg, 4 March 1918, box 9, file 1, and 6, 15, and 16 March 1918, box 55, file 16, AC. The quotation is from 6 March.

[16] The first quotation is from Charles A. Tovey to J. Schlossberg, 10 July 1920, and the second quotation is from H.D. Rosenbloom to J. Potofsky, 16 Sept. 1920, box 55, file 17, AC.

[17] ATJBM, 11 June 1925

[18] The quotation is from ATJBM, 10 Feb. 1927. On this incident see also 22 Feb. 1927. For other examples of friction in this union, see 22 July and 17 Aug. 1926.

[19] ATJBM, 18 August 1927

[20] AGEBM, 27–29 Nov. 1930, 9, box 165, file 14

[21] The quotation is from H.D. Langer to D. Dubinsky, 6 July 1937, box 88, file 1b, DDP.

[22] For general information on the nationalist orientation of the ACCL see, for example, Abella, *Nationalism, Communism, and Canadian Labour*, 44.

[23] LG, Dec. 1933 and April, 1934; ATJBM, 9 and 22 Nov. 1933

[24] M. Finch to W.T. Burford, 5 Feb. 1934, vol. 95, file: "Clothing Workers of Canada ..." CLCC. See also K, 9 March 1934.

[25] CU, May 1935

[26] M. Finch to W.T. Burford, 5 Feb. 1934, vol. 95, file: "Clothing Workers of Canada ..." CLCC

[27] M. Finch to W.T. Burford, 5 Feb. 1934, and [W.T. Burford] to M. Finch, 7 Feb. 1934, vol. 95, file: "Clothing Workers of Canada ..." CLCC

[28] On Finch's ethnocentrism see M. Finch to N.S. Dowd, 9 Dec. 1937 and 6 Dec. 1939, vol. 95, file: "Clothing Workers of Canada ..." CLCC.

[29] E. Smith to Ontario's attorney-general, 21 March 1933, box 9, file: "ILGWU, 1933," RDLO, Office of Deputy Minister, General Subject Files. On Smith's leading role in the ACCL's needle-trades activities in Toronto see, for example, ATJBM, 20 Aug. 1931.

[30] M. Finch to N.S. Dowd, 1 April and 11 Nov. 1938, and 18 March 1939, vol. 95, file: "Clothing Workers of Canada ..."

CLCC. ACCL records also document the NCWC's deep collusion with the employer at another of the few shops this union managed to organize. The actions of the NCWC at this shop were so unethical and so compromising that the ACCL's head office had to repudiate the actions of its own affiliate in this case. See W.T. Burford to W.J. Douglas, 14 Feb. 1935, vol. 159, file: "Toronto N.L. Council, 1935," CLCC. See also Minutes of the National Labour Council of Toronto (ACCL), 15 March 1936, reel M2294, Labour Council of Metropolitan Toronto Collection. Interference in other garment unions' strikes seems to have been the NCWC's main form of organizing.

[31] A. McCormack to A.W. Miller, 27 Jan. 1915, box 20, file 44, IC

[32] A. McCormack to A.W. Miller, 2 March 1915, box 20, file 44, IC

[33] Interview with Ed Hammerstein

[34] IFWUGEBM, meeting of subcommittee of GEB, 12 Aug. 1931, box 3, file 15, 4. For further evidence of ethnic tensions within Toronto's IFWU, see IFWUGEBM, 25–28 Jan. 1937, box 3, file 22.

[35] YZ, 21 July 1932

[36] YZ, 22 and 27 July 1932

[37] YZ, 29 Aug. 1932. See also YZ, 8 Aug. 1932, and W, 13 Aug. 1932.

[38] YZ, 21 Aug. and 4 Sept. 1932; interview with Ed Hammerstein

[39] Interview with Ed Hammerstein

[40] Interview with Jacob Black

[41] Interview with Ed Hammerstein

[42] On the impact of key Canadian businessmen on immigration policy see, for example, Avery, "Dangerous Foreigners," 16–38.

[43] T, Sept. 1912

[44] LGW, April 1912

[45] On the union's defeat in this strike see, for example, LGW, Jan. 1913 (in Yiddish).

[46] YZ, 4 Jan. 1920

[47] YZ, 21 Aug. 1924

[48] YZ, 22 Jan. 1925. See also 5 Feb. 1925.

[49] J, 12 Aug. 1927

[50] RCPSMPE, 4573

[51] Ibid., 4492. See also NC, 4 Aug. 1934. For an earlier incident of the same kind, see, for example, YZ, 27 Aug. 1919.

[52] The quotation is from T, June 1913. See also Dec. 1912 and June 1914.

[53] The quotation is from Cotton's Weekly, 17 Aug. 1911. See also 20 July 1911.

[54] Ibid., 14 Sept. 1911

[55] Ibid., 17 Aug. 1911

[56] Ibid., 20 July 1911

[57] Ibid., 17 Aug. 1911

[58] IB, 1 Dec. 1916

[59] The quotation is from LGW, Feb. 1917. See also June 1917.

[60] See, for example, Biss, "The Dressmakers' Strike," 367.

[61] YZ, 3 Feb. 1925

[62] The quotations are from Charles A. Tovey to J. Schlossberg, 10 July 1920, box 55, file 17, AC. For details on the 1919–20 agreement see the copy of the agreement in PACM.

[63] ATJBM, 13 Aug. 1925

[64] Ibid., 21 Oct. 1926

[65] Biss, "The Dressmakers' Strike," 367. See also IGEBM, 10–16 Feb. 1931, 26.

[66] A. Desser to Charles Zimmerman, 16 June 1935 (enclosure), box 4, file 3, CZP

[67] Interview with Ida and Sol Abel

[68] Fraser includes Toronto in his generalizations about the ACW, failing to notice Toronto's different ethnic composition in this sector and the different timing of Jewish immigration to Canada. Other problems with Fraser's analysis, even as it pertains to New York City, include his lack of understanding of the Jewish nature of the American Jewish labour movement. See Fraser, "Landslayt and Paesani."

Select Bibliography

Manuscript Collections

International Ladies' Garment Workers' Union Archives, New York
David Dubinsky Papers
ILGWU's general executive board minutes

National Archives of Canada, Ottawa
Canadian Labour Congress Collection

Labour Council of Metropolitan Toronto
 Collection

Interviews (pseudonyms have been used for many of the key interviewees)
Ida and Sol Abel, Toronto, 1983
Jacob Black, Toronto, 1971 and 1984
Jim Blugerman, Toronto, 1971 and 1973
Ed Hammerstein, Toronto, 1977, 1983, and 1984

Newspapers
Garment Worker (New York)
Tailor (Bloomington, Illinois)
Western Clarion (Vancouver)
Der Yiddisher Zhurnal (Toronto)

Government Publications
Ontario, Department of Labour, *Vocational Opportunities in the Industries of Ontario: A Survey: Bulletin No. 4: Garment Making* (Toronto 1920)

Books, Pamphlets, Articles, and Theses

Abella, Irving Martin. *Nationalism, Communism, and Canadian Labour: The CIO, the Communist Party, and the Canadian Congress of Labour, 1935–1956.* Toronto 1973

Avery, Donald. *'Dangerous Foreigners': European Immigrant Workers and Labour Radicalism in Canada, 1896–1932.* Toronto 1979

Baron, Salo W. *The Russian Jew Under Tsars and Soviets.* New York 1964

Biss, I.M. 'The Dressmakers' Strike.' *Canadian Forum* 11, 130 (July 1931): 367–9

Fraser, Steven. "*Landslayt* and *Paesani*: Ethnic Conflict and Cooperation in the Amalgated Clothing Workers of America," in Dirk Hoerder, ed., *"Struggle a Hard Battle": Essays on Working-Class Immigrants.* Dekald, Ill., 1986, 280–303

Kumove, Shirley. *Words like Arrows: A Collection of Yiddish Folk Sayings.* Toronto 1984

CHAPTER II

PROLETARIAN IDEOLOGY

CARMELA PATRIAS

$\mathcal{P}$roletarian ideology, in sharp contrast to the accommodationist stance of the patriotic camp, assaulted the very foundations of the established order. Unlike patriotic leaders, whose fear of radicalism led them to assuage the frustration and anger that immigrants felt in response to the difficulties that they experienced, proletarian spokesmen acknowledged these feelings as legitimate reactions to intolerable conditions. Indeed, they tried to focus and harness the immigrants' anger. Through their speeches, the pages of the *Munkás*, and the activities of proletarian associations, communist organizers attempted to explain the causes of the newcomers' plight and to hold out to them a program for radical change.

EXPLAINING THE NEWCOMERS' PLIGHT
Canadian Society and Immigrant Workers
Bringing the whole capitalist system to task, proletarian leaders did not hesitate to point accusingly at those agents of the system whom they considered most directly responsible for the predicament of the immigrants.[1] Among these culprits, Canadian "railway barons" figured prominently. The Canadian railways,

explained the *Munkás* in 1930, benefited most from the exploitation of immigrants. As shareholders in steamship companies, they made profits on steamship tickets sold to them. They profited even more from the sale of railway tickets to these same people, who were forced to travel thousands of kilometres to the west, following their arrival in Canada. The railway magnates continued to exploit the newcomers even after they reached their destination: "On the tremendous expansion of railway lines, which were being extended ever northward, there was a need for cheap labour. Slave labour. To this, immigrant workers who were unfamiliar with the local language and customs, were an easy prey. In the absence of militant labour organizations, they fell defenseless into the clutches of the railway barons." The railway owners also stood to gain from the policy of directing immigrants to the agrarian sector. By breaking the soil, and making it more fertile, as homesteaders or as agricultural labourers, newcomers raised the value of lands owned by the railways. Moreover, these companies also reaped a profit from transporting the product of their labour.[2]

Thus, far from being, as the patriots would have it, the last remaining sector in which immigrants could still find a place under the approving gaze of Canadian authorities, the agrarian sector was just another part of the exploitative capitalist system. Small farmers in Canada, argued proletarian spokesmen, were every bit as exploited as rural labourers and urban workers. They "were the prey of tax collectors, bank collectors, various usurers and a whole swarm of other profiteers and exploiters," and even when their crops were bountiful they could not always provide the barest necessities for their families.[3]

In its discussions of the agrarian sector, the proletarian press paid special attention to the "stoop jobs" in which many Hungarians were engaged. The *Új Előre*, for example, described the exploitation of sugar beet workers, referring specifically to a Hungarian steamship agent, Joseph Schwartz of the Colonists' Service Association in Calgary, whom hundreds of his co-nationals would have encountered during their search for labour: "A Hungarian goes to see him: 'Mr. Schwartz, I heard that you can place beet workers.' 'Yes,' answers the hyena. 'What are the conditions?' 'They are as follows: you have to prepare the soil, buy the seed, do the planting, hoeing, harvesting and cleaning, then transport the produce and perhaps you'll get half of it.'"[4] In the 1930s, when large numbers of Hungarians were forced to seek seasonal agricultural work in central Canada as well, the *Munkás* gave increasing attention to beet and especially tobacco work in southern Ontario.[5]

To convince Hungarians that they would face the injustices of the capitalist system no matter where they turned, the *Új Előre* and the *Munkás* talked about the difficulty of finding work throughout Canada. They explained that the system created a reserve army of unemployed, which permitted it the better to exploit workers.[6] The papers described and condemned practices, such as speed-ups and hav-

ing to bribe the básc (boss) in order to obtain jobs, to which immigrants were forced to acquiesce if they wanted to keep working.[7] They stressed that because of discrimination by employers, immigrants faced greater difficulties than the "English" and "French": "Because we are in a strange land, and we are unfamiliar with its language and customs, our situation is far worse than that of those who are native born or who have lived here for decades. Factory owners know about our vulnerability. When they give us work it is the worst, least well paid, most dangerous work."[8] Proletarian publications carried descriptions of oppressive conditions and low wages in mining, logging camps, construction, factories, and domestic service—all the areas where newcomers were likely to find employment. They paid special attention to the wage-work that women performed at home, "imprisoned" away from fellow workers.[9] These descriptions were unabashedly partisan, calculated to appeal to the emotions:

> At the American Seinement Company of Niagara Falls, a chemical and artificial fertilizer plant, shocking conditions reign. The bodies of the men who work there are being infected by the dust and noxious fumes that the chemicals emit, and scorched by the heat. The municipal authorities want to force the plant to relocate because of the noxious fumes that it emits. In order to put an end to the emission of these fumes, however, the management simply shut off the ventilation system which had removed the gases from the factory, so now the workers breathe in the killer gases. There are absolutely no safety devices, or only very primitive ones which offer no real protection. To acquire new ones would cost money and the company which makes millions of dollars in profits, would

rather sacrifice workers than see its millions diminish by a few dollars.[10]

Proletarian leaders also addressed crowded living conditions in Hungarian boarding-houses. Adam Schaeffer, one of the local editors of the *Munkás*, observed that everywhere in Canada's wealthy cities he had seen immigrants sleeping four to a bed. Undoubtedly with the intention of directing their discontent against the patriotic camp, he added, "I heard one of the Hungarian priests say, about the residents of these boardinghouses, that they should be ashamed of themselves, because they ruin the reputation of the Hungarians in the eyes of English speaking people."[11]

A description of a working-class neighbourhood in Hamilton by Joseph Dohány, the communist organizer who launched the *Munkás*, shows that even experienced proletarian writers did not shy away from exaggeration in order to drive their points home:

I stand in a corner observing the dilapidated shanties. Gaping doors reveal the dirty interiors of these makeshift structures, with broken windows, which are called houses. The abandoned building over there signals that this is the city of Hamilton's working-class quarter. One end of the building is collapsing, while several families live in the other. Their neighbours are the rats, who promenade through the building's abandoned section. I draw closer, so as to be able to take a look among the ruins. The air is stifling. The smell of mold mixes in with the smell of oil which prevails in the area. Among the ruins, working-class children play "house." Just as I approach, one of the girls is saying to the little boy beside her, who appears to be about 6 years old: "Why are you so lazy? Why do you sleep so much? Now you are late for work."[12]

The paper's partisan approach struck a responsive chord. Béla Vágó, for example, decided to join the proletarian camp because of the *Munkás*'s treatment of the condition of workers in Canada: "it spoke explicitly about unemployment and the exploitation of the worker," he explained, "which many of us recognized in time, and therefore we supported the *Munkás* with great enthusiasm…. Of course, it was not a paper that I couldn't understand because of its high level, but what we needed."[13] According to Helen Czukár, one of the oldest members of the proletarian camp in Hamilton, the *Munkás* "was a teacher to the people, who were simple people, they had more time here than back home, they picked up newspapers for the first time and compared them, and they ended up here [in the proletarian camp]. This was their newspaper."[14] Mary Kisko recalled that during the Depression unemployed Hungarians would crowd into the Workers' hall in Welland to read the *Munkás*. Some of them read with such difficulty that it took them hours to finish a single page, she added, but "they sure remembered what they read."[15] Looking back on the role that the paper's explanations played in the lives of Hungarians, another Hungarian-Canadian proletarian explained: "naturally it wrote in such a way as to teach the worker. In my opinion, those who read the *Munkás* developed, and learned to see the world differently from those who did not read our paper."[16]

For if proletarian reporting was more polemical than objective, much of it showed considerable psychological insight. However exaggerated their style, proletarian leaders, through their speeches and writings, communicated their empathy with the plight of immigrant workers. They recognized that a radical explanation of the sources of contemporary ills could mitigate not only the frustration and anger but even the humiliation and helplessness of newcomers unable to make a living. Such analyses of the social and economic problems that racked the capitalist system were especially important during the Depression.

Through stories and letters, the *Munkás* conveyed an understanding of the predicament of unemployed and underemployed immigrants whose relatives in Hungary, not understanding why they stopped sending money home, continued to beg them for financial assistance. The hero of a story that appeared in the *Munkás* almanac in 1936 is János, the native of a small village on the banks of the Tisza, who is forced to migrate to Canada by his family's indebtedness. His father and uncle assume new debts to pay for the journey, but once János gets to Canada he finds work only intermittently, and his meagre earnings are all eaten up by the cost of travelling in search of new work and by the cost of boarding during periods of unemployment. Consequently, he is unable to reimburse his father and uncle. Soon his relatives begin to send him letters full of complaints. After he waits in vain for two years to be repaid, his father's letters become bitter. "You don't want to work," he writes, "because if you wanted to, you would have money. You have probably become a rake in the midst of plenty … but you should know, that soon all our possessions will be auctioned off, and in our old age we will be homeless." János's uncle warns him that he will drive his father to his grave. János, who has not yet joined the proletarian camp, simply despairs. His father commits suicide, leaving behind an accusing note, which János's relatives forward to him in Canada.[17]

In a fictitious letter that appeared in the *Munkás*, another young Hungarian finds himself in a similar situation. Unlike János, however, this man is acquainted with proletarian ideology. He is therefore able to explain to his mother why he is unemployed: "because in their eyes I am a lousy worker, the scum of this social order which rests on the exploitation of workers. I have less value than a dog, although they maintain their thieving reign through my, and our, that is the workers', sweat and blood. Because inner economic problems, the warning signs of the collapse of capitalism, which is on its last legs, require that their regime, condemned to extinction by historical development, be injected with my misery, my hunger and my being thrown out on the street."[18]

Just how closely these didactic, melodramatic accounts reflected the plight of unemployed workers with families in Hungary is illustrated by the similarity between János's letter and that of Sándor Hajas to his aged parents in Böhönye, Somogy county, which was confiscated by the Hungarian Ministry of the Interior.[19] The letter conveys the pain and guilt that Hajas felt because he was unable to help his parents. It also shows that some newcomers found deliverance from guilt and despair by adopting the explanations that proletarian leaders offered. Hajas tells his parents that his "world view in its entirety has completely changed." He offers a rather confused description of the workings of the capitalist system and of the causes of the Depression, revealing that the change in his thinking was brought about by contact with communist ideas. Hajas's letter suggests that even if he did not have a very thorough understanding of these ideas, they did provide him with hope. He concludes by assuring his parents: "we are getting closer and closer to liberation by the day."[20]

FIGURE 11.1: "This is how government relief provides for unemployed workers," *Kanadai Magyar Munkás*, **13 July 1933.**

World Affairs

In keeping with the Communist party's internationalist line, proletarian leaders placed discussion of the class struggle, and of the Depression as the ultimate manifestation of the inherent instability of capitalism, in a global context. The *Munkás* relied on the *Új Előre* and on the English-language communist press for its coverage of international affairs.[21] The paper, the speeches of proletarian leaders, and discussions in proletarian associations dutifully followed the party line in their treatment of world events.

Until 1935, in keeping with Comintern directives, proletarian leaders were bent on demonstrating to Hungarians that capitalist states were attempting to unleash an imperialist war to destroy the Soviet Union and with it the hopes of workers everywhere.[22] After 1935, when the Comintern's Popular Front policy was officially proclaimed, differences between Western democracies and the USSR were minimized and the need for all anti-fascist forces to cooperate against Hitler was stressed.[23]

While it raged, the Spanish Civil War dominated the international concerns of the proletarians. Leaders explained that the Republican forces in Spain were at the forefront of the struggle against fascism, and they attempted to mobilize the Hungarians behind them. One hundred and ten young immigrants responded by going to fight—12 of them to die—for the Republican cause.[24]

The participation of the young volunteers heightened proletarian awareness of the struggle against fascism. The civil war became one of the main subjects of discussion within Workers' clubs.[25] Committees were established within all proletarian organizations to aid the Republicans, and the pages of the *Munkás* were filled with letters from the volunteers who were fighting in Spain.[26]

The signing of the Nazi-Soviet pact in August 1939 placed proletarian leaders, like all communists in the West, in an awkward position. They had to explain how the "fatherland of the proletariat" could conclude a treaty of friendship and non-aggression with the world's leading fascist power. The *Munkás* played down the importance of the pact and continued to print anti-fascist articles. In contrast to the Popular Front days, however, it now minimized the differences between Hitler's Germany and western European democracies. It dubbed Britain and France the "Munichist" powers and claimed that their readiness to betray the Soviet Union forced it to conclude the pact with Hitler.[27]

Horthyist Hungary

But while Hungarian immigrants were thus exposed to communist analysis of world events, examples of the evils of capitalism were still most commonly situated in Canada or in Hungary, the two countries with which they were most immediately concerned. We have already seen how some of those aspects of Canadian society that were of special relevance to immigrant workers were treated by the proletarian leaders.

Vigyázzatok — VÉRES!

Magyar Testvérek!

A „MAGYAR FELTÁMADÁS" című film — történelmi HAMISÍTVÁNY! A Felvidék magyarsága — sajnos! — nem támadt fel, hanem a KISEBB bajból a NAGYOBBA esett. A TŰRHETŐBB csehszlovákiai kisebbségi sorsból, a DEMOKRÁCIÁBÓL beleesett, belezuhant a TŰRHETETLENBE, a fojtogató FASIZMUS karmaiba!

SAJÁT véreitek leveleinek hisztek-e inkább, vagy a hazaáruló labanc HORTHYNAK és az ő ügynökségének: a RE-TA filmtársaságnak?

VÉREITEK panaszkodnak!

„CSALÓDÁS ÉS KESERŰSÉG LETT AZ, AMINEK ÖRÖMNEK KELLETT VOLNA LENNIE!"

Horthy meghozta a „feltámadást"? A magyar és szlovák urak egymásra uszították a magyar és szlovák népet. GYILKOLTAK és GYILKOLJÁK őket!

Bombáztatták KASSÁT, ROZSNYÓT, IGLÓT!

S mi lett a vége? HITLER marsolt be a FELVIDÉKRE! Ezért kellett a csehszlovák demokráciát szétrobbantani? Ezért kellett a revízió? EZÉRT! Mert úgy parancsolta Hitler és Mussolini a magyarul csak gagyogó Horthynak!

HORTHY csak eszköze, BÉRENCE — Hitler-Mussolininek!

Magyarországot KI AKARJÁK FOSZTANI! Már fosztják is!

A magyar népet KENŐCSNEK SZÁNTÁK a fasiszta tengelyre!

Ne higyj (demokratikus) magyar a (fasiszta) németnek!

Magyarországnak DEMOKRÁCIA és SZABADSÁG kell! — Kanadának is!

KIK vannak a RE-TA mögött? Kérdezzétek meg a wellandi szövőgyári munkásokat és akiket miattuk kidobtak a munkából. Pacsuta András a kanadai királyi biztosság által a leleplezett éhbérek és sorvasztó munkaviszonyok miatt indított szövősztrájk elárulója, a „nem-sztrájkolók" elnöke volt 1937-ben. Imre József, a „filmtársaság" ügynöke e hetekben jött vissza Magyarországból, 1937-ben a szövőbárók rendelkezésére bocsájtotta Kis Ujságját a sztrájkoló katolikusok, reformátusok és a többiek ellen!

LE A FASIZMUSSAL! — KI INNEN AZ ÜGYNÖKEIVEL!

Ne tűrjük a magyar név és becsület beszennyezését!

VÉDJÜK MEG A KANADAI DEMOKRÁCIÁT

a Torontói Magyar Kultúr Klub.

●

The RE-TA is showing a FASCIST film!

This film is glorifying the killing of czechoslovak democracy! Horthy as the "Saviour" of the Hungarian people!

HORTHY is a TRAITER!

He is a hireling, a dirty tool of

HITLER and MUSSOLINI!

Imre and Pacsuta of the Re-Ta were the breakers of the wavers' strike in Welland, 1937. Imre just come back from Budapest.

DOWN WITH FASCISM! — OUT WITH IT'S AGENTS!

DEFEND THE CANADIAN DEMOCRACY!

The Hungarian Cultural Club of Toronto.

FIGURE 11.2: Proletarian flyer denouncing *Hungarian Resurrection*, Toronto, 1939.

For more general discussions of politics and current events, they relied on their English-Canadian comrades. The *Munkás*'s staff, for example, regularly borrowed articles from the *Worker*, the English-language newspaper of the Communist party in Canada, and translated them into Hungarian.[28]

The proletarian movement's relentless criticism of Horthyist Hungary formed an integral part of its competition with the patriotic camp for the hearts and minds of immigrants. Proletarian leaders feared that under the combined impact of homesickness and the revisionist campaign of the Horthyist regime, expatriates would forget the harsh conditions that forced them to emigrate and would ally themselves to the patriotic camp.[29]

By refuting the argument that the Treaty of Trianon was the main cause of social and economic problems in interwar Hungary, and hence also of emigration, proletarian spokesmen struck at the central tenet of the patriotic camp. They reminded the newcomers that even before the First World War the lives of workers and peasants in Greater Hungary, whatever their ethnic origin, had been extremely difficult.[30] To the disinherited, they argued, the redrawing of borders changed only the nationality of their exploiters. The condition of workers in the successor states was no worse than that of their brothers and sisters in Hungary.[31] Those seriously affected by the nation's loss of two-thirds of its prewar territory belonged to the upper and middle classes—large landowners, whose estates now fell under the jurisdiction of foreign governments, and civil servants in the employ of the government when it lost control of Slovakia and Transylvania. According to proletarian leaders, these groups, hiding under the guise of patriotism, but motivated entirely by self-interest, were partly responsible for the launching of the revanchist campaign.[32] Their bellicose propaganda was intended to convince workers to shed their blood for the capitalists and landowners in the eventuality of war with the successor states, just as they had done during the First World War.

Proletarian spokesmen further claimed that the campaign for revision of Trianon served the interests of landlords and industrialists whose properties fell entirely within post-Trianon Hungary. According to them, the ruling classes promoted revisionism because, by fanning the flames of lower-class patriotism, they could distract workers and peasants from terrible economic oppression.[33] Not only were urban and rural workers paid poorly, argued the *Munkás*, but they also carried almost the total weight of the nation's taxes.[34] Even small holders were fast sinking into the ranks of the proletariat under that burden.[35] Their great poverty led peasant women to seek abortions, and although this step was the product of necessity, not choice, they were nevertheless liable to severe punishment if caught.[36]

According to the *Munkás*, the Hungarian system was so unjust that the ruling class could not rely solely on the promotion of patriotism among the lower classes to safeguard capitalism. Consequently, it deliberately kept workers and peasants ignorant by depriving them of proper education. The Horthy regime, moreover, ruthlessly crushed any individual or group for attempting to enlighten them about the unfairness of their predicament and to encourage them to struggle against the oppressor.[37]

Not Trianon, argued proletarian spokesmen, but economic exploitation, reinforced by political oppression, forced emigration: "We are here because for the past 15 years the Hungarian ruling class, the executioners of the Hungarian people, have been spilling the blood of our brothers, and keeping thousands of them behind somber prison walls. Those who are not in jail, are starved, overtaxed, surrounded by stool pigeons and punished harshly for crimes they did not commit. They banished us from our native land by depriving us of our livelihood, by oppression, by inequity and by tyranny."[38] Relatives and friends who remained at home, argued the proletarians, were still subject to these intolerable conditions.[39]

This analysis was readily accepted by some Hungarian immigrants and convinced them to join the proletarian camp. George Palotás, drawn to the Montreal Workers' Club by a need for companionship, began to pay close attention to the political discussions held in the evenings. Members spoke about conditions prior to emigration: "they spoke about how we were exploited, like three million beggars in Hungary, and until then I never heard this, and that there was great poverty in Hungary and so on … and how the Hungarian bourgeoisie exploited us, and about the war, the orphans, and I was one."[40]

The Patriotic Camp

According to the leaders of the proletarian camp, the activities of patriotic leaders in Canada constituted a mere extension of the efforts by Hungary's ruling class to manipulate and exploit workers and peasants in the homeland.[41] Not only Budapest's official representatives in Canada, but also patriotic leaders, editors of patriotic newspapers, and clergymen, acted as the regime's agents. Through the pages of the Új Előre and the Munkás, and through their speeches, proletarian leaders purported to reveal the methods and institutions whereby these "Horthyist agents" tried to manipulate Hungarians in Canada. They correctly identified the Kanadai Magyar Ujság,[42] books and flags sent by the Hungarian government to immigrant associations in Canada, and such promotional activities as the Perényi tour, the

erection of the Kossuth statue in the United States, and the organization of international congresses for expatriates as means devised by the regime to transmit its propaganda to co-nationals abroad.[43] But the proletarians readily saw the hands of Budapest even behind such patriotic institutions as the non-subsidized patriotic press, and the Canadian Hungarian Association, which were actually founded by members of the ethnic group.[44]

Some immigrants, such as István Tóth, welcomed this analysis. Before he discovered the Munkás, Tóth had stopped reading Hungarian newspapers in Canada because "they did nothing but praise Hungary—the country which we were forced to leave by the thousand." The Munkás's analysis of Hungarian society was one of the factors that drew him into the proletarian camp.[45]

Proletarian leaders believed that patriotic ideology was itself manipulative. The patriots claimed to be politically neutral in order to gain immigrants' support for objectives with distinct political content, while they denounced as political, and hence somehow reprehensible, everything done on behalf of the working class.[46] According to their opponents, moreover, the patriots were willing enough to appropriate and use folk culture in order to arouse public sympathy for Hungary in Canada, but they deliberately neglected to explain to Canadians under what conditions the creators of this folk culture were forced to live in their native land.[47]

Proletarian critics also rejected the patriots' accommodationism. In response to a call from Reverend Ferenc Nagy of Welland for lawful, orderly behaviour, the Munkás wrote bitterly: "that we are being kicked out of factories, that we are being deported, that doctors do not make house calls to the unemployed, all of this is nothing. We should forget it and be good citizens."[48] The condition of immigrant workers defied accommodation to the status quo. Proletarians saw in Ottawa's policy of deporting indigent immigrant workers the clearest example that Hungarians would be acquiescing in victimization and exploitation if they followed the advice of patriotic leaders. Their only salvation was to organize and demand unemployment insurance.[49]

Proletarian accounts claimed, moreover, that economic, as well as ideological, considerations moved members of Hungary's ruling class to follow immigrants to Canada. Former army officers, gendarmes, and bureaucrats accompanied them on their journey because they recognized that in the New World these people would easily fall prey to their machinations because of their inability to speak English and their ignorance of Canadian laws and customs. In Canada, these men, whom the *Új Előre* described as "hyenas,"[50] served as the newcomers' bankers, notaries, employment agents, and steamship and real estate agents, all the while robbing their unsuspecting customers. Proletarian spokesmen were not above levelling unfounded accusations against steamship agents who in fact acted in keeping with accepted business practices. Despite explicit proletarian criticism of anti-Semitism, some members even used anti-Semitic slurs in an effort to discredit steamship agents.[51] The fact that these agents, most of whom also sold life insurance, presented direct competition to the Canadian Hungarian Mutual Benefit Federation undoubtedly contributed to the acrimony of the denunciations. Yet the proletarians argued that these "class enemies" of the ordinary immigrant, motivated by gain, were alone responsible for dividing the newcomers. Vehement opposition to the left was fuelled by recognition that radicals "stood in their way to the workers' pockets."[52]

Of all attacks against the patriots by the proletarians, however, the most relentless were

those against the clergy. Indeed, proletarian anti-clericalism was so ruthless that even some members of that camp found it offensive.[53] But their leaders persisted. Their anti-clericalism had its roots in the anti-religious traditions of the left. The virulence of this campaign, however, which equalled that of the patriots' anti-communist efforts, suggests that this element was also an integral part of the competition with the patriots to win over the immigrants. Communist organizers recognized that within the ethnic group clerics were their most formidable opponents. Consequently, in trying to discredit these "agents who trafficked in heavenly peace,"[54] no attacks seemed too ungentlemanly. Proletarians accused the clergy of appropriating funds collected by the church and of performing religious and social services only in return for hefty fees.[55] Since proletarian leaders knew that Hungarian clergymen in Canada received their salaries from Canadian churches, they also accused them of having entered the service of domestic capitalism. Behind the readiness of the churches to train Hungarian missionaries, to pay their salaries, and to subsidize their newspapers, they saw the hand of Ottawa anxious to train leaders who could "pacify, calm and quiet down the bankrupt, hungry, dissatisfied masses."[56]

PROPOSALS FOR CHANGE

Women were seen as the chief victims of manipulation by the clergy, and hence as the principal purveyors of "reactionary" attitudes within the ethnic group. Accordingly, communist organizers, in their campaign to raise class consciousness, paid special attention to the reeducation of women. "We working-class mothers are doubly exploited under the capitalist system, first as wives and mothers and secondly as breadwinners," argued the *Munkás*.[57] Women were encouraged to participate as equals in all the activities of proletarian associations, "to get away from their enslavement in the kitchen."[58] To free them to do so, the *Munkás* urged Hungarian men to begin their political activism in their homes, to make their households "democratic" by helping with domestic chores.[59] Through the press and pamphlets, proletarian leaders attempted to introduce Hungarian women to the writings of such prominent members of the communist movement as Alexandra Kollontai and Klara Zetkin.[60]

Unfortunately, the vagaries of party line rather than deep conviction seemed to inform the proletarian approach to women's issues. In 1934, the *Munkás* firmly supported women's right to abortions, pointing out that laws against it were class legislation: bourgeois women with money could obtain safe abortions despite the laws, whereas working-class women were forced to go to back-alley abortionists and many died as a consequence. By late 1936, when a new ruling made abortions illegal in the Soviet Union, the *Munkás* also reversed its position.[61]

The proletarian analysis of the evils of capitalism in Canada and in Hungary, of the machinations of its agents within the ethnic group, and of the oppression of women were counterbalanced by highly idealized accounts of life in the USSR. The preoccupation with the USSR was undoubtedly a response to the Comintern's directive that workers all over the world should be mobilized in support of the "fatherland of the proletariat," which stood in grave danger from the bellicose, imperialist designs of the world's capitalist nations.[62] But stories about full employment, short workdays, excellent working conditions, full equality between the sexes, free medical care, paid vacations, and the like in the Soviet Union, also served to underline the inequities of capitalism, and to provide more clearly defined dimensions to the type of alternative system that workers should strive to bring about.[63]

If proletarian leaders were circumspect concerning the relationship between their organizations and the Communist party, they stated quite openly that immigrants could hasten the advent of a Soviet-type society both in Canada and in Hungary by supporting that party.[64] In this respect, as in all others, Hungarian communists in Canada conscientiously followed the party line.

Until 1934, when communists everywhere took the first steps towards creating a Popular Front against fascist forces, Hungarian communist organizers in Canada argued that in this country only the Communist party represented the interests of the working class, and they denounced as "social fascists" more moderate, reformist parties such as the Co-operative Commonwealth Federation (CCF).[65] They urged Hungarians to join only unions that belonged to the communist-led Workers' Unity League (WUL).[66] Trades and Labour Congress (TLC) unions, these organizers argued, only pretended to represent workers; in reality they acted on behalf of employers.[67] Since, of all the areas in which WUL unions were active, Hungarians were represented in significant numbers only in mining, much of the proletarian discussion of the relative merits of the two types of unions centred on a comparison between the Mine Workers' Union of Canada and the United Mine Workers of America. The former was denounced as a fascist organization that discriminated against "foreigners."[68] The proletarians' campaign to organize immigrant workers extended to the unemployed. They urged unemployed Hungarians to join the Unemployed Workers' Association, explaining that participation did not increase the threat of deportation, since indigence, as well as radicalism, was grounds for such action.

Similarly, until introduction of the Popular Front policy, the proletarian camp in Canada accepted only the small, illegal Hungarian Communist party as the legitimate and sincere defender of the interest of workers and peasants in the homeland.[69] Accordingly, the arrests and trials of communists in Hungary received extensive coverage in the *Munkás*, as did the campaigns organized by the International Red Aid on behalf of these imprisoned communists.[70] Members of proletarian groups in Canada participated actively in these campaigns, by raising funds for the defence of the prisoners, by circulating petitions demanding their release, and by sending letters of protest to Hungarian authorities.[71] The most intensive effort focused on Mátyás Rákosi. Arrested and imprisoned in 1925 for his role in the Communist party, Rákosi, a member of the Hungarian party's Central Committee, was retried in 1934, just as his first sentence was about to come to an end, and he was reincarcerated. The illegality of this treatment aroused international protest.[72]

Following introduction in 1934 of the Popular Front policy, however, support for reformist parties, and for non-communist trade unions, suddenly became permissible and even encouraged.[73] Communist organizers now encouraged Hungarians in Canada to collaborate with the CCF and to join the mainstream of the Canadian labour movement, and after 1937 they threw their full support behind the American-based Committee for Industrial Organization (CIO).[74]

The proletarian view of politics in the homeland also changed. After the Communist party there allied itself with the populist movement, which advocated radical agrarian reform among other goals, the *Munkás* frequently published articles by and about populist writers.[75] In the late 1930s, when the financial situation of their organizations was improving, proletarian leaders also printed and disseminated copies of books and pamphlets by such leading Hungarian populists as József Darvas, Gyula Illyés, and Péter Veres.

In an effort to comply with the Popular Front policy, proletarian leaders even tried for rapprochement with the patriots. They approached patriotic associations, asking them to participate in protests against unemployment.[76] On a number of occasions they also sought joint commemoration of Hungarian national holidays.[77] Within the ethnic group, however, the reversal in attitudes that the Comintern's new policy required was not very successful. Despite their conciliatory gestures, proletarian leaders apparently found it impossible to suppress their hostility. In the proletarian press, for example, attacks on the clergy persisted even while proletarian delegates visited Hungarian-Canadian congregations and asked for their cooperation.[78] Not surprisingly, the patriots viewed the abrupt change with suspicion and generally rejected these overtures.[79]

Whatever the vagaries of party line, however, the proletarians' program ultimately implied transcendence of ethnic boundaries. Proletarian leaders apparently saw no contradiction between promoting the preservation of the Hungarian language and encouraging collaboration with workers from other ethnic groups. "The cultivation of our language and culture [is a question] of life and death for Hungarian Canadians," argued one leader. Rank and file members stated that the company of fellow nationals and speeches and performances in their own language were among the features that inspired them to join the proletarians.[80] Like the patriots, they too feared that unless their children were taught their language and culture, generational conflict would develop.[81] Yet, as we see below, Hungarians were mobilized through the Benefit Federation and through the Workers' clubs to become involved in the struggle of the working class alongside people from other ethnic groups, as well as the Canadian-born.[82]

The internationalism of proletarian ideology, like its anti-clericalism and its revolutionary attitude towards women and the family, exemplifies the radical reorientation in thought that communist organizers hoped to bring about among Hungarian immigrants. They recognized that the newcomers might initially be more responsive to the patriotic call for ethnic preservation than to proletarian internationalism. The *Munkás* stated: "The majority of Hungarian workers ... find it difficult to understand that they must join the same organization as other immigrant workers and native workers and that united we must take up the struggle against the attacks of organized capitalism. The majority of Hungarian immigrant workers are chauvinistic, filled with patriotic feelings, which obscure from their view the suffering of workers who speak different languages."[83]

But the communist organizers sent from the United States were not deterred by the formidable task of convincing immigrants to abandon their traditional views. Indeed, because of their involvement in the oppositionary, and at times illegal, socialist and communist movements, these organizers were well prepared to carry out programs of recruitment and politicization under adverse conditions.

Notes

1 *Új Előre*, 16 June 1928; *Munkás*, 24 July 1930, 24 August 1934.

2 *Munkás*, 24 July 1930.

3 *Új Előre*, 2 April 1927; *Munkás*, 3 July 1930, 20 October, 25 August 1932, 5 February 1935.

4 *Új Előre*, 16 June 1928; see also 29 January 1927. *Munkás*, 26 May 1932, 15 June 1933, 20 January 1937.

5 See, for example, *Munkás*, 12 February 1931, 3 February, 21 July, 22 September, 27 October 1932, 15 June, 17 August 1933, 15 February, 25 December, 28 December 1934.

6 Ibid., 22 January 1930.

7 *Új Előre*, 5 November 1926; *Munkás*, 5 June 1930, 5 March 1931.

8 *Munkás*, 16 July 1929.

9 On home work, see *Munkás*, 3 April 1930. On discrimination against immigrant workers, see *Munkás*, 9 June, 7 July 1932, 24 August 1934.

10 Ibid., 12 September 1929.

11 Schaeffer, "Munkássorsok gazdag Kanadában," 50.

12 *Munkás*, 5 September 1929.

13 Interview with Béla Vágó, November 1976, Toronto.

14 Interview with Helen Czukár, March 1980, Hamilton.

15 Interview with Mary Kisko, 3 March 1980, Welland.

16 Interview with Mary Polyoka, 26 February 1980, Hamilton.

17 Marczi, "Az utolsó állomás."

18 *Munkás*, 30 December 1929.

19 See above, 73.

20 Sándor Hajas to József Hajas, n.d., Interior records, 651f2/1933-6047, IPH. Because of Hajas's involvement in the proletarian camp, the ministry kept a file on him. The file contains copies of his letters home, which were intercepted by postal officials. It also contains a letter from Sándor's father to the Immigrant Aid Bureau in which he explains that he is very concerned about his son, who sent him a picture "and he is so thin, you can barely recognize him. This hurts a parent." Hajas humbly inquires whether the bureau could not help to bring Sándor home. He explains: "although we are very poor, if only we could see our dear child once more, we would be rich."

21 Blaskó memoirs, 70; Vörös, *American Commissar*, 203, 206.

22 See, for example, speech by Lautner, an organizer from the United States, to Windsor Workers' Club, *Munkás*, 13 November 1930; see also 20 July, 27 July, 12 October 1929.

23 *Munkás*, 14 January, 16 January, 25 January 1936.

24 Blaskó memoirs, 107; Szőke, *We Are Canadians*, 80.

25 *Munkás*, 1 October 1936.

26 Ibid., 16 October 1936, 19 August, 12 June, 19 July, 14 August 1937.

27 Ibid., 26 August, 29 August 1939.

28 Vörös, *American Commissar*, 206.

29 *Új Előre*, 1 February 1929.

30 Ibid.; *Munkás*, 22 August 1929, 27 August, 20 May 1931, 14 September, 19 October 1934.

31 *Munkás*, 11 June 1935, 6 August 1931, 16 November 1934.

32 Ibid., 12 June 1930.

33 *Új Előre*, 8 January 1929; *Munkás*, 22 August 1929.

34 Speech given by József Dohány to Toronto workers, *Munkás*, 24 July 1929.

35 Ibid., 16 July, 24 October 1929, 2 August, 21 August 1934.

36 Ibid., 31 May 1934.

37 Ibid., 31 May 1934, 16 July 1929.

38 Ibid., 29 August 1929, 19 March 1931. István Szőke to World Federation of Hungarians, 14 August 1938, Federation records, P 975, Ka 139, NAH.

39 *Munkás*, 26 July 1934.

40 Interview with George Palotás, July 1980, Szamosszeg, Hungary.

41 Speech by Mihály Pásztor, Hamilton, *Munkás*, 10 October 1929; speech by József Dohány, Toronto, ibid., 24 July 1929; *Új Előre*, 11 February, 28 February, 28 December 1928.

42 *Új Előre*, 20 November 1925.

43 Ibid., 28 December 1928; *Munkás*, 11 October 1933; *Új Előre*, 19 April, 31 March 1928; *Munkás*, 24 July 1929, 13 March, 17 April 1930.

44 *Új Előre*, 26 August 1926, 27 February, 20 March, 26 March 1928; *Munkás*, 24 October, 24 July 1930.

45 Tóth, *23 év*, 156–7.

46 *Munkás*, 15 September 1932, 5 January 1934; *Úttörő*, 22 October 1936.

47 *Munkás*, 29 May 1937. Medgyesi, "Munkás kulturát," 99.

48 *Munkás*, 14 September 1934.

49 Ibid., 16 June 1932, 30 June 1932, 22 January 1930, 9 March 1933.

50 *Új Előre* 7 May, 8 January 1928. See also *Munkás*, 29 August 1929.

51 *Munkás*, 29 April 1931, *Úttörő*, 3 October 1929.

52 *Új Előre*, 8 January 1929.

53 Interviews with Mary Gabura, 31 January 1977, Toronto, and Sándor Egyed, June 1982, Niagara Falls; *Munkás*, 25 May 1933.

54 *Új Előre*, 8 July 1927.

55 Ibid., 2 November 1927, 1 October 1928; *Munkás*, 21 November 1929, 13 March, 20 March 1930, 2 July 1931, 12 July 1935.

56 *Munkás*, 28 August 1934.

57 Ibid., 12 July 1934.

58 Ibid., 8 March 1935.

59 Minutes, 27 August 1933, Central Committee of the Workers' Clubs, Records of Workers' Clubs, Puskás collection, MHSO; *Munkás*, 27 March, 3 April 1930, 15 February 1934, 8 March 1935.

60 The *Munkás* had a special women's column. See, for example, *Munkás*, 1934, 1937; on the distribution of pamphlets by Communist women, report on Mrs. János Lancsa, of Windsor, Interior records, 651f2/1936-4298, IPH.

61 *Munkás*, 16 August 1934, 15 October 1936.

62 Carr, *Twilight of Comintern*, 8.

63 *Munkás*, 21 August 1934, 30 November, 31 December 1930, 13 July 1933.

64 Ibid., 24 October 1929, 3 July 1930, 20 May, 21 July 1931, 17 November 1932, 24 May 1934, 2 January 1937.

65 Ibid., 28 April, 12 May 1932, 27 July, 23 February 1933, 8 January, 8 March, 21 June, 19 July 1934.

66 Ibid., 12 September 1929, 7 September, 2 October 1934.

67 Ibid., 5 September 1929, 22 January 1930.

68 See, for example, ibid., 18 September 1930, 1 April 1931, 21 July 1932, 12 October 1933.

69 Ibid., 4 September 1930.

70 See, for example, ibid., 10 July 1930, 17 August, 25 August 1932, 4 May, 24 August 1933, 7 September, 14 September, 21 September 1934, 19 April 1935.

71 Ibid., 12 February 1935, 16 August 1936.

72 Kovrig, *Communism*, 97, 99, 132.

73 *Munkás*, 5 March 1935.

74 Ibid., 18 February, 18 May 1937, 13 April 1932. For a discussion of CIO activities in Canada and the Communist party, see Abella, *Nationalism*, chap. 1.

75 *Munkás*, 22 October 1936, 23 January, 13 February, 20 May 1937.

76 *50 éves a Szent Erzsébet*, 10; Minutes, 6 February 1935, Church Council, Records of the First Hungarian Presbyterian Church of Toronto, MHSO.

77 *Munkás*, 15 March 1934; Minutes, 14 November 1934, Hungary.

78 *Munkás*, 12 July, 19 July, 26 July, 30 July 1935, 18 July 1938; *A Kanadai Magyar Munkás Naptára* (1937), passim.

79 See, for example, *Munkás*, 18 January, 19 February 1935, 27 June 1936, 20 February 1937.

80 Interview with George Palotás, July 1980, Szamosszeg, Hungary.

81 *Munkás*, 18 May 1937.

82 See below, chap. 10.

83 *Munkás*, 8 September 1932.

SELECT BIBLIOGRAPHY

Manuscripts

Hungary

Budapest

Institute for Party History (IPH)
Records of the Ministry of the Interior (Interior records).

Canada

TORONTO

Multicultural History Society of Ontario (MHSO)
Records of the John Calvin Hungarian Presbyterian Church, Hamilton.

Interviews

Hungary

Budapest

Collection of Julianna Puskás (Puskás collection). 6 interviews.

Canada

Hull

Museum of Civilization. Folk Studies Centre
Collection of Linda Degh and Andrew Vázsonyi (Degh-Vázsonyi collection). 110 interviews.

Montreal

Collection of Rev. Aldár Komjáthy. 2 interviews.

Toronto

Collection of Carmela Patrias. 60 interviews.

Multicultural History Society of Ontario (MHSO)
Collection of Julianna Puskás (Puskás collection). 13 interviews.
Collection of Susan Papp-Zubrits. 5 interviews.
Delhi Project. 17 interviews.

Newspapers and Periodicals

Kanadai Magyar Munkás (Munkás) (Hamilton and Toronto).
Új Előre (New York).

All Other Sources

Carr, E.H. *Twilight of Comintern.* London: Macmillan, 1982.

Marczi, György. "Az utolsó állomás" (The Last Stop). In *A Kanadai Magyar Munkás naptára* (Almanac of the Canadian Hungarian Worker), 116–19, 134–6. Toronto: Kanadai Magyar Munkás, 1936.

Schaeffer, Ádám. "Munkássorsok gazdag Kanadában" (Workers' Destinies in Wealthy Canada). *A Kanadai Magyar Munkás naptára* (Almanac of the *Kanadai Magyar Munkás*), 47–52. Toronto: Kanadai Magyar Munkás, 1936.

Szőke, István. *We Are Canadians: The National Group of Hungarian Canadians.* Toronto: Hungarian Literature Association, 1954.

Vörös, Sándor. *American Commissar.* Philadelphia and New York: Chilton Co. Book Division, 1961.

FURTHER READING

Avery, Donald. *"Dangerous Foreigners": European Immigrant Workers and Labour Radicalism in Canada.* Toronto: McClelland and Stewart, 1979.

This is a well-researched account of the contribution of immigrant workers in Canada's economic development. It outlines the circumstances and conditions of their work, as well as the appeal of labour radicalism in the scattered railway construction, lumbering, and mining camps. Avery clearly demonstrates that many immigrant workers were not simply agriculturalists gone astray; they were brought into the country by the government (often at the behest of large companies) to do the dirty and unpleasant work most Canadians and North European immigrants refused to do. This is an important book about immigration and labour radicalism in Canada.

Carter, Sarah A., *Lost Harvests: Prairie Indian Reserve Farmers and Government Policy*. Montreal and Kingston: McGill-Queen's University Press, 1990.

Sarah Carter's book examines Canada's policies and Native responses over the past century as they apply to western agricultural development. Her book succeeds in dispelling the myths of indolence and cultural inferiority that pervade attitudes toward the failures of Native farmers. Carter's research shows that the Plains Indians recognized early on a need to turn to an agricultural base in order to feed themselves in the future. Not only did they display a strong willingness to learn and desire to succeed as farmers, but they also showed an admirable perseverance and patience in the face of misguided and paternalistic government policies that served only to subvert their best efforts.

PART IV

GATE-KEEPING: ENEMIES WITHOUT AND WITHIN

From the turn of the century until World War II (and beyond), Canada was concerned with policing its borders both from within and without. Similar to its concern with "dangerous" workers, the state, through various official and unofficial agents of state power, actively policed Canada's borders, literally as well as figuratively. They assumed, and were entrusted with, the responsibility for determining who belonged in Canada and who did not.

Here we will be focusing on aspects of the overarching theme of gate-keeping, which figured so prominently in turn-of-the-century race and immigration debates and the internment of the Japanese during World War II. In both instances, there was a clear relationship among ideas about "race" and racial hierarchies, culture, and national belonging.

The first two chapters, by Mariana Valverde and Angus McLaren, explore the link between ideas about "racial purity" and "racial hygiene" and how these ideas were mobilized to inspire a racially exclusive vision of nation building. Various players articulated and endorsed these ideas in order to influence the shape of immigration (including deportation) policy. Many of the restrictive measures enshrined in early 20th century Immigration Acts (1906 and 1910) were a consequence of the influence of these "moral reformers." The legacy of these early attitudes and acts endured until well into the post–World War II era.

The last two chapters are concerned with another unsettling era in the history of racial thought in Canada and a contentious issue in Canadian historiography: the internment of Japanese Canadians during World War II. Peter Ward's piece recounts the story of Japanese internment and provides a culturally, socially, and economically informed causal framework to attempt to explain why events unfolded as tragically as they did. Jack Granatstein and Gregory A. Johnson's chapter challenges what has been called the "received wisdom" of Japanese internment, and in the process spark a lively intellectual debate on the nature and interpretation of historical evidence.

CHAPTER 12

Racial Purity, Sexual Purity, and Immigration Policy

Mariana Valverde

"The Purity of Our National Lifeblood": Race and Morality in Turn-of-the-Century Thought

The clean souls and bodies prized by social purity were not only symbolically but literally white. The profound racism of Anglo-Saxon Canadians at the turn of the century had many different roots, some in common with the U.S. and some specific to Canada; racist ideas and strategies permeated the economics, politics, and social policy of early twentieth-century Canada. There is a growing literature on immigration history, but it has generally neglected to examine the sexual/moral components of Canadian racism.

Sexual morality was an important component of what was known as "character," in turn an important part of the project of building a nation that was moral as well as prosperous. As the Presbyterian social reform leader Rev. George Pidgeon said on the occasion of the fortieth anniversary of Confederation, Canada can be "proud of [the] growth of natural resources, of [its] place in the Empire ... [but it] must not forget that the source of national wealth and power lies in the character of its people."[1] White people were seen as having more character, as a group, than Native people or people of colour; and among whites, people of British descent were regarded as having the most character.

Character was both presupposed by and acquired through activities such as clearing prairies and building transcontinental railways; but it was also centrally related to the ability to control one's sexual needs and wants. That the civilization Europeans believed they had brought to North America was built on sexual self-denial was taken almost for granted by most educated, middle-class Canadian Protestants during this period. In the words of Charlotte Whitton (who spent the first four years of her working life under Dr. Shearer in the Moral and Social Reform Council), the ruling group saw "the regulation and control of instinct and emotion as the basis of civilization."[2] The Anglo-Saxon "race" was regarded as much more capable of controlling their instincts than other races; the Anglo-Canadian educated elite accepted without a thought John Stuart Mill's statement that "both in a good and a bad sense, the English are farther from a state of nature than any other modern people. They are, more than any other people, a product of civilization and discipline.... In England, rule has to a great degree substituted itself for nature."[3]

This "rule" or "regulation and control of instinct" was crucial for gender formation, for class order, and for racial and ethnic organization. If blacks and East Indians were undesirable immigrants, it was not because they had no capital and no schooling (many British immigrants were poor and unskilled), but rather because they were "savages," that is, people who could not control their sexual desires and were thus unlikely to lead orderly and civilized lives, saving for rainy days and postponing gratification.[4] Any moral regulation brought to bear on these people would have to be external and coercive. This caused no moral or theoretical problems in Africa or India, where British rule was unabashedly undemocratic. It was, however, a problematic choice for Canada, both for pragmatic reasons and because of the inherent contradictions facing liberal democracies undertaking coercive measures to uphold moral or social values. (Liberal democracies have a structural commitment to a "private" sphere and to juridical equality among all citizens; as I have argued elsewhere, this helps to explain the key role of extra-state voluntary organizations in moral reform campaigns in liberal democratic states.)[5]

In the Canadian context, internalized control was seen as the best foundation for a social order envisioned as built primarily through consensus and genuine, internalized respect for authority, and only exceptionally through coercion and force. As the political economist James Mavor put it, the essence of "the social question" was to ensure "spontaneous regulation" among "the mass of the people," and only the failure of self-regulation would make "compulsory action" necessary.[6] The British system was held up as embodying both respect for authority and (somewhat paradoxically)

self-control, self-regulation.[7] The Moral and Social Reform Council of Canada was "persuaded that in a new country, whose stream of national blood contains strains from almost every nationality and race in the world, it is of vital importance that the traditional British respect for law, order, and authority should be maintained at all costs." Britishness, a peculiar mixture of social order and individual freedom, functioned as a sign of both sexual and civic self-policing.

The sovereign individuals agreeing to respect authority composed the nation; but this nation was not so much a mechanical addition of individuals as an organic whole, whose bloodstream—identified with "the race"—had to be guarded against contamination by external poisons.[8]

This national "blood" had metonymic associations with other bodily fluids. This can be seen in the following text, by Rev. S.D. Chown, head of the Methodist Church and key social purity activist:

> The immigration question is the most vital one in Canada today, as it has to do with the purity of our national life-blood.... It is foolish to dribble away the vitality of our own country in a vain endeavour to assimilate the world's non-adjustable, profligate, and indolent social parasites.... It is most vital to our nation's life that we should ever remember that quality is of greater value than quantity and that character lies at the basis of national stability and progress.[9]

The national blood is here unconsciously linked to the semen individual men and boys were constantly admonished not to "dribble away." The taboo on masturbation is thus combined with unconscious fears of miscegenation, as the link between individual character and nation-building is mobilized in the service of an exclusionary and racist immigration policy. Chown does not have to state that the "parasites" he has in mind are of Asian, black, or Jewish origin; his audience would have supplied those images from the repertoire available to them.

The links between sexual excess, mental and moral degeneration, and the decline of the nation were made repeatedly. It was not a view to be argued for but rather a premise the moral reformers took for granted and elaborated with images, prejudged examples, and rhetorical figures of speech. In a meeting of the Canadian Council on the Immigration of Women, a report authored by Dr. C.K. Clarke (Canada's most famous psychiatrist) shows how racism was constructed by a medical authority—and quickly transposed into the religious key by a clergyman who was present. Clarke's opinion about plans to bring to Canada Jewish children caught in the Ukraine famine was very negative. Since Jews were known to often be educated professionals, Clarke had to resort to complicated discursive twists to support his frankly fascist views:

> It must be remembered that the Jewish children of this type [immigrants] belong to a *very neurotic race*, and while many of them are of unusual ability, yet a certain proportion prove to be mental defectives or are already showing evidence of mental disease…. [They] should be kept for several days under inspection, *and the weaklings weeded out remorselessly*.[10]

On hearing this, Rev. Chisholm, who made his living welcoming immigrants and attempting to direct them to Presbyterian churches, added almost automatically that "Jews have much to do with commercialized vice" (prostitution). The minutes do not record any dissent from the chain of associations being assumed here: Jews—neurosis—disease—vice—prostitution. As Barbara Roberts has shown, the eugenic ideas prevalent among Canada's doctors gave racist immigration policies a scientific veneer: the inquiry into medical inspection of immigrants (which resulted in social purity activist Dr. Peter Bryce being named as head of the federal medical immigration inspection) concluded that "racial criteria were even more important than medical ones" and that "immigrants from northern stock could be rehabilitated and remain healthy in good clean Canadian conditions."[11]

Although many reformers agreed that British people and their descendants were by nature morally superior, Clarke's extreme eugenicist views—shared by important government officials in the 1910s and 1920s—were not the main framework through which moral reformers organized their racism.[12] Unlike the doctors and bureaucrats who came increasingly to monopolize social issues, the evangelical reformers tended to put more emphasis on the role of centuries of parliamentary rule, civilized sexual habits, and Protestantism in producing what they thought was the highest "race." "Race" was not for them a strictly biological concept; it was organized through traditions as well as through genes. This belief was necessary in their evangelical efforts, since if character were completely biologically determined there would be little point in converting Chinese Canadians or Native people to Protestant habits of life. Although they certainly did not think that a Christian Chinese person was the equal of a Christian of British descent, the more hopeful among them thought that in a few generations the objectionable culture of non-British immigrants might disappear, even if the physical ethnic types remained.

The appeal to British traditions put Canadian reformers in a difficult position, since at the same time that they were trying to infuse "foreigners" with the moral values of Tennyson and Ruskin they were also beginning to assert the autonomy of Canada within the Empire, an assertion that necessitated finding specifically Canadian cultural traits. This contradiction was suppressed through an interesting discourse on "nativism" and "traditions" that erased not only Native peoples but also French Canadians through the claim that the (Anglo) Canadian nation's life "extends over milleniums [sic]."[13]

"Nativism" was perhaps also a disingenuous term in the eastern U.S.; but it was downright fantastical in western Canada, which until quite late in the nineteenth century was not even administratively white. Probably because of the precariousness of white/European western Canadian life, the efforts to invent a "native" Anglo-Canadian tradition were most vigorous there.[14] By 1914 this invented tradition was so well accepted that a Methodist newspaper could defend the exclusion of Asian immigrants (in the *Komagata Maru* incident) on the basis of the "evident" statement that white Europeans were native to British Columbia: "it is evident that each race is better off on its own natural environment ... the unrestrained mixing of the races on this coast would lead to economic disaster and ethical demoralisation."[15]

The races, needless to say, only began to be mixed when the whites came. And contrary to the racist fears of whites being swamped by other races, the population of B.C. was in fact becoming increasingly white during the period under study: in 1880–81 almost half of B.C.'s 50,000 inhabitants were Indian, but by 1901 the Indian population remained at about 25,000 while the total population increased dramatically to 180,000. The much-feared Chinese, on their part, made up slightly less than 10 per cent of the B.C. population in 1880–81 (before the great railway boom), more than 10 per cent of the B.C. population in 1901,

but less than 6 per cent by 1921: their numbers, like those of the Native people, had remained fairly stable, but the white population grew tremendously.[16]

As Howard Palmer has pointed out in his study of racism in Alberta, white Canadians of European descent did not generally study demographic trends or react to people of colour and/or immigrants out of economic rationality; their actions were the product of a complex sets of cultural constructs.[17]

* * *

Anglo-Saxons could see themselves as a specific race only in contrast to others. These others were not all identical: there was an elaborate classification system that ranked national and ethnic groups according to a combination of geographical, physiological, and moral criteria. Generally speaking, northerners were to be preferred to southerners (and the role of old European ideas about the sexually passionate nature of southerners and easterners cannot be underestimated in this context); lighter-skinned people were to be preferred to dark-skinned people; and Protestants were far preferable to Catholics, with Christians in general being preferable to non-Christians. These general principles of classification, including the idea of "character" as sexual self-control, then gave rise to a taxonomy that bore little relation to the self-representation of the peoples in question.

The principles of immigration taxonomies were rarely articulated explicitly. For instance, in what was probably the major work on the topic, J.S. Woodsworth's *Strangers Within Our Gates* (1909), the chain of racial being is laid out not through a reasoned discussion but through the simple process of organizing the chapters on each immigrant group in a descending metaphysical order. That this was the "correct" order of precedence would not be questioned by the intended readership. The first group is "Immigrants from Great Britain"; then, those from the U.S., followed by the Scandinavians. The Germans are then discussed, followed by the French (Germans were more likely to be Protestant and hence higher in Woodsworth's scale). Then the book moves on to the "non-preferred" categories: Austria-Hungary; the Balkan states; the Jews, portrayed as though they were a single geographical group; the Italians; a peculiar conglomerate known as "the Levantine races," which includes Greeks, Turks, Armenians, Syrians, and Persians; and finally, the most alien of all, "the Orientals" and the "Negro and the [East] Indian."[18]

This taxonomy, which was not Woodsworth's invention but was part of the dominant culture of the time, is perhaps best illuminated by looking at the fate of the most despised groups, namely Asians and blacks. With respect to Asians, the terms "Chinese" and "Oriental," which were used interchangeably, did not refer so much to geography or physical appearance as to the mythical image of "Oriental" derived from European and American views of China.[19] Central to this myth was the view that the Orientals were not savages (since Marco Polo, Europeans had had a certain awe of China) but were, on the contrary, so civilized that they had degenerated. Theodore Roosevelt's evocation of "the over-civilized man, who has lost the great fighting, masterful virtues" was probably a reference to the Chinese; and the Canadian Royal Commission on Chinese and Japanese immigration of 1902 took it for granted that immigrants from these two countries could not possibly ever be granted citizenship status because of the vices inherent in "an ancient and effete civilization."[20] The young women from university branches of the Dominion YWCA typically heard a lecture on "Japan and its Degeneration" in 1910.[21] In discussions of the opium trade, suggestions were made that Chinese sexual vice was not characterized by impulsive aggression but rather by a loss of manhood and consequent need for drugs to induce sexual desire.

This view of the Chinese as hopelessly degenerate, as a nation in evolutionary and moral decline, was the justification for the policy of not allowing Chinese labourers to set up permanent families and communities in Canada. (It also helped to justify the total exclusion of Chinese immigrants in 1923.) The Royal Commission on Chinese Immigration of 1885 held the generally accepted view that the Chinese were a "non-assimilable race," and Sir John A. Macdonald, who overrode the objections of the British Columbia government and allowed Chinese contractors to bring in labourers to build the railway, assured the anti-Chinese immigration forces that there need be "no fear of a permanent degradation of the country by a mongrel race."[22]

Given this official discourse, it is not surprising that grassroots racism against the Chinese flourished in subsequent decades.[23] Chinese stores in Calgary were wrecked by a racist mob in 1892 with the acquiescence of the local police force; in 1907, an anti-Chinese riot in Lethbridge resulted in restaurants being attacked and their owners being roughed up; and Vancouver's Asiatic Exclusion League incited a major riot in 1907 without suffering any legal consequences.[24]

The moral/sexual overtones of anti-Asian racism were made quite explicit by moral reformers. In 1910, the staff inspector in charge of Toronto's morality division accused the Chinese of enticing white girls into vice:

Immorality among young girls is increasing, caused by too much liberty to roam the streets, and the consequent results therefrom. The lure of the Chinaman is also developing among this class of girls, to their utter demoralization in many instances.[25]

The theme of "the lure of the Chinaman" was explored at length by the well-known conservative feminist Emily Murphy. In 1922 Murphy published as a book a series of articles that had appeared in Maclean's on the drug trade in Canada. This book, *The Black Candle*, shows that social-purity ideas about vice and sexuality were suffused by racism—and vice versa, ideas about race were partly shaped by ideas about the sexual practices of different groups. Murphy raised the spectre of white women being lured through drugs and taken into opium dens; although sexual practices are only hinted at, there are enough hints to indicate that the fear of miscegenation was a profound one in Murphy's mind.

Interestingly, Murphy's sensationalist photographs of drugged individuals included a photo of a *black* man apparently in bed with a white woman. Canadians were at this time exposed to American panics about the sexual influence of black men over white women, and Murphy's picture has to be interpreted in the context of the significant rise of Ku Klux Klan activity in Saskatchewan and Alberta. Black men, who were generally portrayed as oversexed and hence as probable rapists, became the target of a combined sex-and-race panic in Alberta in 1910–11, when a group of black Oklahoma farmers sought to emigrate to Alberta (ironically, to escape Klan persecution in their own country). Although white farmers were being courted as immigrants at this time, the black farmers were strongly discouraged; the federal government even sent a black doctor to Oklahoma to warn potential immigrants that they might die of cold in northern

climes. Women's organizations added their own gender-specific racism to the discussion, as seen in a petition by the International Order of Daughters of the Empire:

> We do not wish that the fair name of western Canada should be sullied with the shadow of lynch law, but we have no guarantee that our women will be safer in their scattered homesteads than white women in other countries with a Negro population.[26]

As William Calderwood has shown, Protestant ministers were quite active in the Saskatchewan KKK in its heyday and this activity was not seen as untoward by their congregations; rather, it shows the continuity between mainstream or "ordinary" racism and the activities of racist groups perceived as marginal to Canadian history.[27]

But if race (as a socially constructed category, not as experience or as anthropological fact) was a crucial variable in the attempt to stem sexual and social degeneration, it was not the only one. British urban working-class immigrants came increasingly under scrutiny. Some Canadians (such as Charlotte Whitton and Peter Bryce, head of the medical inspection of immigrants) went so far as to deny that the urban poor of Britain were more desirable as immigrants than the ethnically inferior but healthier farmers of central Europe. Others preferred to take an environmentalist approach and argue that the degeneration taking place at the heart of the Empire could be reversed after immigration to Canada, at least in the following generation. Moral reformers usually preferred this latter view, as expounded by the Missionary Society of the Methodist Church in 1910:

> It should not be forgotten that while many of these immigrants have deteriorated … they

belong to a race which is the first among the strong ones of the earth—a race that hitherto has had no equal in the work of colonizing … [getting prairies cleared] and covered with yellow harvests; and with beautiful and rich possessions.

> Under the free sky of this Dominion … the children of these people will grow up into healthy and worthy manhood. Blood will tell. The race will assert itself and reproduce in the children of these people the old English character and the old English strength.[28]

The final point to be considered in this section is yet another ambiguity in the meaning of "race." In the days of Sir John A. Macdonald, to be Canadian was to be British, and the existence of Quebec was not a barrier to this unproblematic identification. As the decades wore on, however, Canada developed certain economic conflicts with Britain, mostly in respect to tariffs, and in the cultural realm there began to be an assertion of a Canadian nationalism. In a typical attempt to assert a national identity but still uphold the ideals of the Empire, the popular novelist Sara Jeanette Duncan presented a small-town Ontario hero who is a staunch imperialist but also a Canadian nationalist. Duncan's glorification of Canadian open spaces, healthy work, and democratic lack of class difference does not prevent her hero from waxing mystical about England: "I see England down the future the heart of the Empire, the conscience of the world, the Mecca of the race."[29] Other Canadian writers, however, began to see Canadians as a distinct "race"; as the Vancouver racist agitator Charles E. Hope put it, "we must remember we are trying to evolve a Canadian race as well as Canadian nation,"[30] Hope and others, however, simultaneously believed in the Anglo-Saxons as a race: when they spoke of a Canadian "race" they probably meant a culture, and saw this culture as based on Anglo-Saxon "racial" characteristics.[31]

The nationalist view was vividly presented in a poem, published in the Methodist magazine *Missionary Outlook* in 1905, celebrating the defeat of Native peoples and the rise of a powerful, masculine Canadian nation/race:

> And still the tide flows westward,
> Toward the land of the setting sun;
> And the call goes forth into all the world,
> Until now, where the smoke of the wigwam curled,
> A new life has begun.
> For see! 'Tis the birth of a nation!
> And the men who will mingle now
> The blood of the nation of every land,
> Are founding a race, 'neath whose sovereign hand
> The knee of the world shall bow.[32]

But an article a few months later in the same publication spoke matter-of-factly about the "English-speaking race," and this latter usage remained popular until World War One.[33]

Emily Murphy, the conservative feminist who as a magistrate of women's courts enforced social purity ideals, firmly believed the views about Anglo-Saxon superiority already described, but she added a peculiarly Canadian hypothesis:

> I think the proximity of the magnetic pole has something to do with the superiority of the Northmen. The best peoples in the world have come out of the north, and the longer they are away from boreal regions in such proportion do they degenerate.[34]

* * *

Making Strangers into Neighbours: Race, Ethnicity, and Sexuality in the Work of Home Missions

Missionary work was one of the chief activities of Christian churches in Canada. It was particularly important for churches other than Catholic or Anglican, since both of these had a clear ethnic and national base and were in some ways not keen to disrupt their ethnic homogeneity by indiscriminate recruiting. Methodists, Presbyterians, and Baptists, by contrast, had organized not national churches but conversion-based groups that needed revivals and constant outreach to maintain and increase their base. These Canadian churches, like their counterparts in the U.S. and Britain, developed extensive foreign mission efforts from the mid-nineteenth century on, Canadians concentrating primarily on China, Japan, and India.[35] Unlike British churches, however, Canadian Protestants had the additional task of reaching out to those who had been made into foreigners in their native land, that is, the Native peoples; and, after Laurier's open-door policy came into effect in 1897, much effort was devoted to converting "foreigners" (non-British and non-American immigrants) to Canadian brands of Protestantism.

Foreign missions had been the first concern of both women and men in the Protestant churches, and from the beginning "foreign" included Native peoples. Although work with Native people was sometimes re-classified under the newer category of home missions, the original conceptualization of the missionaries as the real natives of Canada was retained. With the rise of the social gospel movement, a somewhat more progressive attitude developed, church people sometimes speaking against corruption among Indian Affairs officials or against extreme acts of racism. But even

social gospel texts, which present the church as a maternal force mediating between the weak Indians and the sometimes harsh paternal government, portrayed Native peoples as savages who routinely killed their old people, tortured their slaves, and treated women as mere drudges.[36] (Evidence of matrilineality and egalitarian gender roles was, however, also treated as an index of *lack* of civilization.) Although the sexual practices of Native peoples were rarely mentioned, there were veiled references to their disregard for monogamous legal marriages, and more generally to their susceptibility to the passion of the moment. Trying to give these attitudes an anthropological veneer, the missionary educator Rev. Gunn stated that many Native "languages, while rich in combinations and names of material things, are poor or absolutely without such abstract words as faith, hope, and love."[37]

The work of church missionaries with Native peoples was thus firmly based on the belief that only European Christianity could provide the basis of character development. While some church people tried to prevent Native people from being wiped out or ruthlessly exploited, none even contemplated the possibility of self-determination. Even the self-appointed friends of the Indian carried out a contradictory policy best expressed by the deputy superintendent of the Department of Indian Affairs in 1924:

> The policy of the Dominion has always been
> to protect the Indians, to guard their identity as a race and at the same time to apply
> methods which will destroy that identity and
> lead eventually to their disappearance as a
> separate division of the population.[38]

Whether Native peoples were categorized under foreign or home missions, they were part of a vast group of people who came to be known, in the early twentieth century, as "strangers." The term applied paradigmatically to non-English speaking immigrants, but also, by analogy, to Native peoples and even to those whose poverty or vice made them appear as racially distinct. In 1899, a Presbyterian newspaper proclaimed that "a healthy morality" and "a national spirit" depended on making strangers into non-strangers: "It is not to be dreamed of that the Church is to neglect these strangers. Neglect means national peril and religious decline."[39]

Strangers had to be turned into "neighbours," a process sometimes captured by using the word "neighbour" as a verb, as was done by the historian of the Methodist Women's Missionary Society in her description of the contrast between foreign and home missions:

It may be we find it easier, through our missionaries, ... to *neighbour* with those thousands of miles away than we do to visit the foreign woman at the other end of the city. 'Love the *stranger*' is the command.[40]

This dichotomy was clearly set out in the work of J.S. Woodsworth, the foremost Canadian spokesperson on the morals of strangers: in 1909 he published his popular book on immigrants, *Strangers Within Our Gates*, and two years later he published a similar volume on urban problems titled *My Neighbor.*

As "foreign" immigrants began to claim more attention than Chinese and Japanese "heathen," the churches rearranged their budgets accordingly. For instance, the Methodist Women's Missionary Society (MWMS) tripled the number of its missionaries working in Canada between 1906 and 1916; the number of foreign missionaries also went up but far less dramatically.[41] Equally significant is the increasing amount of space devoted to home missions in church publications. And while the Methodist Missionary Society's annual reports put foreign ahead of home missions until 1909, in the year of Woodsworth's *Strangers Within Our Gates* home missions began to be listed first. That same year, the aims of home missions were described as follows: first, "sanitation"; second, "education"; and, a poor third, "evangelistic and social work."[42]

The term "sanitation" referred primarily to physical hygiene, but since in the minds of social reformers soap and water were spiritual as well as physical cleansers, sex hygiene and moral uplift were also intended. The degree of impurity affecting immigrants, however, was a hotly debated point. Some reformers thought immigrants were basically healthy and only needed some training in the English language, self-control, and self-government in order to become good Canadians, while others saw "foreign" immigrants as inherently degenerate in body and spirit. The latter, more racist view was often put forward by church leaders who did not directly work with immigrants but were responsible for lobbying the government and speaking to the public. Rev. S.D. Chown's view of non-Anglo-Saxon immigrants as a potential poison in the Canadian national bloodstream have already been cited; his views were echoed by an editorial in the Methodist *Missionary Outlook* on the topic of strangers:

They come to us with a manhood that has been dwarfed; ... with low ideals of family and social life; with a sullen dislike of law and government and those by whom the law is enforced ... an ominously large number may be classed with the idle and vicious, the incapable, the physically and morally degenerate, the pauper and the criminal.[43]

The imminent danger to Canadian virility posed by strangers was also highlighted by the Presbyterian Church's Rev. G.C. Pidgeon, whose metaphors, however, were more gastronomic than sexual: "Any foreign substance in the body corporate [is] as fatal to its life as an indig.[estible] mass in a liv.[ing] organism…. Moral problems involved."[44]

Some of the front-line workers, nonetheless, had a more benevolent attitude. The home missions textbook issued by the interdenominational Canadian Council for Missionary Education Movement called for "hospitality" to be shown toward the new immigrants from southern and eastern Europe and stated that "we can avoid snap judgements on whole races, based on the few moral failures that are reported in our papers."[45] Without directly criticizing the white-slavery campaign or other moral/sexual panics in which the churches had taken an active role, Gunn tries to shift the onus of moral responsibility by claiming that quite often "pure" immigrants are corrupted upon their arrival in Canadian cities: "The immigrant has to meet the 'Devil's Missionaries' of the liquor traffic, the brothel and the corrupting politician." In this way, "races long known for purity of family life have seen their young women and young men fall down and become a notorious stain upon the national life."[46]

* * *

THE DEPARTMENT OF THE STRANGER: PHILANTHROPIC DEPORTATION

The Presbyterian Church shared the concern shown by Methodists and other representatives of respectable Canadian opinion for contacting and assimilating immigrants. Much of their work was with Scottish immigrants: it sent a minister to work in Glasgow to prepare immigrants and notify appropriate Canadian congregations of the impending arrival of new Scots Presbyterians, and after the Great War they became heavily involved in both obtaining and controlling Scottish single women coming as immigrant domestics. Nonetheless, they also funded a handful of projects for Ukrainian and other non-Anglophone immigrants in the Prairies, most notably schools and nearby boarding homes for rural children in Wakaw and Teulon, and a hospital in Vegreville.[47]

By 1911, the Presbyterian Home Mission Board was paying for Rev. Hunter Boyd in Glasgow and for three immigration chaplains in Quebec, Montreal, and Winnipeg. These tried to direct incoming immigrants to appropriate local churches, but they also helped with the practical details of arrival. That year, Mrs. Ethel West, who was on the executive of the Women's Missionary Society, tried to convince the male-dominated Home Mission Board that special work by women among women immigrants was necessary, adding that girls and women moving within Canada could benefit from an organization such as the proposed Department of the Stranger. The clergymen on the Board agreed that immigration was a key area of work; but they made it clear that they would expect a Department of the Stranger to concern itself "not only with the women and children, but with the men and boys," and they furthermore insisted that the new department be put under the supervision of the Home Mission Board, with the Women's Missionary Society acting in an "auxiliary" role.[48]

Despite the men's formal victory, Mrs. West got herself appointed as head of the Department of the Stranger, and although accountable to the Board of Home Missions she appears to have had considerable latitude in which to use her boundless energy and superior organizational skills. In 1912, the Home

Mission Board prepared forms on which congregations could both report new arrivals or departures or be apprised of immigrants or other strangers in their area. By 1913, Mrs. West had nine Toronto agencies report Presbyterian (and possibly all Scottish) female strangers to her, and many congregations across the country had set up "Strangers' secretaries" to do similar work: the department as a whole handled over 15,000 names in 1913.[49]

Mrs. West, who appears to have been the wife of a Toronto businessman and who had much experience in home mission work, bombarded the Strangers' secretaries of local congregations with requests for reports and circulars giving advice on how to track down strangers. Throughout, her concern for the well-being of immigrants was overshadowed by her greater concern for the moral order of Canadian cities. Before her system of surveillance was established, "girls went to work where Chinamen were employed, where liquor was used," and to prevent these evils she gives suggestions:

> The strangers should be visited immediately and kept in close touch for about three months....You will find that you need to study the environment of the stranger as much as the stranger....We had a group of 62 Scotch girls come to Toronto in one batch, and we have followed their environment most closely.[50]

* * *

The state's work in moral regulation was facilitated by the allegedly philanthropic work of the Presbyterian immigration chaplain in Montreal, Rev. John Chisholm, "an exploring missionary in the interior of British Columbia" transferred from work among Native peoples and lumbermen to work in an urban setting.

Hired in 1912, by 1913 he had already formulated his own sociology of immigrants, proclaiming that Canada might be improved by the addition of "the impulse of the Celt, the endurance of the German, the patience of the Slav, the daring of the Northman, and the romance of Italy." This parade of clichés, however, led him to worry about other character traits that were adding "seasoning" to Canada: "as we view the uncouth ways of many, their lusty morals, their alien ideas, their ignorance and superstition, we have reason to fear that to us is coming a tremendous contribution of the worse."[51] Both Chisholm and his Quebec colleague, Rev. Patterson, mentioned the dangers of "the white slave traffic" as being part of their work. This type of work has generally been described as philanthropic settlement and Canadianization, but it had a darker side that can be called "philanthropic deportation."

During the war there was little need for chaplains to meet the small numbers of immigrants, but after the war the work was renewed. In the meantime, Chisholm, wanting to know how many of the "129,480 immigrant girls" coming to Canada in the pre-war years "made contribution" to the social evil, had got in touch with "prominent social service workers in the USA, among them the late Anthony Comstock."[52]

In an interesting transition from philanthropy to the state, he says he was then "strengthened in his research work" by the "Department of Justice creating me a member of the Federal Secret Service." Since there was no such body, it is difficult to know what Chisholm meant; perhaps he was simply granted the powers of immigration officials. Be that as it may, his official status apparently gave him entry into venereal-disease hospitals, where he heard "from the lips of those poor girls, detailed descriptions" of the causes of their fall. His new status, however, did not merely strengthen his research: he also undertook direct "law enforcement." He mentions rescue work as something that is important but is being done by other church workers; his own specialization, law enforcement in clergyman's disguise, is described as a twofold task: "(1) For the stranger's protection. (2) For the stranger's correction."

* * *

The career in home missions of Mrs. Ethel West, which is unusually well documented, allows some conclusions to be drawn about the transformation of moral reform work into the post-war period. First, there is clearly more collaboration by the state, and notably immigration officials, in the work that was previously done by volunteers for primarily evangelistic reasons. Far from the state supplanting philanthropy, however, what we see is a curious transformation—at its most extreme in Rev. Chisholm—of moral reform itself, and a conscious and deliberate use of volunteer organizations by the state for undertaking work that would otherwise be both too coercive and too expensive.

Second, we see how racial, class, and sexual fears were not only connected but were in some cases merged into a single moral panic—the unfit immigrant—which could be interpreted as primarily a gender/class problem (as in the case of British domestics unfit by reason of their low morals) or primarily a racial problem (as in the case of the "neurotic" Jews).

Third, we see that there was no clear distinction between the work of providing help for those in need—single women needing a place to stay, immigrants requiring basic survival information—and the work of controlling, regulating, and even deporting those deemed undesirable because of their sexual irregularities or because of their "race." The fact that the Department of the Stranger exercised coercive power should not lead us to the one-sided conclusion that nobody obtained generous help from it or was able to use it to track down lost friends or relatives. As in the case of so many of the moral reform projects undertaken in this time period, coercion and protection were but two sides of the same coin.

NOTES

1 UCA, Pidgeon Papers, Box 32, File 529, notes for a sermon on "National Righteousness," first preached in 1907.

2 Quoted in P.T. Rooke and R.L. Schnell, *No Bleeding Heart: Charlotte Whitton, a Feminist of the Right* (Vancouver, 1987), p. 25.

3 J.S. Mill, *On the Subjection of Women* (Cambridge, Mass., 1970 [1869]), p. 67. For the acceptance of this view of the Anglo-Saxon "race" among English-Canadian intellectuals, see S.E.D. Shortt, *The Search for an Ideal: Six Canadian intellectuals and their convictions in an age of transition 1890–1930* (Toronto, 1976).

4 See N. Chabani Manganyi, "Making strange: race, science, and ethnopsychiatric discourse," in Francis Barker et al., eds., *Europe and its Others* (Essex, 1985), vol. I, pp. 152–70; Sander L. Gilman, "Black Bodies, White Bodies: Toward an Iconography of Female Sexuality in Late 19th century Art, Medicine and Literature," in H.L. Gates, Jr., ed., *'Race', Writing, and Difference* (Ithaca, N.Y., 1986), 223–61.

5 See Mariana Valverde and Lorna Weir, "The Struggles of the Immoral: Preliminary Remarks on Moral Regulation," *Resources for Feminist Research* 17, 3 (1988), pp. 31–35.

6 James Mavor quoted in Shortt, *The Search for an Ideal*, p. 134.

7 The self-image of British people as inherently self-regulated is critically explored in Geoffrey Pearson, *Hooligan: A History of Respectable Fears* (London, 1983).

8 NAC, CCC, Box 29, Minutes of Annual General Meeting of Moral and Social Reform Council of Canada, September, 1912. English chauvinism and racism was of course not new; there was a great deal of anti-Irish racism in the 1840s and 1850s. Houston, "The Impetus to Reform." Post-Darwinian theories of racial evolution, however, changed the character of English, Canadian, and American racism toward the end of the century.

9 UCA, S.D. Chown Papers, Box 13, File 376, undated address, "Law and Morality."

[10] UCA, Presbyt. WMS, Dept. of the Stranger Papers, Box 4, File 41, Minutes for 7 October 1920 of the Canadian Council on the Immigration of Women. Emphasis mine.

[11] Barbara Roberts, "Purely Administrative Proceedings: The Management of Canadian Deportation, Montreal, 1900–1935" (Ph.D. thesis, University of Ottawa, 1980), p. 313.

[12] See Angus McLaren, *Our Own Master Race: Eugenics in Canada, 1885–1945* (Toronto, 1997).

[13] UCA, Pidgeon Papers, Box 32, File 529, sermon on "National Righteousness," first preached in 1907.

[14] See Eric Hobsbawm and Terence Ranger, eds., *The Invention of Tradition* (Cambridge, 1983). Terence Ranger's essay in this volume on the way in which British colonial administrators managed to invent not only British but even "African" traditions is quite relevant to the white Canadian project to imagine "Indians" and try to sell these images back to Native people as their own.

[15] Quoted by Peter Ward, *White Canada Forever: Popular Attitudes and Public Policy Toward Orientals in B.C.* (Montreal, 1978), pp. 90–91. For the political economy of race, see B. Singh Bolaria and Peter S. Li, *Racial Oppression in Canada* (Toronto, 1988; 2nd ed.).

[16] Alicya Muszynski, "Race and gender: structural determinants in the formation of BC's salmon cannery labour forces," *Canadian Journal of Sociology*, 13, 1-2 (1988), p. 105; Ward, *White Canada Forever*, p. 15. See also Donald Avery, "Canadian Immigration Policy and the 'Foreign' Navvy, 1896–1914," in Michael Cross and Gregory Kealey, eds., *The Consolidation of Capitalism*, Readings in Canadian Social History, vol. 4 (Toronto, 1983), pp. 47–73. On the political economy of Native people's relations with whites, see Ron G. Bourgeault, "Race and Class under Mercantilism: Indigenous People in 19th century Canada," in Bolaria and Li, *Racial Oppression in Canada*, pp. 41–70.

[17] Howard Palmer, *Patterns of Prejudice: A History of Nativism in Alberta* (Toronto, 1983).

[18] J.S. Woodsworth, *Strangers Within Our Gates: Or, Coming Canadians* (Toronto, 1909).

[19] For an examination of the origins of this, see Edward Said, *Orientalism* (New York, 1979); see also R. Valerie Lucas, "Yellow Peril in the Promised Land," in Barker et al., eds., *Europe and its Others*, vol. I, pp. 41–57. Peter Ward, in *White Canada Forever*, mentions that white British Columbians saw Japanese immigrants as a slight variation on the Chinese, at least until the Russo-Japanese War of 1905, which caused them to think of Japan as a much more successful and aggressive nation than China.

[20] Roosevelt quoted in Richard Hofstadter, *Social Darwinism in American Thought 1860–1915* (Philadelphia, 1945), p. 155; Royal Commission quoted in Ward, *White Canada Forever*, p. 60. Asian Canadians, even if born in Canada, were not allowed to vote as late as World War Two.

[21] Pedersen, "'The Call to Service,'" p. 21.

[22] Avery, "Canadian Immigration Policy and the 'Foreign' Navvy," p. 52.

[23] See Bolaria and Li, *Racial Oppression in Canada*, ch. 5.

[24] On Alberta riots, see Palmer, *Patterns of Prejudice*, pp. 20, 34; on the Vancouver riot, see Ward, *White Canada Forever*, pp. 67–74.

[25] Staff Inspector Kennedy, in *Annual Report of the Chief Constable*, 1910, p. 31.

[26] Quoted by Palmer, *Patterns of Prejudice*, p. 36.

[27] William Calderwood, "Pulpit, Press and Political Reactions to the Ku Klux Klan in Saskatchewan," in S.M. Trofimenkoff, ed., *The Twenties in Canada* (Ottawa, 1972), pp. 191–215.

[28] UCA, 86th annual report of the Missionary Society of the Methodist Church, 1910, p. 36. These views were similar to those held by Sara Jeanette Duncan's protagonist Lorne Murchison. In his visit to London he recognizes the "degeneration" of the English working classes and of the English nation as a whole, seeing Canada as offering a place for the "race" to regenerate itself, growing wheat and making steel under blue skies. S.J. Duncan, *The Imperialist* (Toronto, 1971 [1904]), esp. pp. 122–23.

[29] Duncan, *The Imperialist*, p. 124.

[30] Quoted in Ward, *White Canada Forever*, p. 137.

[31] See Carl Berger, *The Sense of Power: Studies in the Ideas of Canadian Imperialism 1867–1914* (Toronto, 1970).

[32] UCA, *Missionary Outlook*, March, 1905, p. 58.

[33] UCA, *Missionary Outlook*, January, 1906.

[34] Emily Ferguson [Murphy], *Janey Canuck in the West* (Toronto, 1910), p. 38.

[35] Ruth Compton Brouwer, *New Women for God: Canadian Presbyterian Women and India Missions, 1876–1914* (Toronto, 1990).

[36] See, for instance, the missionary textbook by Rev. W.T. Gunn, *His Dominion*, pp. 143–46. Gunn states that the Riel rebellion would not have happened if missionaries had had more power.

[37] Ibid., p. 134.

[38] Duncan Scott, in *Handbook of Canada* (Toronto, 1924), p. 19.

[39] Quoted in Marilyn Barber, "Nationalism, Nativism and the Social Gospel: The Protestant Church Response to Foreign Immigrants 1897–1914," in R. Allen, *The Social Gospel in Canada* (Ottawa, 1975), p. 192.

[40] Elizabeth S. Strachan, *The Story of the Years* (Vol. III, 1906–1916) (Toronto, Women's Missionary Society of the Methodist Church, 1917), pp. 308–09.

[41] In 1906 the MWMS paid for thirty-two missionaries in Japan and China, and twenty-one in Canada; in 1916, there were fifty-six in Japan and China, and sixty-four in Canada. Ibid., p. 309.

[42] UCA, *86th Annual Report of the Missionary Society of the Methodist Church in Canada*, p. 33.

[43] UCA, *Missionary Outlook*, January, 1906, editorial, p. 3.

44 UCA, Pidgeon Papers, Box 33, File 583, "Our Dominion—God's Dominion," sermon, July, 1916.

45 Gunn, *His Dominion*, p. 206.

46 Ibid., pp. 218, 221. This theme of North American cities corrupting European immigrants, especially their young people, was also pursued in the U.S. by progressive reformers such as Jane Addams.

47 UCA, PWMS, Department of the Stranger (henceforth PDS), Box 1, and also reports of the Board of Home Missions, in the annual *Acts and Proceedings of the General Assembly of the Presbyterian Church in Canada*, 1910–1925.

48 UCA, PDS, Box 5, File 43 (typescript history of PDS); and Report of the Board of Home Missions (in *Acts and Proceedings* …, 1913, p. 18).

49 It is unclear whether this includes the immigrants met by the immigration chaplains (who had risen to six by 1913); the chaplains reported directly to the Home Mission Board and not to Mrs. West. But be that as it may, the bureaucratic network of the Department of the Stranger was remarkable.

50 UCA, PDS, Box 4, File 40, circular dated 22 January 1920.

51 UCA, Rev. John Chisholm's report, included in the Report of the Board of Home Missions, in *Acts and Proceedings* …, 1913, p. 62. The reports of Chisholm and other immigration chaplains indicate that they performed many of the functions later taken over by immigration officials, from giving information about accommodation or money exchange to singling out undesirables. For biographical information, see his obituary in the Presbyterian Montreal-Ottawa Conference Minutes for 1936.

52 UCA, PDS, Box 2, File 15; typescript report, undated but undoubtedly 1922.

CHAPTER 13

STEMMING THE FLOOD OF DEFECTIVE ALIENS

ANGUS MCLAREN

At the 1914 Social Service Congress of Canada conference Helen MacMurchy rose to declare that the problem of defective children could only be solved if special education and medical inspection were complemented by restriction of immigration. "It is well known to every intelligent Canadian," she asserted, "that the number of recent immigrants who drift into institutions for the neuropathic, the feeble-minded and the insane is very great."[1] The same sentiments were expressed at the Congress's 1924 meeting, where it was asked:

> What are the eugenic effects of bringing in thousands of boys and girls, a considerable proportion of whom have sprung from stock which, whatever else may be said of it, was not able to hold its own in the stern competition in the motherland?

Such an influx, came the response, added to "our national burden of pauperism, vice, crime and insanity."[2]

For those Canadians preoccupied in the first decades of the twentieth century by what they chose to call "racial degeneration," there appeared to be two obvious threats: the first was the reproduction *in* Canada of the unfit; the second was the immigration *to* Canada of the unfit. [...]

To put such concerns in context it has to be recalled that Canada was, in the first decades of the twentieth century, welcoming millions of immigrants. This necessarily frightened many Anglo-Saxons. Few non-British migrants came to Canada for most of the nineteenth century due to their preference for the United States. Indeed, so many native-born Canadians were lured south that the country's population scarcely grew. But in the 1890's the closing of the American frontier, the upturn in the Canadian economy, the completion of the transcontinental railway, and the launching of an aggressive immigration campaign by Laurier's Liberal government had dramatic results. Between 1896 and 1914 three million immigrants came to Canada. In the single decade between 1901 and 1911 the population jumped 43 per cent in what had become the world's fastest growing country. In 1913 alone over 400,000 immigrants arrived. What preoccupied their hosts was not so much the astonishing numbers as the fact that many (about 800,000 in the first decade of the twentieth century) came from the non-Anglo-Saxon world.[3]

In English-speaking Canada the arrival of newcomers fostered an ideology of "Canadianization" or what might more accurately be described as the goal of assimilating newcomers into Anglo-conformity. English Canadians assumed that white Anglo-Saxons were racially superior and immigrants were welcomed according to the degree to which they approached this ideal.[4] British and Americans were viewed as the most desirable, next northern and western Europeans, after them the central and eastern Europeans (including the Jews), and last of all the Asians and blacks. Thus one found in an eminently respectable history such as Sir G. Arthur Doughty and Adam Shortt's *Canada and Its Provinces* (1914–17) the Galicians presented as mentally slow; the Italians as devoid of shame; the Turks, Armenians, and Syrians as undesirable; the Greeks, Macedonians, and Bulgarians as liars; the Chinese as addicted to opium and gambling; and the arrival of Jews and Negroes as "entirely unsolicited."[5] James S. Woodsworth, the Social Gospeller and future founder of the CCF, followed a similar line of categorization (based on his reading of eugenics) when describing his mission work among the immigrants of pre-World War One Winnipeg. He contrasted the Scandinavians and Icelanders ("clean-bodied" and "serious-minded as a race") to the Slavs and Galicians ("addicted to drunken sprees" and "animalized").[6]

The government, however, was far more pragmatic in its view of immigrants' potential. Sir Clifford Sifton, who became Minister of the Interior in 1896, whatever his personal prejudices, was intent on having Canadian immigration agents ship out to Canada the thousands of central and eastern Europeans who seemed most willing and able to face the rigours of prairie winters.[7] Similarly, in British Columbia the railway companies brought in cheap and plentiful Chinese and Sikh labour. The practical political and economic concerns of the federal government and the railways in settling the West necessarily ran counter to the ideological preoccupations of many Anglo-Canadian intellectuals.[8] Most realized that Canada needed immigrants to do the hard, dirty work of building a country, but they worried about the sort of country that would result.

Opposition to the great wave of non-Anglo-Saxon immigration of the 1890's quickly surfaced. A virulent mix of nativism, racism, anti-radicalism, and anti-Semitism coloured most of the opposition to the arrival of the new Canadians. English Canadians paraded their concern for protecting "democratic institutions" and maintaining an Anglo-Saxon civilization. Such sentiments could manifest themselves in a variety of ways, ranging from the humanitarian concern to "Canadianize" and assimilate newcomers "for their own good" to the desire to shut Canada's borders and repatriate or deport troublemakers.[9] No one was embarrassed to speak of the need to protect the race; what was meant by "race," however, was not always made clear. Some used the term in the biological sense to refer to the purportedly fixed and permanent features that separated superior Anglo-Saxons from inferior groupings; others employed the concept in the cultural sense to refer to British traditions and customs that outsiders could, only with some difficulty, be taught.[10]

* * *

For all their talk of protecting the "race," the eugenicists did not see themselves as racists or nativists. Eugenics was, its followers claimed, both an international movement and a science. Most therefore made an effort to distance themselves from simple-minded nationalists. Calls for restriction of immigration based on eugenic arguments, so their proponents suggested, would not be based on prejudice, personal bias, or old-fashioned notions of patriotism but rather on progressive, sophisticated, and scientifically informed analyses of the worth of individual immigrants.

But in voicing their concern for sorting out the "degenerate," experts were making the unfounded assertion that they had the ability to identify accurately intellectual, moral, and physical strengths. In fact, in most cases it was appropriate cultural behaviour that they took as the best indicator of intelligence. MacMurchy, for example, in the midst of a plea for more sophisticated methods of medical examination and mental testing, made the amazing comment that she paid particular attention to an apparently dim-witted Scottish boy because she *knew* that Highlanders were shrewd.[11] Eastern and southern Europeans were not given the benefit of the doubt. In short, eugenic arguments provided apparently new, objective scientific justifications for old, deep-seated racial and class assumptions.

Eugenic concerns that the quality as opposed to the quantity of immigrants be the government's first priority moreover served specific class interests inasmuch as they enhanced the pretensions of the helping professions. Doctors, so the eugenicists argued, would necessarily play a key role in screening new arrivals because only physicians had the training that permitted the accurate determination of hereditary complaints. The leading eugenic reformers were, of course, doctors who could not help but appreciate the fact that their profession would gain if the government paid greater attention to their concerns. The federal Department of Health was only established in 1919, but for decades the government had relied on the medical profes-

sion in administering its immigration legislation. Eugenics-minded doctors in the early twentieth century therefore had real expectations that their lobbying for tougher immigration restrictions reflecting hereditarian concerns would meet with some success.[12] Many psychologists, social workers, and teachers would also be ultimately drawn to eugenics, in part because by embracing what they took to be a scientific approach to social problems they could enhance their professional standing.

Doctors took a leading role in employing eugenic arguments in the immigration debate. The belief that there existed real hereditarian differences that could not be overcome by an improvement of the environment was repeatedly expressed in the leading medical journals.[13] Dr. J.G. Adami, a Montreal expert on tuberculosis, appealed in 1912 to the Canadian Medical Association to combat the "puerile view" that "it is perfectly sound policy for this country to welcome as citizens those of degraded or depraved parentage."[14] An editorial in *Canada Lancet* for 1908–09 declared, along similar lines, "Degenerates among people are worse than bad weeds to a farmer."[15] Dr. Charles Hastings, medical health officer of Toronto, asserted that Canada was committing "race suicide" in sacrificing the well-being of its own youth to the care of newcomers. He informed the readers of the *Canadian Journal of Medicine and Surgery* that it cost the federal government

> … nearly three quarters of a million annually for immigration purposes alone. Thousands are being imported annually of Russians, Finns, Italians, Hungarians, Belgians, Scandinavians, etc. The lives and environments of a large number of these have, no doubt, been such as is well calculated to breed degenerates. Who would think of comparing for a moment, in the interests of our

country, mentally, morally, physically or commercially, a thousand of these foreigners with a thousand of Canadian birth?[16]

Eugenically inclined physicians claimed that they were providing a more sophisticated analysis than that of the older racists who denigrated all Slavs, Jews, Orientals, and blacks while trumpeting the virtues of all Anglo-Saxons. Indeed, hereditarians frequently pointed out that some of the worst sorts of immigrants were from Britain. Dr. Peter H. Bryce, for example, went out of his way to castigate the abilities of the "riotous Glasgow Jew" and the stroppy Cockney.[17] A 1909 editorial in the *Canadian Journal of Medicine and Surgery* asserted that Canada had become the "garbage pail of England, Ireland, and Scotland."[18] As professionals, eugenicist doctors were asserting that the old racial labels were too crude; the establishment of family pedigrees was required, as were sophisticated medical examination and mental testing. Only the specialist could determine the importance of such issues.

The hereditarians' assertion that foreigners were "inferior" was not original. Their most important contribution to the anti-immigration agitation was in specifying that it was the mental defectiveness of immigrants—a defectiveness that in 80 per cent of cases was inherited and could be scientifically determined—that justified their exclusion.[19] The country had the right to prevent itself from being swamped by carriers of hereditary feeble-mindedness. Helen MacMurchy, as the nation's expert on the subject, raised the alarm that the arrival of such degenerates threatened the fabric of Canadian society. In the same reports to the Ontario government that called for special education of the backward, she recommended as well that entry to the country of the feeble-minded be barred. In her *Fifth Report* (1910) she pointed out the

need for the medical inspection of immigrants.[20] In her *Eighth Report* (1914) she lamented the fact that in 1913 forty-seven feeble-minded immigrants were detained but twenty-four were eventually released.[21] Basing her calculations on the work of Dr. Henry H. Goddard, who employed intelligence testing at the Vineland, New Jersey, Training School for Feeble-Minded Boys and Girls, she estimated that Canada was admitting more than a 1,000 feeble-minded immigrants a year. And as we have seen, MacMurchy claimed that feeble-mindedness was in turn responsible for poverty, unemployment, alcoholism, and prostitution.[22]

MacMurchy was not the first to claim that immigrants were swamping asylums, prisons, and hospitals. Dr. T.J.W. Burgess, superintendent of the Verdun Protestant Hospital, warned in his 1905 presidential address to the American Medico-Psychological Association that Canada was "flooded" with "defective immigrants."[23] Dr. Peter H. Bryce reported in *Canada Lancet* that the percentage of foreign-born in the hospitals had jumped from 20 per cent in 1903 to 30 per cent in 1906. "Whole families of degenerates have come out," he reported; at the Toronto Asylum they were overrepresented in the ranks of "sexual perverts, the criminal insane, slum degenerates, general paralytics and other types of weaklings."[24] Dr. J.D. Pagé, chief medical officer of the port of Quebec, informed the Public Health Association meeting in Toronto in 1915 that the Canadian situation mirrored that found in the United States, where the proportion of the foreign-born feeble-minded was four times as high as that of the native-born.[25]

A variety of experts claimed that these foreign degenerates were swamping the existing charity institutions. A.P. Knight, professor of biology at Queen's University, accused the federal government in 1907 of allowing the entry of an increasing number of mental degenerates and physical weaklings from Europe:

> Our asylums, jails, hospitals and other charitable institutions show an increasing percentage of men and women, emigrants from the older lands, who are handicapped by a bad heredity, and quite unfit to make their way in the new world. Their children are equally unfit. They are underfed and undersized; they inherit the unsound minds and diseased bodies of their parents and are doomed to suffering and inferiority from the very beginning of their lives.[26]

Reports in the *Canadian Practitioner and Review* and *Canada Lancet* for 1908 and 1909 asserted that the block settlement of such settlers contained the "riff-raff from Europe, colonies of immigrants spreading crime, disease, and ignorance."[27]

It was the immigrant's purported contribution to Canada's crime rate that particularly alarmed observers. In a Rhode Island workhouse, reported Dr. F. McKelvey Bell of Ottawa, over 76 per cent of the criminals were foreign-born. In Canada, according to Bell, the situation was just as bad: "we have only 13 per cent of foreigners in the Dominion, [but] 40 per cent of our convicts are of foreign birth and no doubt many others are children of foreigners."[28] Similarly, Michael Steele, MP for South Perth, resorted to American sources in quoting from Dr. Goddard when informing Parliament in 1917 that "there is no such thing as hereditary criminals, it is hereditary feeble-mindedness that accounts for the conditions. Criminals are not born, they are made, and probably fifty per cent of all criminals are mentally defective."[29] Reflecting on all the vices imported to the New World by the foreigner, James Russell, superintendent of the Hamilton

Asylum, warned his colleagues in the American Medico-Psychological Association in 1908 that to welcome such degenerate hordes could only put the Anglo-Saxon race in peril. "The immense virility of the Anglo-Saxon race like the sturdy oak may resist the encroachments of the canker worm for generations," he wrote, "but unless purged and purified of disease it will at last crumble and decay."[30]

Russell, in referring to the question of the declining "virility" of native Canadians, was addressing a fear raised by Dr. Peter H. Bryce. Bryce (1853–1932), educated at Upper Canada College and the University of Toronto, served the Ontario and federal governments in a variety of capacities as a medical expert. He was, from 1882 to 1904, the first secretary of the Ontario Board of Health and, from 1904 to 1921, chief medical officer of the Department of Immigration. In the latter capacity his hereditarian views clearly influenced the way in which immigration policy was carried out.[31]

Bryce's concern that the fertility of the native Canadian was disturbingly low and that of the immigrant alarmingly high was rooted in his early findings when on the Ontario Board of Health. In 1885, sitting on a provincial committee established to determine how to deal with the distressing problems of infanticide and child abandonment, he first had forced on his attention the fact that not all births were welcomed.[32] In 1889, as deputy registrar general, he expressed his disquiet at finding that Ontario cities had a fertility rate distinctly lower than that of the countryside. According to Bryce such developments were due—not to economic pressures—but primarily to the propaganda of both male and female neo-Malthusians.

> It is natural that amongst such writers many should be women; some moved thereto, at

times, doubtless, from womanly sympathy for their sisters amongst the poor, borne down with the cares of children; others have been urged to speak from the standpoint of the emancipated woman, whose ambition it is to enter the arena of public affairs and dispute the field with men, and yet a still larger number have adopted this new philosophy from the standpoint of personal selfishness, and declare that they will recognize no duty which will deprive them of the right to enjoy the fullest whatever society may bring them of pleasure, and utterly refuse to undergo, if it can be avoided, the pains and inconveniences of maternity, while accepting the social protection, privileges and joys which marriage can bring them.[33]

In returning to the issue in his 1903 report Bryce argued that Ontario's low fertility could only be taken as evidence "that natural conditions are being interfered with, or being supplanted by those of a preventative character and criminal in tendency."[34] Those intent on following such practices, according to Bryce, could count on the support of chemists, physicians, and purveyors of "every form of nostrum and mechanical appliance." The danger was that if such social degeneracy continued it could threaten the destiny of the Anglo-Saxon race in playing "the dominant part over inferior races in the march of progress."[35]

Bryce's major preoccupation was with the declining fertility of Canadians, which he attributed in part to the degenerative effects of urbanized, industrialized society. Relying on such European theorists as Max Nordau, whose *Degeneration* (1895) had quickly become the classic attack on modernization, Bryce advanced the view that urbanism produced "neurasthenia," an acquired characteristic passed on from generation to generation. But though

Bryce attributed declining family size in part to sterility caused by neurotic fatigue, he also blamed it on individual egoism. "How many parents," he asked, "have such clear ideas of their duty to the state that they are prepared to be inconvenienced in their pleasure by rearing a normal number of children?"[36]

* * *

The editor of *Canadian Practitioner and Review* was appalled by such findings. It was, he declared in a 1908 article, "a question of who are to be the fathers of the future children of Canada."[37]

* * *

By 1914 the basic line of the eugenicist anti-immigration argument was laid out. Beginning with the premise that certain inherited traits could not be attenuated by a changed environment, eugenicists proceeded to attribute all social problems associated with the immigrant experience to the innate characteristics of the individual, not to the problems posed by a strange, new homeland. Doctors, in equating intelligence to competency in dealing with an Anglo-Saxon culture, not surprisingly found high levels of feeble-mindedness in the immigrant population. Feeble-mindedness they then posited as the root cause of most of the stresses and strains experienced by their young nation. And such problems threatened to worsen over time because, the eugenicists warned, the fertility of inferior immigrant families was not only distressingly high, it appeared to have the effect of forcing down the fertility of superior native Canadians.

To judge by the continual barrage of complaints, one might have assumed that Canada had placed no restrictions whatsoever on the entry of immigrants. In fact, as early as 1869 the nation's first Immigration Act contained provisions against the entry of lunatics and idiots.[38] In 1901 the United States began medical inspections at the Canadian border and Canada soon followed suit by beginning its own medical inspections. By 1902 amendments added to the list of undesirables those who suffered from any loathsome, dangerous, or infectious disease. Orders-in-council in 1902 stipulated that spot medical inspections would take place at Quebec, Halifax, Saint John, Montreal, and Winnipeg. Their purpose was to prohibit the entry into Canada of persons with a specified physical disability or disease, persons diseased, crippled, or deformed or with a mental disorder, and persons suffering from a physical disease of a curable nature. Bryce oversaw these regulations from the time of his appointment as chief medical officer of the Department of Immigration in 1904.[39]

By 1906 the feeble-minded, idiots, epileptics, insane, deaf, dumb, blind, infirm, and those afflicted with a loathsome, contagious, or infectious disease were specified as belonging to the prohibited groups. The Immigration Act of 1910 divided the prohibited classes into three broad categories, which were in turn subdivided.[40] The mentally defective included idiots, imbeciles, feeble-minded, epileptics, and insane; the diseased included those afflicted with any loathsome disease or a contagious or infectious disease that might become dangerous to the public health; and the physically defective included the dumb, blind, or otherwise handicapped. Dr. Charles A. Bailey described to the readers of *Public Health Journal* in 1912 how the rapid "sizing up" of new arrivals by the medical inspector at the port of entry played its part in the conservation of the race.[41]

* * *

The campaign of MacMurchy and others to alert the public to the danger of the feeble-minded began to bear fruit just before the outbreak of World War One. In the spring of 1914 C.K. Clarke, superintendent of the Toronto General Hospital and professor of psychiatry at the University of Toronto, established the Social Service Clinic in Toronto for the mentally defective. Commissioner Boyd of the Juvenile Court sent troubling cases to Clarke for examination—many of them involving immigrant juveniles.[42] In Quebec Dr. Pagé, medical superintendent of the Immigration Hospital at Sans Bruit, was authorized by the Minister of the Interior to hire a psychologist provided by Goddard's Vineland clinic. Pagé reported that thanks to Miss Mateer's help two mental defectives per 1,000 immigrants were detected as opposed to the usual five per 100,000 found when close examination was not possible.[43] What the eugenicists wanted, however, was a thorough medical inspection along the lines adopted by the American government to take place in the immigrant's country of origin. If defectives were to be prevented entry, what MacMurchy referred to as the "loopholes" in the immigration law had to be closed.

* * *

Canadian commentators tended to draw much of their information on the hereditary taints of foreigners from American authors and called on the Canadian government to follow the U.S. lead in restricting immigration. Thus, J.S. Woodsworth concluded *Strangers Within Our Gates* (1909) with the suggestion that Canada should seriously observe the workings of the American Restriction League.[44] MacMurchy, likewise, described in envious fashion the facilities at Ellis Island where American physicians had the power of rejecting thousands of unfit immigrants each year.[45]

World War One abruptly ended both the massive flow of immigrants and the protests that their arrival engendered. The post-war slump of 1918–22 further impeded the resumption of new arrivals; indeed, the federal government actively employed its powers of deportation in 1919 to crush labour unrest.[46] But by 1925 business was again buoyant and a second major wave of immigration to Canada began. Largely as a result of the influence of eugenicists, the United States put into place in 1921 and 1924 restrictions on the entry of central and southern Europeans. Evidence that such immigrants were therefore choosing Canada as a destination led to calls that it should likewise adopt a quota system. Restrictions were imposed but only in the sense that illiterates were excluded and categories of "preferred" northern and "non-preferred" southern and eastern European immigrants were drawn up. Some journalists commented that it was strange that having just fought Germany, Canada should employ immigration laws that would allow the entry of the Kaiser but exclude the Pope. No one protested the fact that Asian immigration was all but ended and that the government—by determining after 1923 that only citizens of predominantly white Commonwealth countries could be deemed British subjects— effectively excluded blacks.[47]

Eugenicists were also pleased that the war, in forcing on the public's attention the importance of national health, was instrumental in leading the federal government to establish in 1919 the Department of Health.[48] Its mandate was to suppress a number of afflictions that endangered the efficiency of the population— venereal disease, infant mortality, tuberculosis, and feeble-mindedness. Many also presumed that the new department would strike at the root of a number of these problems by help-

ing to police immigration. Speaking in favour of the creation of such a department, Charles Sheard reminded his colleagues in the House of Commons, "We have had in the past, rushing into this country, without restraint, inspection or restriction, the diseased, the mentally defective, the criminal, the unhappy, the uncertain, the infamous."[49] Dr. Michael Steele, a long-time proponent in Parliament of public health measures, stated that in his estimation the main reason for the establishment of the Department of Health was to prevent the arrival in Canada of feeble-minded immigrants, whom he likened to a "social virus."[50] The department included in its roster of experts several key personalities sympathetic to eugenic arguments—Peter H. Bryce, medical officer of the Department of Immigration; John Andrew Amyot, deputy minister of health; J.D. Pagé, chief of quarantine; Helen MacMurchy, head of the Child Welfare Bureau; and J.J. Heagerty, head of the Venereal Disease Control Branch.

In revealing the traumas suffered by shell-shocked troops, the war had also provided doctors with arguments that innovative preventive measures were needed to protect the nation's mental health. One such measure was the use of mental testing on troops, which was employed in the United States but, to the disappointment of Canadian psychiatrists, not employed in Canada.[51] In this context the Canadian National Committee for Mental Hygiene was established in 1918 by C.K. Clarke and Clarence Hincks to draw attention to the fact that both the native and immigrant populations would have to be tested if their true potential was going to be determined. The CNCMH set as its agenda a campaign against crime, prostitution, and unemployment, which it asserted were all related in one way or another with feeble-mindedness. The underlying argument of the Committee was that the old methods of dealing with such problems by institutionalization were expensive and ineffective; preventive methods, beginning with examination and testing, were necessary.[52] The Committee provided anti-immigrationists with added ammunition by asserting that its surveys proved that there was a direct correlation between immigration and insanity, criminality, and unemployment.

* * *

In Canada Peter Sandiford, professor of education at the University of Toronto, was among the foremost proponents of intelligence testing. "Intelligence," he stated in a 1927 article that summed up his views, "is a trait that is passed on by heredity."[53] He attempted to prove the superiority of nature over nurture in some of the earliest studies of twins and in the employment of data drawn from observations of the Dionne quintuplets.[54] The fact that some nationalities did better at the American army tests than others (the English and Scots had the highest grades and the Belgians and Poles the lowest) he attributed to Darwinian selection, not to the cultural blinders of the testers. Similarly, by ignoring the fact that Who's Who measured professional success rather than intelligence, he could conclude that "Obviously if America wants to restrict her immigration by means of the 'Quota' she should aim to keep out as far as possible Russians (Poles), Italians, and Greeks and encourage in their stead Canadians, Britishers, Germans and Danes."[55] The lesson Sandiford drew from such work was that Canada, too, had to prevent itself from being made a "dumping ground for misfits and defectives."[56]

In 1924 Sandiford carried out his own testing of British Columbia school students and was pleased to find, as predicted, that among whites those of British and German stock did best and those of Slavic and Latin stock did most poorly. He advanced as proof of the hereditary nature of intelligence the fact the parents of the brightest students were from the professional classes and the slowest from the unskilled. Sandiford, like so many hereditarians, revealed his basic conservatism in equating financial success with intelligence.

But Sandiford's tests also produced results that he found "profoundly disturbing"—they appeared to indicate that the Japanese were the most intelligent racial group and the Chinese the second. Further tests proved "more encouraging" in that white scores were higher than the Chinese, but the Japanese still came in first. Sandiford concluded that the evidence had to be taken to mean that only those few exceptionally clever Asians immigrated to Canada; it was clearly unthinkable that they were racially superior to Anglo-Saxons. Nevertheless, the ability of the Japanese and Chinese to compete successfully with whites posed, in Sandiford's words, "a problem which calls for the highest quality of statesmanship if it can be solved satisfactorily."[57] Like so many of the intelligence testers, Sandiford knew in advance what results his surveys were supposed to produce. When such tests did not confirm the superiority of the white race a "problem" was said to exist that required the intervention of government. Sandiford, the self-proclaimed social Darwinist, was ambivalent about the struggle for survival. On the one hand he declared that quality would always win out, but on the other he called on the government to protect native Canadians from the competition of immigrants by subjecting them all to stringent mental, physical, and possibly even "moral" tests.[58]

Sandiford claimed that intelligence testing was turning psychology into a "true experimental science." An indicator that psychology was finally "put on the map" in Canada occurred in 1931 when the Department of Educational Research at the Ontario College of Education received a $30,000 grant from the Carnegie Foundation. And yet Sandiford himself, while lauding the fair and reliable nature of the intelligence tests, was led to wonder why it was only in North America that there was such enthusiasm for them. "Is it the presence of the immigrant," he mused, "that has led to this anomalous state of affairs?"[59] Sandiford managed to stifle these qualms and was joined in his enthusiasm for this kind of testing by such leading hereditarians as Helen MacMurchy, Eric Clarke, and Clarence Hincks.[60]

Medicine and psychology were not the only professions to exploit an Anglo fear of the feeble-minded immigrant. Social work, much of which had been carried out on a volunteer basis by women's groups in the early twentieth century, became increasingly professionalized in the interwar period and emphasized the need to have trained experts police new arrivals. A number of its leading proponents clearly turned to the profession's advantage the spectre of foreign degeneration.

In the pre-war period the National Council of Women, whose members were engaged in most of the significant philanthropic agencies, was torn by its conflicting desires: on the one hand it wanted to restrict immigration; on the other, its middle-class members wanted a ready supply of cheap domestics.[61] Aroused by the carnage of the First World War, which in the eyes of the NCW was killing off the fit while allowing the degenerate to breed, the Council petitioned the government in 1915 for the medical inspection of immigrants to weed out mental defectives. "Contagious diseases have long been controlled by legislation," it noted, "but this more deadly, transmittable disease of feeble-mindedness is still uncontrolled."[62] In 1919 Helen Reid, a member of the Dominion

Council of Health, wrote that it was necessary to prevent the entry into Canada of those British women "who in addition to their lack of training for domestic service, bring with them only too often, serious mental and moral disabilities. These women either glut the labour market here, reducing the wages of working men, or end up, alas! too frequently, in our jails, hospitals, and asylums."[63]

In the 1920's the colourful and flamboyant Charlotte Whitton, director of the Canadian Council on Child Welfare and the leading advocate in Canada of the creation of social work as a profession, carried on the campaign against the entry into Canada of the mentally deficient.[64] She claimed that Britain sought to dump its surplus labour on the dominions and that pre-war "unregulated immigration" was responsible for Canada's post-war economic problems. What Whitton objected to in particular was the entry of the feeble-minded.

> Statistics abound to show the alarming degree to which an immigration policy that sought not quality but quantity has contributed to the social problems of this young country. Fortunately the war stemmed the human tide temporarily at least, and allowed us to take stock of the population that has flowed into this country.... Our strength and resources are bent to the task of keeping this country strong, virile, healthy, and moral, and we insist that the blood that enters its veins must be equally pure and free from taint.[65]

In fact, for all her avowed professionalism, Whitton undertook her survey of immigrant children with the clear purpose of tracking down as many cases of degeneration as possible.[66]

The approach taken by Whitton was illustrated in the Social Service Council of Canada's 1924 study, *Canada's Child Immigrants*. It drew evidence from a vast range of social agencies to paint a portrayal of the failures of juvenile immigration. Among its damning evidence it cited figures from C.K. Clarke's psychiatric clinic in Toronto, which showed that out of 125 immigrant girls examined, seventy-seven were mentally deficient, thirty-six were prostitutes, thirty-one suffered from venereal disease, and eighteen had illegitimate children.[67] Such a sample, of course, was in no way representative, but it was all grist for the mill of those complaining of the lack of "scientific selection" of immigrants. With similarly sifted evidence the Canadian Council on Child Welfare, of which Whitton was director, reported in 1929 that immigrant feeble-mindedness, spreading with "cancerous tenacity," was responsible for "filth, disease, criminality, immorality and vice."[68] It was with such fears in mind that in 1924 the United Farm Women of Alberta's convention struck a committee to seek to have debarred from entry into Canada the feeble-minded, epileptic, tubercular, dumb, blind, illiterate, criminal, and anarchistic. The same organization claimed in 1927 that 75 per cent of the mental patients in the province were migrants.[69]

By the mid-1920's potential British immigrants were being medically examined in the United Kingdom. Ultimately, nearly 1,500 doctors overseas co-operated in providing inspections, and by 1928 twenty-eight medical officers of the Department of Immigration were at work in Britain and Europe. Over 10,000 persons were forbidden entry to Canada in the 1920's, but this did not silence the critics.[70] The *Canadian Medical Association Journal* complained that low-grade immigrants with high fertility continued to flood Canada. Preliminary medical inspection was only compulsory for specific categories of immigrants—unaccompanied women, children on private immigration schemes, and those on government-assisted passage.[71]

In the 1920's the Canadian government employed neither intelligence testing nor a quota system to limit immigration. The country's policy was less restrictive than that of the United States—not because of greater humanitarianism but because money was to be made from new arrivals. In the mid-twenties powerful interest groups—in particular the railway companies that stood to benefit from having immigrants on their ships, on their trains, and on their land—pressured the Mackenzie King government to reopen Canada's doors to the central and eastern Europeans needed to farm the Prairies. Although the federal government launched a variety of schemes to encourage "preferred" British immigration, it also entered into the Railways Agreement with CPR and CNR in 1925 that eventually brought to Canada 165,000 central and eastern Europeans and 20,000 Mennonites.[72]

The shipping companies had their own inspections of immigrants and were fined by the federal government for each deportee. But even the government's own examination system at ports of entry was mainly a matter of form and, in any event, frequently avoided by ministerial permits. The western provinces continued to point out the inadequacy of the inspection system; they were, of course, going to pay for the mistakes made by either the railways or the federal government.[73] Concerns were also expressed by westerners that many of the new immigrants were not fulfilling their appointed task of taming the land but, because the wheat boom had passed and the best farmlands were already occupied, were turning to the cities. This second wave of immigration raised the ire of the eugenicists and precipitated a backlash from a variety of nativist groups, including the Ku Klux Klan, the Native Sons of Canada, and the Orange Order.

Obligatory inspection overseas along American lines only came in 1928 as part of an attempt by the Mackenzie King government to stem the tide of anti-immigration sentiment. The Railways Agreement was the focus of the attack of a motley collection of restrictionists, including leaders of the Trades and Labour Congress, members of the United Farmers of Alberta, Anglo-Canadian bigots led by George Lloyd, Anglican bishop of Saskatoon, nativists of the National Association of Canada, and the Ku Klux Klan. R.B. Bennett, the new Conservative leader, also threw his party's support behind what was obviously a popular issue.[74]

Between February and May of 1928 a Select Committee on Agriculture and Colonization heard representatives of the railway companies, the churches, the social services, and other interested parties give their views on immigration policy.[75] There was no official eugenicist presence; the Committee's time was mainly divided between the representatives of the shipping companies, who wanted a free hand to bring in eastern Europeans, and the representatives of British interests, who fought to ensure that Anglo-Saxon settlers received preferential treatment.

But eugenic preoccupations clearly coloured the discussions. In Parliament a few MPs, such as J.S. Woodsworth (who had turned away from eugenics once he recognized that it was being used as a stick with which to beat the working class), Samuel Jacobs, and Michael Luchkovich, made spirited attacks on the arguments of the hereditarians. "I challenge any member of this House or any scientist," asserted Luchkovich, "to prove biologically that one race of people could not do as well as another race under similar circumstances."[76] Outside of the House Robert England, whose credentials as an objective commentator on immigration matters were somewhat compromised by the fact that he had worked for the CPR, kept up a barrage of criticisms of what he described as "the scientific determinist, geog-

rapher or eugenist" and "the violent rantings and fantastic claims of Gobineau, Stoddard, or McDougal in their well-known books."[77]

The immigration committee's final report, submitted on June 6, 1928, called for the implementation of stricter controls; the Conservative government elected in 1930 erected the barriers that put an end to Canada's interwar wave of immigration. The CNCMH hailed the closing of Canada's borders as a victory, but in fact it was the depression that terminated large-scale immigration to Canada.

Had the hereditarians been successful in imposing their views on others? For one thing, it was not always clear what those views were. Some eugenicists wanted certain ethnic groups given preference, others wanted all to be subjected to standardized examinations. Nevertheless, the general assumption was widespread that the hereditarians had popularized the idea that some immigrants demonstrated by their social incompetency the presence of a hereditary taint. Such arguments against immigration were employed by a vast range of organizations—the Church of England Council for Social Service, the Canadian National Committee on Mental Hygiene, the National Council of Women, the Social Service Council of Canada, the National Child Welfare Association. Knowing what they were looking for, each easily dredged up from the files of asylums, orphanages, rescue homes, penitentiaries, industrial schools, and psychiatric clinics sensational accounts of the social cost of admitting immigrants to Canada. Opposition to immigration in the late nineteenth century had been raised by nativists, nationalists, and labour leaders opposed primarily to the quantity of incoming foreigners; the opposition of the interwar period was increasingly led by professional groups—doctors, social workers, and psychiatrists—employing eugenic arguments to attack the quality of the new arrivals. Such onslaughts were clearly self-serving in that they allowed professions to be established and careers to be made by those who presented themselves as vital agents dedicated to the definition and defence of the race.

Canadian eugenicists were not as successful in 1928 as their American counterparts had been in 1924. This was because the self-proclaimed defenders of "intelligence" found in the Canadian shipping companies redoubtable opponents. The forces of "materialism" were so strong that as late as 1925 the Railways Agreement gave the CNR and the CPR in effect a free hand in the importation of "non-preferred" immigrants. And the closing of Canada's doors, so desperately sought by the hereditarians, was brought about, not as a result of scientific argument, but because of the economic constraints of the 1930's.

The chief "success" of the hereditarians (if one wishes to so qualify it) did not consist of seriously impeding the entry of immigrants to Canada. The hereditarians' success lay in popularizing biological arguments to perpetuate the argument—so beloved by the anxious—that the nation's problems were largely the product of the outsider. The dividing line separating the old racist from the new eugenicist was rarely as clear as the latter claimed. The message of the eugenicist was far more radical in style than in content; new intelligence tests, medical examinations, questionnaires, and surveys might be brandished, but the purpose was the old one—defence of Anglo-Saxon dominance. This was not, however, quite the same thing as defence of the social status quo. The immigration debate revealed cleavages within the middle classes and pitted professionals against business interests. Some members of the helping professions consciously employed eugenic fears as a means of forcing their way into the establishment. The more cautious were aware that such a strategy could be pushed too far. Conservative Canadians would always view with suspicion those who constantly harped on such unseemly subjects as race and sex.

NOTES

[1] Helen MacMurchy, "Defective Children," *Social Service Congress: Ottawa 1914* (Toronto: ssc, 1914), p. 101.

[2] Social Service Congress, *Canada's Child Immigrants* (Toronto: ssc, 1924), pp. 16, 33. See also Neil Sutherland, *Children in English Canadian Society* (Toronto: University of Toronto Press, 1976), p. 73.

[3] Howard Palmer, ed., *Immigration and the Rise of Multiculturalism* (Toronto: Copp Clarke, 1975), pp. 4–12.

[4] Howard Palmer, "Reluctant Hosts: Anglo-Canadian Views of Multiculturalism in the Twentieth Century," in *Multiculturalism as State Policy* (Ottawa: Queen's Printer, 1976), pp. 84–97. For the best contemporary expression of this ideology, see Ralph Connor [Charles William Gordon], *The Foreigner* (Toronto: Westminster, 1909).

[5] W.D. Scott, "Immigration and Population," in *Canada and Its Provinces* (Toronto: Glasgow, Brook, 1914–17), VII, pp. 531, 561, 565, 568, 569, 570.

[6] James S. Woodsworth, *Strangers Within Our Gates or, Coming Canadians* (Toronto: Methodist Mission, 1909), p. 92; see also Terry L. Chapman, "The Early Eugenics Movement in Western Canada," *Alberta History*, 25 (1977), pp. 9–17; Marilyn Barber, "Nationalism, Nativism, and the Social Gospel: The Protestant Church Response to Foreign Immigration in Western Canada, 1897–1914," in Richard Allen, ed., *The Social Gospel in Canada* (Ottawa: National Museum of Man, 1975), pp. 186–226.

[7] David J. Hall, *Sir Clifford Sifton* (Vancouver: University of British Columbia Press, 1981–85), I, pp. 262–69, II, pp. 66–72, 300–02. Immigration was a branch of the Department of Agriculture until 1892 when it was hived off to the Department of the Interior. A separate Department of Immigration and Colonization existed from 1917 to 1938 when it was subsumed under the Department of Mines.

[8] Donald Avery and Peter Neary, "Laurier, Borden and a White British Columbia," *Journal of Canadian Studies*, 12 (1977), pp. 24–34; Donald Avery, *"Dangerous Foreigners": European*

Immigrant Workers and Labour Radicalism in Canada, 1896–1932 (Toronto: McClelland and Stewart, 1979).

9   Robert F. Harney and Harold Troper, Immigrants: A Portrait of the Urban Existence, 1890–1930 (Toronto: van Norstrand Reinhold, 1975), ch. 4.

10 Carl Berger, The Sense of Power: Studies in the Ideas of Canadian Imperialism, 1867–1914 (Toronto: University of Toronto Press, 1970), pp. 117, 131, 148–52.

11 MacMurchy, The Feeble-Minded in Ontario: 5th Report, 1910 (1911), p. 52.

12 Not all doctors were so damning of immigrants. See, for example, J.M. Shaver, "Civic Problems Caused by Immigrants," PHJ, 7 (1916), pp. 433–37.

13 Bator, "'Saving Lives on the Wholesale Plan,'" p. 219.

14 CMAJ, 2 (1912), p. 980.

15 "Defectives and Insane Immigrants," CL, 42 (1908–09), p. 62.

16 "Medical Inspection of Public Schools," Canadian Journal of Medicine and Surgery [hereafter CJMS], 21 (1907), p. 73.

17 "Medical Inspection in Schools," PHJ, 7 (1916), pp. 59–62; see also Peter H. Bryce, The Value to Canada of the Continental Immigrant (Toronto, 1928).

18 "Why is the Immigrant Act Not Enforced," CJMS, 25 (1909), pp. 251–53.

19 On American developments, see Samuel B. Thielman, "Psychiatry and Social Values: The American Psychiatric Association and Immigration Restriction, 1880–1930," Psychiatry, 48 (1985), pp. 299–310.

20 MacMurchy, The Feeble-Minded in Ontario: 5th Report, p. 32.

21 MacMurchy, The Feeble-Minded in Ontario: 8th Report, 1913 (1914), pp. 17–18. See also 9th Report, pp. 10–11; William W. Lee, "Effects of Immigration on National Health," PHJ, 4 (1913), pp. 134–36.

22 MacMurchy, The Feeble-Minded in Ontario: 10th Report, 1915 (1916), pp. 32–33.

23 Proceedings of the American Medico-Psychological Association [hereafter PAMPA], 4 (1905).

24 CL, 41 (1907–08), pp. 944–45.

25 PHJ, 6 (1915), p. 558.

26 "Medical Inspection in the Schools," QQ, 15 (1907–08), p. 140.

27 Canadian Practitioner and Review [hereafter CPR], 33 (1908), pp. 477–78; CL, 42 (1908–09), p. 140.

28 "Social Maladies," QQ, 16 (1908–09), p. 50; see also A.H. Desloges, "Immigration," PHJ, 10 (1919), pp. 1–5.

29 House of Commons, Debates, 2 May 1917, p. 994.

30 PAMPA, 7 (1908), pp. 106–07.

31 See Canadian Journal of Public Health, 40 (1949), p. 84.

32 Ontario Sessional Papers, 74 (1886), pp. 128–32.

33 Ontario Sessional Papers, 32 (1899), pp. 20–21.

34 Report of the Registrar General, 9 (1903), p. 8.

35 Ontario Sessional Papers, 32 (1899), p. 21.

36 "Feeble-Mindedness and Social Environment," American Journal of Public Health, 8 (1918), p. 656.

37 "The Undesirable Immigrant," CPR, 33 (1908), p. 477.

38 Manpower and Immigration, A Report of the Canadian Immigration and Population Study Two: The Immigration Program (Ottawa: Info Canada, 1974), pp. 1–6.

39 J.D. Pagé, "Trachoma and Immigration," Dominion Medical Monthly, 25 (1905), p. 306; see also PHJ, 4 (1913), pp. 641–46.

40 Zlata Godler, "Doctors and the New Immigrants," Canadian Ethnic Studies, 9 (1977), p. 8.

41 "The Medical Inspection of Immigrants," PHJ, 3 (1912), p. 435.

42 Helen MacMurchy, "The Mentally Defective Child," PHJ, 6 (1915), p. 85.

43 J.D. Pagé, "Immigration and the Mentally Unfit," PHJ, 6 (1915), pp. 554–58; see also MacMurchy, The Feeble-Minded in Ontario: 9th Report, pp. 10–11.

44 Woodsworth, Strangers, p. 264. On the American experience, see John Higham, Strangers in a Strange Land: Patterns of American Nativism, 1860–1925 (New York: Atheneum, 1955); Barbara Miller Solomon, Ancestors and Immigrants (Cambridge, Mass.: Harvard University Press, 1956), pp. 146–57.

45 MacMurchy, The Feeble-Minded in Ontario: 9th Report, p. 11.

46 Avery, "Dangerous Foreigners," pp. 81–82; Barbara Roberts, Whence They Came: Deportation from Canada, 1900–1935 (Ottawa: University of Ottawa Press, 1988).

47 On Asians, see Howard Palmer, "Patterns of Racism: Attitudes Towards the Chinese and Japanese in Alberta, 1920–1950," Histoire sociale/Social History, 13 (1980), pp. 137–60; H.F. Angus, "Canadian Immigration: The Law and Its Administration," American Journal of International Law, 28 (1934), pp. 74–89; Peter Ward, White Canada Forever: Popular Attitudes and Public Policy Towards Orientals in British Columbia (Montreal: McGill-Queen's University Press, 1978). On American blacks, see Harold Troper, Only Farmers Need Apply (Toronto: Griffin House, 1972), pp. 121ff.

48 McGinnis, "From Health to Welfare: Federal Government Policies Regarding Standards of Public Health For Canadians, 1918–1945."

49 Sheard cited in Janice Dickin McGinnis and Suzann Buckley, "Venereal Disease and Public Health Reform," Canadian Historical Review, 63 (1982), pp. 345–46.

50 House of Commons, Debates, 2 May 1917, p. 992.

51 O.C.J. Withrow, "Mentally Defective Recruits for Army Service," PHJ, 8 (1917), pp. 109–11; Tom Brown, "Shell Shock in the Canadian Expeditionary Force, 1914–1918: Canadian Psychiatry in the Great War," in Charles Roland, ed., Health, Disease, and Medicine: Essays in Canadian History (Toronto: Hannah Institute, 1984), pp. 436–64.

[52] *CMAJ*, 8 (1918), pp. 551–52.

[53] Peter Sandiford, "The Inheritance of Talent Among Canadians," *QQ*, 35 (1927), p. 2. Elsewhere he wrote, "The eugenists are right so far as they stress the importance of stock, for, as every farmer knows, if one desires well-favoured offspring the best procedure is to start with first class parents." *Foundations of Educational Psychology: Nature's Gift to Man* (Toronto: Longmans, 1938), p. 42.

[54] Sandiford was a student of the Columbia University psychometrician E.L. Thorndike, who also worked on twins. See Sandiford, *The Mental and Physical Life of School Children* (London: Longmans, 1913), p. 13; "Education," *PHJ*, 7 (1916), pp. 496–97; "I.Q.," *CJMH*, 3 (1922), p. 40; A.H. Wingfield and Peter Sandiford, "Twins and Orphans," *American Journal of Educational Psychology*, 19 (1928), pp. 420–21. See also Wingfield's book-length attempt to prove that intelligence was an inherited trait, *Twins and Orphans: The Inheritance of Intelligence* (Toronto: Dent, 1928).

[55] Sandiford, "Inheritance," p. 8.

[56] Sandiford, *Comparative Education* (Toronto: Dent, 1918), p. 431.

[57] Sandiford, "Inheritance," p. 17. Sandiford's findings were critiqued in Helen Reid and Charles Herbert Young, *The Japanese Canadians* (Toronto: University of Toronto Press, 1938), pp. 135–36. On school testing elsewhere, see Gillian Sutherland, *Ability, Merit, and Measurement: Mental Testing and English Education, 1880–1940* (Oxford: Clarendon Press, 1984); Clarence J. Karier, "Testing for Order and Control in the Corporate Liberal State," in N.J. Block and Gerald Dworkin, eds., *The I.Q. Controversy* (New York: Pantheon, 1977), pp. 154–80.

[58] Sandiford, "Inheritance," p. 18; see also E. Jamieson and P. Sandiford, "The Mental Capacity of Southern Ontario Indians," *Journal of Educational Psychology*, 19 (1928), pp. 536–51. Canada did produce one of the most notable critics of claims made for racial differences in intelligence— Otto Klineberg. After obtaining his B.A. at McGill, Klineberg pursued graduate work at Columbia and was much influenced by Franz Boas. Klineberg demonstrated that the fact that northern U.S. blacks obtained higher test scores than southern blacks was due not to the more intelligent moving north, as the eugenicists claimed, but to their improved social and educational environment. H.A. Tanser, a Canadian student of psychology, sought to counter Klineberg's findings. Tanser argued that since the iq scores of blacks who had lived in Kent County, Ontario, since the 1850s were fifteen to twenty points lower than those of whites, there was a basis for believing in "innate racial inferiority." See Otto Klineberg, *A History of Psychology in Autobiography*, 6 (1974), pp. 163–82; H.A. Tanser, *The Settlement of Negroes in Kent County, Ontario and A Study of the Mental Capacity of Their Descendants* (Chatham: Shepherd Publishing, 1939). Curiously enough, Tanser's obscure study, which was cited by the racist journal *Mankind Quarterly* in 1960 as providing proof of black inferiority, was republished in 1970 by the Negro Universities Press of Westport, Connecticut.

[59] Sandiford, "Research in Education," *University of Toronto Quarterly*, 3 (1934), pp. 314, 315, 319.

[60] On support of testing, see Colin K. Russell, *CMAJ*, 8 (1918), p. 551; William D. Tait, "Science and Education," *Scientific Monthly*, 29 (1929), pp. 132–36; Eric Clarke (son of Charles K. Clarke), "Mental Hygiene in Toronto Schools," *PHJ*, 13 (1922), pp. 126–30; Clarence Hincks, *PHJ*, 9 (1918), pp. 102–05; Chester E. Kellogg, "Mental Tests and Their Use," *Dalhousie Review* [hereafter *DR*], 2 (1922–23), pp. 490–99. E.J. Pratt noted that low standards of living seemed to affect intelligence: "Mental Tests in Toronto," *PHJ*, 12 (1921), p. 150; H.B. Moyle of the Ontario Hospital at Mimico warned that iq tests only revealed "school acquirement," not raw intelligence, and so posed the danger of labelling a still developing child. "Childhood," *CJMH*, 3 (1921), p. 257.

[61] On the women's organizations and eugenics, see Bacchi, "Race Regeneration and Social Purity"; Barbara Roberts, "A Work of Empire: Canadian Reformers and British Female Immigrants," in Kealey, ed., *A Not Unreasonable Claim*, p. 189. On domestics, see *A Conference of the Canadian Council of Immigration of Women* (Ottawa: King's Printer, 1928); Strong-Boag, *The Parliament of Women*, p. 248.

[62] *The Yearbook of the National Council of Women* (Toronto: ncw, 1915), pp. 237, 241.

[63] Marilyn Barber, "The Women Ontario Welcomed: Immigrant Domestics for Ontario Homes, 1870–1930," in Alison Prentice and Susan Mann Trofimenkoff, eds., *The Neglected Majority: Essays in Canadian Women's History*, vol. II (Toronto: McClelland and Stewart, 1985), pp. 112–13.

[64] On Whitton, see Patricia T. Rooke and R.L. Schnell, *Discarding the Asylum: From Child Rescue to the Welfare State in Canada, 1800–1950* (New York: University Press of America, 1983), p. 247; see also Rooke and Schnell, "Child Welfare in English Canada, 1920–1948," *Social Service Review*, 55 (1981), pp. 484–506; and on the place of eugenics in the rise of social work, see Roy Lubove, *The Professional Altruist: The Emergence of Social Work as a Career* (Cambridge, Mass.: Harvard University Press, 1968), pp. 66–69.

[65] Charlotte Whitton, "Mental Deficiency as a Child Welfare Problem," National Archives of Canada (nac), mg 30 e 256 vol. 19.

[66] Rooke and Schnell, *Discarding the Asylum*, p. 237. On the child immigrants, see Joy Parr, *Labouring Children: British Immigrant Apprentices, 1869–1924* (London: Croom Helm, 1980).

[67] Social Service Council of Canada, *Canada's Child Immigrants* (Ottawa: sscc, 1924); see also Mrs. J. Breckinridge McGregor, *"Several Years After": An Analysis of the Histories of a Selected Group of Juvenile Immigrants Brought to Canada in 1910 and in 1920 by British Emigration Societies* (Ottawa: cccw, 1928), p. 5.

[68] *Report of the New Brunswick Child Welfare Society, 1928–29* (Ottawa: cccw, 1929), p. 205. The journal *Social Welfare* carried a steady stream of articles denigrating immigrants. See, for example, 1 (1919), pp. 130, 138–39; 2 (1920), pp. 175–77.

69 *United Farmers of Alberta*, 26 February 1924, p. 12; 2 February 1925, p. 20; 16 April 1927, p. 5. Agnes MacPhail, Canada's first woman Member of Parliament, followed Whitton's line in saying too many immigrants ended up in "jails, asylums, and hospitals." House of Commons, *Debates*, 7 June 1928, p. 3885; 27 May 1929, p. 2874.

70 J.D. Pagé, "Medical Aspects of Immigration," *PHJ*, 19 (1928), pp. 366–73; D.A. Clark, "Medical Aspects of Immigration," *PHJ*, 17 (1926), pp. 371–73.

71 "Our Immigration Laws," *CMAJ*, 17 (1927), p. 349. On deportations and rejections (the vast majority of which were due to civil rather than medical problems), see the *Annual Report of the Department of Immigration*, 1918–1938.

72 Palmer, "Reluctant Hosts," p. 91.

73 McGinnis, "From Health to Welfare," pp. 50–54.

74 Avery, *"Dangerous Foreigners,"* pp. 106–11; Mary Vipond, "Nationalism and Nativism: The Native Sons of Canada in the 1920s," *Canadian Review of Studies in Nationalism*, 9 (1982), pp. 81–95. On Bennett, see House of Commons, *Debates*, 7 June 1928, p. 3925.

75 Select Standing Committee on Agriculture and Colonization, *Minutes and Proceedings* (Ottawa: King's Printer, 1928).

76 On Jacobs, see House of Commons, *Debates*, 7 June 1928, pp. 3895–97; 27 May 1929, pp. 2894–95; on Luchkovich, 27 May 1929, p. 2903; on Woodsworth, 7 June 1928, pp. 3900–01.

77 Robert England, *The Threat to Disinterested Education* (Toronto: Macmillan, 1937), p. 10; *The Central European Immigrant in Canada* (Toronto: Macmillan, 1929), p. 198. See also his *The Colonization of Western Canada* (London: King, 1936); "Continental Immigration," *QQ*, 36 (1929), pp. 719–28; J. Murray Gibson, "The Foreign Born," *QQ*, 27 (1920), pp. 331–50, L. Hamilton, "Foreigners in the Canadian West," *DR*, 17 (1938), pp. 448–60; D. Walter Murray, "Continental Europeans in Western Canada," *QQ*, 38 (1931), pp. 63–75; Watson Kirkconnell, "Western Immigration," *Canadian Forum* (July, 1928), pp. 706–07. On those desiring more restrictions, see Duncan McArthur, "What is the Immigration Problem?" *QQ*, 35 (1928), pp. 603–14; W.A. Carrothers, "The Immigration Problem," *QQ*, 36 (1929), pp. 517–31; A.S. Whitely, "What Need of Immigration," *DR*, 9 (1929), pp. 225–29.

CHAPTER 14

EVACUATION

PETER W. WARD

*B*etween late 1937 and early 1942 resurgent nativism once more flooded white British Columbia. Three waves of anti-Orientalism swept across the province, in 1937–38, 1940, and 1941–42, each of them of several months' duration. The third was by far the greatest in magnitude. Indeed, its crest was broader and higher than that of any previous racial outburst in the history of the province. Never before had west coast whites been so intensely aroused. Never before had their protests been so vociferous. Never before had they confronted the federal government with such insistent demands. And in the end, never before had the response of Ottawa been as drastic as it was on this occasion.

The Japanese were the sole targets of these three new outbursts. While anti-Chinese sentiment found intermittent voice in British Columbia during the 1930s, mounting anti-Japanese prejudice had largely eclipsed it since the last days of Chinese immigration. During the depression years images of Japanese militarism came to dominate white attitudes toward the Japanese. To growing numbers of British Columbians, Japan seemed bent on a program of conquest which might well sweep the entire

north Pacific rim. On this account the Japanese minority on the west coast appeared more threatening than ever. In the eyes of white observers, its unwillingness to abandon Japanese culture was proof of continuing loyalty to the new Japanese Empire, and even more unsettling was the inference that the Japanese immigrant community harboured subversive elements, men and women who would undermine the nation's defence efforts in the event of war with Japan. At bottom, of course, these assumptions were variations of the longstanding popular belief in Asiatic unassimilability. They had been buried in white racial thought since the Russo-Japanese war. What brought them to the fore during the early 1930s was the resumption of Japan's military adventures in Manchuria. Her subsequent attack on China in 1937 placed them in even sharper relief.

It was the invasion of China in the summer of 1937 that touched off the first of these incidents. In Canada reports of this aggression provoked the first strong outburst of anti-Oriental feeling in a decade. Much of it was directed at Japan herself. Across the nation indignant Canadians boycotted Japan's products and protested her war atrocities.[1] Meanwhile British

Columbians aimed new barbs at the local Japanese. Animus was most intense in coastal centres—especially Vancouver and Victoria, and their surrounding districts—where provincial nativism traditionally had been strongest. To some extent the Japanese were made scapegoats of Japan's militarism. But many whites also saw in them another cause for concern, for the attack fused old racial antipathies with vague, new anxieties in the minds of west coast residents. Suddenly the region's longstanding fears of isolation and vulnerability were stirred to life again, and this new, tense atmosphere breathed fresh life into the community's dormant racial hostility. At the same time the menace inherent in the Japanese image was once again confirmed. Japan, it was presumed, had designs on British Columbia. Rumour had it that hundreds of illegal Japanese immigrants were present on the coast, that Japanese spies and military officers lived surreptitiously in the community, and that a potential Japanese fifth column was growing in the province. The result was a new upsurge of anti-Asian sentiment.

Archdeacon F. G. Scott, a popular Anglican wartime padre, precipitated the new outbreak in mid-November 1937, one week after the Japanese had taken Shanghai. In a widely reported interview with the *Toronto Daily Star* he suggested that Japanese officers were living, disguised, in fishing villages along the west coast.[2] A few coastal residents ridiculed Scott's claims. Others, however, vouched for their truth, and his supporters won the day for a public outcry followed in the wake of his remarks. Capt. MacGregor Macintosh, a Conservative member of the legislature, first endorsed Scott's report and then, early in 1938, raised charges of widespread illegal Japanese immigration.[3] Led by A. W. Neill, by now a perennial foe of the Oriental immigrant, provincial members of Parliament from all parties demanded a halt to Japanese

immigration.[4] Simultaneously Alderman Halford Wilson urged Vancouver City Council to limit the number of licenses for Japanese merchants and to impose zoning restrictions upon them.[5] Meanwhile Vancouver's major daily newspapers launched their own anti-Japanese campaigns.[6] In Ottawa the prime minister received a flurry of protest notes while the outspoken Alderman Wilson's mail brought him letters of support.[7] The chief object of public concern was the persistent rumour that hundreds of illegal Japanese immigrants were living in the province, a tale made all the more credible by memories of serious immigration frauds which had been discovered early in the decade.

Judged in the light of previous anti-Oriental incidents, this was not a major outburst. Its central figures, Wilson and Macintosh, made no attempt to organize a protest movement. They merely spent their energies in making public demands for more restrictive legislation. Nor was popular hostility as intense as it had been in the past. Because the level of animosity was relatively low and dynamic organizational leadership was absent, this precluded the development of a major racial crisis. Nevertheless all signs pointed to increasing public tension, and the weight of this concern was soon felt in Ottawa.

Prime Minister Mackenzie King was loath to grasp such a nettle as this. King probably wished to placate British Columbia's nativists, or at least quiet them if he could. At the same time, he was subject to countervailing pressures. He was anxious not to embarrass British interests in Asia by taking any initiative which might provoke Japanese ire. Japan's renewed militarism had heightened his own inherent sense of caution. But demands from the west coast grew so insistent that ultimately he could not ignore them. Urged first by Premier T. D. Pattullo of British Columbia and then by Ian Mackenzie, the only west coast representative in the cabinet, King early in March 1938 promised a public enquiry into rumours of illegal Japanese entrants.[8]

But the mere promise of an investigation did not still demands for an end to Japanese immigration. Macintosh went even further and called for the repatriation of all Japanese residents in Canada, regardless of their citizenship.[9] On March 24 the Board of Review charged with the investigation held its first public hearing in Vancouver. During the next seven weeks it conducted a series of additional meetings in major centres throughout the province, and once the hearings commenced, popular unease appeared to dissipate. The hearings themselves put an end to scattered public protest by offering a forum to the vociferous. Furthermore, the meetings forced critics to prove their allegations or remain silent, and many chose the latter refuge. Public concern subsided to such an extent that when the board concluded, early in 1939, that rumours of illegal Japanese immigration had been greatly exaggerated, its report attracted little notice.[10]

But while hostility ebbed appreciably, it was not completely dispelled, and for the next two years the west coast Japanese remained the targets of rumour, suspicion, and criticism. Repeated calls rang out for an end to all Japanese immigration (now fallen to less than 60 per year) while the Vancouver City Council tried to restrict the number of trade licenses issued to Orientals.[11] Then, in the spring of 1940, the second wave of animosity began to well up. In this instance the anxious wartime atmosphere created by Canada's recent belligerency heightened traditional prejudices and aggravated racial tensions in west coast society. At the same time, and for the same reason, Japan's Asian military campaign again began to rouse concern. The growth of general unease once more strengthened feelings of vulnerability and insecurity in the community. Prompted by mounting anxiety, the cry went up that illegal Japanese immigrants were infiltrating the country; renewed demands were made for an end to all Japanese immigration as well as for stronger Pacific coast defences. Tales of the Japanese subversive threat also circulated freely.

* * *

While provincial and federal authorities grew increasingly alarmed at the prospect of racial turmoil, senior military officers in British Columbia were also concerned by the presence of Japanese on the coast. Intelligence officers had kept watch on the Japanese community since 1937 and from the outset had accepted the prevailing assumption that Japanese residents, regardless of their citizenship, would endanger national security in time of war. As early as June 1938 the Department of National Defence had explored the prospect of widespread Japanese wartime internment.[12] In 1940, during the summer's crest of popular anti-Japanese feeling, the Pacific Command's Joint Service Committee approved contingency plans to meet both an external Japanese attack and an internal Japanese insurrection. The committee also endorsed an intelligence report which warned of possible sabotage by the west coast Japanese fishing fleet. Japanese residents, it reported, "could very easily make themselves a potent force and threaten the vital industries of British Columbia." If war broke out, the committee believed, every Japanese resident in British Columbia should be considered a potential enemy.[13]

On the other hand the RCMP tended to minimize the Japanese threat. Since 1938 officers in "E" Division, stationed in Vancouver, had also kept the Japanese under surveillance. In 1940 they assigned three constables to observe the community and also employed Japanese informants. On the basis of continual investigation, the force concluded that Japanese residents posed no real threat to Canada. On the contrary, it observed what it believed to be convincing evidence of Japanese loyalty to Canada. Signs of this were especially clear in the community's strong support for Victory bond drives and Red Cross work, the Nisei desire to volunteer for military service, and the widespread Japanese wish not to arouse white antagonism. "This office," the Officer Commanding at Vancouver reported late in October 1940, "does not consider that the Japanese of British Columbia constitute a menace to the State."[14]

Was there substance to this apparent threat of Japanese subversion? The Board of Review in 1938 had found no proof of wholesale illegal immigration. Nor had the RCMP discovered any indication of serious danger, and surely this was the organization best able to judge.[15] It had scrutinized the Japanese community more carefully than had any other agency. Neither military intelligence nor popular rumour was founded on such close observation, and the claims of each should be judged accordingly. All available signs pointed in one direction only: no significant evidence of Japanese treachery could be seen at this time. Nor would any be discovered at a later date. The threat of Japanese subversion was created by the union of traditional racial attitudes and perceptions shaped by the fears and anxieties conjured up by war. Yet despite its insubstantial basis, the threat was real enough to many British Columbians, and it was the goad which stirred popular animus to life once more.

* * *

In the final months before Pearl Harbor was bombed, racial tensions began to abate. Nevertheless conditions remained favourable to a new anti-Japanese outburst. Influenced by the community's xenophobia, its traditional racial cleavage, and its anxieties borne of war and isolation, white British Columbians continued to suspect their Japanese neighbours. The west coast Japanese could not be trusted. Their allegiance was in doubt. Given the opportunity, it was assumed, some among them would betray the province to the enemy. For its part the federal government, while alarmed by the Japanese problem, was ill-prepared to meet the issue head on. It feared that Japan might use a racial disturbance as a *casus belli*, but aside from forming the Standing Committee it had done very little to prevent an outbreak.

The third and final wave of hostility, in force and amplitude surpassing all previous racial outbursts, was touched off in December 1941 by Japan's assault on Pearl Harbor. This sudden, dramatic attack roused the racial fears and hostilities of white British Columbians to heights never before attained. In turn they loosed a torrent of racialism which surged across the province for the next eleven weeks. This outbreak of popular feeling demanded an immediate response from the King government. In attempting to placate white opinion it offered a succession of policies, each one aimed at further restricting the civil liberties of the west coast Japanese. As it proved, nothing short of total evacuation could quiet the public outcry.

The outbreak of war with Japan immediately raised the problem of public order for the King government because it greatly increased the likelihood of violent anti-Japanese demonstrations in British Columbia. It also created a new enemy alien problem, for the declaration of war altered the status of many Canadian residents of Japanese origin.[16] Faced with the prospect of racial incidents as well as that of an alien menace, the Dominion government quickly took preemptive action. A few hours after war was declared, thirty-eight Japanese nationals were interned on the grounds that they might endanger the community. At the same time the west coast Japanese fishing fleet was immobilized. On the advice of the RCMP, all Japanese-language newspapers and schools voluntarily closed their doors. Meanwhile Prime Minister King, senior police and military officers, and Vancouver's major newspapers all reassured the public and called for calm. As King told the nation in a radio address on December 8, "the competent authorities are satisfied that the security situation is well in hand. They are confident of the correct and loyal behaviour of Canadian residents, of Japanese origin."[17]

But many west coast whites were not so easily mollified. Neither prompt federal action nor loyal protestations from leading Japanese did much to assuage their concern. War's outbreak once more opened the floodgates of fear and hostility. As a result the west coast quickly resumed its attack on the province's Japanese. Once again enmity was strongest in and around Vancouver and Victoria, long the province's two focal points of anti-Asian sentiment. In the week following Pearl Harbor some Japanese in Vancouver were victimized by scattered acts of vandalism. Several firms began discharging their Japanese employees. Fear of Japanese subversion again spread in the province.[18] In private, British Columbians began protesting to their members of Parliament. The weight of public concern also bore down on provincial newspapers. Columnist Bruce Hutchison informed the prime minister's office that at the *Vancouver Sun*, "we are under extraordinary pressure from our readers to advocate a pogrom of Japs. We told the people to be calm. Their reply was a bombardment of letters that the Japs all be interned."[19]

To encourage calm, police, government, and military officials issued further assurances that the Japanese problem was well in hand.[20] But their statements seemed to have little effect. Popular protest continued to grow, and in response alarm in government and military circles increased too. On December 20 F. J. Hume, chairman of the Standing Committee, told King:

> In British Columbia particularly, the successes of the Japanese to date in the Pacific have to a great extent inflamed public opinion against the local Japanese. People here are in a very excited condition and it would require a very small local incident to bring about most unfortunate conditions between the whites and Japanese.[21]

Maj.-Gen. R. O. Alexander, commander-in-chief of the Pacific Command, was also concerned.

> The situation with regard to the Japanese resident in British Columbia is assuming a serious aspect. Public feeling is becoming very insistent, especially in Vancouver, that local Japanese should be either interned or removed from the coast. Letters are being written continually to the press and I am being bombarded by individuals, both calm and hysterical, demanding that something should be done.[22]

Alexander feared that public demonstrations, which according to rumour were to be held in the near future, might lead to racial violence.

After a brief lull over Christmas the public outcry grew more strident than ever. Increasing numbers of west coast whites, regardless of all reassurance, were certain that the local Japanese community endangered west coast security. By early January 1942 patriotic societies, service clubs, town and city councils, and air raid precaution units, most of them on Vancouver

Island or in the Vancouver area, had begun to protest.[23] Repeatedly they urged that all Japanese, regardless of citizenship, be interned as quickly as possible. Other spokesmen suggested somewhat less drastic action, but whatever the precise demands of the public, they all assumed the need for some form of Japanese evacuation. And with each passing day opinion seemed to grow more volatile. Even moderates like J. G. Turgeon, Liberal MP from Cariboo, were alarmed at the seeming danger. On January 6 he warned the prime minister:

> The condition in this province is dangerous, so far as the Japanese are concerned. If the Government do not take drastic action, the situation will get out-of-hand. The Government will suffer, and so will the Japanese, personally and through destruction of property.
>
> I am therefore forced to recommend that very strong measures to [sic] taken,—and quickly. Either delay, or lack of thorough action, may cause violence.[24]

Under heavy pressure, both popular and political, the federal government ordered yet another review of the Japanese problem. On January 8 and 9, 1942, a committee of federal and provincial government, police, and military officials met in Ottawa to discuss means of allaying west coast alarm. The central question explored was whether or not the Japanese should be removed from coastal areas; but the meeting could not agree on an answer. Several representatives who had just arrived from British Columbia, together with Ian Mackenzie, the meeting's chairman, argued that all able-bodied male Japanese nationals should immediately be removed. The majority of the delegates, however, few of whom had recently been in British Columbia, opposed such drastic action. Consequently the meeting submitted a moderate report which

suggested both an extension of existing minor restrictions on the liberties of all Japanese and the creation of a quasi-military work corps for Canadian Japanese who wished to support the war effort.[25]

But the conference's report was only one opinion. From British Columbia there came ever more insistent demands for an evacuation program, and within the cabinet Ian Mackenzie, King's closest political friend from the province, pressed for such a solution.[26] Consequently, when the government announced its revised plans on January 14, the new policy bore the unmistakable imprint of west coast opinion. The King government accepted most of the Ottawa conference's proposals, but in addition it proposed to remove all enemy aliens, regardless of age, sex, or nationality, from protected areas soon to be defined in British Columbia. The program was aimed primarily at Japanese nationals although it embraced Germans and Italians as well. The statement also promised that a Japanese Civilian Corps would soon be formed for work on projects deemed in the national interest.[27] The covert hope was that Japanese Canadian men would volunteer for it in large numbers, thus permitting the government to remove them from the protected areas without an unpleasant resort to compulsion.[28]

It was felt that, by yielding to some of the west coast's demands, the partial evacuation policy would calm British Columbian fears. Concerned for the safety of Canadian prisoners in Japan's hands, anxious to avoid needless expense and disruption in time of war, and touched with a lingering sense of justice and humanity, the King government refused to make further concessions. But the plan was also rather equivocal in that it neither defined the protected areas nor promised when evacuation would begin. In effect, it still gave the federal government considerable freedom of action.

For a few, brief moments the gesture seemed satisfactory. Premier John Hart of British Columbia, whose government had already demanded similar measures, applauded the decision and the *Vancouver Sun* praised the King government's common sense. The storm of protest abated temporarily.[29]

Within ten days, however, agitation began to increase once again. The public outcry mounted throughout February until, during the last week of the month, it reached unprecedented volume. Pressed by the irrational fear of enemy subversion, thousands of west coast whites petitioned Ottawa for the immediate evacuation of all Japanese. Individuals, farm organizations, municipal councils, civil defence units, constituency associations, service clubs, patriotic societies, trade unions, citizens' committees, chambers of commerce—even the Vancouver and District Lawn Bowling Association—all demanded the total evacuation of Japanese from coastal areas.[30] One group of prominent Vancouver residents telegraphed Ian Mackenzie that, "owing to wide spread public alarm over enemy aliens on the Pacific coast and especially respecting those astride vital defence points and with a view to stabilizing public opinion and in the interest of public safety," they urged the immediate evacuation of all Japanese.[31] Never before had west coast race relations been so seriously strained.

Parliament reconvened on January 22 as the racial crisis mounted. Members of Parliament from British Columbia, no doubt as concerned as their protesting constituents, began to press for total evacuation. Howard Green, the Conservative member from Vancouver South, opened the attack in the Commons on January 29.[32] The threat of Japanese treachery confronted the Pacific coast, he said, and therefore all Japanese should be removed from the province. During the next three weeks other British Columbian members made similar claims in the House. In private they were even more insistent. On January 28 British Columbians in the Liberal caucus demanded that Japanese Canadians who failed to volunteer for the Civilian Corps be evacuated as quickly as possible. In succeeding weeks, as popular protest reached its greatest heights, King faced successive demands for relocation from provincial politicians, Conservative, Liberal, and independent alike.[33]

Meanwhile government officials in British Columbia sustained their pressure as well. At the height of the popular outcry the attorney-general of British Columbia told Ian Mackenzie:

> Events have transpired recently which add to the danger we have always been subjected to by the presence of Japanese on this Coast.
>
> I cannot urge too strongly the seriousness of this situation and the danger the people of British Columbia feel upon this matter.
>
> Nothing short of immediate removal of the Japanese will meet the dangers which we feel in this Province.[34]

At the same time the minister of labour campaigned for total evacuation. The lieutenant-governor informed the prime minister that he had "rarely felt so keenly about any impending danger as I do about the Japanese on this coast being allowed to live in our midst." He suggested that at the very least Japanese males be quickly interned. Since mid-January senior officers of the Pacific Command had grown more concerned as well. By the time public protest reached its peak, they too subscribed to demands for total evacuation.[35]

It was Ian Mackenzie who ultimately bore the brunt of this storm of protest. First he received warnings and notes of alarm, then petitions urging evacuation, and finally demands that he resign. But on this matter Mackenzie had long shared the concern of his constituents. In the first weeks after the outbreak of war he grew convinced that all able-bodied Japanese men should be removed from strategic areas. In consequence he considered the partial evacuation policy inadequate. He also believed that the April 1 deadline was too remote. As pressure upon him grew, Mackenzie's alarm at the instability of public opinion increased in like proportion. On February 22, when news reached him of a series of mass protest meetings planned for March 1, his anxiety reached a peak.[36] Two days later he informed cabinet colleagues of the heated state of west coast opinion and of a call for his own resignation. As he told the minister of justice:

> The feeling in British Columbia in regard to the Japanese is so aflame that I consider we should take the necessary powers (if we have not got them now) to remove Canadian Nationals, as well as Japanese Nationals, from the protected areas.
>
> I have no report on how the Vancouver Corps has succeeded, but I greatly fear *disorder* from reports actually received unless all able-bodied males of Japanese origin are immediately evacuated.[37]

Publicly Mackenzie appeared unperturbed, urging calm on his west coast correspondents, but privately he was extremely exercised.[38]

Within the cabinet others shared something of Mackenzie's alarm, particularly his concern for possible public disturbances. The prime minister agreed that there was "every possibility of riots" on the west coast, and feared that in such an event there would be "repercussions in the Far East against our own prisoners." The

situation was awkward, he recognized, because "public prejudice is so strong in B.C. that it is going to be difficult to control."[39] Under such heavy external pressure, and alarmed by the evident danger of racial violence, the federal government finally took decisive action. On February 24, only hours after Mackenzie had written his warning to cabinet colleagues, the government approved an enabling measure which permitted total evacuation. Three days later the announcement was made that all persons of Japanese ancestry would have to leave the protected zones.[40] The King government had once more capitulated to public pressure.

* * *

In the weeks that followed, a series of military reverses continued to play on west coast fears. By mid-January Japanese troops had overrun much of Malaya, the Philippines, Burma, and British North Borneo. They had occupied Thailand, captured Hong Kong (taking more than 1,600 Canadian troops prisoner), sunk Britain's most modern battleship, and crippled her Pacific fleet. Late in January they had laid siege to the island of Singapore. News of this swift succession of decisive victories dominated the front pages of the provincial press. These accounts repeatedly emphasized that Japanese subversion and fifth column activity had played a central role in Japan's program of conquest. Already convinced of their own vulnerability, British Columbians grew more alarmed when worse news succeeded bad, and increasingly hostile toward the Japanese minority. The combined effect of Japanese militarism and the province's legacy of racial tension was to reveal the old image of the Yellow Peril in a new and lurid light. As many British Columbians peered through the fog of their anxieties, they saw little but the menacing outline of Japanese subversion. A growing sense of crisis narrowed their perceptions, which in turn intensified public unease. Thus social tensions and racial imagery were mutually reinforcing. Had British Columbians seen their Japanese neighbours clearly, they would have observed an isolated, defenceless minority, gravely alarmed by its plight and anxious to demonstrate its loyalty to Canada. But fear and prejudice obscured their vision. The local Japanese seemed nothing but a grave and growing threat.

A further sign of mounting social pressure was the increasing incidence of rumours of Japanese subversion. Some told of Japanese who owned high-powered vehicles and short wave equipment, who lived near sites of great strategic value, who swelled with insolent pride at Japan's successive victories. Others hinted at active Japanese disloyalty, and in the hothouse atmosphere of growing public tension stories grew to outlandish proportions. Military intelligence officers were informed in mid-January that Japanese in Vancouver had fixed infra-red and ultraviolet beacons on their roofs, devices which, when viewed through special binoculars, would guide enemy flights over the city.[41] Rumour is usually the product of serious social and psychological stress,[42] and these persistent rumours were one more indication of the growing racial crisis on Canada's west coast. The outbreak of war with Japan had spread a grave sense of looming threat among west coast whites. Yet for all its immediacy the threat remained somewhat vague and nebulous. The enemy was identified; his whereabouts were not. Rumours helped resolve this ambiguity. They suggested that some of the enemy were very close at hand. While this in itself was cause for concern, it also helped to clarify the confusions of war with a distant, elusive power. Because rumours singled out the nearest available enemy, they helped reduce the ambiguity

which had spawned them in the first place. Once in circulation, they too stirred the ever-widening eddies of hostility and alarm.

It seems clear that a further, immediate reason for the renewed upsurge of protest in February was that many British Columbians, anxious for total evacuation, had misinterpreted the government's policy announcement of January 14. The *Sun* had taken it to mean that "all Japanese and other enemy aliens" were to be removed from protected areas, an assumption shared by several British Columbia members of Parliament. "My understanding," wrote Ian Mackenzie, "was that all able-bodied, adult enemy aliens would have to be removed from protected areas. My further understanding was also that all able-bodied *Canadian nationals* would have to be moved, but that *first* they should be given an opportunity to volunteer in the Civilian Corps."[43] Added complications arose from the failure of the federal government to implement its program immediately. Neither the evacuation plans nor the designated protected areas were announced until January 23, and the delay itself provoked some concern. When finally announced, the plans indicated that evacuation was not to be completed before April 1, a date which seemed far too remote to those who believed the Japanese threat was imminent. Once the plans were made public there was a further delay while the relocation machinery was set up. The task of arranging to move, house, and care for several thousand Japanese proved a time-consuming one and it was complicated further by the strong opposition of residents in the British Columbian interior, especially the Okanagan Valley, to proposals that all the Japanese be settled inland.[44] Several times the immediate departure of Japanese from Vancouver was announced and then postponed. Consequently few, if any, Japanese left their homes before mid-

February. In the eyes of concerned west coast whites the government's partial evacuation policy increasingly seemed a mixture of confusion, delay, and prevarication. It appeared that Ottawa did not understand, let alone sympathize with, British Columbia's predicament.

Three elements thus combined to generate social strain in the province after the bombing of Pearl Harbor: reports of Japan's military campaigns in Asia, rumours of impending Japanese attack on British Columbia, and federal delays in implementing the wholesale evacuation policies advocated on the west coast. The first two projected a Japanese military threat to the province and assumed that the local Japanese community would play a subversive role in the anticipated conflict. The third expressed the frustrations of whites when the precautions they deemed necessary were not immediately taken. In each case the roots of this strain were fundamentally psychological.

The pattern of mobilization of this outburst is also revealing, for, by and large, British Columbians reached their conclusions about the Japanese menace with little prompting. More or less simultaneously, thousands recognized an obvious threat and identified the equally obvious solution. In the generation of this consensus, neither popular leaders nor popular journalism played a predominant role. Halford Wilson and MacGregor Macintosh, once the two chief critics of the west coast Japanese, were submerged beneath the rising tide of hostility. In fact, the protest movement had no preeminent leaders whatsoever. Nor did provincial papers become leaders of opinion, even though some took up the popular cry. During the crisis west coast journalism helped sustain the prevailing mood, but most papers merely reflected the popular mind. In other words the outburst was both widespread and largely spontaneous.

The very structure of the protest movement supports this contention for it clearly revealed how extensive was the anti-Japanese consensus. Although public anxiety had flared up immediately after Pearl Harbor, no effective anti-Japanese movement began to emerge until late January. In its earliest stage protest was random; it had no central leadership and no institutional focus. When the movement did begin to take form, protest was mobilized concurrently by a broad range of the traditional social, economic, administrative, and political organizations already entrenched in British Columbia. The Provincial Council of Women, the Vancouver Real Estate Exchange, the Canadian Legion in Gibson's Landing, the Kinsmen's Club of Victoria, the North Burnaby Liberal Association, the BC Poultry Industries Committee, the Corporation of the District of Saanich, the National Union of Machinists, Fitters, and Helpers (Victoria Local Number 2), and scores of other similar groups all pressed their demands for evacuation. Not only did these organizations represent major interest groups in the province, but their influence cut across most social, economic, and political bounds in west coast society. They represented the interests and opinions, the fears and hostilities of tens of thousands of British Columbians. If there were some provincial whites who did not share prevailing attitudes, they remained largely silent in the face of the consensus.

In addition, the forces opposing the outburst were relatively weak. In this case ultimate responsibility for control rested with the King government. Throughout the eleven-week crisis its chief concern remained constant: to reduce the level of racial tension in west coast society. For King and those of his ministers who were preoccupied with the problem, the first task was to prevent the torrent of racist rhetoric from spilling over into overt violence. Beyond that they wished to moderate racial hostility. But they had few tools at their disposal with which to achieve these ends. Physical protection of the minority by police or military forces was never seriously considered. Nor, save in a limited way, was counter-publicity used to refute the claims of the nativists and encourage public calm. Instead the government employed appeasement to mollify British Columbia. Its first step, taken immediately, was a policy of selective internment and increased restrictions on Japanese civil liberties. The second was a plan to remove that segment of the Japanese population which seemed most immediately dangerous. The third and final step was wholesale evacuation. As a means of attaining the primary goal of lower social strain, the King government selected this as the path of least resistance. Whether any alternative policy could have succeeded is now a moot point.

That the King government chose this solution is not at all surprising, for west coast opinion weighed down upon a group of politicians quite susceptible to prejudice against Asians. Ever since Confederation, anti-Orientalism had pervaded the political culture of the province beyond the Rockies and on many occasions provincial representatives had thrust their opinions upon Ottawa. Usually their words had received a fairly sympathetic hearing, and past governments had repeatedly acquiesced in their major demands. Ian Mackenzie, on whom much of the burden of west coast opinion fell in 1942, had long been confirmed in his anti-Asian sentiments, though not outspokenly so, and on the eve of war in the Pacific most British Columbian politicians held the same convictions that he did. Consequently, when anti-Japanese feeling welled up after Pearl Harbor, they shared the public's growing concern and transmitted it with alacrity to Parliament and cabinet.

In Ottawa Mackenzie King also faced the rising tide of protest. His experience with west coast hostility toward Asians had been longer and more intimate than that of any other federal politician. In 1907 and 1908 he had held three royal commissions to investigate Oriental immigration and racial disturbances in Vancouver. In the 1920s and 1930s, as prime minister, he was repeatedly confronted by the issue. As was usual with King, his comments on the Oriental problem were always extremely circumspect. Prior to his premiership he had concluded that the roots of west coast tensions were economic, not racial, and he envisaged their satisfactory resolution through negotiation with Asian nations to seek mutually acceptable immigration levels.[45] In office, he proceeded to use both diplomacy and legislation to restrict immigration from China and Japan. During the later 1930s, however, when anti-Japanese feeling increased on the west coast, King felt constrained from any further restrictive action by international tensions. His view of the issue after the outbreak of war with Japan remains unclear. He did not share the anxieties of west coast residents, yet he ultimately accepted the possibility of a Japanese invasion of British Columbia.[46] Probably his primary concern was for the instability of west coast opinion and the threat to public order which it posed. If subsequent government policy is any measure of his thought, he was willing to adopt any expedient that would reduce public tension.

When the final announcement was made, the province did not immediately breathe a sigh of collective relief. Tension remained high for several days thereafter. In Ottawa Ian Mackenzie believed that public disorder was still possible. Slowly, however, the strain of racial crisis began to ease. The two mass meetings held on March 1 were quiet and orderly. Mackenzie received a note of praise from supporters in Vancouver. The flood of protests to Ottawa began to recede.[47]

When the cabinet approved the order which permitted evacuation, the editors of the *Sun* looked forward to the day the move would be complete. They hoped that the coast was "Saying Goodbye, Not Au Revoir" to the Japanese.[48] But while some had undoubtedly seen the crisis as a chance to solve the province's Japanese problem for all time, this scarcely explains the previous weeks' outburst of hostility. War with Japan had sharpened the animus, narrowed the vision, and intensified the fears of a community already profoundly divided along racial lines. In the minds of west coast whites, intimations of vulnerability and isolation had long nursed a sense of insecurity, and after Pearl Harbor many British Columbians had felt themselves exposed as never before to attack from Japan. In addition, they had grown convinced that the resident Japanese were a threat to the community's security. These beliefs had virtually no foundation in fact. In essence they were facets of the traditional Japanese image held by white British Columbians, stereotypes further distorted in the heat of war. Its fears fed by these perceptions, the west coast loosed a torrent of hostility. Sensitive to the public temper, and alarmed by the prospect of racial disturbance, the federal government attempted preventative action. But neither minor restrictions on civil liberties nor the promise of partial relocation satisfied west coast whites. They demanded total Japanese evacuation. In the end their wishes were met.[49]

* * *

Yet, more openly than ever before, a small but growing number of whites simultaneously declared support for the Japanese minority. Campaigns by whites in favour of Oriental civil rights were not entirely new by the 1940s. During the interwar years, to a very limited extent, west coast attitudes toward Asians had begun to liberalize. British Columbia trade unionism gradually abandoned its intense nativism. Undoubtedly racism persisted within the labour movement, but union leaders and policies were no longer outspokenly anti-Oriental and limited support for racial equality could be found in union circles. Of greater importance was the fact that Asian minorities had gained a political voice for the first time during the 1930s; the CCF took their cause to the public, calling for the franchise for second-generation Orientals, albeit with due regard for the party's political fortunes. Liberal protestantism also lost its obsession with the seeming need to assimilate Asiatics and commenced open advocacy of minority group interests. Together these various developments marked the dawn of a reassessment of traditional white assumptions about the Asian immigrant in British Columbia, and it was on these foundations that the first shift in attitudes during and after World War II was based.

The wartime advocates of the Japanese-Canadian cause demanded just treatment for all evacuees and urged positive government policies to extinguish anti-Orientalism forever. In the forefront of this movement were a handful of Protestant clergy and laymen and a few members of the CCF. Early in 1942 they formed the Vancouver Consultative Council, a group of between thirty and forty men and women from civil libertarian backgrounds.[50] Soon they were joined by the Fellowship for a Christian Social Order, a Christian socialist organization with branches in Toronto, Vancouver, and other Canadian cities. Both groups denounced racism and campaigned for government action to eliminate discrimination and encourage Japanese integration into Canadian society. They believed that the only way to solve the racial problem for all time was to disperse the

Japanese community throughout Canadian society. In the words of Dr. Norman F. Black, a leading member of the VCC:

We feel very strongly that our Japanese problem can be solved only by prompt and systematic geographic and occupational dispersion ... *we foresee bloodshed on the streets of Vancouver* if, at the termination of the war, twenty thousand or ten thousand or even five thousand homeless and workless Japanese and Canadians of Japanese ancestry suddenly crowd back into this locality when war passions are still surging. The reasons for such anxiety are too manifest to require explanation. And we feel that, unless in the meantime these people have established real homes and become absorbed into the general currents of Canadian economic and social life, an intrinsically hopeless situation will inevitably develop.[51]

Similar sentiments were echoed by the provincial CCF.[52]

Late in the war this movement broadened as leaders of the second-generation Japanese joined church groups, civil libertarians, and CCF politicians in a protest against the federal disenfranchisement of those Japanese Canadians who lived outside the province of British Columbia.[53] An even more vigorous campaign opposed the King government's plan for mass Japanese deportation, a policy intended to send to Japan some 10,000 persons of Japanese ancestry who during 1944 and 1945 had declared their wish to go and had not retracted their decision before the Pacific war had ended; the majority of them had subsequently changed their minds and thus were to be deported against their will. In this instance protest was marshalled by Japanese-Canadian civil rights groups and the Co-operative Committee on

Japanese Canadians, a Toronto-based coalition of local and national organizations, among them churches, youth clubs, trade unions, welfare councils, the YMCA, YWCA, and civil liberties associations. This was by far the most vigorous opposition yet mounted against anti-Oriental government policies. Ultimately it was successful for the King government relented and repatriated only those who still wished to be sent.[54]

These campaigns marked a fundamental shift in white attitudes toward Orientals, the first in the lengthy history of their presence in Canada. In British Columbia and across Canada liberal views on race relations were suddenly ascendant. In the later 1940s nativists still voiced their views in public but they were clearly on the defensive. One sign of this change in public opinion was the relative swiftness and ease with which discriminatory legislation was dismantled. The federal government repealed the Chinese Immigration Act in 1947, although sharp limitations on the number of entrants were to continue for years. Of greater symbolic significance was the removal of the franchise restrictions which had long been imposed upon all Asiatics. Chinese and East Indian Canadians gained the vote both provincially and federally in 1947. After a further two-year delay, symptomatic of greater white prejudice, Japanese Canadians were also given the franchise. Soon all of the legal disabilities affecting Orientals had been removed. By the early 1950s discrimination in law against residents of Oriental ancestry was a thing of the past. Undeniably nativism still lurked in white British Columbia, but its public spokesmen had vanished. Lacking public legitimacy, racial discrimination was henceforth forced to assume its many subtler forms.

The motives which lay beneath this major change in public opinion are too complex for analysis here. But among the many possibilities, four seem especially significant. First, and of most immediate importance, the end of the war and the Japanese dispersal had finally erased the image of a Japanese menace in Canada. Henceforth this minority group ceased to seem a military and economic threat. As a result, those attitudes which had once formed the core of anti-Japanese feeling could no longer be maintained. Second, the postwar revelations of German war atrocities cast racist doctrines into unprecedented disrepute in western societies. This revulsion underlay the growing trend toward public declarations of basic human rights, ideals which found open expression in the United Nations' charter and the liberal internationalist rhetoric of the postwar years. So articulate were the champions of this new idealism and so pervasive were their beliefs that by the early 1950s they had reduced Canadian nativists to virtual silence. In the third place, China had been a wartime partner of the Allies and this may have encouraged more positive public attitudes toward the Chinese in Canada, in any case a group which had already ceased to seem a major threat in the eyes of most British Columbians.

Finally, acculturation had greatly reduced the social distance between whites and Asians, particularly those of the second generation. In defiance of all that nativists had long predicted, the Chinese, Japanese, and East Indians had in varying degrees absorbed the social and cultural norms of western Canadian society. Thus they had taken great strides toward eliminating the fundamental source of British Columbian racism. The unassimilable Oriental was becoming assimilated.

NOTES

1   A. R. M. Lower, *Canada and the Far East—1940* (New York: Institute of Pacific Relations, 1940), pp. 23–28.

2   *Sun*, Nov. 17, 1937.

3   *Sun*, Nov. 24, 1937; *Colonist*, Jan. 19, 1938.

4   Canada, *Commons Debates*, Feb. 17, 1938, 550–75.

5   *Province*, Feb. 22, 1938.

6   *Province*, Feb. 2, 17, 18, and 24, 1938; *Sun*, Feb. 10, 12, 14, and 28, 1938.

7   Two representative letters to King are: Dr. R. S. Hanna to King, Feb. 14, 1938, King Papers, MG 26, J2, vol. 147, file I-209; Forgotten Native of Japanada to King, n.d., ibid. Letters to Wilson in 1938 can be found in the Wilson Papers, vol. I, file 1.

8   Pattullo to King, Jan. 26, 1938, King Papers, MG 26, J1, vol. 256, 218388–89; Mackenzie to King, Feb. 26, 1938, ibid., vol. 253, 216060; King to Mackenzie, Mar. 1, 1938, ibid., 216062–63A.

9   *Sun*, Mar. 23, 1938.

10   The Board of Review estimated that about 120 Japanese were then living illegally in the province. Board of Review [Immigration], *Final Report*, Sept. 29, 1938, p. 38.

11   British Columbia, *Journals*, Dec. 9, 1938, 120; *Sun*, Oct. 12 and 18, 1938.

12   L. R. LaFleche to F. C. Blair, June 2, 1938, Canada, Department of National Defence Records, file H.Q. 6-0-7, Department of National Defence Archives, Ottawa.

13   Brig. C.V. Stockwell to the Secretary, Department of National Defence, Sept. 4, 1940, Defence Records, file H.Q.S., v.s. 38-1-1-1, vol. 5.

14   Supt. C. H. Hill to the Commissioner, Aug. 25, 1938, Canada, Immigration Branch Records, vol. 86, file 9309, vol. 16; Asst. Comm. R. R. Tait to Keenleyside, Oct. 28, 1940, External Affairs Records, vol. 2007, file 212, pt. I. The entire contents of this file substantiate the observations made in this paragraph.

15   The RCMP did, however, identify a small number of Japanese who might endanger the state in time of war and these individuals were arrested and detained immediately after war on Japan was declared.

16   All Japanese nationals immediately became enemy aliens and restrictions imposed upon them were also imposed upon all Japanese Canadians naturalized after 1922.

17   Forrest E. La Violette, *The Canadian Japanese and World War II: A Social and Psychological Account* (Toronto: University of Toronto Press, 1948), p. 44; Declaration of the Existence of a State of War Between Canada and Japan, Dec. 8, 1941, King Papers, MG 26, J5, D58190–94; *Sun*, Dec. 8, 1941; *Free Press*, Dec. 8, 1941; *Province*, Dec. 8, 1941.

18   After Pearl Harbor the major daily newspapers in Vancouver and Victoria published a steady stream of letters on the Japanese problem, most of which voiced suspicion of the west coast Japanese and demanded federal action to remove the threat which they posed. For reports of vandalism see

Province, Dec. 8, 9, and 11, 1941. For rumours of Japanese subversion see Weekly Internal Security Intelligence Report, Dec. 13, 1941, Western Air Command, Defence Records, file H.Q. S67-3, vol. 1. With the exception of fishermen, most Japanese who lost their jobs were soon reabsorbed by the labour market. Hill, Intelligence Report, Dec. 16, 1941 and Jan. 13, 1942, External Affairs Records, file 3464-G-40, Department of External Affairs, Archives Branch (EAA).

19 Hutchison to Pickersgill, [Dec. 16, 1941, King Papers, MG 26, J4, vol. 347, 239219-20.

20 *Province*, Dec. 19, 1941; Hill to the Commissioner, RCMP, Dec. 20, 1941, External Affairs Records, file 3464-H-40C, EAA.

21 Hume to King, Dec. 20, 1941, External Affairs Records, vol. 1868, file 263, pt. IV, PAC.

22 Alexander to Chief of the General Staff, Dec. 30, 1941, Defence Records, file H.Q. 6-0-7. Alexander's concern was shared by those officers commanding Canada's Pacific coast naval and air forces. Commodore W. J. R. Beech to the General Officer Commanding-in-Chief, Pacific Command, Dec. 27, 1941, ibid.; Air Commodore L. F. Stevenson to the Secretary, Department of National Defence for Air, Jan. 2, 1941, Defence Records, file H.Q., S67-3, vol. 1. In Ottawa the Chief of the General Staff did not subscribe to these fears. Lt. Gen. K. Stuart to Keenleyside, Dec. 26, 1941, External Affairs Records, file 3464-H-40C, EAA.

23 Petitions to the federal government can be found in King Papers, MG 26, J2, vol. 294, file P.309, vol. 14; Ian Mackenzie Papers, vol. 24, file 70-25, vol. 1; ibid., vol. 25, file 70-25, vols. 2 and 3; ibid., vol. 25, file 70-25E, PAC; External Affairs Records, file 773-B-1-40, pts. I and II, EAA.

24 Turgeon to King, Jan. 6, 1942, ibid., pt. I.

25 Conference on the Japanese Problem in British Columbia, Minutes, Jan. 8 and 9, 1942, External Affairs Records, vol. 1868, file 263, pt. IV, PAC; Mackenzie to King, Jan. 10, 1942, Mackenzie Papers, vol. 32, file x-81; Keenleyside to Mackenzie, Jan. 10, 1942, ibid. The minority recommendation for partial evacuation was appended to the report.

26 Mackenzie to King, Jan. 10, 1942, ibid.; Pacific Command to National Defence Headquarters, Jan. 12, 1942, telegram, Defence Papers, file H.Q. 6-0-7.

27 Statement of the Prime Minister, Jan. 14, 1942, Mackenzie Papers, vol. 24, file 70-25, vol. 1. Two protected zones were ultimately defined. The larger embraced the area west of the Cascade Mountains, a range which ran parallel to the coast about 100 miles inland. The smaller encompassed the city of Trail and vicinity.

28 Mackenzie to B. M. Stewart, Jan. 23, 1942, Mackenzie Papers, vol. 32, file x-81, vol. 2; Keenleyside to Mackenzie, Jan. 26, 1942, ibid.; Keenleyside, "The Japanese Problem in British Columbia," Memorandum to N.A. Robertson, Jan. 27, 1942, ibid.

29 *Sun*, Jan. 14, 1942; the lull was obvious to military intelligence officers in British Columbia. Maj. H. C. Bray to the Director, Military Operations and Intelligence, National

Defence Headquarters, Jan. 29, 1942, Canada, Department of Labour Papers, Lacelle Files, vol. 174, file 614.02:11-1, vol. 1, PAC.

30 See above, n. 23.

31 M. C. Robinson and others to Mackenzie, Feb. 23, 1942, Mackenzie Papers, vol. 25, file 70-25, vol. 2.

32 *Commons Debates*, Jan. 29, 1942, 156-158.

33 Mackenzie to Robertson, Jan. 28, 1942, Mackenzie Papers, vol. 32, file x-81, vol. 2; R. W. Mayhew to King, Feb. 12, 1942, King Papers, MG 26, J1, vol. 330; G. G. McGeer to King, Feb. 13, 1942, Gerald Grattan McGeer Papers, box 2, file 9, PABC; O. Hanson and others to King, Feb. 21, 1942, King Papers, MG 26, J1, vol. 336.

34 R. L. Maitland to Mackenzie, Feb. 17, 1942, Mackenzie Papers, vol. 32, file x-81, vol. 2.

35 G. S. Pearson to A. Macnamara, Feb. 17, 1942, Labour Records, Lacelle Files, vol. 174, file 614.02:11-1, vol. 2; *Sun*, Feb. 16, 1942; Lt. Gov. W. C. Woodward to King, Feb. 11, 1942, King Papers, MG 26, J1, vol. 336; Alexander to the Secretary, Chiefs of Staff Committee, Feb. 13, 1942, Defence Records, Chiefs of Staff Committee, Miscellaneous Memoranda, vol. 3, February 1942; Joint Services Committee, Pacific Coast, Minutes, Feb. 19 and 20, 1942, ibid.

36 Mackenzie to L. St. Laurent, Feb. 14, 1942, Mackenzie Papers, vol. 24, file 70-25, vol. 1; Mackenzie to King, Feb. 22, 1942, King Papers, MG 26, J1, vol. 328.

37 Mackenzie to St. Laurent, Feb. 24, 1942, Mackenzie Papers, vol. 25, file 70-25, vol. 2. At the same time Mackenzie sent similar letters to colleagues King, C. G. Power, J. L. Ralston, A. Macdonald, and H. Mitchell.

38 Mackenzie to J. R. Bowler, Feb. 26, 1942, ibid.

39 King Diary, Feb. 19, 1942, King Papers, MG 26, J13.

40 Order in Council P.C. 1486, Feb. 24, 1942; *Commons Debates*, Feb. 27, 1942, 917-20.

41 Weekly Internal Security Intelligence Report, Jan. 17, 1942, Western Air Command, Defence Records, file H.Q. S67-3, vol. 1. For another example of rumour see Gwen Cash, *A Million Miles from Ottawa* (Toronto: Macmillan, 1942), pp. 25-26.

42 On the nature and significance of rumour see Gordon W. Allport and Leo Postman, *The Psychology of Rumor* (New York: Russell and Russell, 1965), especially chap. II.

43 *Sun*, Jan. 14, 1942; Mackenzie to Stewart, Jan. 23, 1942, Mackenzie Papers, vol. 32, file x-81, vol. 2. The emphasis was Mackenzie's.

44 Although some fruit and vegetable growers in the Okanagan Valley requested Japanese workers for the duration of the war in order to ease the wartime labour shortage, the proposal roused a strong outburst of bitter opposition in the valley. Protest was channelled through municipal councils, newspapers, boards of trade, and dissenting farm organizations. Proposals that the Japanese be moved east of the Rockies met opposition from several provincial governments. *Penticton*

Herald, Jan. 15, 22, and 29, 1942; *Kelowna Courier*, Jan. 22 and Feb. 12, 1942; Keenleyside, Memorandum for Robertson, Feb. 4, 1942, External Affairs Records, file 3464-G-40, EAA.

45 W. L. Mackenzie King, *Industry and Humanity: A Study in the Principles Underlying Industrial Reconstruction* (Toronto: Thomas Allen, 1918), pp. 75–76.

46 King Diary, Feb. 20, 23, and 24, 1942, King Papers, MG 26, J13.

47 Cash, *A Million Miles*, p. 33; *Province*, Mar. 2, 1942; *Colonist*, Mar. 3, 1942; A. Thompson to C. N. Senior, Feb. 27, 1942, Mackenzie Papers, vol. 25, file 70-25, vol. 2.

48 *Sun*, Feb. 26, 1942.

49 While racial tensions swelled in British Columbia after Pearl Harbor, a similar crisis occurred on the American Pacific Coast. There, as in Canada, residents in coastal areas who were of Japanese origin, were forced to move inland to camps constructed for their reception. The American decision for evacuation, however, was based solely on military consider-ations and was taken by military officers who had been given a free hand by President Roosevelt. There seems to have been no collaboration between the Canadian and American governments in the decision-making process, and, while the events of the two evacuations ran in close parallel, neither country's policy appears to have had much influence upon that of the other. For accounts of the American evacuation see Morton Grodzins, *Americans Betrayed: Politics and the Japanese Evacuation* (Chicago: University of Chicago Press, 1949); Stetson Conn, "The Decision to Evacuate the Japanese from the Pacific Coast (1942)," *Command Decisions*, ed. Kent Roberts Greenfield, prepared by the Office of the Chief of Military History, Department of the Army (New York: Harcourt, Brace, 1959), pp. 88–109; Roger Daniels, *Concentration Camps USA: Japanese Americans and World War II* (New York: Holt, Rinehart and Winston, 1972).

50 Interview with Rev. Howard Norman, July 26, 1973.

51 Black to G. Dorey, Jan. 4, 1943, United Church of Canada, Board of Home Missions, United Church Archives, Toronto.

52 Grace MacInnis and Angus MacInnis, *Oriental Canadians—Outcasts or Citizens?* (n.p., n.d.) pp. 17–20.

53 Carol F. Lee, "The Road to Enfranchisement: Chinese and Japanese in British Columbia," *BC Studies*, no. 30 (Summer 1976), p. 52.

54 Ibid., 60; La Violette, *The Canadian Japanese and World War II*, chaps. X and XI.

CHAPTER 15

The Evacuation of the Japanese Canadians, 1942:
A Realist Critique of the Received Version

J.L. Granatstein and Gregory A. Johnson

The popularly accepted version of the evacuation of the Japanese Canadians from the Pacific Coast in 1941–1942 and the background to it runs roughly like this. The white population of British Columbia had long cherished resentments against the Asians who lived among them, and most particularly against the Japanese Canadians. Much of this sprang from envy of the Japanese Canadians' hard-work and industry, much at the substantial share held by Japanese Canadians of the fishing, market gardening and lumbering industry. Moreover, white British Columbians (and Canadians generally) had long had fears that the Japanese Canadians were unassimilable into Canadian society and, beginning early in this century and intensifying as the interwar period wore on, that many might secretly be acting as agents of their original homeland, now an aggressive and expansionist Japan. Liberal and Conservative politicians at the federal, provincial and municipal levels played upon the racist fears of the majority for their own political purposes. Thus when the Second World War began in September 1939, and when its early course ran disastrously against the Allies, there was already substantial fear about "aliens" in British Columbia (and elsewhere) and a desire to ensure that Japanese Canadians would be exempted from military training and service. The federal government concurred in this, despite the desire of many young Japanese Canadians to show their loyalty to Canada by enlisting.

After 7 December 1941 and the beginning of the Pacific War, public and political pressures upon the Japanese Canadians increased exponentially. Suspected subversives were rounded up by the RCMP in the first hours of the war, and over the next ten weeks a variety of actions took place that resulted in the seizure of fishing vessels, arms, cars, cameras, radio transmitters and short-wave receivers owned by Japanese Canadians, and then escalated through the evacuation from the coast of male Japanese nationals between the ages of 18 and 45 to the removal of all Japanese, whether Canadian citizens by birth or naturalization and regardless of age or sex, into the interior. The legalized theft of the property of these Japanese Canadians then followed, and even before the war ended the government moved to deport large numbers to Japan. These events occurred despite the facts that the RCMP and Canada's senior military officers considered the removal of the Japanese from the coast unnecessary, there being no credible military or security threat; that the responsible politicians in Ottawa, and particularly Ian Mackenzie, BC's representative in the Cabinet, knew that the Japanese Canadians posed no threat to national security and acted out of a desire to pander to the bigotry of some whites or for political motives relating to the conduct of the war at home.

This bald summary is based on such books as Ken Adachi's *The Enemy that Never Was* (Toronto, 1976), the second volume of Hugh Keenleyside's *Memoirs* (Toronto, 1982), and Ann Gomer Sunahara's *The Politics of Racism* (Toronto, 1981), as well as on the National Association of Japanese Canadians' brief to the federal government, *Democracy Betrayed: The Case for Redress* (1985). There are variations of emphasis in these accounts, naturally enough, but the received version is a composite that does not pay much attention to these differences.

That Canadians should be interested in the events of 1942 is understandable. That they should attempt to fix blame for the events of those days is no less so, and historians, whose trade obliges them to rummage with more or less science through the past, have not been immune from this tendency. It is the responsibility of historians, however, to try to put themselves back into the circumstances of the past and, while never becoming apologists for the horrors of those times, to seek to understand why people acted as they did. This paper is an attempt to do precisely that, and to look afresh at some points which are encompassed in the received version of the 1942 evacuation and open for examination and some which are not.

THE INTELLIGENCE SERVICES

The first question that must be raised, and one that has not been asked before, is this: what resources did Ottawa's civil, military and police authorities have on the West Coast before the outbreak of war to secure information about the 22,000 Japanese Canadians living in British Columbia? The answer is readily available.

The responsibility for internal security rested with the RCMP, assisted as necessary by the armed forces.[1] In July 1941, five months before the outbreak of war with Japan, the RCMP's "E" Division responsible for the Pacific Coast had on its staff three persons concerned with gathering intelligence on the Japanese Canadians in British Columbia: a sergeant who did not speak Japanese, a constable who did, and a civilian translator. These three were in charge of the "active personnel intelligence work on enemy and potential enemy aliens and agents." There was, in addition, a lieutenant-commander at Naval Headquarters in Esquimalt charged with intelligence duties who was "greatly interested in the Japanese problem generally," but who had many other tasks. The Royal Canadian Air Force's intelligence section in the province, which like the Royal Canadian Navy's had a wide range of duties over and above collecting information on Japanese Canadians, consisted of two officers, both of whom had lived in Japan and spoke Japanese. The senior officer, a Squadron Leader Wynd, however, could read Japanese only with difficulty; whether his colleague was any more fluent is uncertain. The army's intelligence on the coast was in the hands of two very busy officers, neither of whom spoke Japanese. In addition, the British Columbia Provincial Police had four officers working in the Japanese-Canadian community. Cooperation between the various services was hampered by RCMP regulations that forbade the Mounties to share information with their colleagues without first securing permission from Ottawa headquarters. Even so, the West Coast Joint Intelligence Committee had been created to coordinate the information collected by the military and police.[2] There is one additional point worth mentioning: the British intelligence services had some representation on the West Coast, and there exists in RCMP files one very long (and very inflammatory) report on "Japanese Activities in British Columbia," prepared by someone unnamed for William Stephenson's British Security Coordination.[3]

This intelligence presence did not amount to very much. As Hugh Keenleyside of the Department of External Affairs, a British Columbian who had served in the Legation in Japan and who was genuinely sympathetic to the Japanese Canadians, wrote in June 1940, there was a danger of subversive activities on the part of some elements in the Japanese community. "The police," he went on, "are not in a position to ferret out the dangerous Japanese as they have done with the Germans and Italians; they have lines on a few Japanese who might be expected to take part in attempts at sabotage.... But that would not really solve the problem."[4] Even, therefore, in the view of someone in a position to know (and understand), the intelligence information gathered on the Japanese Canadians was strictly limited, the officers involved pathetically few in number and largely baffled by the impenetrability of the Japanese language and the tendency of the Japanese Canadians to stay together, separate, and (with good historical reasons) not to trust whites.

The discussion thus far has said nothing about the quality of the information gathered. The available intelligence evidence on the Japanese Canadians is very slim (and the Privacy Act prevents us from seeing whatever else there might be), but we can state with confidence that when the RCMP looked at Communist questions, towards which it had a definite *idée fixe*, or the activities of suspected Nazis in this period, its work was far from competent.[5] In November 1939, J.W. Pickersgill of the prime

minister's office complained that the force could not distinguish between facts and hearsay, or discriminate between legitimate social and political criticism and subversive doctrine. There was, moreover, "no suggestion that there is any co-ordination with Military Intelligence, or with the Immigration authorities, or with the Department of External Affairs, or even with the Censorship." More disturbing still to Pickersgill was "the evidence of a total lack of the capacity, education and training required for real intelligence work...."[6] Whether the RCMP's efforts on the Japanese Canadians were any better remains speculative, at least until all the files are open to research; the existing documents offer no grounds for optimism.

There is little more information available on the quality of military intelligence gathered. But as the regular forces before the war were tiny and as military intelligence, a skill requiring years of preparation, was not among the best-developed areas of the permanent forces, there is no reason to believe that the army, navy or air force by 1941 were any less clumsy or more sophisticated in their ability to gather and assess information on the Japanese Canadians than the RCMP. Evidence for this conclusion is suggested by the efforts of the Examination Unit, a secret operation of External Affairs and National Defence set up under the shelter of the National Research Council, among other things to attempt to decipher Japanese diplomatic and military wireless messages in response to a British request before Pearl Harbor. As the just declassified manuscript history of the Examination Unit notes, two people were engaged for this purpose in August 1941, a Mr. and Mrs. T.L. Colton. "It was hoped that Mrs. Colton, who was very well educated in Japanese but could not handle translation into English, might be able to explain the contents of messages to her husband who could then write them out in English. This system," the history notes dryly, "did not prove very satisfactory" and the Coltons were replaced in April 1942.[7]

In this atmosphere of improvisation and amateurism, many of the available reports by the RCMP and the military on the Japanese Canadians tended to focus on investigations of alleged "unlawful drilling [with weapons]" by male Japanese Canadians, reports of caches of Japanese rifles and ammunition, and accounts of suspicious fishing parties of well-dressed Japanese who did not appear to be fishermen. Rumours, plain and fanciful.[8] On the other hand, there were just as many assertions offered with great confidence that 95 percent of Japanese Canadians were law abiding and satisfied with their lot in Canada and that "No fear of sabotage need be expected from the Japanese in Canada." That last statement by Assistant Commissioner Frederick J. Mead of the RCMP, one of the Mounties' specialists in security matters and Communist subversion, was, he added, "broad [but] at the same time I know it to be true."[9]

Mead was soon a member of the British Columbia Security Commission where, activist *Nisei* (or second generation Canadian Japanese) correctly believed, he depended on intelligence from Etsuji Morii, a man suspected of blackmailing other Japanese Canadians and a notorious underworld figure. Morii was in turn the Commission's appointed chairman of the "Japanese Liaison Committee," whose mandate was to convey news and information in 1942 to the community.[10] As Mead was the senior RCMP official on the coast early in 1942, he was almost certainly the main source for RCMP Commissioner S. T. Wood's defence of Morii and his assertion to William Stephenson (in response to the British Security Coordination report mentioned earlier) in August 1942 that "we have searched without letup for evidence detrimen-

tal to the interests of the state and we feel that our coverage has been good, but to date no such evidence has been uncovered."[11] The RCMP's firmly-stated position may have been correct, but again the small size of its resources and the lack of sophistication of all its operations in this period tend to raise doubts. From 45 years distance, the fairest thing that can be said is that the RCMP had uncovered relatively little hard information about possible subversion among the Japanese Canadians before 7 December 1941, if there were indeed subversive intentions within the community, because it lacked the competence and skills to do so. Moreover, much of the information that the RCMP had before and after that date came from sources that even many Japanese Canadians considered self-interested and tainted.

THE ROLE OF THE JAPANESE CONSULATE
Such intelligence information as there was tended to agree that the Japanese Consulate in Vancouver was the focus of Japanese nationalism, propaganda and possible subversive activities in BC. One RCMP report surveying the general activities of the Japanese Canadians noted that the Consul and his staff regularly visited areas where Japanese Canadians lived to deliver speeches and to talk privately with individuals about the Tokyo government's views of world events. One RCAF intelligence officer was sufficiently alarmed by these activities to tell his superior that he considered British Columbia's Japanese Canadians to be "directly under the control of the Japanese Government through their consul at Vancouver."[12] The Consul was also thought to exercise considerable influence on the local Japanese language schools and press. Roles of these sorts, of course, were well within the bounds of diplomatic niceties. And since, under Japanese law, *Nisei* born abroad before

1924 were considered as Imperial subjects, while those born abroad after that date could register at Japanese consulates and secure Japanese citizenship in addition to their status as British subjects, the Consul in Vancouver had substantial work to do in dealing with the approximately 7,200 Japanese nationals, 2,400 naturalized British subjects, and the unknown (but very large) number of Japanese Canadians holding dual citizenship in the BC community.[13] A military intelligence paper surveying the situation on the coast added that the Consul "through his agents, and through the Japanese schoolmasters, and the Japanese patriotic societies cultivates a strong Japanese spirit and a consciousness among the BC Japanese of being 'sons of Japan abroad' rather than Canadian citizens."[14] That was no different than the role of the Italian and German consuls in this pre-war period.

There were, however, grounds for believing that in this instance the Japanese Consulate's officials had duties of a more dangerous kind. On 28 February 1941, Vincent Massey, the high commissioner in London, reported to Prime Minister Mackenzie King that "reliable information of a most secret character" had revealed that "official Japanese circles" were taking great interest in the British Columbia Coast. "Reference is also made to large number of Japanese settled in British Columbia and on Western Coast of United States, who are all said to have their duties,"[15] an ominous phrase.

The source of that information was possibly Britain's Government Code & Cypher School which had been reading some Japanese military and diplomatic messages since the 1920s,[16] or more probably "Magic," the name given by the Americans to their armed forces' decryption operation that in January 1941 had cracked the "Purple" code used for the most secret Japanese diplomatic traffic. Britain and the United States soon started to cooperate in

reading Japanese codes, and by the spring of 1941 the two countries had pooled their intelligence.[17] The Americans also began reading their hitherto unbroken files of Japanese messages back to 1938.

The decryption team had intercepted important telegrams from the Foreign Office in Tokyo to the Japanese Embassy in Washington dated 30 January 1941, which gave the *Gaimusho*'s orders to its officials in North America to de-emphasize propaganda and to strengthen intelligence gathering. Special reference was made to "Utilization of our 'Second Generations' [Nisei] and our resident nationals" and to the necessity for great caution so as not to bring persecution down on their heads. Those messages were copied to Ottawa and Vancouver as "Minister's orders"—instructions, in other words, that were to be carried out in Canada just as in the United States. The Consulate's success in carrying out these orders remains unknown.

A further message from Tokyo to Washington, dated 15 February 1941, was also sent to Ottawa and Vancouver as a "Minister's instruction." In this telegram, the Foreign Ministry specified the "information we particularly desire with regard to intelligence involving US and Canada," especially the strengthening of Pacific Coast defences, ship and aircraft movements. In a telegram the day before, the Consulate in Vancouver was instructed to pay special attention to paragraph 10 of the order to Washington: "General outlooks on Alaska and the Aleutian Islands, with particular stress on items involving plane movements and shipment of military supplies to those localities." The next month, the Consulate was asked to report on RCN ship movements. Whether these particular telegrams were the basis for Massey's despatch to Ottawa is unclear.[18]

A thorough search of the "Magic" intercepts in the United States National Archives makes clear that at least as early as 1939 intelligence and counter-intelligence work was carried on from the Vancouver Consulate, exactly as was taking place in the Japanese Consulates all over the United States and throughout the Western Hemisphere. As we have seen, the 1941 telegrams also stress efforts to involve the resident nationals and the second generation *Nisei*, at whom radio broadcasts from Tokyo had been deliberately aimed for some years. How much, if anything, Ottawa knew of all this, beyond the RCMP's suspicions and the information conveyed in the Massey telegram, is still indeterminate. But surely there was ample justification in the light of the Massey telegram for the government to have increased surveillance on the Consulate and the Japanese-Canadian community. There is no sign that it did so.[19]

One contemporary assessment of the Canadian situation by an RCAF intelligence officer noted that "espionage and subversive activity is largely carried on by a few key Japanese working under the Consul and *seriously* involves only a few—say 60 at most—Japanese individuals." This same officer then tried to assess the response of Japanese Canadians in the event of war, particularly if the Japanese authorities instructed them to engage in sabotage, and if such orders were reinforced by "disorderly demonstrations of white antipathy." His answer was that "No one knows; but no one in his senses would take a chance on Japanese loyalty under those circumstances."[20]

THE PRE-WAR PRO-JAPAN ACTIONS OF JAPANESE CANADIANS

If that sounds harsh, there were reasons why it should not. Throughout the 1930s and especially after 1937, Japan had aggressively expanded its influences in northern China, and the Imperial Japanese Army had campaigned with great brutality in that country. The Japanese government, naturally enough, tried to put the best face possible on its actions, and it encouraged the creation and spread of propaganda on its behalf abroad, something in which Japanese Canadians directly assisted by writing and distributing leaflets. The most widely distributed pamphlet, dated 1 October 1937 and published by the Canadian Japanese Association, the largest Japanese-Canadian association with over 3,000 members, was "Sino-Japanese Conflict Elucidated," a far from unbiased examination of the struggle in China, despite its claim to be circulated "in the interests of truth, to meet unfair and untrue propaganda." Moreover, money, comforts for the troops, medical supplies and tin foil were collected for Japan by first generation *Issei* and second generation *Nisei* groups.[21] There was, of course, nothing remotely improper about this, and other ethnic groups in Canada at that time (Italians, say, during the Italo-Ethiopian war) and more recently (Jews during the Arab-Israeli wars, for example) have acted similarly in comparable circumstances.

But the wholly justifiable outrage in Canada over such incidents as the brutal rape of Nanking, with its estimated 200,000 or more dead (and Japanese army assaults on Canadian missionaries stationed there) led many Canadians to boycott Japanese products and to call upon the federal government to take steps to cease strategic metal exports to Japan. Such measures were eventually taken.[22] And the *New Canadian*, the newspaper of British Columbia's *Nisei*, began publication in late 1938, noted its founder, Edward Ouchi, the General Secretary of the main *Nisei* organization, the Japanese Canadian Citizens' League, to counter the "vicious" anti-Japanese propaganda of North American Chinese that was hurting Japanese-Canadian businesses. Although the newspaper did not offer frequent support for Japan's war in China in its pages, it did give close and favourable coverage to the activities of the Consul in Vancouver and even ran an occasional rotogravure section of propagandistic photographs on life in Japan.[23]

Inevitably Japanese-Canadian support for Japan's war on China focussed much attention upon the *Issei* and *Nisei*. As Professor Henry Angus of the University of British Columbia wrote in October 1940:

> The young Japanese understand the position well enough. At first they (in all good faith I think) distributed a good deal of pro-Japanese, anti-Chinese propaganda. Now they say, "we are not responsible for what Japan may do." I tell them that they have unfortunately made people feel that they are identified with Japan by their action in distributing propaganda, and that it is very difficult to find a way of removing this impression.[24]

Angus was always very sympathetic to the Japanese Canadians (and after he had joined External Affairs, he and Hugh Keenleyside would find themselves under attack in Parliament because of the vigor of their resistance to the evacuation in January and February 1942),[25] but he was surely correct in his assessment. Even such supportive British Columbia politicians as CCF Member of Parliament Angus MacInnis agreed.[26] The Japanese Canadians by their support for Japan "impaired [their] standing with those circles most disposed to press [their] cause," Professor Angus lamented.[27]

We can say today that Canadians should have understood the difficulties that a small minority would have faced in not supporting its belligerent mother country in those days in the late 1930s and early 1940s. But after the Pearl Harbor attack and the fall of Hong Kong, British Columbians, already predisposed to expect the worst of the Japanese Canadians and

motivated by deep-rooted racism against them, and Canadians generally could not reasonably have been expected to make such judgements. Many Japanese Canadians had supported Japan against China before 7 December and few, if any, had opposed her; after Pearl Harbor, China was an ally and Japan an enemy. Therefore, the supporters of Japan before 7 December were now supporters of Canada's enemy and possibly (or probably) disloyal, particularly as there seemed no way of distinguishing the active few from the passive majority. The syllogism was flawed (and certainly the vast majority of German and Italian Canadians had been treated far differently in the comparable circumstances of September 1939 and June 1940), but few were prepared to challenge its logic.

Norman Robertson, the under secretary of state for external affairs, a British Columbian and no bigot, expressed something of the same reasoning when he told Pierrepont Moffat, the American minister to Canada, on 8 December 1941 that "the Government had hoped not to have to intern all Japanese. However, this might be very difficult in view of the treacherous nature of the Japanese attack, [and] the evidences of premeditation...."[28] Robertson's description of the attack mirrored the public's response: "In the wake of Pearl Harbor, the single word favoured by Americans as best characterizing the Japanese people," John Dower has noted, "was 'treacherous'...."[29]

THE ATTITUDES OF JAPANESE CANADIANS AFTER 7 DECEMBER

In August 1944, Prime Minister King told the House of Commons that "no person of Japanese race born in Canada has been charged with any act of sabotage or disloyalty during the years of war." In his account, Ken Adachi added that "no alien Japanese or naturalized citizen had ever been found guilty of the same crime."[30] Those statements are undoubtedly true, but they do not tell the whole story.

Thirty-seven or 38 Japanese nationals were arrested and interned by the RCMP at the outbreak of the war, presumably because they were thought to be engaged in espionage or subversive activities. None of the standard accounts offers any detailed information on the allegations against or the fate of these people.[31]

More important, it seems certain that support for Japan remained strong among some Japanese Canadians after the war began. The *Issei* Takeo Nakano, in his book *Within the Barbed Wire Fence*, notes that "We Japanese, largely working-class immigrants, were, generally speaking, not given to sophisticated political thinking. Rather we had in common a blind faith in Japan's eventual victory." John J. Stephan's study, *Hawaii Under the Rising Sun*, cites the conclusions of Japanese historians Nobuhiro Adachi and Hidehiko Ushijima that most first-generation Japanese in Hawaii remained loyal to Japan: "even among those who considered the Pearl Harbor attack a betrayal were many who believed in and hoped for an ultimate Japanese victory.... Radio reports of Japanese advances ... confirmed for many their motherland's invincibility." Nakano's book demonstrates that the same response existed in British Columbia, and even Sunahara notes that the Japanese vice-consul encouraged some Japanese Canadians to seek internment as a gesture of support for Japan.[32] Those of Japanese origin, of course, formed a greater proportion of the Hawaiian population (about 35 percent) than did the Japanese Canadians in British Columbia (about three percent). Moreover, at this point it is impossible to determine if the links between the Japanese Canadians and Japan were stronger or weaker than those between Hawaiian Japanese and the mother country. These two factors could certainly have affected the situation.

* * *

THE ROLE OF THE MILITARY IN THE EVACUATION

There is no doubt that senior officers of the armed forces and the RCMP in Ottawa were remarkably unperturbed by the presence of large numbers of Japanese Canadians in British Columbia.[33] General Maurice Pope, the vice chief of the General Staff, attended the Conference on the Japanese Problem in British Columbia in Ottawa on 8–9 January 1942, which brought together representatives from British Columbia, the federal bureaucracy, and political figures, and his memoir provides the standard account. The navy, he wrote, had no fears, now that the Japanese-Canadian fishing fleet was in secure hands; the RCMP expressed no concern, and Pope himself, offering the army position, said that if the RCMP was not perturbed, "neither was the Army." Pope adds that several days after the meeting adjourned, the angry and frightened British Columbians who had attended "must have got busy on the telephone" for "we received an urgent message from the [Army's] Pacific Command recommending positive action against the Japanese in the interests of national security. With the receipt of this message, completely reversing the Command's previous stand," the minister of national defence, Colonel J.L. Ralston, "was anything but pleased."[34]

The evidence simply does not support Pope's account. While it is clear that the Department of National Defence's representatives on the Special Committee on Measures to be Taken in the Event of War With Japan agreed in mid-1941 with the Committee's recommendation to Cabinet that "the bulk of the

Japanese population in Canada can continue its normal activities,"[35] and while it is equally certain in mid-December the Chiefs of Staff Committee told the Cabinet War Committee that fears of a Japanese assault on BC were unwarranted,[36] there is absolutely no doubt that the military commanders *in* British Columbia and the military members of the Permanent Joint Board on Defence were seriously concerned about the possible threat posed by the Japanese-Canadian population both before and after 7 December 1941. The real question that remains unanswered is why in this instance the generals, admirals and air marshals in Ottawa were so ready to ignore the advice of their commanders in the field.

* * *

After Pearl Harbor, but before the Conference in Ottawa, ... three senior officers on the coast wrote to Ottawa with their views. Major-General R.O. Alexander, the GOC of Pacific Command, told the chief of the General Staff on 30 December that he believed "internment of Japanese males between the ages of 18 and 45, their removal from the coast and their organization into paid units on public works ... would be advisable." Such action, Alexander added, "might prevent inter-racial riots and bloodshed, and will undoubtedly do a great deal to calm the local population." There is no doubt that General Pope saw this letter, because he sent a copy of it to Hugh Keenleyside of the Department of External Affairs and Keenleyside wrote back to him with suggestions on 3 January—before the "Japanese Problem" conference in Ottawa took place.[37]

The senior RCAF officer in BC shared the view of his army colleague. Air Commodore L.F. Stevenson informed RCAF headquarters in Ottawa on 2 January that security "cannot

rest on precarious discernment between those who would actively support Japan and those who might at present be apathetic." If the government had doubts about the wisdom of moving the Japanese out, Stevenson said, "I suggest a strong commission be appointed immediately to ... obtain the opinion of a good cross section of the BC public and the officers charged with the defence of the Pacific Coast." The senior naval officer agreed, Commodore W.J.R. Beech telling his headquarters on 27 December that "Public opinion is very much against the Japanese all over the Queen Charlotte Islands and in view of the strategic position of these Islands I would strongly recommend that all the Japanese be removed."[38]

All three officers stressed public opinion at least as much as military needs, and it is reasonable to assume that their positions often put them in close contact with politicians and journalists likely to be pressing for stern action. But this does not alter the fact that the responsible military commanders in British Columbia, after 7 December and before the Ottawa conference, called for removal of the Japanese Canadians from all or part of the coastal region; so too had their staffs urged removal before 7 December from the vicinity of military bases and after Pearl Harbor from coastal areas of the province.[39] Moreover, on 13 February 1942, the Joint Services Committee, Pacific Coast, decided that in view of "the deterioration of the situation in the Pacific theatre of war ... the continued presence of enemy aliens and persons of Japanese racial origin [in the coastal areas] constitutes a serious danger and prejudices the effective defence of the Pacific Coast of Canada."[40] And as late as 26 February, the RCN commanding officer on the coast was advised by his security intelligence officer that "The removal of all Japanese from this coastal area would undoubtedly relieve what is becoming more and more a very dangerous situation from the point of view of sabotage and aid to the enemy as well as the great danger of development of interracial strife."[41] Again, public opinion was given equal weight with the fear of sabotage, but it is significant that this advice was proffered after adult male Japanese citizens living on the coast had been ordered inland.

* * *

Was There a Military Threat to the Coast?

Whether there was a direct military threat to the coast from the Imperial Japanese forces is also worth some consideration, if only because the received version denies any. In September 1941, RCAF headquarters in Ottawa had been confident that the United States Navy was the ultimate guarantor of the safety of the Pacific Coast: "Unless the United States Navy is seriously defeated or loses its northern bases," Air Vice Marshal G.M. Croil told his Minister, C.G. Power, all Canada had to do was remain in "watchful readiness" on the West Coast.[42] With that attitude in the ascendant, the coast of British Columbia was left "poorly defended," the words employed to describe matters by Robert Rossow, Jr., the American Vice-Consul in Vancouver, in August 1941.[43] After Pearl Harbor, however, the worst possible case seemed to have occurred, and Canada was largely unprepared. Certainly there were few modern aircraft, few ships, and relatively few trained soldiers in the area until the outbreak of war,[44] and it took some time before more could be rushed to the coast.[45] That caused concern.

So too did the course of the war. The Japanese hit Pearl Harbor on 7 December and simultaneously attacked Malaya, Hong Kong, the Philippines, and Wake and Midway Islands. On 8 December, Japan occupied Thailand, captured Guam on 13 December, Wake on 24 December, and Hong Kong on 25 December. Manila fell on 2 January, Singapore followed on 15 February, a staggering blow to the British position in Asia (and something that frightened British Columbia)[46] and the Imperial Japanese Navy crushed an allied fleet in the Java Sea on 27 February, the date that the Canadian government's decision to move all Japanese Canadians inland was in the newspapers. Closer to home, a Japanese submarine had shelled Santa Barbara, California on 23 February, two days later the "Battle of Los Angeles" took place with much ammunition expended against (apparently) imaginary targets, and there were submarine attacks on points in Oregon. (On 20 June a Japanese submarine shelled Estevan point on Vancouver Island.) The Dutch East Indies and most of Burma were then captured in March, capping an extraordinary four months of conquest.

At the beginning of June, the Japanese launched what H.P. Willmott, the leading historian of Pacific war strategy, called "their main endeavour, a twin offensive against the Aleutians," designed to draw the American fleet to battle to protect their territory, "and against the western Hawaiian Islands," intended to lead to an invasion once the Americans' Pacific Fleet had been destroyed. At least two plans for such an invasion existed before and after the attack on Pearl Harbor, and one plan saw the capture of Hawaii "as preparatory to strikes against the United States mainland."[47] (Whether attacks against the Canadian Coast were intended remains unclear until such Japanese military records that survived the war are searched.) Dutch Harbor, Alaska was attacked by carrier-based aircraft on 3 June as part of this plan. Four days later Kiska and Attu in the Aleutian Islands were taken.

Although in retrospect the American naval victory at Midway in June, aided beyond measure by "Magic" intercepts, put an end to the Hawaiian adventure and truly marked the beginning of the end for Japanese imperial ambitions as a whole, its significance was not quite so apparent in mid-1942 as it has since become. Certainly the Canadian government did not slacken its defence efforts on the coast after the American victory. In mid-February 1942, a military appreciation prepared by the chiefs of staff for the minister of national defence's use at a secret session of Parliament noted that "probable" Japanese strategy included containing "North American forces in America" by raids on the North American Pacific seaboard. "Possible" enemy aims included an "invasion of the West Coast of North America," although the chiefs noted that "Under present conditions" such invasion was "not considered to be a practicable operation of war."[48]

The next month, with the Japanese forces seemingly roaming at will throughout the Pacific and with the politicians anxious to satisfy the public clamour for stronger local defences in British Columbia, the chief of the General Staff in Ottawa was estimating the possible scale of a Japanese attack on the Pacific Coast to be two brigades strong (i.e., two Japanese regiments of three battalions each or approximately 5,200 to 6,000 men), and he was recommending the raising of new forces.[49] At the beginning of April, President Roosevelt used the occasion of the first meeting of the Pacific Council, made up of representatives of all the belligerent allies, to say that he had invited Canada because "he thought that Canada might do more than she was now doing."[50] That disturbed Ottawa, perhaps because it mirrored British Columbia public opinion so clearly, and Mackenzie King hastened to discuss the matter with the president.[51]

Later that month, after Lieutenant Colonel James Doolittle's B-25 bombers, launched from the carrier *Hornet*, had hit Tokyo, Canadian intelligence reports predicted that enemy aircraft carriers would launch retaliatory attacks against the West Coast in May.[52] By June, there were nineteen battalions on the coast, a response to Japan's invasion of the Aleutians and continued and growing public concern. Even so, the military commanders were far from satisfied. The Joint Canadian United States Services Committee at Prince Rupert believed that military strength in the area was "entirely inadequate against many types of attack that are possible and probable from the West."[53] The air officer commanding on the coast asked for sixteen squadrons to deal with the maximum scale of attack by battleships, cruisers and carrierborne aircraft. There were also blackouts and dimouts, and active plans underway in July and August 1942 for the evacuation of Vancouver Island and the lower mainland in the event of a Japanese attack.[54]

The Cabinet War Committee was assured by the chief of the General Staff in late September that he saw "no reason to fear any invasion from the Pacific Coast at present time,"[55] but two months later the Combined Chiefs of Staff, the highest Allied military authority, determined that while "carrier-borne air attacks and sporadic naval bombardment" were the most probable form of attack, the possibility of "a small scale destructive raid cannot be ignored." By that, the British and American planners meant "a force comprising 10/15 fast merchant ships carrying up to two brigades."[56] And as late as March 1943, there was a flurry of reports of Japanese activity in North American waters that stirred fears about a possible attack of the precise sort the planners had anticipated.[57] In other words, and contrary to the arguments of those who have argued that there was never any threat from Japan to the coast and hence no justification on grounds of national security for the evacuation of the Japanese Canadians, there *was* a credible—if limited—military threat into 1943.

* * *

None of this alters the conclusion that the Japanese Canadians were victims of the racism of the society in which they lived and an uncaring government that failed to defend the ideals for which its leaders claimed to have taken Canada and Canadians to war. Even so, this paper does maintain that there were military and intelligence concerns that, in the face of the sudden attack at Pearl Harbor, could have provided Ottawa with a justification for the evacuation of the Japanese Canadians from the coast. The government in December 1941 was unaware of much of the data that has since

emerged, and even if it had had it all, it simply lacked the assessment capability to put it together. If it had had the information and the intelligence capacity to appraise it properly, the arguments for evacuation would certainly have appeared far stronger than they already did.

However arguable this case, there is, of course, no necessary connection between the later confiscation of property and the still later effort to deport the Japanese Canadians and the reasons for the evacuation that seemed compelling to some in January and February 1942. The anger that persists at the evacuation might be misplaced; that at the confiscation of property and the attempt at deportation still seems wholly justifiable. In any case, this paper should demonstrate that there remains ample room for further work, broader interpretations and, perhaps, a changed emphasis in this area of research.

NOTES

[1] National Archives of Canada (NA), Department of National Defence Records, mf reel 5257, f. 8704, "Instructions for the Guidance of General Officers Commanding-in-Chief Atlantic and Pacific Commands," 26 February 1941

[2] NA, Department of External Affairs Records, vol. 2007, f. 1939-212, pt. 2, "Report on the State of Intelligence on the Pacific Coast with Particular Reference to the Problem of the Japanese Minority," 27 July 1941; Department of National Defence Records, vol. 11913, "Japanese" file, Cmdr Hart to R.B.C. Mundy, 21 August 1940

[3] PAC, RCMP Records, declassified report, "Japanese Activities in British Columbia" and attached correspondence. See also External Affairs Records, vol. 2007, f. 1939-212, pt. 2, "Report on the State...."

[4] External Affairs Records, vol. 2007. f. 1939-212, pt. 1, Keenleyside to H.F. Angus, 28 June 1940. After the order to remove the Japanese from the coast, Keenleyside noted that American "control of enemy aliens seems to be rather more severe than ours while their action with regard to their own citizens is somewhat less severe than ours." Ibid., Acc. 83-84/259, box 171, f. 2915-40, pt. 1, Keenleyside to Wrong, 14 March 1942

[5] See, e.g., Robert H. Keyserlingk, "'Agents Within the Gates': The Search for Nazi Subversives in Canada During World War II," *Canadian Historical Review*, LXVI (June 1985), 216–17; J.L. Granatstein, *A Man of Influence* (Ottawa, 1981), pp. 81ff; Reg Whitaker, "Official Repression of Communism During

World War II," *Labour/Le Travail*, XVII (Spring 1986), 137 and *passim*.

[6] NA, W.L.M. King Papers, "Note on a War-Time Intelligence Service," 27 November 1939, f. C257903ff. We are indebted to Professor W.R. Young for this reference.

[7] Department of National Defence Records, Declassified Examination Unit Files, memorandum for chairman, Supervisory Committee, 15 August 1941, Lt C.H. Little memorandum, 18 April 1942, Draft History, chapter VI, "Japanese Diplomatic Section," 1

[8] The spy scares in British Columbia sound much the same as those in Britain before the Great War. See Christopher Andrew, *Secret Service* (London, 1985), 34ff.

[9] Department of National Defence Records, vol. 11917, f. 5-1-128, 1938-9, RCMP report, 3 June 1938; ibid., vol. 11913, "Japanese" file, "Vancouver" [an agent] to Cmdr Hart, 30 June and 13 July 1940; External Affairs Records, vol. 2007, f. 1939-212, pt. 2, RCMP report, 29 July 1941; Ann Sunahara, *The Politics of Racism* (Toronto, 1981), 23

[10] See Roy Miki, ed., *This is My Own: Letters to Wes & Other Writings on Japanese Canadians, 1941–48 by Muriel Kitagawa* (Vancouver, 1985), 98–9.

[11] RCMP Records, declassified material, Commissioner S.T. Wood to Stephenson, 5 August 1942

[12] Department of National Defence Records, vol. 3864, f. N.S.S.

1023-18-2, vol. 1, memorandum, F/L Wynd to senior air staff officer, 24 June 1940

13 External Affairs Records, vol. 2007, RCMP report, 29 July 1941. Under a Japanese law of 1899, Japanese men liable for military service did not lose Japanese nationality upon naturalization abroad unless they had performed their military service. After 1934, Canada would not accept Japanese for naturalization without certification that they had completed military service. See ibid., Acc. 83-84/259, box 171, f. 2915-40, pt. 3, memorandum, "Postwar Treatment of Japanese in Canada," n.d.; John J. Stephan, *Hawaii Under the Rising Sun* (Honolulu, 1984), 24; and Ken Adachi, *The Enemy That Never Was* (Toronto, 1976). Adachi, 175, says that in 1934 86 percent of *Nisei* were dual citizens. The population numbers used here are those in the *Report and Recommendations of the Special Committee on Orientals in British Columbia, December 1940* (copy in NA, Privy Council Office Records, vol. 1, f. C-10-3), not those of the 1941 Census which were, of course, not available at the time.

14 External Affairs Records, vol. 2007, f. 1939-212, pt. 2, "Report on the State.... " See also the pamphlet by the Vancouver unit of the Fellowship for a Christian Social Order, "Canada's Japanese" (Vancouver 1942?]), 7–8, with its explanation of the role of the Consulate.

15 External Affairs Records, f. 28-C(s), Massey to prime minister, 28 February 1941. This telegram was discussed by the Cabinet War Committee, the key comment being that by Angus L. Macdonald, the minister of national defence (naval services), that there was "little danger of serious attack by Japan" on the Pacific Coast. Privy Council Office Records, Cabinet War Committee Minutes, 5 March 1941. This type of attitude presumably was responsible for the fact that, as late as July 1941, as we have seen above, the RCMP still had only three people responsible for Japanese-Canadian questions. For a plausible hypothesis on how the information might have reached Massey—from US under secretary of state, S. Welles, to the British ambassador, Halifax, to London and thence to Massey—see Ruth Harris, "The 'Magic' Leak of 1941 and Japanese-American Relations," *Pacific Historical Review*, L (1981), 83.

16 Andrew, 261, 353; Ronald Lewin, *The American Magic* (New York, 1982), 44ff

17 Ibid., 45–6

18 United States National Archives (USNA), General Records of the Department of the Navy, RG 80, "Magic" Documents, box 56, Tokyo to Washington, 30 January 1941 (2 parts); ibid., Tokyo to Washington, 15 February 1941; ibid., Los Angeles to Tokyo, 9 May 1941; ibid., Tokyo to Vancouver, March 1941. USNA, Records of the National Security Agency, RG 457, "Magic" Documents, SRH 018, SRDJ nos. 1233-4, 1246-9, 1370, 1525, Vancouver to Tokyo, 7, 14 July, 11, 19 August 1939. Some of this information is contained in *The "Magic" Background to Pearl Harbor* (Washington, 1977), I, no. 131, and especially no. 135, which is the Tokyo to Vancouver, 14 February 1941, telegram referred to. See also *New York Times*,

22 May 1983, and Gregory A. Johnson's doctoral research paper, "Mackenzie King and the Cancer in the Pacific" (York University. 1984).

19 Indeed, as late as 21 October 1941, and despite the Massey telegram referred to above, Hugh Keenleyside, the assistant under secretary of state for external affairs, told the under secretary that "While it might be possible to find Japanese nationals in British Columbia against whom some meagre suspicion exists, there is certainly no Japanese national at large in that Province or elsewhere in Canada against whom any really convincing case can be made out." That comment likely reflected both RCMP advice, which is suspect, and Keenleyside's own extensive knowledge. Whether his certainty was justified—in the light of the Consulate's activities—is another question. D.R. Murray, ed., *Documents on Canadian External Relations*, vol. VIII: *1939–41*, pt. 2 (Ottawa, 1976), 1169

20 External Affairs Records, vol. 2007, f. 1939-212, pt. 2, "Report on the State.... " Cf. H.F. Angus' critique of this report in Department of National Defence Records, f. 212-39c, 15 August 1941, and his memorandum of an interview with the officer, F/O Neild, 15 August 1941. We are indebted to Professor Patricia Roy for the Angus critique. It is worth noting that even missionaries shared alarmist views. A United Church China missionary, in Vancouver in January 1941, wrote that "I have had too much experience with the Japanese to trust them ... there is a war in progress and we in Vancouver are in the front line. And the front line is no place for thousands of enemy citizens." United Church Archives, Board of Foreign Missions, Honan, box 11, f. 174, Stewart to Reverend Armstrong, 20 January 1942

21 Adachi, 184–5. Membership figures for the Canadian Japanese Association are in University of British Columbia Archives, Japanese Canadian Collection, Miyazaki Collection, f. 6-4. A copy of the pamphlet is in ibid., P.H. Meadows, Japanese Farmers Association Papers.

22 Granatstein, 98ff; King Papers, f. C144716ff, contains petitions and other material on Canadian policy to Japan after 1937. See also Murray, 1203ff, for extensive documentation on metals export policy.

23 Ed Ouchi, ed., *'Til We See the Light of Hope* (Vernon, BC, 1982[?]), 70. *The New Canadian* is available in the UBC Archives. For support for the war, see the 20 October 1939 issue; on the consul, see, e.g., 8 September 1939. The rotogravure section began in late 1939 and ran well into 1940. On the economic boycott launched by Chinese groups, see UBC Archives, *Chinese Times* translations for 1937.

24 NA, J.W. Dafoe Papers, Angus to Dafoe, 15 October 1940. Mackenzie King told the Japanese minister to Canada in January 1941 that Japanese Canadians would not be called up for NRMA service: "he must remember that Japan and China were at war and we might be encouraging a little civil war if we supply both Chinese and Japanese with rifles etc., in BC at this time. He laughed very heartily at that." King Papers, Diary, 8 January 1941

25 University of British Columbia, Special Collections, H.F. Angus Papers, vol. 1, folder 2, draft memoir, 320-1; H.L. Keenleyside, *Memoirs of Hugh L. Keenleyside*, vol. II: *On The Bridge of Time* (Toronto, 1982), 171

26 University of British Columbia Archives, Special Collections, MacInnis Papers, Box 54A, f. 8, MacInnis to the Canadian Japanese Association, 11 December 1937; ibid., f. 12, MacInnis to T. Umezuki, 18 April 1939. The CCF did not live up to its ideals once the Pacific War started and the BC party supported removal of Japanese Canadians. See Werner Cohn, "The Persecution of Japanese Canadians and the Political Left in British Columbia, December 1941–March 1942," *BC Studies*, LXVIII (Winter 1985–6), 3ff.

27 H.F. Angus, "The Effect of the War on Oriental Minorities in Canada," *Canadian Journal of Economics and Political Science*, VII (November 1941), 508

28 Harvard University, J. Pierrepont Moffat Papers, "Memorandum of Conversations with Mr. Norman Robertson...," 8 December 1941

29 John W. Dower, *War Without Mercy: Race and Power in the Pacific War* (New York, 1986), 36. See also Christopher Thorne, *Racial Aspects of the Far Eastern War of 1941–1945* (London, 1982) and chapter II of his *The Issue of War* (London, 1985).

30 Canada, House of Commons *Debates*, 4 August 1944, 5948; Adachi, 276

31 RCMP Records, "Japanese Activities in British Columbia," Appendix 6, lists the names. Adachi, 199, says 38 were arrested. Sunahara, 28, agrees.

32 Takeo Nakano, *Within the Barbed Wire Fence* (Toronto, 1980), 8; Sunahara, 70; Stephan, 171

33 To what extent the post-7 December military response was a reflection of pre-war contempt for Japanese military capabilities remains unknown. Dower, 98ff, discusses the responses of the American and British military and civilians both before and after the outbreak of war.

34 Maurice Pope, *Soldiers and Politicians* (Toronto, 1962), 176–8. Escott Reid, who attended the Conference for the Department of External Affairs, later wrote that delegates from BC "spoke of the Japanese Canadians in a way that Nazis would have spoken about Jewish Germans. I felt in that room the physical presence of evil." "The Conscience of a Diplomat: A Personal Testament," *Queen's Quarterly*, LXXIV (Winter 1967), 6–8

35 External Affairs Records, Acc. 83-84/259; box 115, f. 1698-A 40, "Report of Special Committee...," 28 July 1941. Ottawa had not always been so calm. The Joint Staff Committee at Defence Headquarters on 5 September 1936 had foreseen circumstances in which "the Western Coast of Canada will be within the area of hostilities and is likely to be attacked not only by Japanese naval and air forces, but, in the case of important shore objectives, by Japanese landing parties operating in some strength." An abridged version of the document is in James Eayrs, *In Defence of Canada*, vol. II: *Appeasement and Rearmament* (Toronto, 1965), 213ff. Two years

later Defence Headquarters had concluded that "there was a problem of possible sabotage in wartime and recommended that Japanese Canadians not be allowed to purchase property adjacent to areas of military importance." Cited in John Saywell, "Canadian Political Dynamics and Canada-Japan Relations: Retrospect and Prospect," 26, a paper published in Japanese only ("Nikkakankei No Kaiko To Tembo," *Kokusai Seiji* (May 1985), 121–36)

36 W.A.B. Douglas, *The Creation of a National Air Force*, vol. II: *The Official History of the Royal Canadian Air Force* (Toronto, 1986), 405. The British and American planners meeting at the Arcadia conference later in December agreed. Ibid., 410. On 29 December 1941, the chief of the General Staff told the Cabinet War Committee that he had just returned from the Pacific Coast where he found the military and police more concerned with the possibility of attacks on Japanese Canadians than with subversion. Cabinet War Committee Minutes, 29 December 1941. The enormous difficulties that the military would have faced in dealing with racist attacks on Japanese Canadians should not be underestimated: the limited number of trained troops in the area and the very real problem of using white troops against white British Columbians in defence of Japanese Canadians would have frightened any realistic commander.

37 RCMP Records, vol. 3564, f. C11-19-2-24, General Alexander to CGS, 30 December 1941; ibid., Keenleyside to Pope, 3 January 1942

38 Mackenzie Papers, vol. 32, f. X-81, "Extracts from Secret Letters," 30, 27 December 1941. See also C.P. Stacey, *Six Years of War* (Ottawa, 1955), 169, and W.A.B. Douglas, "The RCAF and the Defence of the Pacific Coast, 1939–1945," an unpublished paper presented to the Western Studies Conference, Banff, Alberta, January 1981, 8.

39 Department of National Defence, Directorate of History, f. 193.009 (D3), Pacific Command, Joint Service Committee, minutes, 9 January 1942

40 Department of National Defence Records, Acc. 83-84/216, f. S-801-100-P5-1, minutes of Joint Service Committee, Pacific Coast, 13 February 1942

41 Ibid., vol. 11767, f. PC019-2-7, P.A. Hoare to commanding officer, 26 February 1942. The Joint Service Committee recommended on 20 February that all aliens and all Japanese regardless of age and sex should be removed from certain areas on the coast, particularly those near defence installations and in isolated areas. Cited in Patricia Roy, "Why Did Canada Evacuate the Japanese?" unpublished paper, 6–7

42 Privy Council Office Records, vol. 3, f. D-19-1, Pacific Area, memorandum, AVM Croil to minister for air, 11 September 1941

43 Department of State Records, 842.20 Defense/100, "Observations on the General Defense Status of the Province of British Columbia," 1 August 1941

44 See Stacey, 165ff, and Department of National Defence Records, vol. 2730, f. HQS-5199X, "Memorandum of the Joint Service Committee, Pacific Coast, on the Matter of

the Defences of the Pacific Coast of Canada," 12 July 1940; Privy Council Office Records, vol. 3, f. D-19-1, Pacific Area, appreciations of 18 November 1941 and 10 December 1941.

45 See, e.g., Dafoe Papers, Bruce Hutchison to Dafoe, January 1942; Mackenzie Papers, vol. 30, chief of air staff to minister for air, 16 March 1942 and various memoranda.

46 Dower, 112, notes that, as the Japanese victories continued through early 1942, "Suddenly, instead of being treacherous and cunning, the Japanese had become monstrous and inhuman … invested in the eyes of both civilians and soldiers with superhuman qualities."

47 The best accounts of Pacific war strategy are H.P. Willmott, *Empires in the Balance* (Annapolis, 1982) and *The Barrier and the Javelin* (Annapolis, 1983). On the Aleutian and Midway plans, see Willmott, *Barrier*, chapter 3; Stephan, chapters 6-7. Note, however, Willmott's cool assessment of the difficulties Japan would face in trying to take Hawaii. *Empires*, 437. The importance of the Aleutian thrust was seen by the Americans' Special Branch, Military Intelligence Service, based on an analysis of "Magic" traffic. See USNA, RG 457, box 2, SRS-668, supplement to Magic summary, 30 July 1942, and on the Special Branch, Lewin, 141ff. One interesting assessment of the Japanese attack in the Aleutians was offered to Japanese Ambassador Oshima in Berlin by General von Boetticher, a former military attaché in Washington: "the Aleutian attack has closed the only practicable route for an attack on Japan and is a serious threat to Canada and the West Coast." Ibid., box 1, SRS-640, Magic summary, 26 June 1942

48 NA, J.L. Ralston Papers, vol. 72, Secret Session file, chiefs of staff appreciation, 19 February 1942

49 Stacey, 171. See also Cabinet War Committee Minutes, 18 February 1942, and National Defence Records, vol. 2688, f. HQS-5159-1, vol. 2, "Report of Meeting Held at Headquarters, 13th Naval District Seattle, … 6 March 1942," where Canadian and American commanders agreed with the Canadian estimates of scales of attack and suggested that "nuisance raids" were most likely. Additional information on defence preparations is in John F. Hilliker, ed., *Documents on Canadian External Relations*, vol. IX: *1942–1943* (Ottawa, 1980), 1162ff. For a good example of hindsight 20/20 vision on the impossibilities of a Japanese attack on the coast, see Adachi, 207–8.

50 Privy Council Office Records, vol. 14, f. W-29-1, "First Meeting of the Pacific Council in Washington," n.d. 1 April 1942 and attached documents

51 Ibid., "Memorandum re Prime Minister's Visit to Washington, April 14th to 17th, 1942"

52 Department of National Defence Records, vol. 11764, f. PC05-11-5, naval message to NOI/C, Vancouver and Prince Rupert, 29 April 1942

53 Ibid., vol. 11764, f. PC010-9-18, memorandum, "Defence of the West Coast," 7 July 1942

54 See *Vancouver Sun*, 10 August 1942; *Vancouver Province*, 13 August 1942; documents on External Affairs Records, Acc. 83-84/259, box 216, f. 3942-40; Douglas, *Creation*, 354. We are indebted to Professor John Saywell for his recollections of this period on Vancouver Island and to his father's book, John F.T. Saywell, *Kaatza: The Chronicles of Cowichan Lake* (Sidney, BC, 1967), 197–8, which briefly details the role of the Pacific Coast Militia Rangers, a force largely of skilled woodsmen and hunters.

55 King Papers, f. C249469, memorandum for file, 25 September 1942. See also Cabinet War Committee Minutes, 25 September 1942, where the chief of the General Staff said he would be "surprised" if the Japanese attacked the coast.

56 USNA, RG 218, Records of the US Joint Chiefs of Staff, mf. reel 10, f. 39322ff, Combined Chiefs of Staff, "Probable Maximum Scale of Attack on West Coast of North America," CCS 127, 29 November 1942. See also ibid., f. A4024ff, CCS 127/1, "Probable Scale of Attack on the West Coast of North America," 16 January 1943. Not until August 1943 (in CCS 127/3) did the Combined Chiefs declare the possibility of any serious attack on the coast "very unlikely." Douglas, *Creation*, 368–9. C.P. Stacey's comment in *Arms, Men and Governments* (Ottawa, 1970), 46, that "No informed and competent officer ever suggested that the Japanese were in a position to undertake anything more than nuisance raids" seems exaggerated in the light of the CCS papers. It is worth recalling that the Canadian raid on Dieppe involved about 5,000 men and was intended, among other purposes, to lead the Nazis to strengthen the French Coast at the expense of the Eastern front. The Japanese planners could (and should?) have been thinking similarly. Certainly a raid in force would have resulted in a massive public demand for the stationing of more troops on the coast; indeed, the simple prospect of such a raid did lead to the strengthening of defences.

57 Department of National Defence Records, vol. 11764, f. PC05-11-7, naval messages, 30–31 March 1943. This may have been based on false information. A secret US Federal Communications Commission project had reported on landing barges in the area; Washington discounted these reports but turned the information over to Canada, which sent them to the West Coast and then back into the American intelligence net where "they were believed to be authentic. Hence military action was ordered." See USNA, RG 457, SRMN-007, memorandum, 19 April 1943.

FURTHER READING

Adachi, Ken. *The Enemy That Never Was.* Toronto: McClelland and Stewart, 1979.

An acclaimed history of Japanese Canadians, this book spans the years from 1877 to 1975. It was commissioned by the National Japanese Canadian Citizens Association. *The Enemy That Never Was* was republished in 1991 in the wake of the redress movement, which resulted in a formal apology to Japanese Canadians by the Canadian government.

Cook, Ramsay. *The Regenerators: Social Criticism in Late Victorian English Canada.* Toronto: University of Toronto Press, 1985.

This book is an exploration of the nature of social criticism at a time when faith encountered a crisis within the dichotomy of industrial science and religion. Cook analyzes the thoughts of a wide cast of characters, from evolutionists to rationalists, freethinkers, feminists, spiritualists, socialists, communists, and many more, in this presentation of an often bewildering array of 19th-century beliefs.

Iacovetta, Franca, Roberto Perin, and Angelo Principe, eds. *Enemies Within: Italian and Other Internees in Canada and Abroad.* Toronto: University of Toronto Press, 2000.

In the campaign led by the National Congress of Italian Canadians to gain redress for compatriots interned during the Second World War, leaders claimed that the Canadian state had waged a war against ethnicity. Their version of history, argue the editors of this book, draws on selective evidence and glosses over the fascist past of some Italian Canadians. The editors have assembled here scholars who seek to stimulate informed debate through their writings. *Enemies Within* is the first study of its kind to examine the formulation and uneven implementation of internment policy, and the social and gender history of internment.

Roberts, Barbara. *Whence They Came: Deportation From Canada, 1900–1935.* Ottawa: University of Ottawa Press, 1997.

According to the author, immigration policy was, until recently, largely in the hands of a small group of bureaucrats. Barbara Roberts explores these government officials, showing how they not only kept the doors closed, but also managed to find a way to get rid of some of those who did break through the carefully guarded barriers. Roberts's important book utilizes an objective style to explore a dark history.

PART V

THE POST-WAR ERA: NEW RIGHTS AND NEW RACISMS

*I*t is perhaps a cliché, but nonetheless true, that the long post-war era—from the immediate end of the Second World War to the present—is a watershed period in race and immigration in Canada. With the end of the war, the world began to slowly understand the scope of the genocidal atrocities that had been unleashed, principally upon European Jewry, but also upon the Romany people and other "inferior" populations who were the unfortunate targets of Adolf Hitler's final solution. As images of emaciated bodies—both of the dead and survivors—in concentration camps in places such as Dachau and Auschwitz were broadcast internationally, the world came to understand the chilling reality of unchecked racism and the terrible toll that had resulted from it. Some six million (or more) Jews were dead, as well as countless others, including hundreds of thousands of Roma: a generation forever lost.

Canadians did not change generations of racial attitudes overnight. Nonetheless, the horror of these atrocities began to mobilize public sentiment against the overt racism of the pre-war period, both globally and in Canada. In 1948 the United Nations issued a Universal Declaration of Human Rights, a document that enshrined the fundamental equality and dignity of all human beings, regardless of their origin. In Canada, there were many developments in this area, and many of the changes were spearheaded by minority activists who pressed governments to protect minority rights. As a consequence of these struggles, legislation such as Ontario's Racial Discrimination Act of 1944, the 1947 Saskatchewan Bill of Rights, and Ontario's Fair Accommodation Practices Act of 1954, to name just a few, was passed.

There were also changes to Canada's immigration policy during this era, but they came a little more slowly than developments on the human rights front. During the immediate post-war era, Canada remained committed to maintaining its system of racially preferential immigration. In 1947 Prime Minister Mackenzie King delivered a speech to the House of Commons on Canada's immigration policy. In it he maintained that Canada's post-war immigration policy was not to differ in any way from what had existed prior to the war. King stated three main positions. Firstly, admission was to be seen as a privilege and a matter of the government's discretion.

Secondly, immigrants were to be viewed in terms of what they could bring to the country. Thirdly, immigration was not to change the fundamental character of the country.

As the post-war era unfolded, the Canadian government began to gradually change its position due to a touch of altruism and, of course, self interest. Canada's economy was booming and it needed labourers. The so-called displaced persons, or DPs, of Europe, languishing in the Allied-controlled camps, were actively targeted for emigration to Canada. As the supply of DP's dwindled, the government turned to other previously undesirable groups such as Italians. The government also began to alter its immigration policies. In 1962 the Diefenbaker government removed racial preferences from immigration policy, and in 1967 the government introduced the points system, which was designed as a method to facilitate the new colour-blind admissions policy, one that assigned points based on factors such as one's occupation and knowledge of Canada's official languages.

While it is true minorities have benefited from the revolutionary changes in attitudes and policies that have taken place during the post-war era, this age of new rights is also, paradoxically, an age of new racisms. Although the post-war era has given marginalized groups important formal equality before the law, subtler and systemic forms of racism have displaced the older, more overt forms that once were a more common fact of Canadian life. After 1962 Canada, by virtue of its new commitment to colour-blind immigration, began to admit non-white immigrants in unprecedented numbers. It is clear, however, that many—though certainly not all—non-white immigrant groups tend to languish at or near the bottom of Canada's socio-economic ladder. They often face a daunting number of covert, systemic barriers to full inclusion in the mainstream of Canadian political and economic life. In addition, many non-whites in Canada, such as domestics and agricultural workers, are allowed in the country for their labour but denied the benefits of Canadian citizenship.

The first two chapters are about rights in a sense that is broader than (but inclusive of) legislated rights: the agency exercised by everyday people who struggled for equality during and after the Second World War. Written by Dionne Brand and Franca Iacovetta, these articles show the importance of the post-war era in creating the conditions where two groups of women claimed their rights to new kinds of paid labour, with mixed results for both. The third chapter, by Daiva Stasiulis and Abigail Bakan, and the fourth, by Grace-Edward Galabuzi, show us that racialized minorities continue to face struggles in the labour market, and with immigration policies.

CHAPTER 16

"WE WEREN'T ALLOWED TO GO INTO FACTORY WORK UNTIL HITLER STARTED THE WAR": THE 1920S TO THE 1940S

DIONNE BRAND

The purpose of this essay is to review, through oral accounts, the experiences of Black women in Canada between the wars, their location in work outside the home, and the impact of the Second World War on their job opportunities. Using the accounts of several women born between 1900 and 1924, I will examine how race and gender structured life for Black women in this country during the period 1920 to 1946. The oral accounts used here are from the oral history project that I coordinated between 1988 and 1990—"Lives of Black Working Women in Ontario"—which was sponsored by the Immigrant Women's Job Placement Centre. Some fifty women were interviewed. These oral accounts can be found in their entirety in my book *No Burden to Carry: Narratives of Black Working Women in Ontario 1920s–1950s* (Toronto: Women's Press 1991).

In order to locate the women who speak in this essay it is necessary to look briefly at the lives of their mothers and grandmothers as described by them. Canadian history and Canadian women's history has given us little if any information of the existence of these women who survived slavery and the Underground Railroad. As a feminist recorder

facing the problem of white and biased documentation, I found that oral history opened up that vast and yet untapped well of events, knowledge, and experience that Black women live and have lived in this country. The abolition of slavery, the institution that gave rise to the presence of their great-grandmothers and grandfathers on Canadian soil, was not one hundred years old when the women in the oral accounts were born.

Still, the abolition of slavery did not eradicate racism as an organizing principle within the social, economic, or political life of Canada and the United States. The mothers and grandmothers of the women in these accounts worked in fields, tended chickens and hogs, washed, ironed, cooked and cleaned for a wage, and took care of children, grandchildren, and family. For Black women in Canada, however, the availability of work outside the home—long an imperative in their lives—was structured by both their gender and their race. They found themselves in the gender- and race-bound work of their day, which placed them at the lower end of the economic strata. But they had to work, and their place in the economy reflected the prejudices that Canadian society imprinted on their character. Black women of the time had inherited not only the burdensome legacy of a labour force stratified by race and gender but also a social milieu steeped in racial hatred.

* * *

In the small Black farming communities of Ontario and in cities like Toronto and Windsor, with their small Black populations, the approach of the Great Depression only compounded the difficulties of daily life. Accounts show more than a passing similarity of experience between rural and urban women as the Depression saw many farm daughters move to the cities to join their urban counterparts seeking work in the twenties and thirties. Addie Aylestock was one such farm daughter. Born near Elmira, Ontario, in 1909, she went on to become the first woman to be ordained in the British Methodist Episcopal Church.

There was four of us—four girls. It seemed like we had the idea in our head to leave. Most of us left home pretty early because our parents were poor and weren't able to look after us.

My sister was doing domestic work, getting her room and board. And there was a friend, in the BME Church, of my mother's and my sister's. When I came to Toronto I used to spend a lot of time at her home, so she sort of was chaperoning us. I was not quite sixteen.

Toronto was like a big city to me then, but not near as big as now. You can't compare: it wasn't built up like it is now. The city was three- or four-storey houses—I thought that was high!

When I worked as a domestic I didn't have much to do. I just got up and got out—got my breakfast and got out in the morning—and

back at two o'clock in the afternoon and then I got the dinner ready.

I think they gave me enough for car fare—I really don't remember, but it wasn't very much. I know when I first came to Toronto there weren't many opportunities for Black girls, in those days anyways. And then again, my parents were satisfied that I had a job in housework that I would stay in. I think I got fifteen dollars a month at the start—that was supposed to be enough for your clothes and your car fare. I lived in the west end of Toronto then, on Brighton Avenue.

I guess the Depression started when I came here to Toronto. It didn't really seem like a Depression to me. The reason I knew about the Depression was that I heard mother and dad talking about it. I didn't realise that's what it was, but I knew that sometimes we were getting the same thing to eat, like beans, turnips, maybe something the farmers would give us. My parents didn't have money to go out and buy much.

Addie Aylestock

* * *

In her essay "Domestic Service in Canada 1880–1920," Genevieve Leslie argues that domestic service changed with industrialization. "The period 1880–1920 … was a transitional period which clearly revealed the incompatibility of domestic service and modern industrial trends … In 1891 domestics accounted for 41 percent of the female work force, and were by far the largest single group of workers; by 1921 domestics represented only 18 percent of all employed women but were still the second largest category of female workers."[1] Since their arrival in Ontario, first as slaves then as fugitives from slavery, in the early 1800s, Black women had worked on farms, in domestic service, and at home. Indications are that not until 1940 or so did any significant number of them work at industrial labour. Leslie does not talk about Black women in domestic service, and we can assume her statistics reflect only white women working in domestic service, because certainly up to the Second World War at least 80 per cent of Black women in Canadian cities worked in domestic service.[2] Industrialization did not have the overwhelming impact on Black women wage-earners that it did on white women, but race clearly blocked their entrance into industrial labour. Bee Allen, Eleanor Hayes, and Rella Braithwaite, born between 1911 and 1923, recount the difficulties of navigating the race barrier.

I had wanted to be a teacher but when I was young there weren't that many blacks teaching in Toronto.

My first job was, as with many Black girls, in service. I had not been in any kind of work, but I felt I could take care of a child, so I took that job. That's what I did prior to marriage, and not for too long, because I would then be sixteen, maybe seventeen.

In service situations I always asked, "Do you hire coloured?" because I did not have financial means to go running up to some place up in Rosedale from where I lived and be turned down when I got to the door— that was car fare spent for nothing. Sometimes they would say, "Well, I'm sorry." Other times I would phone and they would say, "Well, are you dark?" and I would say, "Well, I'm not dark," and then they might say, "I'm sorry, the reason I'm asking is because we'd like our coloured help to be unquestionably coloured." These were domestic jobs; you were going to live in, in many cases, and they did not want to have their friends or relatives wondering at you.

I guess probably some white people lived with the idea that they would live with a coloured person in their home if they were not extremely dark, and that was because they just keep showing up in their face all the time. Others wanted you to be dark because mostly coming from the States they were accustomed to Black help and this is what they wanted.

It was when I was trying to find service jobs that this business about being Black came up. Black women had not really had that long of a life in other jobs because it was the war that opened it. The war brought in the necessity for hiring women.

I lived in for maybe one job, but I didn't stay there very long. In a lot of these service jobs you lived in, and you only had Thursday afternoon off and maybe every other Sunday. Some general domestics were doing everything: they were doing the cooking and they were also serving. They were part of the family, but the mistress didn't want any of your life to keep you from getting up early and getting her breakfast.

I stayed home during the first year of our marriage and then I had the daughter. In '31–'32—her first year—I was quite ill and spent some five or six weeks in the hospital and came home from that time. Then I got this opportunity to go work in the shoe factory; once I got into working in the shoe factory then I never went back into domestic service. I never did because I felt I had now an opening tool.

Bee Allen

Some of us who have been there … can talk about it without shame. One woman was saying how much she was getting paid and she was getting five dollars a week in old clothes.

If you were lucky—if the lady was nice—five dollars a week and old clothes. Back then I worked for fifteen dollars a month, with car fare. That's nothing! They used to say with car fare or without car fare. A friend of mine was getting twenty dollars a month, but she didn't get car fare. Tokens were four for a quarter. When I was in high school the girls who wanted to take commercial courses or secretarial courses they weren't encouraged to do so. We were told, 'Well, who would want to hire you?' There were a few businesses that would hire you but very, very, very few! There are women today living here in Toronto who were the first this and the first that: the first Black secretary in the government is living today; the first Black nurse to train in a hospital is living today; the first Black to work in Eaton's is living today.

That's where the openings were—garment factories or knitting mills—anything that wasn't too, too visible. The excuse they had was that the other employees might object. Now you hear them say that there's no discrimination here, but it's beneath the surface. But it wasn't beneath the surface then—they were very, very frank about it.

Eleanor Hayes

* * *

These accounts outline the limitations of Black women's job mobility before the Second World War, as well as the difficult conditions they encountered in the households in which they worked.

The situation of Black women engaged in waged work seems to have been similar in the United States. Jacqueline Jones, in her exhaustive treatment of Black women and work there, points out: "In 1940 one third of all white, but only 1.3 percent of all black working women

had clerical jobs. On the other hand, 60 percent of all black female workers were domestic servants; the figure for white women was only 10 percent."[3] Ruth Pierson, in her book *"They're Still Women After All": The Second World War and Canadian Women*, states: "Canada's War effort, rather than any consideration of women's right to work, determined the recruitment of women into the labour force. The recruitment of women was part of a large-scale intervention by Government into the labour market to control allocation of labour for effective prosecution of war."[4] This was no less true for the women in these accounts. Nor was racial desegregation an objective of the war effort. Ghettoized up to then in domestic work of one sort or another—mother's helpers, housekeeping, laundry work, general help—Black women were released by the war effort from the racialized, segregated, female employment that domestic work was for them, and were given entry into industrial labour and clerical work. "Things opened up," many women say.

After Reliable Toy, I worked in a factory down on John Street; they made suits. There was lots of that domestic work, going and cleaning up other people's dirty place. Really and truly, we weren't allowed to go into factory work until Hitler started the war, and then they'd beg you, "Would you like a job in my factory?" But we weren't allowed in [before]. We were left more or less to clean their dirty houses. Which I never did, I'll tell you that. Then we had a chance to go and work in the ammunition dump.

They called it GICO. That's where Centennial College is now—used to be the war plant. I lasted about a week there. I couldn't stay because I started to haemorrhage. [The work] was filling magazines, little pellets with gunpowder for the soldiers.

I kept menstruating—the humidity was too high or something, I couldn't stay. I have pictures of some of us that were out there. There were many Black women out there. I had to go back to other factory work.

Marjorie Lewsey

* * *

As many in these accounts attest, Black women would not have needed much encouragement to flee race-bound domestic work. Most were well within the age group most favoured for recruitment, single and 20–24 years old. Though some were married, by mid-1943 the National Selective Service was recruiting them too.[5] Indeed, given the extent of the labour shortages there was a lot of room for Black women. "By mid 1943 there were labour shortages in service jobs long dependent on female (*i.e., white*) labour. Women were leaving these for higher paying employment in war industries. Hospitals, restaurants, hotels, laundries, and dry cleaners were clamouring for help, but the labour pool of single women available for full time employment was exhausted."[6] Then too, as Pierson points out, even non-essential jobs like those in candy, tobacco, and soft-drink companies,[7] were experiencing labour shortages.

The widespread expansion of goods and services that the war occasioned made possible and palatable the employment of Black women in jobs where their employment was once unacceptable, in terms of both their race and their sex. But the nation-wide publicity campaigns undertaken by the NSS to persuade women to sign up for work were not directed towards Black women, nor were their slogans of patriotism instrumental in recruiting Black women. Simply put, Black women needed the work—they needed the money—and waged work had been an essential part of their daily lives. Again, James St G. Walker points out that "in 1941, 80% of Black adult females in Montreal were employed as domestic servants."[8] By all accounts, this was also the case in Toronto and other Black communities. And as domestic workers, usually beginning their working lives at fifteen, Black women received wages of from fifteen to thirty dollars a month in conditions of employment that could subject them to such arbitrary demands as forgoing time off, having to work sixteen hour days, and receiving clothing in lieu of wages. Racism created an atmosphere in which Black women's presence was on sufferance. So, the industrial wage (such as it was), the wholesale war recruitment that suggested that one's chances were as good as anyone else's, the anonymity of industrial labourers, and the indications of Black progress that this opportunity signalled were all a boon to Black women and to the Black community as a whole—despite the laissez-faire racism on the job in the war plants and other industries.

There is some evidence that suggests the kind of treatment Black women as a whole experienced in the munitions plants. Grace Fowler refers to working on the "high explosives side" in one munitions plant.

It was in '44 I went to work at the war plant. November. And so I got a job in the war plant. I worked on what they call the high explosives side, where you got paid a little extra because you were workin' with dangerous powders. We made detonators for torpedoes. And it wasn't a bad job. I learned every job on the line because it was awful boring just to stay in one.

Grace Fowler

Fern Shreve remarks that she felt that another Black woman was given a certain dangerous position on the line, making grenades, because of her race.

> I remember in the munitions factory—Chatco Steel in Chatham—that was where there were more Blacks than any other job that I think that I worked on. I don't know why, but there were whites there. I guess if I wanted to make a case of it I could probably say that the Blacks were doing the dirtier work, but I can't prove that. There was a lady, an older lady, Mrs. Selby, and they had what they called the oven. These things were dipped in varnish, and then they were cooked, and they'd go around, and poor Mrs. Selby would sit under there and take those things off. Today I would just think that would be the most horrible thing that I could think of. We were also so much younger than she—we should've been doing some of the dirty work. That was really terrible. We worked nights. She'd be sitting there nodding, see the fire burning and go "Oh!" I think back on it now and think that's just dreadful! Why was she chosen to do that particular job?
>
> *Fern Shreve*

"Things opened up" also meant that Black women felt freer at least to argue against racism on an equal footing with the white woman they encountered during the war.

> When I worked in that war plant, especially on the night shift, when all the machinery breaks down we used to get into some real good discussions. This one night we talked about nursing, and I was saying how they wouldn't let Black girls go into nursing at that time, and she was trying to explain to me why they didn't and was trying to be delicate about it and she was saying, well you

know your people have a different odour and somebody sick they don't want somebody around them. I said, "I work alongside of some of these women. If I smelled as bad as them, I'd shoot myself, so don't talk to me about bad smell."
>
> *Grace Fowler*

The narrative of one woman on war work also suggests that she encountered for the first time the unusual circumstance of "more Blacks in any other jobs that I worked on." Another left teaching in the Maritimes for service in Ottawa, having been recruited through the Selective Service. Still another became a teacher, recruited through a government war program that offered grade twelve and thirteen students forty-five dollars to train as teachers, and another cites the fact that male teachers had been recruited into the armed forces, precipitating the recruitment of women as teachers.

> We finished high school at Merlin. That was grade twelve and part of grade thirteen, only part because I took sick. It was during the war. The government offered any grade twelve or thirteen student who would become interested in teaching anywhere in Ontario forty-five dollars. It was a lot of money in that time—just take a six-week teacher training course. I got excited in May when this came through: I'm going to apply and I'm going to be able to make some money for the family, I thought.
>
> Teaching was the last thing I had wanted to do because I had wanted to be a secretary, like my aunt. Norma Brown and I went to London to take this course. Both of us had our jobs before we left. Norma was in Shrewsbury. I had my school in Chatham Township.
>
> *Cleata Morris*

Though teaching was the other traditional job for a Black woman (there being segregated one-room schoolhouses in Black communities in the Maritimes and Ontario), the Second World War obviously opened up the number of jobs available in the profession.[9] It changed the make-up of their classrooms from comprising mainly Black students to including white students.

According to Pierson, along with the recruitment of women into industries and services, there was also recruitment of women into agriculture "to fill some of the gaps in farm power with female labour." In all provinces farmers' wives and daughters took over farm work in the absence of male relatives and farm workers who had left the land to join the armed forces or to work in industry.[10]

Some Black women, particularly those from south-western Ontario, might have been part of the Women's Land Brigade and Farm Girls Brigade of the Farm Labour Service, as some recount not only working in their own fields but also hiring out as farm help. However, either option would not have been unusual for these women under ordinary circumstances, since some of them had husbands, brothers, and fathers who worked on the railroads as porters, and the women were already carrying the load of farm work. Others already worked planting tobacco or picking tomatoes and cucumbers.

When we worked in Chatham in the Libby's factory, we worked side by side with all the white women. After the war all the country people had to leave all the factories and come back. We did other jobs and then they hired the people from the city of Chatham. A lot of us worked on farms around here. A lot of women went to the fruit orchards out on Highway 3, the fruit farms. We all worked out there. There used to be a great big truck used to come down here. All the bunch came out to the fruit farm. You'd get much more than you'd get for a day's work. It's according to how you picked: if you picked steady all day, you'd make good. But a lot of time a lot of them their legs was tired.

… A lot of women went out to the corn fields. Here in Chatham they come out in the country and they pick tomatoes, and a lot of them suckered corn in the spring. You go along and take the little riffs that come out in the corn—you break them off so the ears grow. Women worked in the corn, then they worked in the plants in Chatham.

June Robbins

As Pierson[11] has found, despite the recruitment campaigns that stressed patriotic duty, the principal motivation for women in entering the wartime job market was indeed not the need to do patriotic service, but economic necessity. This was perhaps even more true for Black women workers of the time.

After I married, until my son was born I was doing some work on my own, and when the war came on I was doing war work out there. They had a place set up out in Scarborough. There wasn't too many coloured people working there from what I can remember, but there was some.

I guess if I was thinking about it today maybe I wouldn't have done that with the way you feel about war. But at that time it was good money; we were really filling these shells. When I come to think of it—my goodness, the place could've blown up! You didn't really think too much about it, not when you're younger. When you went in you took a shower; when you went out you took a shower, in case the powder gets on you—and I never did like showers. I always liked baths.

I don't think the war years was very much different from the way the people'd been feeling, even in other races, all along. I think young men are just eager; I don't think they're thinking about what might happen. Personally, I don't like to think of war because you're just wondering if they'll ever come back. Even now, especially in the States, young men are going for different things, and they're not expecting things to happen, but they're killing people. But the war gave a lot of different work to women. I think maybe that was the part: the women kind of started doing work.

Bertha McAleer

It was quite a traumatic experience for somebody who had lived in the city. Barrie was very small and it was made up of retired farmers. The war had just started, so there were people there from all over living in rented rooms and anything they could get to live in.

For a while I worked at the tannery. There were a lot of women hired—women had been there for years—and they dyed the skins as they came on the belt. And, of course, I wanted something to do and I wanted more money. So finally with the war on they really needed women: they needed help because the men just weren't there, so finally I got a job there, in the early 40s, over my husband's objections.

I think the whole thing opened up with the war: more was demanded and consequently they had to have more people in jobs; this was the turning point for Blacks.

Vi Aylestock

When I came back from London in 1945 I went to work in a munitions plant, working with hand grenades. We were preparing these shells—we didn't have anything to do with the explosives—they were dipped and scrapped and stuff like that. We weren't making much money there—they didn't pay money in those days, but you could get work like it was going out of style. It was night work—we worked nights all the time in the munitions plant. I decided that wasn't quite enough money for me, so I'd go out on Saturday and work extra. I went to the unemployment office and they sent me to this lady's house to wash. When I get there she wants me to wash her bathroom, and as slow as I worked I think I made two dollars—and it was something like fifty cents an hour I was being paid. I didn't go to work anymore Saturdays!

Fern Shreve

Black women did see these jobs as a gain for the race, but much to their chagrin, no sooner had they fled domestic work than the retrenchment of women workers began, supposedly back "into traditionally female occupations."[12] In their case, "traditionally female occupations" would mean domestic work, but retrenchment was also accompanied by an infusion of Black Caribbean women recruited by the Department of Immigration for domestic work in Canada.

While no Canadian historian has traced the course, consequences, and significance of Black women's war work in Canada, Jacqueline Jones, in her formidable historical study of Black women and work in the United States, writes of the period: "From official United States Government posters to short stories in popular women's magazines, recruitment propaganda was aimed exclusively at white women of both the middle and working classes. When Black women were mentioned in connection with the national manpower crises at all, they were exhorted to enter 'war services' by taking jobs that white women most readily abandoned—laundry, cafeteria, and domestic work ... While male workers might absent themselves from the factory as a result of overindulgence the night before, (white) female workers stayed home periodically to catch up on their washing, cleaning, and grocery shopping. Black women thus were supposed to form a behind-the-scenes cadre of support workers for gainfully employed white wives."[13]

Though the proportion of Black women was smaller in Canada, the same racial and sexual division of labour determined their entry into and location in war work. Black women in the United States had a longer history of factory work than Black women in Canada. While the former had what Jones describes as a "weak hold on industrial position" from the twenties to the forties (7 per cent of Black women in 1920, 5.5 per cent in 1930, 6 per cent in 1940),[14] Black women in Canada seemed to have had no hold at all. Repeatedly, in these narratives, the women say that Black women could not get any position but that of domestic work before the war.

Their foothold in factory work in the 1940s was, therefore even more precarious than their sisters' to the south. Isolated, in smaller numbers in Toronto, Windsor, Chatham, and smaller communities in Ontario, their chances of collective action were much more slim, though not non-existent. The experiences on the wartime ship floor inspired a militancy that would carry two of the women in these narratives on to union organizing in Barrie and Chatham. The similarities between their experience in war work and that of Black women in the United States is worth noting in a Canada that sees itself as being apart from the legacy of racism at the core of social, political, and economic development in Canada and the United States. Of the experience of Black women in the United States during the war Jones writes: "often black women found their hard-won jobs in industry were not only segregated but the most dangerous and gruelling ones that a factory had to offer. During the war, certain men's jobs were converted to women's work and in the process down graded to lower pay and status, but others were converted to black women's work of ever greater inferiority. In aeroplane assembly plants, black women stood in stifling 'dope rooms' filled with the nauseating fumes of glue, while white women sat on stools in the well ventilated serving room ... Elsewhere black women worked in ammunitions and gunpowder, poisonous plastic and acetone, scaling mud and hazardous equipment ... Furthermore, they were routinely assigned 'disengaging' night shifts that imposed additional burdens on them as wives and mothers."[15]

Albeit dressed up in patriotism, war factory work in the 1940s could not have been a bed of roses for white women either, but racism could be counted on to structure the shop floor and to exact the most harsh penalties from Black women. One example can be cited to show that every step of the way to equality was a fight and that mere entry into industrial labour could not eradicate racism: in 1946, Viola Desmond, a Black woman in New Glasgow, Nova Scotia, was arrested, spent a night in jail, went to trial, and was fined for sitting in the white section of a movie theatre. But as an old Black saying goes, "you cut your dress to suit your cloth." So despite the endemic racism in work and social structures, Black women (and men) in Canada grabbed on to the industrial wage and hung on for dear life.

My husband was overseas a couple of years. All of the men remember that they went overseas and gave up jobs or lost out on education and everything, and when they came back it was very hard to get a job. He retrained when he came back, along with the rest of the soldiers, but it was not easy. He remembers the long line up when they came back: nearly everybody else white and he was standing in it—he and one other Black soldier. They pointed right to my husband and they called him up to the front and they told him right away: "You! You go to the porters and get a job there." They just picked him right out of the line up like that, but he really didn't want to go there.

Rella Braithwaite

They did not wish to return to the white people's kitchens where there was isolation, no fair wage, no chance of mobility, nor any recourse for the "personalized" racism of the employer. In a look at what she calls "Black Women Workers Demobilised and Redomesticated," Jacqueline Jones examines the impact of the end of the war on Black women workers: "a government researcher noted that reconversion affected Negroes more severely than white workers: from July 1945 to April 1946, for example, unemployment rates among non-whites increased more than twice as much as among whites … By 1948 most of the gains that blacks had derived from the wartime boom had been wiped out, and labour analysts predicted that, given the persistent marginality of black workers, their well being depended almost entirely on a strong economy."[16]

Escape as they tried, domestic work stared Black women in the face once again. Most of the women in these narratives did escape, but they faced hard times combining part-time work, child-rearing, and efforts to seek work and careers outside of domestic work. But if they were reluctant to go back to domestic work, their Black Caribbean sisters were not. Fleeing the bust of Caribbean economies in the 1950s, these women came to Canada to fill the shortages in domestic workers.

Linda Martin and Kerry Seagrave have examined the state of domestic work in Canada after the war. "At the end of the war the Canadian housewife faced the same domestic crisis (as in the U.S.). For Canada the solution lay in immigration, with thousands to be admitted into the country to become domestics. This practice was aided and abetted by the Canadian Government which did the recruiting in Europe. The Senate Committee on Immigration and Labour in an August 1946 report specifically mentioned the desirability of letting experienced foreign servants into the country."[17] What Martin and Seagrave overlook is that when by 1949 the importation of European servants failed to make up the shortage, Black Caribbean women were imported to do the job. Nowhere do they mention race as a factor in the Canadian "servant problem." They do not mention the Caribbean Domestic Worker Scheme of the fifties (some were threatened with deportation in the 1970s), or the undoubtedly dubious but nevertheless racial distinction between European women imported as "nannies" and Caribbean women as "domestics." While European women imported for domestic work would later blend into the white face of Canada, Black Caribbean women brought in as domestic workers would reinforce the stereotype of the Black woman as servant. Well into the sixties and beyond Black women continued to fight for a foothold in non-domestic labour. Even today, a disproportionate number of Black women work in institutionalized domestic work as nursing attendants and health-care aids, and in other service-sector jobs.

NOTES

1 Genevieve Leslie in J. Acton et al., eds., *Women at Work, 1850–1930* (Toronto: Women's Press 1974), 71.

2 James St G. Walker, *A History of Blacks in Canada: A Study Guide* (Ottawa: Ministry of State for Multiculturalism 1981), 132.

3 Jacqueline Jones, *Labor of Love, Labor of Sorrow* (New York: Vintage Books, Random House 1985), 200.

4 Ruth Roach Pierson, *"They're Still Women After All": The Second World War and Canadian Womanhood* (Toronto: McClelland & Stewart 1986), 22.

5 Pierson, *"They're Still Women"*, 27.

6 Ibid.

7 Ibid.

8 Walker, *History of Blacks*, 132.

9 Robin Winks, *The Blacks in Canada* (Montreal: McGill-Queen's University Press 1971), 388.

10 Pierson, *"They're Still Women"*, 32.

11 Ibid., 47.

12 Ibid., 61.

13 Jones, *Labor of Love*, 236–7.

14 Ibid., 208.

15 Ibid., 240.

16 Ibid., 257.

17 Linda Martin and Kerry Seagrave, *The Servant Problem* (North Carolina and London: McFarland and Co. 1985), 55.

CHAPTER 17

FROM CONTADINA TO WOMAN WORKER

FRANCA IACOVETTA

One Thursday in mid November 1956 Maria Rossi and her daughter arrived in Toronto from their peasant farm in Italy. They were met at Union Station by Rossi's husband, who had left them a year previously for work in Toronto. After eating dinner with relatives, Rossi was ushered into her new home in a basement flat in the house of a Calabrian family who had settled in the city a few years earlier. Next day, the couple went shopping for household necessities, including an espresso coffee-maker and pots for cooking spaghetti, at Honest Ed's discount department store. (It was known as "la polizia" [the police] because of the uniformed security guards.) To Rossi's delight, the next morning the Santa Claus parade passed by their Dupont Street home. At seven o'clock Monday morning Rossi went directly to work at a nearby laundry where a sister-in-law had secured her work as a steampress operator at $37 a week. For twenty years Maria Rossi worked at many low-skilled jobs—sewing, cooking, tending a grocery store, and operating a cash register—when she finally withdrew from the work force to care for her dying husband.[1]

Performing demanding roles as immigrants, workers, wives, and mothers, women played a critical role in the immigration of southern Italian families to postwar Toronto. Their active commitment to the family helped bridge the move from Old World to New as women's labour, both paid and unpaid, contributed towards the material well-being of their families. The transition from *contadina* (peasant woman) to worker did not require a fundamental break in the values of women long accustomed to contributing many hours of labour to the family. As immigrant workers, however, they confronted new forms of economic exploitation and new rhythms of work and life. Women at home similarly performed valuable support roles and endured the alienating aspects of urban industrial life. Bolstered by networks of kin and paesani, women not only endured these hardships but displayed a remarkable capacity to incorporate their new experiences as working-class women into traditionally rooted notions of familial and motherly responsibility.

Women and children, of course, figured prominently in the flow of Italian immigrants who entered postwar Canada. By the mid-1950s they made up half of the annual Italian volume. More than 81,000 Italian adult women came as part of the first major wave of immigrants who entered Canada during the decade of the 1950s, a figure representing over 30 per cent of the total volume of Italian immigration in this period. Young peasant women sponsored by their husbands or families predominated, although those from artisan and merchant backgrounds also came. Only a minority of women arrived as trained domestics, hairdressers, and seamstresses, while even fewer entered the country under nominated terms—as immigrants sponsored by Canadian employers. After 1951, as the process of family reunification got underway, the number of female immigrants entering Toronto roughly equalled that of male arrivals. By 1961 almost 42,000 Italian women had entered Toronto; another 29,000 arrived during the subsequent decade.

During the years following the Second World War, Italian women, like men, fell victim to North American sentiments regarding the supposed inferiority of southern Italians. However, as women they confronted additional prejudices. This was particularly true of married peasant women. Because Canadian government officials did not expect such women to work and make a direct economic contribution to the country, they ignored them. In the rare descriptions of peasant women contained in the Immigration Branch files, Italian women emerge as helpmates and housekeepers but never as farmers in their own right. Following a lengthy discussion of the work routines of southern peasants, one official summarized women's contribution in a single sentence: "Where cattle were owned they were often tended by the women."[2] A 1950 agreement that removed customs duties on Italian bridal trousseaus entering Canada recognized women's role in setting up a home in the new society.[3] Yet it also reflected prevailing notions about married women's prescribed roles as wife

and mother and reinforced the assumption that married southern Italian women, most of whom had obtained low levels of formal education and possessed few marketable skills for an industrial economy, were inferior immigrants. This position of inferiority was reinforced by the fact that most of them entered Canada under the family classification scheme—as dependants who, along with their children, were officially deemed to be the responsibility of their husbands. This status also rendered them ineligible to apply for government assistance or training programs.[4]

WORKING ON THE FARM

Contrary to contemporary assumptions that women were little more than part of the male newcomer's cultural baggage, southern Italian women, like their compatriots who came from Italy's other regions, were active agents in family migration. A consideration of their role must begin with life in rural Italy where […] peasants generally resided in simple households, each of which made up an agricultural work group. Also, each family drew on the labour power of every household member and combined incomes from a variety of sources—farming, agricultural or other forms of wage labour, and selling home-made goods such as cloth and produce.

The literature on southern Italy, which consists largely of the postwar ethnographic accounts of social anthropologists, emphasizes the segregation and subordination of women and virtually excludes consideration of how women's work contributed to family survival. In his study of a Calabrian village, anthropologist Jan Brøgger stresses the predominance of "female exclusion"—a code of conduct that imposed severe restrictions on women's interaction with males outside of their own house-

252 | PART V: The Post-War Era: New Rights and New Racisims

hold. Whenever they found themselves in mixed company, including harvest time when two or more families joined forces, he notes, women were prohibited from engaging freely in conversation with men and were closely chaperoned by their parents or female kin. John Davis, who studied a postwar village in Basilicata, treats the entire issue of women's farm labour as a potentially dishonourable activity. Although he readily concedes that women regularly performed critical field duties, he posits the view that the presence of a woman working in the fields called into question the husband's ability to support his family and, unless she was obviously working, cast doubt on the woman's chastity.[5]

While such extreme views must be rejected—indeed, a careful reading of the anthropological texts reveals that, as in most cultures, the actual practice of the villagers repeatedly contradicted the ideal types so carefully charted by academics—it is clear that, as in the past, the patriarchal organization of the southern family and the cultural mores of southern society significantly shaped gender relations inside and outside the family in the postwar south. Such factors imposed heavy restrictions on the choices and behaviour of women. The age-old concept of familial *onore* (honour) that pervaded the culture not only of southern Italians but of many European and rural societies rested in large part on the sexual purity of wives, daughters, and sisters, the men's successes in guarding the virtue of their women, and the men's ability as family breadwinners. While men were expected to provide for their wives and children through hard work and self-deprivation, women were to reciprocate by remaining sexually faithful. Linked to prevailing notions of male self-esteem and authority was the corollary—the fear that a woman might engage in pre- or extra-marital sex and thereby bring shame to her family. Supervision of

women's public activities was the inevitable result.[6]

As in other European cultures, male privilege within Italian society was exercised widely within the public sphere. Within the towns and villages of southern Italy, men were freer to socialize outside the household, and they led the religious and social feasts celebrated in the paese. Considered the family's chief decision-maker, the male head acted as the family's representative in its dealings with the outside world—making annual rental payments to absentee landlords or their agents, journeying out of the region in search of work, or acting as the main marriage negotiator for children. One Calabrian woman, Vincenza Curtola, recalled, for instance, how her father spent two weeks consulting people, including the town cleric and doctor, before granting final approval to his daughter's prospective husband.[7]

A model of male-dominance/female-submission is ultimately too simplistic to account for peasant women's experiences in the Mezzogiorno. It ignores the complexity of gender relations in Italy and underestimates the importance of female labour to peasant family production. The dictates of the household economy regularly drew women outside of the home to participate in agricultural production. Though the supposed natural link between women and domestic labours persisted, women's work roles included domestic and farm duties. And both involved back-breaking efforts.

Domestic responsibilities included cooking, cleaning, and childcare, as well as weaving, sewing clothes, and, especially during the winter slack, producing embroidered linens and crocheted tablecloths for bridal trousseaus. Well into the years after the Second World War, such labours remained time consuming and arduous. As Guiseppina Mazoli, a Molisan woman recalled, doing laundry involved fetching water from the town well, boiling it, soaking the items for an hour, and then carrying them out to a nearby stream where they were rinsed and laid out on the rocks to dry. Cooking over open wood stoves was hot and dirty work, and the stoves required constant maintenance and cleaning.[8]

Women and girls also farmed—clearing the plots, sowing and planting, hoeing, and sharing in the overall work of the summer grain harvest, a project that drew on the help of kinfolk and neighbours. At home, women were responsible for the threshing and winnowing. During the autumn ploughing, women transported manure from the barn to the various plots. Though the task of breaking the ground was usually performed by men, women also did this exhausting work. And throughout the season, they travelled back and forth between town and the fields carrying food and supplies in baskets on their heads.[9]

Because the landholdings of a single peasant family were scattered, the family members worked at some distances from each other. In some parts of southern Italy, such as western Sicily, the gender division of labour was quite rigid: women were responsible for the upkeep of the nearby garden plots, while the men worked the fields farther away from town. But this was not the case for all regions. One woman, Elizabetta Marcone, explained how on her farm in southern Abruzzi the women and men of the family performed similar tasks, each on a different plot of land. Every morning, she said, each of her parents took a few children and set off for a field. They would return each night to the dinner that Marcone's grandmother had waiting for them. The relentless tasks of farming were made more enjoyable, she added, by the camaraderie of the family work group. "We worked very hard, get up at the crack of dawn to work in the *campagna* (fields), but we're singing, happy because we're together."[10]

Female members of the peasant household helped in other ways. They grew vegetable gardens, fed the animals, and herded them into grazing grounds. Women made cheese from the milk of goats and cows, and sold the surplus locally. Many of the women who later migrated to Toronto had also regularly sold wheat, eggs, and vegetables to people who came to the farm from nearby villages. During the harvest, they had threshed wheat and beat out the broad beans that had been insufficiently threshed on the treading floor. In southern regions, women and children also picked olives, nut and fruits growing on their land, or they picked for large landowners on neighbouring estates in exchange for a portion of the product. The women also husked and cracked the almonds. Girls and boys of coastal towns brought home smelts and other small fish. Women preserved vegetables, fruits, and meats, and they helped collect fuel wood from communal lands.[11] In the wintertime, women wove cloth, either for their personal use or for sale to the travelling merchants who passed through town. During the war they also earned money by sewing military uniforms.[12]

While there were few nonagricultural job opportunities in southern towns, some parents, including those who belonged to the peasantry, encouraged their daughters to learn one of the few artisanal trades available to women. Usually, the young women were sent to the local seamstress to learn pattern-making and sewing or to train as a hairdresser. This is what happened to Assunta Cerelli, who in the late 1930s apprenticed with a local seamstress in her hometown in Sicily and later set up her own business as a seamstress and embroiderer in her parents' home. After her husband was killed in the war, she set up shop in a house her parents gave her. She soon established a stable clientele among the local womenfolk.[13]

Other daughters were sent to work in domestic service or in the garment, textile, and silk factories of the region. While some of them lived in chaperoned boarding houses, others moved into the homes of their employers. They regularly sent home their wages. Teenage girls were also employed as live-in domestics in their own hometowns, while small numbers of married women found work as cleaning ladies, toiling on a daily basis in the village offices or in the homes of the local prominenti. Southern peasant women also joined the expanding reserve army of labour employed in the hidden economy of postwar Italy—earning their wages on a piece-rate basis at home by embroidering linens, weaving carpets, or cleaning fish. Predictably, the incomes earned from performing jobs that in Italy became known as *lavoro nero* (black work—that is, work that was performed without benefit of protective industrial legislation) were low, unstable, and even exploitative. But given the critical importance of alternative forms of income to peasant families, the money women earned in this informal economy was highly valued by their families.[14]

In the daily work and family worlds of southern peasants, the distinctions between the work roles of women and men were often blurred, especially during the Second World War. When large numbers of southern men were conscripted into the Italian army, women were left with the responsibility of operating the farm. As one woman put it, "Lots and lots of men went to war. There were only kids and old people in our town and the women. The women worked on the farms then, with their kids helping. They worked hard, like the men. They kept the farm going." Similarly, wives, sisters, and daughters compensated for the absence of men who were making seasonal sojourns. With perhaps a little assistance from their parents, women continued to run the family farm, and many of them were left to make major decisions affecting their children and the family as a whole.[15]

* * *

It cannot be assumed that under patriarchal structures women were simply passive and powerless victims. The emphasis that scholars have placed on the importance of Italian men's public role and of women's modest conduct in mixed company can be very misleading. For it is within the private sphere that women could wield influence over their families; here, some women made extremely effective use of informal means of persuasion, alternatively berating and coaxing a reluctant or disappointing husband. Other women exhibited an impressive capacity to argue, manipulate, disrupt normal routine, and generally make life miserable for men in order to achieve certain demands. By the same token, men who might publicly boast about their authority could act differently once beyond the purview of fellow men. In the privacy of the home, some husbands shared decision-making as a matter of course while others frequently gave in to the demands of a persistent wife. In her study of postwar southern women, Ann Cornelisen captures an element of the public/private dynamic in her description of a married woman who supported her elderly parents. When asked who made the family's decisions, the woman claimed she consulted with her parents. But when Cornelisen confronted her with the fact that she did not usually confer with her parents, she responded: "The Commandments say Honour thy father and thy mother, don't they? No reason to let any one know what happens inside the family." Another woman Cornelisen describes endured months of verbal and physical assault from her husband as she tried to persuade him to work in Germany so they could pay for their son's operations. In the end, however, she emerged triumphant, having secured the necessary work permit and presenting it to her husband as a *fait accompli*. Shortly afterwards he left for Germany.[16]

* * *

Behind the public veneer, then, women exercised considerable power. As the family social convener responsible for arranging visits, gifts, and entertainment, women placed themselves at the centre of wide networks of family, kin, and paesani. Women also wielded great influence over their children; it has often been said that because fathers were the dispensers of corporal punishment, children confided in and felt more emotionally close to their mothers. Mothers would spare their children a spanking or beating by concealing the mischief they had done, or women would act as their children's mediators. According to Elizabetta Marcone, her mother sent instructions in 1955 to her husband in South America asking him to grant formal approval for their daughter's marriage. While the father's role as the family's chief decision maker was symbolically affirmed by the couple's having to await his approval, in fact the wedding preparations had been quietly underway for weeks before his reply arrived.[17]

Far from Ann Bravo's model of the lonely, isolated peasant woman with a truncated self-identity, women's close identification with their families did not preclude bonds of friendship with other women.[18] Peasant society offered numerous opportunities for women to establish friendships, and many did so. Within households, in-laws who worked together at domestic or field chores became close confidants, while tasks undertaken jointly by neighbours permitted women from different households to work together and, during breaks, to chat and gossip. While doing laundry, shelling beans, or making cheese outdoors, women talked endlessly and, very often, they forged close bonds. Of course, not all women were natural allies; rivals could be suspicious of, and cruel to, each other. In many instances, however, relations between female neighbours were more intimate than those between kin who lived at a distance from each other and thus could not maintain daily contact. A sign of the intensity of these female friendships is that many women chose long-time friends to be their children's godmothers.[19]

* * *

THE EXPERIENCE OF EMIGRATION

Women were generally denied a formal voice in the decision of the family to emigrate, but by making use of informal mechanisms of persuasion, they sought to influence the timing and target of migration. Desperate to get married and leave her wartorn hometown in northern Molise, Margherita Caravelle, the eldest of six children, convinced an initially uninterested fiancé that after marrying they should join her sister in Toronto. When she first raised the idea, her husband refused, telling her she was "crazy" even to consider abandoning the small bit of property they had recently inherited from her parents. However, several months later, with a loan from her parents in hand, their bags were packed for Toronto. More daring still was Maria Grande, an unmarried daughter in a large family who, despite her parents' disapproval, arranged her own voyage and joined two brothers who had previously migrated to Toronto. Christina Di'Angelo, however, recalled how her parents initially decided to send her,

her two sisters, and a brother to Toronto to raise money for her father's medical bills and for the family butcher shop in Calabria. It was only after they had settled in the city and successfully found jobs that her parents decided to sell the shop and join the family overseas.[20]

Typically, the married women who dominated the flow of female immigrants from Italy shared with their husbands the desire to immigrate to Toronto. Although anxious about the prospect of leaving home, they believed in the "dream of America" and were convinced that several years of hard work would secure for them "a better life," as it was most commonly put. Several women recalled, for instance, how in the days before the Second World War they had always been impressed by the sojourners who had returned to the home town wealthier men, and they hoped they would be equally fortunate. Others felt firm in their conviction that immigrating to a booming industrial metropolis such as Toronto offered the best possibility of securing a comfortable future for themselves and their children. As Luisa Bacci, a Basilicatan woman who hailed from a town near Naples, put it, "We were full of worries, in those days, 'Am I doing the right thing?' But we knew too that we had to try, and we believed that we could make a better life in Canada, especially in a big city like Toronto. There were lots of jobs and we knew we could work hard. It was a chance to take."[21]

Italian immigration occurred in a comparatively ragged fashion, and the process frequently involved the temporary fragmentation of families. Women in many instances bore the hardships caused by this fragmentation. Consider the case of Rosa Carpi, the twenty-five-year-old daughter of southern Italian peasants, who in the early 1950s married Luigi, a local man she had met during his periodic visits home while he was working for three years in Belgium coal mines. Soon after they married, he returned to Belgium, and two years later, Carpi, now pregnant, followed him there. When they received news that a relative had sponsored Luigi to Canada, the family returned home and Luigi left immediately for Toronto. In 1961, after her husband had sponsored his father and youngest sister, Carpi and her child finally arrived in Toronto.[22]

Significantly, women were familiar with economic strategies that involved the temporary departure of family members, for many had experienced the absence of fathers and brothers who had worked temporarily outside of Italy or served in the war. One woman, Elizabetta Marcone, explained that she had barely known her father because he had spent so many years away from the family—working at a variety of jobs in Albania from 1936 to 1938, in Germany from 1938 to 1939, and in Argentina for six years after the war. Even so, loneliness and hardship ensued, especially for women who were separated shortly after marriage, a situation that also led to a further blurring of gender-linked work roles. With only the occasional help from her father and brother, Angela Izzo ran the family farm in Molise for two years while rearing two children, including a son born just two days before her husband's 1951 departure for a Quebec farm. Immediately after their marriage in Calabria, Evalina Caputti's husband left for two years to work in agricultural and railway repair jobs in Switzerland. He made only two brief visits in as many years, though he respected his familial obligations by regularly sending money home. Eventually, he accompanied a brother to Toronto and, one year later, he called for his wife and child.[23]

In contrast to a previous era, when an earlier generation of immigrants had crossed the ocean in steerage, the postwar immigrants, including Italians, made the voyage in relative comfort, unless, of course, they suffered from seasickness. Women, however, did put up with the additional strain of having to care for their children on board ship. With the crowded conditions that prevailed, it was difficult, for instance, to keep children from wetting themselves before their turn for the washroom came up, and a mother suffering from seasickness found it hard to contend with a sick or otherwise disagreeable child. Still other women feared their children might fall overboard or disturb passengers by crying in the cabin at night. At Halifax, they worried about becoming separated from their children. When one woman arrived in Halifax on a cold day in November 1953, she was embarrassed by her lightly clad sons and feared the Canadian officials might consider her a bad mother. The train ride through eastern Canada evoked concern because the wood-frame houses resembled more the poverty of home than the expected wealth of the New World. As one woman put it, "When I saw all those little shacks I thought, my God, is that what Toronto is going to be like, living in a small crowded place just like in Italy?"[24]

But Toronto brought familiar faces and relief. In many cases, women's most vivid recollections are of the excitement that prevailed at the train station, as relatives and paesani were reunited, and of the comfort they felt at being together with their families.[25]

WOMEN AND IMMIGRANT HOUSEHOLDS

With the arrival of women in Toronto, the system of male boarding gave way to more complex, or blended, household arrangements. In many instances newly arrived or recently reunited families passed through an intermediate step, renting a small flat in a house owned by non-kin or non-Italians until such time as they could afford to enter the housing market. Despite the crowded nature of the extended

family households, most Italian women preferred this setup. Those who spent their early immigrant years living in a rental flat resented daily intrusions on their privacy. As a newly arrived immigrant with two children, one of them born just weeks after her arrival in Toronto in the spring of 1957, Evalina Caputti had been so distressed by the complaints of her landlady, who kept insisting that the children were too loud, that she wanted to return home. What with the family plot and furniture sold to finance the trip, even she knew this was not a likely possibility. Another woman, Elizabetta Marcone, so resented her landlord's complaints about excessive water and electricity bills and her child's ruining the hardwood floors that she made her husband move to other quarters within a month of her arrival in Toronto.[26]

For much the same reason as the men, Italian women preferred the familiari arrangement. Confident that this strategy would enable them to one day own their own home, they tolerated the crowded conditions, the constant noise, and the long line-ups for the bathroom. However, at least in the short term, the crowded household also held particular advantages for women, especially for those whose arrival in early postwar Toronto coincided with the years of childbirth. Women passed on cribs, baby clothes, and advice on breast feeding, and during the labour-intensive projects in which all members of the household participated, such as wine-making and the annual butchering of the pig, expectant mothers could rely on the help of their female housemates. Extended households also let women collectivize housekeeping and exchange confidences. Women who were at home all day—one nursing a newborn, another sewing clothes, and another unemployed—frequently shared domestic chores. In their testimonies, women also commented on how rare serious outbursts were in a house containing up to twenty people. Fernanda Pisani, a Molisan woman who lived for a decade in such a household in the Junction colony, nostalgically recalls those early years as a special time when *parenti* (kin) united during hard times: "Sometimes, it seems, we cared more for each other then than now, when we have our big houses but not so much time for each other."[27]

Far from huddling indiscriminately, people living in these crowded households had a deep-seated sense of propriety and retained as much as possible their sense of nuclear family. At supper, for instance, families sharing a kitchen ate at different or overlapping times as each woman, who alone was responsible for her family's meals, awaited her husband's arrival from work before heating her pot of water for pasta. Individual families shared private quarters and, while several women might be entrusted to do the grocery shopping, each family paid for its share of the supplies.

WOMEN'S UNPAID LABOURS

Whatever the household structure, women at home performed crucial economic roles that contributed to the welfare of their families now struggling to survive in Toronto. Like other working-class women, they stretched limited resources and found ways to cut costs and earn extra cash. Women's labours daily replenished the male breadwinner, and they fed, clothed, and raised children. In extended households, they might take care of extra menfolk who were unmarried or had not yet called for their wives, elderly parents, and in-laws. Since some households lacked refrigerators, women daily purchased perishables such as milk and bread. Without washing machines and often with access only to hotplates located in otherwise unfinished basements, basic chores were time-consuming and arduous.

* * *

WOMEN'S PAID WORK

For thousands of Italian immigrant women who had settled in Toronto in this period, the tasks associated with domestic chores and reproduction swallowed up only a portion of each day. The rest of the time was spent inside the factory walls or at home, bent over a sewing machine or madly packaging novelty items or advertising flyers—all for a nominal wage. More than any other factor, economic need, and the insufficient incomes earned by their husbands, prompted many Italian women to contribute directly to their family's finances by entering the paid labour force. They were part of the dramatic postwar increase of women, including married women, in the Canadian work force.

The proportion of married women in the Canadian female work force increased from 12.7 per cent in 1941 to 30 per cent in 1951; by 1961 it had grown to almost 50 per cent. Immigrant women, including Italians, figured prominently in this movement. In 1961 almost 11 per cent of the million working women in Canada were European-born, of whom Italian-born women represented more than 17 per cent. They made up 15 per cent of the 100,100 or more European-born women workers in Ontario. Some 16,990 Italian women, most of them immigrants, made up 6.5 per cent of Toronto's 1961 female labour force. While working women accounted for more than one-third of the total Italian adult female population in Canada and Ontario in 1961,[28] for Toronto this figure was 41.5 per cent. And these statistics do not cover the numerous women who earned money informally by taking in children or laundry, or by cleaning homes.[29]

While Canadian-born women swelled the ranks of the white-collar work force in the decades following the Second World War, immigrant women, most of whom lacked English and possessed few marketable skills, provided low-paid, unskilled, and semi-skilled female labour in industry. With the approval of employers who considered them hard-working and docile, Toronto's Italian women figured prominently in the city's postwar female immigrant workplaces. Their jobs included garment homework, operating steampresses, sewing, and novelty-making machines, packaging, bottling and labelling, laundry work, and domestic service. And they earned among the lowest incomes in Toronto. In 1961 Italian women whose mother tongue was not English earned an annual average of $1456—about 60 per cent of the average female income.

Manufacturing and domestic service were the largest employers of European immigrant women in Canada. In 1961 almost 57 per cent of the more than 32,000 Italian women workers in Canada were in manufacturing, most of them in clothing, food and beverage, textiles, and leather-goods shops. In service, where 28 per cent were located, three-quarters were domestic servants.[30] Statistics for Toronto reveal similar patterns. The number of Italian women employed in the city grew from under 3000 in 1951 to almost 17,000 a decade later. By 1961 Italians represented 6.5 per cent of the total female work force of 260,633, and 21 per cent of working women who were of European origin. Almost half of the city's Italian women workers were employed in the manufacturing sector, especially in the clothing and leather, textile and knitting categories. Large numbers could also be found in the tobacco, food and beverage, and rubber industries, while the strong new Italian presence in the city's needle trades was most evident in the leather-making shops, where Italians represented fully 40 per cent of the women employed.

The other major employer of Toronto's Italian women in these years was the service sector. Here the Italians, who made up one-third of the female work force, were most concentrated in laundries and dry-cleaning shops. Indeed, by 1961 they represented 28 per cent of Metro Toronto's female laundry workers. Another 14 per cent could be found in personal service work. Most were cleaning ladies employed in private homes, offices, and public buildings. Only 2 per cent of the women employed in service appear to have worked as live-in domestic servants. While agriculture employed comparatively few women in Toronto, Italian women accounted for 15 per cent of those who were employed in temporary jobs picking fruit and vegetables on farms on the outskirts of the city.

* * *

WOMEN'S WORK AND FAMILY ECONOMIES

Italian women's paid labour was part of a well-articulated working-class family strategy of success, one most often measured in terms of homeownership. Female wages helped support families through periods of seasonal male unemployment. Women's earnings were also used for daily living expenses, such as groceries, clothing, and household necessities, while men's paycheques went into savings deposits and towards houses and other investments. Characterized by low wages and high turnover, women's work experience also reflected the gender inequities of the postwar occupational structure. Predictably, the desire of capital for cheap workers and of immigrant working–class families for additional earnings were inextricably linked.[31]

Like many unskilled male and female workers, Italian women worked long hours at either

monotonous or hazardous jobs that were physically demanding. Women employed in drap-
ery and clothing factories endured poor
ventilation and high humidity, as well as speed-
ups and close supervision. Women assembling
items in plastics factories put up with dust and
foul-smelling fumes. Laundry work required
much lifting, and steampresses made the workplace almost unbearable in summer. Constant
bending over a sewing machine led to sore
backs.[32] Italian women in factories also confronted the new time and work discipline of
industrial capitalism and the impersonal relations between employers and workers. At the
same time, the daily experience of the workplace, where Italians learned to speak English
from co-workers and sometimes forged friendships, may also have had a partially empowering impact on women hitherto confined to the
household. By contrast, domestic workers who
cleaned house for middle-class clients toiled in
total isolation from their working sisters.[33]

During the 1950s, Italian women workers
did not articulate a political response to their
exploitation. This resulted in part from their
low status as low-paid and unskilled workers
and from the barriers of language and ethnicity erected in the workplace. Another important factor was the isolation of domestic
workers. Household duties also kept women
away from organizing meetings, and many were
unsure about union organizers who visited
their shops. Since joining a local might endanger their job, they truly feared compromising
their main goal of helping the family's financial situation. Moreover, unionization was made
more difficult by the fact that Italians were in
industries characterized by high concentrations
of unskilled female workers and high labour
turnover rates.[34]

* * *

Oral testimonies and case studies reveal how
women juggled their various familial responsibilities. Shortly after Lenora Fericci immigrated with her parents in 1958, for instance,
she found work as a seamstress on Spadina
Avenue and continued to work there for two
years following her marriage in 1959. One year
later, she left to have a child, and then returned
in 1963 to similar work at a garment factory
on College Street. Three years later she left to
have her second child, and then returned to
the same job two years later. Following the
family's move to the suburbs, she secured work
in a local plastics factory, which she left for a
period of six months in 1971 to have her third
child. Later still, a workplace injury would keep
her out of the work force for a decade. Another
woman had been employed in a garment shop
for two years when she was compelled to quit
in the winter of 1962 on account of her son's
illness. Because her husband suffered a workplace injury shortly afterwards, the family was
able to obtain a loan from the Public Welfare
Department to cover their upcoming mort-
gage payments. One month later, with her son
fully recovered and her husband receiving
workmen's compensation, she returned to her
old job. There were other ways in which
women succeeded in adjusting their work
schedules to meet the needs of their families.
For example, when one woman's son developed serious sinus trouble, she switched from
daytime to nighttime cleaning jobs so she could
take her son to his weekly hospital visit.[35]

When babysitting could not be provided by
female kin, many Italian women put off work
until a sister, in-law, or cousin became available
to watch the children. (These relatives might
themselves be recent immigrants or new mothers earning a little extra cash.) Mothers who
hired landladies or neighbours sometimes felt
uneasy about leaving their children with

strangers unconnected by links of kin or village. One woman recalled how each morning she hated leaving her crying son with the landlady downstairs. Suspecting that her child was being neglected by the babysitter, who had young children of her own, she stopped working for over a year until her mother's arrival in the city in 1959 gave her the opportunity to re-enter the work force. As Ferguson observed in 1962, at least some women could take temporary jobs during the winter months when their husbands were unemployed and took over the childcare duties for a few hours in the afternoon.[36] Opting for a different solution, some women worked as daytime domestics and brought their pre-school children to their clients' homes. Women who turned to industrial homework often did so for the same reason: they could watch over their children while they earned some extra cash.[37]

* * *

The entry of southern Italian peasant women into Toronto's postwar labour force reflected a pattern of continuity, for women had been important contributors to the peasant family economy in the Mezzogiorno. Since women's work was already justified in terms of peasant survival, no dramatic change in values was needed to allow these women to work outside the home. Given the scarcity of resources accessible to southern Italian immigrant families newly arrived in postwar Toronto, additional wages earned by women, including those at home, amounted to an effective familialist response.

Still, women's entry into an urban industrial work force did not occur without difficult adjustments, especially for married women. These strains reflected a dialectical process by which southern peasants became transformed into working-class families. Their familialist and collectivist behaviour was not simply the expression of traditional peasant culture; it also reflected their new economic position as members of working-class families coping with conditions of scarcity and restriction within industrial capitalism. This held particular significance for working Italian women, a fact ignored by scholars who view Italian immigrant women exclusively in terms of family and home. Scholars, too, have ignored the possibility that, even where wages and conditions are poor, paid employment could be an empowering experience for immigrant women who might otherwise have been isolated in their homes. Motivated by a commitment to family, women linked their self-identification as women and mothers to the paid and unpaid labours they performed for the benefit of parents, husbands, and children. In the process they developed a sense of feminine pride that was rooted both in their peasant and in their immigrant working-class experiences. They saw themselves as indispensable to their families. The nature of their labours had been largely transformed when they entered Toronto's industrial economy, but their paid and unpaid work remained critical to the daily survival of their newly arrived families in postwar Toronto.

NOTES

1 Personal interview (pseudonym)

2 National Archives of Canada (NA), Immigration Branch Records (IR), vol. 131, file 28885, G.H. McGee, "Some Observations Respecting Italian Farm Workers," 4 April 1952

3 NA, Department of External Affairs, Statement, 29 March 1950; A.D.P. Heeney, Memorandum, 30 March 1950; House of Commons, *Debates*, 28 March 1960

4 Alan G. Green, *Immigration and the Postwar Canadian Economy* (Toronto 1976), 89–90; Monica Boyd, "The Status of Immigrant Women in Canada," in Marylee Stephenson, ed., *Women in Canada* (Don Mills 1977). See also Sheila Arnopolous, *Problem of Immigrant Women in the Canadian Labour Force* (Ottawa 1979); Laura Johnson, *The Seam Allowance: Industrial Home Sewing in Canada* (Toronto 1982); Alejandra Cumsille et al., "Triple Oppression: Immigrant Women in the Labour Force," in Linda Briskin and Lynda Yanz, eds., *Union Sisters: Women in the Labour Movement* (Toronto 1983); Roxanna Ng and Tania Das Gupta, "Nation-Builders? The Captive Labour Force of Non-English Speaking Immigrant Women," *Canadian Woman's Studies* 3 (1981); Makeda Silvera, *Silenced* (Toronto 1983).

5 Jan Brøgger, *Montevarese: A Study of Peasant Society and Culture in Southern Italy* (Oslo 1971); John Davis, *Land and Family in Pisticci* (New York 1973) 94–5

6 Constance Cronin, *The Sting of Change: Sicilians in Sicily and Australia* (Chicago 1970), chap. 4; Brøgger, *Montevarese*, 106–20; Davis, *Pisticci*, chap. 2; Charlotte Gower Chapman, *Milocca: A Sicilian Village* (Cambridge, Mass. 1971), 41, 72–80, 109–10; A.L. Maraspini, *The Study of an Italian Village* (Paris 1968), 17–18, 73–8, 142–50

7 Personal interview (pseudonym); Leonard W. Moss and Walter H. Thompson, "The South Italian Family: Literature and Observation," *Human Organization* 18 (1959)

8 Personal interview (pseudonym); interviews. See also Judith E. Smith, *Family Connections: A History of Italian and Jewish Immigrant Lives in Providence, Rhode Island 1900–1940* (Albany 1985), chap. 2; Donna Gabbaccia, *From Sicily to Elizabeth Street: Housing and Social Change among Italian Immigrants* (Albany 1984), chap. 2; Edward Banfield, *The Moral Basis of a Backward Society* (New York 1958), 53–4, 63; Davis, *Pisticci*, 46–7; Chapman, *Milocca*, 23–5.

9 Rudolph Bell, *Fate and Honor, Family and Village* (Chicago 1979), 40, 124–7; references in note 8

10 Personal interview. On Sicily see Cronin, *Sting of Change*, 92–4; Chapman, *Milocca*, 32–3; for other regions see interviews and Ann Cornelisen, *Women of the Shadows: A Study of the Wives and Mothers of Southern Italy* (New York 1977), 24, 157–60; Davis, *Pisticci*, chap. 3.

11 Personal interviews; Chapman, *Milocca*, 23–4, 32–4, 64; Bell, *Fate and Honour*, 124–34; Banfield, *Backward Society*, 50

12 Personal interviews; Chapman, *Milocca*, 16–17. See also Thomas Kessner and Betty Boyd Caroli, "New Immigrant Woman at Work: Italians and Jews in New York City, 1880–1905," *Journal of Ethnic Studies* 5 (1978).

13 Personal interview (pseudonym); interviews; Cronin, *Sting of Change*, 92–5

14 Banfield, *Backward Society*, 53; Maraspini, *Italian Village*, 14–15; Ann Cornelisen, *Women of the Shadows*, 44–5; Lucia Chiavola Birnbaum, *liberazione della donna: feminism in Italy* (Middletown, Conn. 1986), 242

15 Personal interview (pseudonym)

16 Cornelisen, *Women of the Shadows*, 222–4, 57–93; Chapman, *Milocca*, 32–40. Oral informants made the same point. By contrast, contemporary studies, such as Harriet Perry, "The Metonymic Definition of the Female and Concept of Honour among Italian Immigrant Families in Toronto," in Caroli et al., *Italian Immigrant Woman*, stress Italian women's subordination within the family. See also Vincenza Scarpaci, "La Contadina, the Plaything of the Middle Class Woman Historian," *Journal of Ethnic Studies* 9 (1981).

17 Personal interview (pseudonym)

18 Ann Bravo, "Solidarity and Loneliness: Piedmontese Peasant Women at the Turn of the Century," *International Journal of Oral History* 3 (1982)

19 Personal interviews; Cornelisen, *Women of the Shadows*, 61–3; Gabbaccia, *From Sicily to Elizabeth Street*, 44–9; Chapman, *Milocca*, 83–4, 116–28

20 Personal interviews (pseudonyms)

21 Personal interview (pseudonym)

22 Personal interview (pseudonym). This pattern was also pronounced among postwar Portuguese immigrants. See David Higgs, *The Portuguese in Canada* (Saint John, NB 1982).

23 Personal interviews (pseudonyms). Valuable discussions of women and migration include Mirjana Morokvasic, "Why Do Women Migrate? Towards an Understanding of the Sex-Selectivity in the Migratory Movements of Labour," *Studi Emigrazione* 20 (1983); Annie Phizacklea, ed., *One Way Ticket: Migration and Female Labour* (London 1983).

24 Personal interviews

25 Personal interviews

26 Personal interviews (pseudonyms)

27 Personal interview (pseudonym). For a contemporary account of boarding among Italian families see Edith Ferguson, *Newcomers in Transition: A Project of the International Institute of Metropolitan Toronto 1962–1964* (Toronto 1964).

28 Married women's statistics cited in Julie White, *Women and Unions* (Ottawa 1980), 37; Toronto data in Canada, *Census*, 1961. See also Patricia Connelly, *Last Hired First Fired: Women and the Canadian Work Force* (Toronto 1978); Pat and Hugh Armstrong. *The Double Ghetto: Canadian Women and Their Segregated Work* (Toronto 1978).

29 This calculation was arrived at by dividing the total number of Italian women in the Metropolitan work force into the total number of women in the Italian ethnic group aged 15–64 in Metropolitan Toronto. Using the same method of calculation, the percentage of women in the work force by ethnic group was as follows: all groups, 44.6; British Isles, 45.0; German, 51.0; Netherlands, 18.9; Polish, 41.5; Ukrainian, 48.5. Canada, *Census* 1961; Dominion Bureau of Statistics, Unpublished Tables on Labour Force, Metropolitan Toronto, 1961

30 Canada, *Census*, 1961. See also Arnopolous, *Immigrant Women*; Monica Boyd, "At a Disadvantage: The Occupational Attainment of Foreign-Born Women in Canada," *International Migration Review* 18 (1984) and "The Status of Immigrant Women in Canada," *Canadian Review of Sociology and Anthropology* 12:4 (1975); Charlene Gannage, *Double Day, Double Bind: Women Garment Workers* (Toronto 1986); Margueritte Andersen, ed., *Histoires d'immigrées* (Montreal 1987); Catherine E. Warren, ed., *Vignettes of Life: Experiences and Self-Perceptions of New Canadian Women* (Calgary 1986); Barbara Roberts et al., *Looking for Greener Pastures: Immigrant Women in the Winnipeg Garment Industry* (Toronto, forthcoming).

31 For a similar argument on an earlier period see Bettina Bradury, "The Fragmented Family: Family Strategies in the Face of Death, Illness and Poverty, Montreal, 1860–1885," in Joy Parr, ed., *Childhood and Family in Canadian History* (Toronto 1982).

32 Personal interviews; AO, IIMT, MU6522, 1963 D, F D; MU6518, 1962 A, A A. For a comparison see Fernanda Nunes, "Portuguese-Canadian Women: Problems and Prospects," *Polyphony* 8 (1986); Roberts et al., *Greener Pastures*.

33 Personal interviews; Ferguson, *Newcomers in Transition*, 127

34 White, *Women and Unions*, chap. 3; personal interviews. See also Sheila Arnopolous, "Immigrants and Women: Sweatshops of the 1970s," in Irving Abella and David Miller, eds., *The Canadian Worker in the Twentieth Century* (Toronto 1983); Rachel Epstein, "Domestic Workers: The Experience in BC," in Briskin and Yanz, eds., *Union Sisters*

35 Personal interview (pseudonym); the case file is in AO, IIMT, MU6517, 1961 P. Q; MU6522, 1963 C.

36 Personal interview; Ferguson, *Newcomers in Transition*, 126

37 Personal interview; AO, IMMT, MU6514, 1962 D; Johnson, *The Seam Allowance*

CHAPTER 18

Marginalized and Dissident Non-Citizens:

Foreign Domestic Workers[1]

Daiva K. Stasiulis and Abigail B. Bakan

The systemic reproduction of migrant domestics as non-citizens within the countries where they work and reside renders them in a meaningful sense stateless, as far as access to state protection of their rights is concerned. This is despite the formal retention of legal citizenship status accorded by their home country, and, often, the legal entry as non-citizen migrant workers in the host country. [...] In this chapter, we consider the lived experiences of domestic workers themselves, based largely on a survey of foreign domestic workers living in Toronto. This chapter offers a comparative analysis of the experiences of two groups of women of colour, those of West Indian and Filipino origin, working in the homes of upper-middle- and upper-class Canadian families resident in Toronto, Ontario in the mid-1990s.

The limited literature on foreign domestic workers in Canada indicates patterns of structural discrimination, ranging from overt physical abuse, to denial of privacy rights, to denial of fair wages and adequate benefits. Our study attempts to identify both common and differential patterns of discrimination among foreign domestic workers originating from the two main regions of the English speaking Caribbean and the Philippines.

Our findings suggest that there are notable differences between West Indian and Filipino domestic workers in terms of immigration status, with a higher concentration of illegal migrants among the former than the latter. The recent pattern of discrimination against the legal entry to Canada of West Indian domestic workers [...] is expressed in this finding. Illegal immigration status among a notable portion of West Indian domestic workers interviewed was indicated in the survey not only in response to directed questions, but also in terms of the impact of such status on working conditions and access to benefits that would otherwise accrue to workers who have legal means of access. Our survey findings suggest further, that upon securing live-in, domestic work with a Canadian family in Toronto, Ontario, there are great discrepancies between employment situations regarding wages, general working conditions, and parameters of employee bargaining rights. However, while certain discrepancies based on immigration status were clear, the findings suggest that other aspects of domestic work bear greater commonality based on similar workplace conditions and systemic structures that favour Canadian citizen employers over their non-citizen employees. The variability of conditions that was discernible in the survey results is reflective of the absence of standards of employment and mechanisms to enforce the labour rights of foreign domestic workers upon their arrival in Canada. The capricious control of private employers explains many aspects of the work experiences of foreign domestic workers, rather than the place of origin of the domestic workers. The commonalities in the overall experiences of these two groups of domestic workers from the West Indies and the Philippines are greater than the differences: both groups are seriously underpaid, overworked, and treated with minimal trust or respect for privacy by their employers.

In sum, we were able to identify two main lines of demarcation revealed in the study. The first is determined by [...] gatekeeping [...]. The changes in immigration policy since the 1980s have tended to disfavour West Indian domestic workers and promote a patronizing racialized favour towards Filipinas that has directly impacted on the workplace experiences of these two groups of workers. However, the more profound line of demarcation appears to be not between the conditions and experiences of West Indian versus Filipino domestic workers, but between the employers on one side, and West Indian and Filipino workers collectively on the other. Racialized relations of exploitation within the private home are expressed in a hierarchy of class and citizenship, reinforced by the gatekeeping structures which overwhelmingly favour citizen/employers over non-citizen/employees. Even in a province such as Ontario, where certain legal rights have been won by domestic workers, the lack of enforcement mechanisms ensures relations of continued discrimination. The exercise of legal rights for domestic workers is dependent upon the registration of a formal complaint; such complaints, raised individually, are assessed by the domestic worker as a calculated risk. Any given complaint may lead to an improvement in the working conditions of the live-in, temporary status, female foreign domestic worker, but it alternatively may lead to a decline in conditions, as in the event of the complaint resulting in the dismissal and loss of job and domicile for the worker. Moreover, the restrictions associated with the FDM and the LCP, federal immigration policies, are not mitigated by labour legislation that resides in the jurisdiction of the provincial state.

Our findings suggest that various negotiating strategies among immigrant women seeking employment in Canada lead them to adopt various paths that culminate in live-in employment in private domestic service. Upon taking up residence and work in the homes of wealthy Canadian citizen employers, common structural conditions that promote systemic exploitation and racialization come into play. Here class exploitation is amplified by racial discrimination, and both of these hierarchical relationships are enforced by systemic patterns across the citizenship/non-citizenship divide.

A note on the survey methodology is in order. The data is drawn from 50 questionnaires, 25 from interviews conducted with live-in domestics from the West Indies, and 25 from those originating from the Philippines.[2] Country of origin was determined by birthplace. The interviews were conducted by female research assistants of the same regional or national origins as the interviewees. They were conducted face-to-face, or in the rare cases when respondents were unable to meet, by telephone. In all cases, individual interviews were about 90 minutes long, and followed a questionnaire guideline. The sample was selected through a snowball approach of community contacts. No more than three names were suggested from each interviewee, among whom no more than one name was subsequently interviewed. Interviewees were asked to respond to all questions, though it was not uncommon for some questions to be declined a response.[3]

Because the study is numerically small, it is of qualitative rather than quantitative significance. However, [...] the Caribbean and the Philippines are not arbitrary reference points in terms of the general experience of Third World migration.[4] Data of this nature is based on generalizing collective patterns of work and living experiences and upon the assumption of social patterns of negotiation. While the size of the sample is small in regard to statistical trends, it is substantially larger than an approach based on individual life histories. The study effectively highlights the working and living conditions of women workers treated as temporary visitors who are compelled to live with their employers and who perform duties of private domestic service. Though they provide labour in serious demand, employers and the Canadian state designate them as menial servants. These findings are explored in more detail below, according to a series of specific topics, notably: immigration status; the live-in requirement and accommodation; working conditions, wages and benefits; and remittances and family support.

IMMIGRATION STATUS

Faced with the threat of deportation for non-fulfillment of duties, domestic workers who live with their employers work long hours for low pay in very isolated and highly regulated conditions. Regarding their immigration experience and status, however, there was a divergence of experience between the two groups of women interviewed in this study. Among the West Indian women, 20 out of 25 responded to a question about place of work immediately prior to working as a domestic in Canada (Q7).[5] Of these, all but two (who had worked in Europe) had worked in the West Indies immediately before coming to Canada. Among the Filipinas, 23 responded to this question; only 11 of these came directly from the Philippines. Others had worked in the Middle East, Asia and Europe, immediately prior to coming to Canada to work.

This finding reflects divergent patterns of migration for the two groups of women, and distinct strategies for negotiating the global restrictions they face. The migration of West Indian domestics to Canada reflects historical and imperial country/region to country ties. In contrast, Philippine migration indicates the aggressive marketing of labour for export on the part of various Philippine governments. The latter process has had the unintentional effect of rendering unskilled or deskilled Filipino women experienced international migrants.[6]

[N]egotiating citizenship involves navigating the selection processes of various gatekeepers. There is a preference among domestic placement agencies in Canada to recruit Filipinas from outside Manila; moreover, the experience requirement of the LCP in Canada has tended to favour those who had previously served as household workers in other countries. This trend is reflected in the survey findings, especially notable given the small size of the sample. In contrast, West Indian women in search of domestic service as a means of emigrating are no longer readily welcomed in Canada. Among the West Indian domestics in our study, ten entered Canada as domestic workers on either the FDM or the LCP, and therefore were legally admitted as foreign live-in domestic workers; 14 entered Canada as visitors, and one claimed asylum as a refugee (Q15). It is illegal to work in Canada while on a visitor visa, and refugee status is almost never granted to those who claim the need for asylum from the West Indies. Refugee claimants can only work with a separately issued work permit. Therefore, the majority of the West Indian respondents entered domestic service in Canada as undocumented migrant workers. Among the Filipinas, 23 had entered Canada on the FDM or LCP programme as foreign domestic workers, while only two entered as visitors.

The divergent patterns of entry into Canada and the subsequent differences in migration status for the two groups indicate the relatively more restrictive access for West Indian women compared with Filipinas. The relatively high proportion of undocumented workers among West Indian women reflects the effectiveness of gate-keepers in Canada in limiting the legal access of these applicants. However, evidence suggests that neither the numbers seeking work as domestics in Canada, nor the demand for live-in domestic service, have declined. Such racialized bias compels more and more West Indian women to enter the country as visitors and work without any formal status in the country. This pattern of increasing numbers in undocumented personal service is widespread in other countries such as the United States and Italy.[7] Despite a general trend towards increasing restrictions regarding the numbers of domestic workers admitted on the LCP, Filipino applicants are currently considered in a racist stereotype to be "good servants," and therefore some continue to find it possible to pass through Canada's closely guarded gates. This legal passage is conditional, however, on their willingness to work as maids and nannies, to arrive on temporary visas and to live with their employers.

In response to another question regarding current immigration status within Canada, the picture changed somewhat (Q16). Among both groups of women workers, several had obtained landed, or permanent resident status, yet continued to work as live-in domestic workers. Among the West Indian domestic workers, 16 had temporary or unidentified status within Canada at the time of the interview, whereas nine had obtained landed immigrant status or actual legal citizenship. Among the Filipino domestic workers, 19 were legal temporary workers, whereas six had obtained landed immigrant status.

The notable feature here is that historically it has been unusual for any worker to accept live-in domestic service in Canada unless they are temporary workers. The implication is that the economy in Canada today is so restrictive for "unskilled" immigrant workers of colour, that even those who are legally eligible to leave live-in domestic service are faced with few or no other options. At least some West Indian workers, and the more recently arrived Filipino workers, continued to work at least partially as live-in domestic servants despite having obtained landed immigrant or citizenship status. This is an unusual phenomenon within the postwar Canadian workforce, and one that has not been formally recognized by the Canadian government.

Regarding immigration status, then, our findings reveal two patterns. First, there are apparently more illegal or undocumented domestic workers among the West Indian sample. Second, the findings suggest that both West Indian women and Filipinas who have the right to work legally in occupations other than domestic service are compelled to remain working as domestics. This second pattern runs counter to the thesis of "ethnic succession" whereby only the most recent of immigrant groups are to be found in the most exploited ("dirty, dangerous and difficult") jobs.

LIVE-IN REQUIREMENT AND ACCOMMODATION

These findings have implications for the live-in requirement of the LCP. The LCP obliges foreign domestics to work and live in their employers' home for two years within a three-year period if they are to be eligible to apply for permanent residence in Canada. Domestic workers will commonly share an apartment for weekend use in order to obtain some privacy and time away from what are often 24 hour on-call obligations. Such arrangements are not incorporated into the LCP, and employers and immigration authorities can challenge caregivers for doing so without their permission.[8]

Those who are illegal, however, and have no hopes of obtaining permanent legal status, would feel no obligation to live in their employers' homes to meet the FDM/LCP regulation. Yet workers with undocumented status are also at greater risk of deportation as they have no legal claim to residence within Canada. Therefore, there is likely more, rather than less, obligation among undocumented workers to live in the employers' home if this is established as a condition of employment. Those who are landed immigrants or citizens, however, would be released from the live-in requirement and would normally seek alternative employment other than domestic service.

Domestic workers interviewed for this study were all "officially" live-in domestic workers; this was a precondition of qualification in the study. However, the respondents indicated that the "live-in" feature for domestic service occupational status did not necessarily mean living with one's employer all week long; and in some cases, officially designated "live-in" workers, actually lived out. In such a case this likely meant that they not only had a residence in the employer's home, but also maintained their own private or shared residence. Among the West Indian domestics, of the 24 who responded to this question, only four lived with their employer during the entire seven-day week (Q28). Thirteen lived with their employer during the five- or six-day working week only; five lived-out; and two had "other" living arrangements that were not specified. Among the Filipinas, of the 24 who responded, only six lived with their employer all week. Sixteen lived with their employer during the working week only; and two lived out.

* * *

While the quality of accommodation varies markedly, the living space for the majority of live-in domestics in Canadian middle-class homes is not designed to provide privacy and separation for live-in workers from employer's families. The resulting lack of privacy and constant employer (and employing family members') surveillance—whether by design or by default—inhibits domestic workers from having any private life of their own. The potential restrictions include barring intimate friendships and familial and sexual relationships, creating conditions that are in direct contradiction with the ideals of autonomous adulthood, so-called "family values" and personal freedom in Canadian society. When asked what changes they would like to see in the LCP (Q36F), 18 of 25 West Indian domestics, and 16 of 23 Filipinas who responded said they favoured changes in the live-in requirement. The commonality of this response among both groups of workers in the interview sample is notable. Upon entering the country and experiencing the pressures of living with one's employer, both groups of foreign domestic workers in Canada encounter a commonly oppressive set of circumstances.

* * *

WORKING CONDITIONS, WAGES AND BENEFITS

We have identified the temporary immigration status of foreign domestic workers in Canada, combined with the compulsory live-in requirement, as the main conditions that render them vulnerable to the arbitrary designs of their employers. These conditions are heightened by the personalistic nature of the employer/employee relationship characteristic of domestic service, and the differential impact of class, race and citizenship status. Among both West Indian and Filipino domestic workers, a substantial majority of respondents surveyed indicated that the two main areas of responsibility associated with their employment were caring for the employers' children, and cleaning the employers' house. For West Indian domestic workers, 22 of 24 respondents who answered this question identified care for the employers' children as part of their current job; among Filipinas, the 24 out of 25 who responded to this question all identified childcare.[9] Moreover, when asked to identify the frequency with which such care was provided (Q4A2A2), all 21 West Indian domestics who responded to this question answered seven days per week; all 24 Filipinas who responded offered the same frequency rate.

This is particularly interesting given the responses to the questions regarding accommodation. Though all of those who answered this question indicated they were expected to care for children seven days per week, a majority of respondents did not actually live in the employers' homes throughout the entire week. This suggests that employers' expectations were for the provision of care every day, every week; however, by arranging to live out for part of

the week, workers were able to get some time off away from their childcare responsibilities.

* * *

Not surprisingly, cleaning house was another major area of work responsibility characterizing the employment situation of West Indian and Filipino domestic workers (Q4A2C1).[10] For the former, the response rate of those who identified housework was 21 of 25; for the latter, 21 of 24. Other common tasks, indicated by at least 18 affirmative responses from both the West Indian and the Filipino respondents, were: serving guests (Q4A2K1); shovelling snow in the winter (Q4A2J1) and gardening (Q4A2L1). Thus, it was common for both Filipino and West Indian workers, hired as nannies, also to be expected to work simultaneously as housekeepers. This is consistent with the association of household labour with "women's work," and defined as combining childcare and housekeeping as part of the same job description. It also indicates the tendency for women of colour to be expected to perform the duties of the employing "woman of the house" in a gendered, hierarchical, heterosexual, nuclear family structure. When paid female domestic labour is employed in the private Canadian home, gendered divisions become altered by class divisions within the home. Women of means employ poor women to perform the domestic duties associated with women's labour; in the process a clear line of demarcation according to class and enforced by citizenship and race come into play. This pattern was common in the study whether the foreign domestic workers came to Canada from the West Indies or the Philippines.

* * *

Doing the laundry appeared in the findings to be a task more universally included in the "house cleaning" job description. Among West Indian domestic workers, 21 of 25 who answered this question (Q4A2G1) did the laundry; for Filipinas, the response rate was 22 of 24. Even here, however, when the question of frequency was asked, variations emerged again. Fourteen of 21 West Indian domestic workers who responded (QA2G2) did the laundry once per week; seven did the laundry on a daily basis. Among Filipinas, of 15 who responded, ten did the laundry once per week, while five did laundry daily. When a question was asked about ironing (Q4A2H1), all 25 of the West Indian domestics who were interviewed responded, among whom 13 indicated this task was part of their job description, performed once a week. For Filipino domestic workers surveyed, again there was a response rate of 100 per cent regarding the task of ironing: 22 indicated that ironing was a regular part of their expected duties. Sixteen of 18 Filipinas who responded indicated that they did the ironing once per week; one ironed every day; and one ironed only once per month.

* * *

Another feature of live-in domestic work is the spatially restrictive nature of the arrangement, where the employer is not only one's boss but also one's landlord. When the landlord is responsible for determining access not only to private residence but also to permanent residence in the country, the regulatory power of the employing family is augmented even further. Employers determine not only what the domestic worker is expected to do, but also what she is expected not to do, or denied access to do at all.

One finding that emerged in the survey data related to job description was conspicuous in this negative sense. A clear majority of respondents indicated that they were *not* expected to perform one duty commonly associated with household labour: grocery shopping (Q4A2I1). Among the West Indian domestic workers, of 25 who answered this question, 21 stated they did not do the grocery shopping; among Filipinas, of 24 who answered this question, 21 had the same response.

We believe this finding is suggestive of a pattern worthy of further exploration among foreign domestic live-in workers. Grocery shopping is unquestionably a task associated with household labour and with meal planning. However, given that there is no obvious correlation between the numbers of respondents responsible for menu preparation and the numbers who do the grocery shopping, this factor alone does not explain the high negative response rate. The survey does not suggest that domestic workers were not asked to plan the meals; what is indicated in the findings is only that they were not asked or expected to buy the groceries for the meals.

Alternatively, we suggest an interpretation of the labour of grocery shopping in relation to the household as a work site. Grocery shopping for a family on a regular basis suggests several forms of behaviour that may be considered distinct from other household duties. It compels fairly autonomous activity outside of the household. It requires transportation, in a car or taxi, that would logically be paid for by the employer, and assumes responsibility in managing this transportation to and from the household work site. It is also dependent upon financial exchange, sometimes in considerable amounts measured over a period of time, both for transportation and especially the purchase of the groceries. Indeed, the grocery bill for an employing family with two or more children, which is typical of employers of foreign domestic workers, may exceed the wages paid to live-in household workers. Given that most of the domestic workers cared for young children, it would also likely require that the children accompany the domestic worker in the activity, where responsibility on the part of the employee is increased. Moreover, as live-in domestics are expected to pay for their board out of wages paid them by the employer, the live-in domestic worker who buys groceries for her own consumption would, in a sense, be paying her own wages from the employer's funds. Grocery shopping is a duty that demands considerable individual discretion—choosing the best products, managing variation in price options, and so on. We believe that it is precisely because grocery shopping encouraged these features of autonomy, increased responsibility, physical distance from the household as a work site, control of family finances, and individual, mature discretion, that domestic workers tended not to be asked to perform this duty. Despite the small size of the interview sample, the uniformity of the responses among both West Indian and Filipino domestic workers is suggestive of the need for further investigation of this dimension of live-in domestic service.

Another set of survey questions regarding working conditions focused on the number of hours worked and the payment of wages. West Indian domestic workers interviewed worked an average of 51.3 hours per week; Filipinas worked an average of 49.2 hours per week. According to Ontario labour legislation, any work performed over 44 hours within a given week is overtime. Overtime pay for domestic workers is expected to be at the rate of 1 1/2 the hourly rate, and time off in lieu is required to be at the rate of one and one-half hours per hour of overtime worked.[11] In response to a question about payment for overtime, however, among 25 West Indian workers who answered

this question, ten received overtime compensation, while 15 did not. Among Filipino domestic workers, of 22 responses, 16 received overtime compensation, while six did not.

There is sufficient discrepancy here to suggest a possible variation between the two groups, indicating that West Indian workers surveyed, who work an average of 2.1 hours more per week, are also less likely to receive overtime pay or time off in lieu for the work they perform. We interpret the discrepancy in overtime pay combined with the longer average work week to have resulted from the absence of security among these workers in demanding adequate compensation from their employers. The larger number of undocumented workers among the West Indian workers surveyed would suggest greater vulnerability in the workplace, and less bargaining power to enforce compensation for overtime. However, the fact that six of 22 respondents among the Filipino workers, indicate lack of compensation for overtime pay is significant insofar as this national group of domestics is predominantly here under the LCP. Our survey indicates that both West Indian and Filipino domestic workers are vulnerable to extreme discrepancies in pay, in part due to the long hours of work associated with private service employment and the difficulty of enforcement of overtime compensation. The more vulnerable the immigration status of the worker, the more likely she is to be unfairly compensated, and the greater the margin of discrimination she is likely to suffer.

The measurement of hours of paid work in the home has long been a contentious and hard-fought issue among domestic advocacy organizations in Canada. In 1987, overtime pay or time off in lieu for domestic workers was recognized in Ontario law, a direct response to domestic workers' demands.[12] Subsequent studies indicate, however, that while a majority of domestic workers routinely work overtime, only a minority receive fair compensation for overtime work performed.[13] For the live-in domestic worker, enforcement of such a provision is dependent upon a separation of work performance in the home as a work site, from time off while resident in the same home as a site of respite from work. Our findings reflect this pattern of contestation surrounding hours of labour performed, a pattern suggested in the findings for both West Indian and Filipino workers.

We can now turn from number of hours worked, to hourly rates of pay. Here, again, there was considerable discrepancy, but the variations in pay were characteristic of both West Indian and Filipino domestic workers. There was wide variation in frequency of pay, with a majority expecting to receive a cheque every two weeks (Q4A122B); 12 West Indians and 14 Filipinas. Others expected to be paid monthly (Q4A12C): four among the West Indian domestic workers and eight among those from the Philippines. Still others expected to be paid weekly (Q4A12A): six in the West Indian group, three among the Filipinas.

While the frequency of pay is variable, this factor taken in isolation is not significant. However, when we combined information from responses regarding frequency of pay with hours of work per week and pay rates, we were able to approximate the hourly wages of West Indian and Filipino domestics in the survey.[14] Accordingly, West Indian workers were paid on average $4.53 per hour; Filipino workers in the survey were paid an average of $4.73 per hour. The 20 cent per hour discrepancy is a relatively small margin of difference given the number of undocumented workers among the West Indian group. What is more noteworthy is the fact that both the West Indian and Filipino workers received hourly wages considerably

below the legal minimum wage in Ontario at the time ($5.40–$6.85 per hour).[15] Not only is the average earned demonstrably low, but it is also merely a statistical average. Among West Indian workers, the pay scale went as low as $2.14 per hour; for Filipino workers, the low end of the hourly pay rate was $1.91 per hour.

Our findings confirm and expose the highly unregulated employment standards applicable to foreign domestic workers in Canada, reflected in arbitrary and unaccountable rates of pay. Since 1987 full-time live-in domestic workers have been entitled to receive at least the minimum wage. Employers are allowed to deduct the costs of room and board, within standards provided in federal guidelines; however, the parameters for arbitrary pay rates are greatly increased by the live-in requirement of the FDM and LCP. The discrepancy in pay demonstrates the unregulated control placed in the hands of employers of live-in domestic workers in Canada. Moreover, the employee does not necessarily retain a formal record of payment for work performed. When asked if a pay slip was received with payment (Q4B4), among the 12 West Indian respondents who answered this question, only one received a pay slip with every payment; three received a pay slip once per year; and seven stated that they never received a pay slip. Among the Filipino workers, 14 responded to this question; three received a pay slip with every payment; 11 never received one. These findings are significant given that under the conditions of the LCP, the "employer is required to include a statement of earning with [each] paycheque."[16] Such a record of employment is necessary should the worker apply for employment insurance benefits, and as proof that the employee has worked the necessary length of time as set out in the federal regulations.[17] Our findings suggest that there is systematic non-compliance of employers with this pay slip requirement.

The survey investigated not only amounts and frequency of pay, but also workplace benefits. While the general conditions of work among the West Indian and Filipino domestic workers in the survey were similar, or similarly varied, certain benefits indicated a different pattern. Live-in domestics in Ontario are entitled to equal pay for equal work, pregnancy leave, paid public holidays, parental leave, regular payment of wages, vacation time, free periods away from work at designated intervals, termination notice and work details in writing.[18] They are also, like all Ontario workers, eligible for health care coverage, workers' compensation, certain tax benefits based on pay scale and employment insurance (formerly referred to as "unemployment insurance" in federal legislation).

West Indian domestic workers were less likely to be guaranteed receipt of these benefits than Filipinas. Regarding health care benefits, among West Indian workers, of 25 respondents who answered this question (Q4A8A), 13 stated that they did receive benefits, eight did not, and four did not know. Among the Filipino workers, among 24 who answered this question, all received health care benefits. Regarding pension benefits (Q48B), of 24 West Indian respondents, four received benefits, 11 did not, while nine did not know. For the Filipino domestic workers, among 22 respondents, 20 did receive pension benefits and two did not. Turning to unemployment insurance (Q4A8D), of 23 West Indian domestic workers who answered this question, three received benefits, 17 did not, and three did not know. Among the Filipinas, of 22 respondents, 20 received unemployment insurance benefits while two did not. Finally, regarding the benefit of receiving a tax refund (Q4A8C), of 24 West Indian domestic workers who answered this question, 12 stated that they did, 11 did not and one did not know. For the Filipino domes-

tic workers, of 22 respondents, 19 stated that they did receive a tax refund while one did not and two did not know.

Despite the small size of this study, these findings fall sufficiently along the lines of nationality to suggest further exploration. These benefits, when received, accrue to the employees from the government, whereas the necessary paper work and ensuring receipt of benefits rests with the employer. Unlike the payment of wages, there is not necessarily a direct cost to the employers in allowing these benefits to be accessed by the employees.[19] However, there are costs involved for the employer in the regularization of the employee/employer relationship, including paying the employer's contributions to various government funds. Given that we discovered that a significant number of the West Indian domestics interviewed had no documented migration status, one of the indicated effects is the inability to access benefits to which legal foreign domestic workers are entitled.[20] Despite the illegality of employing and harbouring an undocumented worker, the lack of regulation of the work process means that the employer gains even greater control and more work for fewer costs. It is likely that the significant gap in the access to employee benefits revealed in the findings is a feature of the undocumented status of many of the West Indian respondents.

REMITTANCES AND FAMILY SUPPORT

Our survey also investigated the role of female domestic workers as the economic supporters of their own families. Immigration to Canada as a means to acquire remittances to support family members "back home" for both groups of workers was a key issue of exploration. This is an important element of the negotiating strategy of migrant communities, particularly of women for whom compensatory paid work sufficient to support their families is limited relative to men in virtually every country in the world. The interviewees were asked to rank the importance—on a five-point scale with "very important" at one end, ranging through "important," "neutral" and "not very important," and with "not important at all" at the other end of the scale—of a number of factors considered in their decision to come to Canada as a domestic worker. Each question was ranked separately.

For a significant number of women workers, among both the West Indian and Filipino groups, the decision to come to Canada was largely linked to their family's financial and social welfare. Among the West Indian domestic workers, of 25 who responded to the statement "I wanted to immigrate to Canada," 24 ranked this as either important or very important (Q12A). Among 25 Filipino workers who responded, 20 ranked this statement in these categories. When asked to rank the statement, "I wanted to bring over my family or certain family members to Canada" among 25 West Indian respondents, 15 placed this reason as important or very important; and among 25 Filipinos who responded to this question, 18 placed this statement in these categories (Q12B). When asked to rank the statement, "I wanted to be able to earn money to send back home," 24 West Indian and 25 Filipino workers responded to this question. Among the West Indian workers, 17 placed this statement as important or very important, as did 19 Filipinas (Q12 H).

Another question, this one open ended, asked "What are the major things you have gained, or hope to gain, in becoming a live-in domestic worker in Canada?" (Q31). Here, there was a differentiated emphasis between the West Indian and Filipino workers. The former stressed personal achievements associated with raising their standard of living, while the latter emphasized the importance of remittances. The largest number of West Indian domestics first mentioned furthering their education (ten of 25 who responded); the second most common answer was about integrating with others or getting to know Canada (eight responses); and the remaining responses were about raising their standard of living, acquiring landed immigrant status or bringing their family to Canada. The Filipino responses were different. Here, sending money home was the most common goal mentioned first (ten of 20 who responded); after this, the most common answers focused on bringing their family to Canada (six responses); and the remaining answers were scattered among educating their children, improving their standard of living and gaining a better job.

The role of remittances figures more highly in the concerns of the Filipina domestics interviewed than among the West Indians. In both cases, remittances are important, but the relative weight is different. When asked to rank their response to the question directly posed, "For your family back home, how important do you feel it is that you send them money from your work in Canada?" (Q25), among 21 West Indians responding, 14 stated very important or important. Out of 25 Filipinas who answered this question, 19 stated very important or important.

This variation in emphasis may in part be reflective of the more recent migration flow of Filipinos to Canada, with more dependents remaining back home in need of overseas support. Around 15 per cent of households in the Philippines receive income from their relatives deployed abroad.[21] Further, the Philippine state is highly dependent upon overseas remittances as the main source of foreign currency, and for this reason often refers to its exploited female migrants abroad as national "heroines." There is a massive network of state and private interests encouraging overseas work for this purpose.[22] The West Indies are, however, also dependent upon overseas remittances. However, the culture of praising immigrants for sending back funds is not as pronounced as in the Philippine case. Another feature in explaining the difference in emphasis is the number of undocumented workers among the West Indian interviewees. Sending money to another country that has been earned under the table is not only challenging, but highly risky to those both at the sending and receiving ends of the funds.

Despite the differences, an interesting similarity regarding remittance payments was also indicated in the survey. A majority in both the West Indian and Filipino groups did not send their remittance cheques to their husbands/partners back home, but to their mothers or other relatives. In answer to the question, "To whom do you generally send remittance cheques?" (Q24), among 20 West Indian respondents, only three stated that money was sent to their husbands. Other responses included their mother (nine); combinations of relatives (six); or another relative or person (two). Among the 23 Filipino respondents who answered this question, only six stated that they sent money to their husbands. Other responses were their mother (nine); combinations of relatives (three); another relative or person (three); and eldest daughter (two).

Of note is the fact that among both groups of women, a greater number directed their remittance cheques to their mothers than to their husbands/partners, and to other relatives in general than to their husbands/partners. This is despite quite divergent marital patterns between the two samples (Q18). Of 25 West Indian domestics who answered a question about marital status, only three were in the category of married/partner prior to arrival in

Canada; one described herself in the category of separated/divorced/widowed; and 21 stated that they had never married. Among the 25 Filipinas who responded, roughly half (12) identified themselves as married/partner; two in the separated/divorced/widowed category; and 11 stated that they had never married. Therefore, there were a larger number of married/partnered Filipinas compared with the West Indian women.

This is a finding consistent with the divergent cultural norms related to the institution of marriage. In the Philippines, the majority of the population are practising Catholics and formal legal marriage is commonly expected of young women. In the West Indies, on the other hand, there is a common tradition of unions without formal marriage, and single-parent families headed by women are far from unusual.[23] In both groups, however, husbands were notably not the principal recipients of the remittance cheques.

This cross-cultural similarity in remittance patterns conforms to worldwide observations that women tend to work to support the basic needs of their families rather than for personal consumption. Moreover, it implies that there should be no automatic presumption that male partners or spouses are part of the familial picture; and if they are, there should be no automatic assumption that they are trusted to distribute the family earnings in accordance with the wishes of the women migrant wage-earners. As a strategy for negotiating citizenship, the financial independence of women workers is therefore an important factor in the process. This finding adds emphasis to the case for considering female migration patterns distinctly from male migration patterns and marital relations, even when considerations of family support as a motivation for immigration are highlighted.[24]

CONCLUSION

Despite the small size of this survey sample, certain discernible patterns are revealed in the findings. The citizenship divide on a global scale, enforced by gatekeeping mechanisms, is expressed within the private homes of Canadian families. Facing profound obstacles, women workers from the West Indies and the Philippines have negotiated strategies motivated overwhelmingly by the basic desire to support themselves and their families. Our study indicates that the restricted immigration status of both West Indian and Filipino domestic workers has a profound impact on their working and living conditions in Canada. More specifically, the greater the restriction faced at the border, the greater the risk of intense exploitation and discrimination. Our research suggests that the increased restrictions against West Indian workers has only served to increase the likelihood of illegal employment, without leading to any concomitant improvement in domestic service working or living conditions for those of Filipino origin. On the contrary, employers of domestic service continue to be subject to minimal regulation that might ensure a transparent standard of work expectation and enforcement of mechanisms to guarantee workers' legal rights.

The identification of the particular matrix of citizenship, class, race and gendered relations among foreign domestic workers in Canada that we suggest to be evidenced by our study is to our knowledge unique. While several studies have identified patterns of abuse, racism and exploitation, these have either traced general trends, or focused largely on a single racial/citizenship group. Rina Cohen has identified a more instrumental connection between race and job performance, tracing a pattern within domestic service where lighter-skinned workers were nannies, and darker-skinned workers

were cleaners and cooks.[25] Our study indicates, alternatively, that there are indeed dramatic variations in the job descriptions and levels of compensation among domestic workers, but these variations are within a general spectrum of exploitation not directly reducible to the country of origin or racial identity of the domestic workforce. Instead, the sharp demarcation in class and citizenship status between the employers and migrant employees, supported by systemic factors in Canada and the world system fundamentally shape the relations of paid domestic labour. As Brigitte Young has aptly summarized:

> The flexibility of the labour market has produced greater equality between educated middle-class women and men while creating greater inequality among women. High value is placed on the integration of professional women into the formal economy while the "paid" reproductive work of women in the informal economy (the household) continues to be undervalued; women's "paid" work outside the home is not equal to women's "paid" work inside it … These changes have produced two categories of women within the household: professional women and maids.[26]

Our findings revealed the complexity of paid reproductive work performed by live-in household workers. Placed in the wider context of the global political economy, West Indian and Filipino women workers are part of a system that Parreñas refers to as the "international transfer of caretaking." In such a system, women from the Third World care for the children of wealthy women in the First World, and in turn support through their labour and remittances the provision of care for their own children back home.

NOTES

1. Sections of his chapter are drawn from Daiva Stasiulis and Abigail B. Bakan, "Negotiating Citizenship Globally: Migrant Domestic Workers as a Case Study," *Feminist Review*, no. 57, London, UK, Autumn 1997.

2. The 50 interviews took place between 1994 and 1995, after the new LCP legislation was enacted. Some of the interviewees arrived in Canada under the previous FDM and others by means elaborated further in the chapter. We would like to acknowledge the research assistance of Maria Leynes, Marcia Williams, and Claudine Charley in conducting interviews for this study.

3. For purposes of security and confidentiality we did not interview the employers of the domestic workers in this survey, upon whom the interviewees depended for their very livelihood and residence in Canada. Interviews with placement agencies documented in the previous chapter provide a reasonable profile of their clients, the employers of domestic workers in Canada.

4. Respondents identified Trinidad and Tobago, Jamaica, Barbados and Guyana as the countries of origin among West Indian domestic workers participating in the survey.

5. The reference "Q" followed by a number refers to the question number of the interview schedule. This chapter is an interpretation of selected findings, relevant to the wider analysis of negotiating citizenship rights. The survey questionnaire is available on request from the authors.

6. See Abigail B. Bakan, "The International Market for Female Labour and Individual Deskilling: West Indian Women Workers in Toronto," *North/South: Canadian Journal of Latin American and Caribbean Studies* (1987), vol. 12, no. 24.

7. See Parreñas, *Servants of Globalization*.

8. According to the Department of Citizenship and Immigration Canada (CIC): "An important requirement of the Programme is that employees must live in the employer's home. The Live-in Caregiver Program exists only because there is a shortage of Canadians to fill the need for live-in care work. There is no shortage of Canadian workers available for caregiving positions where there is no live-in requirement." See CIC, LCP website, www.cic.gc.ca/english/visit/caregi_e2.html#2.

9. Question 4A2A1.

10. The CIC guidelines are silent in regard to house cleaning. However, there is the recommendation of a written contract between the employee and the employer upon acceptance of a job in Canada on the LCP, with the proviso that the federal government has no authority for enforcement and that labour standards vary across the provinces. In the CIC's Sample Contract, "Housekeeping Responsibilities" are, however, listed under the heading of "Care Responsibilities/Duties," and accompanied by two boxes, "Yes" and "No." Then there is room in the sample contract under the heading "Describe,"

to explain the specific duties expected. See CIC, "The Live-in Caregiver Program: Information for Employers and Live-in Caregivers from Abroad," Ottawa, February 1999, www.cic.gc.ca/English/visit/caregi_e2.html.

11. The Ontario Employment Standards Act was amended in 2000, but it continues to permit employers the option to give workers time off in lieu of pay for overtime worked. The law specifies that such an arrangement must be agreed upon by the employee and must be met within 12 weeks after the pay is earned. Ontario, *Employment Standards—Fact Sheet: "Domestic Workers,"* www.gov.on.ca/LAB/es/dome.htm, 2001.

12. See Fudge, "Little Victories and Big Defeats," 119–45.

13. INTERCEDE conducted a study in 1989 of live-in domestic workers, which revealed that fully 65 per cent of the 576 workers surveyed reported they were regularly required to work overtime, but only 33 per cent who were so required received the legal compensation; 43.7 per cent of those required to work overtime received no compensation whatever. (Sedef Arat-Koc and Fely Villasin, *Report and Recommendations on the Foreign Domestic Movement Program*, INTERCEDE report for submission to the Ministry of Employment and Immigration, 1990, 5–7.)

14. This was based on results from Q4A12A, Q4A12B and Q4A12C, where respondents paid weekly, bi-weekly or monthly, respectively, provided their regular earnings over the appropriate time period. These figures were averaged according to the number of respondents, and divided into hourly units according to the average working week for West Indian and Filipino workers.

15. The Ontario NDP government raised the minimum wage from $5.40 per hour to $6.85 per hour on 1 January 1995. Interviews were conducted both before and after this date. The Ontario minimum wage has not been increased since this time.

16. CIC, "The Live-in Caregiver Program: Employers and Live-in Caregivers from Abroad," Ottawa, February 1999, www.cic.gc.ca/English/visit/caregi_e2.html#1, 5.

17. CIC, "The Live-in Caregiver Program": 7.

18. Ontario, *Employment Standards—Fact Sheet*, www.gov.on.ca/LAB/es/dome.htm, 2001.

19. In some provinces and territories, the employer is required to pay the cost of belonging to Canada's national health insurance system, while in others the worker is responsible for paying these costs. See Citizenship and Immigration Canada, "The Live-in Caregiver Program Employers and Live-in Caregivers from Abroad," Ottawa, February 1999, www.cic.gc.ca/English/visit/caregi_e2.html#1, 4.

20. For instance, the Immigration booklet for the Live-in Caregiver lists employment standards that "may" be accessible to domestic workers, depending on provincial/territorial standards as including days off, vacation time with pay, paid public holidays, overtime pay, minimum wage, equal

pay, equal benefits, pregnancy leave and notice of employment termination, employment insurance, Canada pension
plan and old age security. See Citizenship and Immigration,
"The Live-in Caregiver Program": 4.

[21] Peter Stalker, *The Work of Strangers* (Geneva: International
Labour Organisation, 1994), 126.

[22] See Heyzer, Nijeholt and Weerakoon, eds, *The Trade in
Domestic Workers.*

[23] See e.g., Elizabeth Uy Eviota, *The Political Economy of Gender:
Women and the Sexual Division of Labour in the Philippines*
(New Jersey: Zed Books, 1992); Momsen, ed., *Women and
Change in the Caribbean.*

[24] Linda Miller Mattei, "Gender and International Labor
Migration: A Networks Approach," *Social Justice*, vol. 23, no.
3 (1996), 38–54.

[25] See Rina Cohen, "The Work Conditions of Immigrant
Women Live-in Domestics: Racism, Sexual Abuse, and
Invisibility," *Resources for Feminist Research*, 16: 1 (1987), 36–8.

[26] Young, "The 'Mistress' and the 'Maid' in the Globalized
Economy," 315–16.

Bibliography

Arat-Koc, Sedef and Fely Villasin. *Report and
Recommendations on the Foreign Domestic
Movement Program* (INTERCEDE report for
submission to the Ministry of Employment and
Immigration, Ottawa, 1990).

Bakan, Abigail B. "The International Market for
Female Labour and Individual Deskilling: West
Indian Women Workers in Toronto,"
*North/South: Canadian Journal of Latin American
and Caribbean Studies*, 12: 24 (1987).

Cohen, Rina. "The Work Conditions of Immigrant
Women Live-in Domestics: Racism, Sexual
Abuse, and Invisibility," *Resources for Feminist
Research*, 16: 1 (1987), 36–8.

Eviota, Elizabeth Uy. *The Political Economy of
Gender: Women and the Sexual Division of Labour
in the Philippines* (New Jersey: Zed Books, 1992).

Fudge, Judy. "Little Victories and Big Defeats: The
Rise and Fall of Collective Bargaining Rights
for Domestic Workers in Ontario," in A. Bakan
and D. Stasiulis, eds, *Not One of the Family:*
Foreign Domestic Workers in Canada (Toronto:
University of Toronto Press, 1997), 119–45.

Heyzer, Noeleen, Geertje Lycklama à Nijeholt and
Nedra Weerakoon, eds. *The Trade in Domestic
Workers: Causes, Mechanisms and Consequences of
International Migration* (Kuala Lumpur and
London: Asian and Pacific Development Centre
and Zed Books, 1994).

Mattei, Linda Miller. "Gender and International
Labor Migration: A Networks Approach," *Social
Justice*, 23: 3 (1996), 38–54.

Stalker, Peter. *The Work of Strangers* (Geneva:
International Labour Organization, 1994).

Stasiulis, Daiva and Abigail B. Bakan. "Negotiating
Citizenship: The Case of Foreign Domestic
Workers in Canada," *Feminist Review*, No. 57
(Autumn 1997), 112–39.

Young, Brigitte. "The 'Mistress' and the 'Maid' in the
Globalized Economy," in Leo Panitch and Colin
Leys, eds, *Socialist Register, 2001: Working Classes,
Global Realities*, (London: Merlin Press, 2001).

CHAPTER 19

The Economic Exclusion of Racialized Communities—

A Statistical Profile

Grace-Edward Galabuzi

Introduction

[...] In this chapter we use three important measures of economic performance for racialized groups, both immigrant and Canadian-born: unemployment, labour-market participation, and employment income. This approach gives a fuller picture of the condition of racialized group members in the Canadian economy. It also allows us to shift the emphasis away from the debate about measures of discrimination in income and toward a more rounded assessment of the contribution of structures of racial discrimination to the disadvantaged position of the racialized group in the labour market and ultimately in society. The approach also acknowledges other complex factors responsible for the disadvantage, including prolonged periods of economic downturn, mismatched skill sets, and length of stay in the country. These factors are also likely to be experienced by non-racialized group members, although not necessarily in the same way. The other benefit of this approach is that it allows the analysis to draw from broader research done on the employment barriers faced by racialized group members and the income implications of those barriers.

Using both the income and employment measures, we identify a gap between the economic performance of the racialized communities and the rest of the Canadian population. In fact, some data show that among some groups the income gap is growing and income inequality in Canada is increasingly along racial lines. The 1995 Statistics Canada for individual earners data show that about 10% of all people who reported employment income in 1995 (about 1.5 million individuals) were members of the racialized population. According to that data, in 1995 racialized group members' employment income was $22,498, 15% lower than the national average. Employment earnings of immigrants arriving from 1986 to 1990 were $21,538, or 18% of the earnings of non-immigrants. For more recent immigrants, coming after 1990, the employment income was $16,673, or 36% of that of non-immigrants. This gap also coincided with general cutbacks in the levels of government transfers, either in federal employment insurance benefits or provincial social assistance benefits, during much of the 1990s.[1] For racialized women, average earnings were $16,621 in 1996, compared to $23,635 for racialized men, $19,495 for other women, and $31,951 for other men.[2]

TABLE 19.1:   Canada: Income of Racialized Group Individuals, 1995

	Total Population	Racialized group	Difference %
Average	$27,170	$22,498	18%

Source: Statistics Canada, 1996 Census data, available at www12.statscan.ca/english/census01/home/index.cfm.

RACIALIZED GROUPS AS A STATISTICAL CATEGORY[3]

The members of a racialized group correspond to the group defined as such in Statistics Canada data, using the term *visible minority*, as defined by the *Employment Equity Act* of 1986. The act defines "visible minorities" as "persons, other than Aboriginal peoples, who are non-Caucasian in race or non-white in colour." Under this definition, the act's regulations specify the following groups as visible minorities: Chinese, South Asians, Blacks, Arabs and West Asians, Filipinos, Southeast Asians, Latin Americans, Japanese, Koreans, and Pacific Islanders. In the 1996 census, the identification of the racialized group population was achieved using a new census question that asked respondents whether they were members of one of the population groups defined as a visible minority under the provisions of the *Employment Equity Act*. In previous censuses, this information had been derived primarily from responses to the question on ethnic or cultural origin. In this report, we have supplemented some of that data by looking at source-country data as it relates to immigrant populations, especially after 1970.

DATA CONFIRMS UNEQUAL EMPLOYMENT INCOME OF RACIALIZED GROUP MEMBERS

Based on a set of special runs of Survey of Labour Income Dynamics data done for the Centre for Social Justice for 1996–1998, we conclude that racialized groups suffer a considerable disadvantage in employment income in the Canadian labour market.[4] This data, based on individual earnings before taxes, shows that in 1996, racialized Canadians earned an average of $19,227; non-racialized Canadians made $25,069, or 23% lower. The 1996 median before-tax income gap at 29% ($13,648 to $19,111) shows an even more profound inequality because it factors out the highest and lowest earners. This gap grew in 1997 as earnings of racialized individuals increased slightly to $19,558, a gap of 25% when compared to the $25,938 earned by other Canadians. The median before-tax income again betrays a widening inequality, with earnings of $13,413 for racialized groups and $19,602 for others, or a gap of 32%. The tax and government transfers' effect was marginal in terms of closing the gap. The average after-tax income of the racialized groups in 1996 was $16,053, compared to $20,129 for other Canadians, a 20% gap. After-tax incomes grew for both groups in 1997 to $16,438 for racialized individuals, or 79% of the $20,793 for other Canadians, with incomes still showing a marginal growing gap. The median after-tax income for 1996 was $12,991 for racialized groups compared to $16,922 for other Canadians, a gap of 23%. That gap grew in 1997 to 26%, as racialized group individuals took home less at $12,895, while other Canadians increased their earnings to $17,320.[5]

On average, the improving economy resulted in only a marginal change, with 1998 figures showing an average before-tax income for racialized groups of $20,626, which accounted for 74% of the $27,174 for the rest of the population. The median incomes of $14,507 (racialized) compared to $20,517 (non-racialized) left the gap at 30%. Taking the tax and government transfers into consideration, racialized groups earned an after-tax average of $17,376, 80% of the $21,694 for the rest of the population. The median after-tax income was $13,561, compared to $18,146, or 25% lower.

Some have speculated that the income gap is a function of low educational attainment. However, an analysis of the 1998 high school and post-secondary educational levels shows that the gap between low and highly educated groups is similar, ranging from 22–24%. From the employment income data for the year 1998, we are also able to deduce that the proportion of the university-educated racialized population in the top 10% of earners is also much lower, 20.6% compared to 31% for the non-racialized population.

* * *

A decile analysis of the income data confirms the racial stratification by income. With minor variations, racialized groups are disproportionately concentrated in the lower five income deciles (61.1%) as compared to the rest of the population (49%). The income gap is largely maintained when one considers disposable (after-tax) income, suggesting that the tax effect has not sufficiently compensated for the inequality generated in the market. These patterns are repeated for racialized groups in 1997 (60.5%) and 1998 (60.5%). The lowest decile also represents the highest single number of racialized group members: 15.9% in 1996, 15.9% in 1997, and 15.4% in 1998. The figures also hold true for highly educated groups, varying only slightly.

TABLE 19.2: Canada: Income of Racialized Persons by Select Deciles, 1996. Before Tax—1 is the lowest and 10 the highest

Deciles	Total Population	Racialized group(a)	Non- racialized group(b)	Difference (a/b) %
1st	10	15.9	9.2	6.7
2nd	10	12.8	9.6	3.2
3rd	10	11.3	9.8	1.5
4th	10	10.2	9.9	0.3
5th	10	10.9	10.0	-0.9
6th	10	8.5	10.1	-1.6
7th	10	9.1	10.0	-0.9
8th	10	8.3	10.3	-2.0
9th	10	7.1	10.4	-3.3
10th	10	5.8	10.6	-5.8

Source: Centre for Social Justice special run of data from Statistics Canada, *Survey of Labour and Income Dynamics, 1999–2000*, 2001.

TABLE 19.3: Canada: Income of Racialized Persons by Select Deciles, 1996, after Tax

Deciles	Total Population	Racialized group (a)	Non-racialized group (b)	Difference (a/b) %
1st	10	15.9	9.2	6.7
2nd	10	12.8	9.6	3.2
3rd	10	11.4	9.8	1.6
4th	10	10.2	9.9	0.3
5th	10	10.5	10.0	-0.5
6th	10	8.9	10.1	-1.2
7th	10	8.2	10.2	-2.0
8th	10	8.3	10.3	-2.0
9th	10	7.6	10.3	-2.7
10th	10	6.4	10.5	-4.1

Source: Centre for Social Justice special run of data from Statistics Canada, *Survey of Labour and Income Dynamics, 1996–2000*, 2001.

TABLE 19.4: Canada: Income of Racialized Persons by Select Deciles, 1997, before Tax

Deciles	Total Population	Racialized group(a)	Non-racialized group(b)	Difference (a/b) %
1st	10	15.4	9.3	6.1
2nd	10	13.6	9.6	4.0
3rd	10	12.9	9.6	3.3
4th	10	9.7	9.9	-0.2
5th	10	8.9	10.1	-1.2
6th	10	8.6	10.1	-1.5
7th	10	9.4	10.0	-0.6
8th	10	8.0	10.3	-2.3
9th	10	6.9	10.5	-3.6
10th	10	6.6	10.5	-3.9

Source: Centre for Social Justice special run of data from Statistics Canada, *Survey of Labour and Income Dynamics, 1996–2000*, 2001.

A labour-market structure with an over-representation of racialized groups in low-income occupations and sectors, and underrepresentation in highly paid occupations and sectors is bound to produce the documented gap in employment income. Any explanation of the income gap needs to address these racialized labour-market inequalities.

TABLE 19.5: Canada: Income of Racialized Persons by Select Deciles, 1998, before Tax

Deciles	Total Population	Racialized group (a)	Non-racialized group (b)	Difference (a/b) %
1st	10	14.8	9.1	5.7
2nd	10	12.7	9.7	3.0
3rd	10	12.7	9.7	3.0
4th	10	10.6	9.9	0.7
5th	10	9.7	10.0	−0.3
6th	10	9.1	10.0	−0.9
7th	10	8.3	10.3	−2.0
8th	10	8.2	10.3	−2.1
9th	10	7.1	10.4	−3.3
10th	10	6.8	10.5	−3.7

Source: Centre for Social Justice special run of data from Statistics Canada, *Survey of Labour and Income Dynamics, 1996–2000*, 2001.

RACIALIZED GROUP EARNINGS AND UNIONIZATION

As Table 19.6 shows, the only category with a single-digit gap between racialized and non-racialized employee incomes is the unionized sector. The average wages of racialized unionized workers are also comparable to those of employees with university degrees, suggesting that unionization is a serious non-governmental option to deal with the income gap between Canadians of colour and those of European origin. Yet the challenge there is significant too, given that racialized group members are underrepresented in unionized work. Of the 2,905,100 unionized workers in Canada, only 203,100 are racialized group members, or 7% of the union population (as compared to 11.4% in the population).

In a broader framework, what is the impact of unionization on access to the labour market for racialized group members, both Canadian-born and immigrant? A study by Reitz and Verma (2000), dealing with the union coverage of racialized group members based on an analysis of 1994 Survey of Labour and Income Dynamics data, concludes that racialized men

TABLE 19.6: Employment Income of Full-Year/Full-Time Racialized Persons in Unionized Workplaces before Taxes, 1998

	Total Population	Racialized group (a)	Non- racialized group(b)	Difference (a/b) $	%
Average	44,451	41,253	44,919	3,666	8%
Median	41,450	38,755	42,000	3,245	7%

Source: Centre for Social Justice special run of data from the Statistics Canada, *Survey of Labour and Income Dynamics, 1996–2000*, 2001.

have much lower levels of unionization than other men while the levels for women were only marginally lower. Controlling for such factors as gender, recent immigration, education, and occupation, they suggest that employment discrimination affects access to union jobs, especially in certain occupations and industries. The result is a lower unionization rate among racialized group members.[6]

While Reitz and Breton conclude that unionization may not mitigate racial discrimination in the workplace, the findings presented here suggest otherwise. The segregated nature of racialized group participation in the labour market, the overrepresentation in certain sectors, industries, and occupation (many non-unionized and lower paid), would suggest potential improvements of wage levels should those sectors be unionized. Similarly, increased access for racialized group members to sectors, industries, and occupations that are heavily unionized should improve their employment income. Even Reitz and Breton cite studies in the United States that suggest that unionization benefits workers from vulnerable groups like young people and low-skilled people, including African Americans. While their study is not conclusive as to whether that would be the case in Canada (they looked only at 1994 data), it can be speculated that unionization would indeed help workers in precarious forms of work like garment-making, harvesting, kitchen and food service, and some retailing.

Another related issue regards union rules dealing with entry into unionized workplaces; such provisions as seniority represent a barrier to access to and retention of regulated, well-paid work. Reitz and Breton's research would suggest that such barriers do exist, but that the level of impact is unclear. It is also the case that those last hired are usually the most vulnerable, having the least job security. However, labour-

market regulation and union rules also protect workers from employers' arbitrary exercise of power, and would benefit racialized group members as their levels of unionization improve.

MAKING SENSE OF THE NUMBERS

Regarding the observable income differentials between racialized and non-racialized groups, a Statistics Canada analysis concluded that compensating for the key differences between racialized and other Canadian-born earners, such as age, frequency of work, and patterns of labour market participation, reduces the gap between their average employment income from about 30% to 4%.[7] The conclusion raises as many questions as it attempts to answer. It is not clear that we can "compensate" for many of the differences because that assumption ignores the reality that racialized groups experience those variables because of discriminatory structures in the labour market that impede access to full-time, permanent employment. Those variables may reflect the discriminatory effect. From their study, Christofides and Swidinsky (1994) concluded that "raw, unedited evidence" supports the contention that racialized group members, like women, Aboriginal peoples, and people with disabilities, are disadvantaged in the Canadian labour market. These disadvantages derive from discriminatory treatment and account for a significant portion of their inferior income.

Their research, using Employment and Immigration data from 1990 and Statscan Canada Labour Market Activity Survey (LMAS) data from 1989, confirms that racialized group members were more likely, on average, to be paid less than other comparable employees.[8] A further analysis, using the Ordinary Least Squares (OLS) wage regression, demonstrated that "substantial portions of the observed differentials cannot be explained by productivity differences alone."According to Christofides and Swidinsky, these account for 30% of the wage gap. They attribute the unexplained residuals to labour-market discrimination.[9] These findings are consistent with those in a number of other studies, including Li (1988), Reitz and Breton (1994), Gosine (2000), Hou and Balakrishnan (1996), and Wanner (1998).[10]

Their research indicates that the labour-market disadvantages of racialized women are especially acute. It also suggests that racialized group members not engaged in regular paid employment routinely face particularly low wage offers—a condition confirmed by anecdotal evidence from those working for temporary employment agencies. A report by the Toronto-based Contingent Worker Project found that close to 70% of those surveyed from a pool of temporary agency workers, most of whom were racialized minorities, earned less than $1,500 a month.[11] These findings are consistent with Fernando Mata's work, which shows that "Immigrants, visible minorities and Aboriginal groups are experiencing great difficulty in terms of socio-economic integration. They are affected by higher unemployment rates, lower incomes and are more likely to be concentrated in manual jobs than other groups."[12] Akbari's (1989, 1999) examination of discrimination in employment experienced by racialized immigrants confirms these findings, as do numerous studies, some quoted above, dealing with inequality in employment.

The Income Gap between Racialized and Non-racialized Immigrants Is Growing

Fully 80% of racialized community earners were immigrants, most having arrived after 1965. For the racialized immigrant population,

except for the immigrants who arrived in the period between 1956 and 1965, average employment income was lower than that of other immigrants, and the gap grew. More recent immigrants, a majority of whom are racialized group members, have significantly lower earnings. According to 1996 Census data, the average employment income of immigrants who came between 1986 and 1990 was 18% lower than that of non-immigrants. The average employment income of the most recent immigrants, those who came after 1990, was 36% lower than the average earnings of non-immigrants.[13] It is clear that, within almost every period of immigration, this gap grows, from about 2% for 1966–1975 immigrants to 28% for the most recent immigrants. Given the debate outlined previously about the immigration factor in explaining income differentials, it is instructive that the income differential extends to immigrant groups.

The Racialized Gap in 2000

There have been some changes since the late 1990s. An analysis of employment income for the year 2000 shows that while racialized group members made gains towards the end of the century, the patterns of inequality persists. In 2000, there was a significant increase in the median before- and after-tax income of racialized persons—25.1% and 22.5% respectively (average after-tax increase 28.5%), an increase significantly above that of the non-racialized median before- and after-tax income at 7% and 8.4% respectively (average after-tax increase 16.9%).

While the income gap between racialized and non-racialized individual earners diminished over that period, it remained at significant levels and continues to be an important indicator of racial inequality in the Canadian labour market. While the median after-tax income of racialized persons was 23.2% lower than that of non-racialized persons in 1996, the gap fell to 13.3% in 2000 (Table 19.7). The median before-tax income gap fell from 28.6% in 1996 to 16.5% in 2000. While the size and persistence of the gap suggest a continuing problem with income inequality in the Canadian labour market for racialized groups, the higher rates of increase among racialized groups in 2000 point to a time lag in access to the benefits of the expansion of the Canadian economy over that period, an indicator of structural discrimination in employment. Some of that time lag can be explained by the "immigration effect," yet its size compares unfavourably to previous immigration periods.

There were also patterns of income disparity observable among cohorts with post-secondary education, who have an average after-tax income gap of 8.5%, and a 14.6% median after-tax income gap as well as among cohorts with less than high school education, who have average after-tax income gap of 22.6%, and a 20.6% median after-tax income gap (see Tables 19.8 and 19.9).

Time-lag trends are also observable among both the low-skilled and high-skilled groups. The increase in median after-tax incomes for university-educated racialized group members was 17.0% compared to 7.6% for non-racialized. Average after tax increases were 38.2% for racialized compared to 14.2% among non-racialized university educated (1997 and 2000 SLID data).

A decile breakdown confirms that racialized persons are overrepresented in the lower-income deciles, while non-racialized persons are overrepresented in the upper-income deciles (see Table 19.10).

TABLE 19.7: **After-Tax Income of Racialized Persons, Canada, 2000**

	Total Population	Racialized (a)	Non-racialized (b)	Difference (a/b) $	%
Average	23,023	20,627	23,522	2,895	12.3
Median	18,138	15,909	18,348	2,439	13.3

Source: Statistics Canada, Income Statistics Division, *Survey of Labour and Labour and Income Dynamics, Custom Tables, 1999–2002*, 2001.

TABLE 19.8: **After-Tax Income of Racialized Persons, University Degree, Canada, 2000**

	Total Population	Racialized (a)	Non-racialized (b)	Difference (a/b) $	%
Average	38,312	35,617	38,919	3,302	8.5
Median	32,832	28,378	33,230	4,852	14.6

Source: Statistics Canada, Income Statistics Division, *Survey of Labour, and Labour and Income Dynamics, Custom Tables, 1999–2002*, 2005.

TABLE 19.9: **After-Tax Income of Racialized Persons, Less Than High School, Canada, 2000**

	Total Population	Racialized (a)	Non-racialized (b)	Difference (a/b) $	%
Average	15,125	11,958	15,444	3,486	22.6
Median	12,955	10,378	13,068	2,690	20.6

Source: Statistics Canada, Income Statistics Division, *Survey of Labour, and Labour and Income Dynamics, Custom Tables, 1999–2002,* 2005.

TABLE 19.10: **After-Tax Income of Racialized Persons by Select Deciles, Canada, 2000—1 is the Lowest and 10 is the Highest**

Deciles	Total Population	Racialized group (a)	Non-racialized group (b)	Difference (a/b) %
1st	10	15.4	9.3	6.1
2nd	10	11.4	9.7	1.7
3rd	10	11.4	9.7	1.7
4th	10	8.7	10.1	-1.4
5th	10	9.9	10.0	-0.1
6th	10	8.8	10.2	-1.4
7th	10	9.7	10.1	-0.4
8th	10	8.6	10.2	-1.6
9th	10	8.4	10.3	-1.9
10th	10	7.7	10.4	-2.7

Source: Statistics Canada, Income Statistics Division, *Survey of Labour, and Labour and Income Dynamics,* Custom Tables, 2002.

IMMIGRATION AND INCOME DIFFERENTIALS

According to the 1996 census, in 1995, four of every five racialized group earners were immigrants, with almost all arriving after 1965. Of the 2.8 million immigrants who reported employment income, 1.5 million identified as members of racialized groups. While it is still the case that immigrant earnings vary according to period of immigration, there are troubling signs when racialized immigrant earning patterns are considered. Compared to non-racialized immigrants, and also considering compensation in relation to educational attainment, there are significant differentials suggesting the impact of racial discrimination in job attainment and compensation. The overall 1996 immigrant income average was reported at $27,684, which is 5.7% higher than that of non-immigrant Canadians, at $26,193. Much of the positive differential is attributed to higher educational attainment than that of non-immigrants, and a higher average of older earners (42 years to 36 years). An important part of this picture is the earnings of the mostly European pre-1976 immigrants group. Key differences begin to emerge when one focuses on racialized immigrant group employment income. While for the total immigrant population, the average income was $23,928, the racialized immigrant population earned only $18,044.[14]

Tracking immigrant income by period indicates the extent of the racialization factor. Looking at a period during which racialized group immigration has intensified, i.e., post-1986, we find that the employment income for immigrants arriving between 1986 and 1990 was $21,538, or 18% lower than the income of non-immigrants. The employment income level falls further for those arriving between 1990–1995, to $16,673, or 36% of the non-immigrant income. While it can be argued that the key variable here is period of stay, there are two reasons why that explanation is inadequate. First, the average income of racialized immigrants is lower than that of non-racialized immigrants during both the pre-1986 and post-1986 periods. The critical periods for our purposes are 1986–1990 and 1991–1995. The employment incomes of non-racialized immigrants for the periods 1986–1990 and 1991–1995 were $24,533 and $20,809 respectively, compared to $19,960 and $15,042 respectively for racialized immigrants. The second reason is that these patterns of difference are consistent with those of racialized non-immigrants, i.e., Canadian-born racialized earners. Their employment income for 1995 was $18,565, or

30% lower than that of other Canadian earners.[15]

Table 19.11 shows the decline in income attainment over the last 10 years among university-educated immigrants, for both the most recent immigrants as well as the 10-year resident, relative to a similarly educated Canadian population over the same period. According to the data, after one year in Canada, in 1990, a male immigrant with a university degree earned 55.8% ($33,673) of his male Canadian-born counterpart's income, while a female immigrant earned 56.6% ($21,059) of her female counterpart's. By 2000, that amount had fallen to 47.3% ($31,460) and 48.3% ($19,829) respectively. For those who had lived in the country for 10 years, the gap had not closed as was the case in the pre-1980s immigration class; rather, immigrants still lagged behind at 86.2% ($52,060) for males and 87.3% ($32,522) for females in 1990. Even more importantly, by 2000, the gap had grown to 28.6% among males and 20.9% among females. In both cases, while the incomes of immigrant graduates declined, those of the Canadian-born cohort grew, from $60,375 for males in 1990 to $66,520 in 2000 and from $37,235 for females in 1990 to $41,062 in 2000.

Table 19.12 shows the extent to which the income gap is racialized. Among immigrants of comparable stay in the country, there is a

TABLE 19.11: **Average Earnings of Immigrants and Canadian-Born with University Degree, in 2000**

	Male		Female	
	1990	2000	1990	2000
1 year in Canada.	$33	$31.5	$21	$19.8
10 years in Canada	$52	$47.5	$32.5	$32.4
Canadian-born	$60	$66.5	$37	$41

Source: Statistics Canada, "Earnings of Canadians: Making a Living in the New Economy," 2001 Census analysis series (March 11, 2003).

growing gap between the racialized and non-racialized.

CANADIAN-BORN RACIALIZED GROUP EARNERS

According to Statistics Canada data, in 1995, just over 253,000 earners in the racialized group population were born in Canada. Their average employment income of $18,565 was almost 30% below the level reported by all other earners who were Canadian-born. Statistics Canada suggests that age distribution is a possible factor explaining the differential. However, while the median age of the Canadian born racialized group was lower by more than 11 years, the educational attainment of the racialized group earners was higher than that of other Canadian-born earners and should act as a compensatory factor. This is perhaps true only to a point. Some 45% were under the age of 25, while the figure was 18% for other Canadian-born earners. Less than 10% were between 45 and 64, compared with 25% for

other Canadian-born earners. The argument is that older people earn more on average than younger earners, despite educational differentials. Statistics Canada also offered another explanation, that only one third of Canadian-born racialized group members were employed full time for the full year in 1995, compared with one half of other Canadian-born earners. However, it seems disingenuous to use this as an explanation for lower average incomes without commenting on the discriminatory nature of work attainment, especially barriers to full-time work. The higher levels of part-time, contractual, and precarious work that racialized group members experience are not natural phenomena. The explanation overlooks racial discrimination as a factor, which other studies have cited as an important contributor to both work attainment and lower incomes generally.[16] The Statistics Canada position also fails to acknowledge structural causes of the income gap such as the disproportionate participation in low-income sectors and occupations which, as discussed above, many studies

TABLE 19.12: Canada: Number and Average Earnings of Racialized and Non-racialized Immigrants by Period of Immigration

Number and average earnings of visible minority immigrants aged 15 and over by period of immigration, Canada 1995

	Immigrant earners		Average earnings		
	Visible Minority Population	Others	Visible Minority Population	Others	
Period of immigration	Number		Dollars		% Difference
TOTAL	1,247,940	1,570,080	23,298	31,170	-25.3
Pre-1956	6,715	213,380	28,378	34,350	-17.4
1956–1965	28,360	341,155	36,910	34,011	8.5
1966–1975	293,485	488,160	32,852	33,399	-1.6
1976–1985	331,970	260,640	24,279	29,286	-17.1
1986–1990	264,420	139,365	19,960	24,533	-18.6
1991–1995	322,990	127,375	15,042	20,809	-27.7

Source: Statistics Canada, *The Daily* (May 12, 1998).

have identified as a function of employment discrimination.

The higher levels of unemployment and their implications in terms of disproportionate impacts from cuts to Employment Insurance (EI) benefits contribute not just to the income gap but also to higher-than-average levels of low incomes among the racialized Canadian-born group. Limiting the explanation of the income gap to age and full-time employment differentials therefore fails to deal with the key implications of this finding, which include a high incidence of poverty, especially child poverty, an issue that should be the focus of government policy. In the final analysis, the dispute regarding the factors contributing to the employment-income gap does not negate its existence. This gap is growing and demands public attention.

RACIALIZED GROUP FAMILIES' AND NON-RACIALIZED FAMILIES' EARNINGS

According to census data for 1996, racialized husband-and-wife families earned a median income of $38,308, compared to $52,066 for non-racialized families, or an average of $13,758 (26%) less per year. Interestingly enough, this 26% disadvantage does not occur when the couple is mixed (one racialized group member and one not).[17]

This inequality is quite consistent across most of the major racialized groups. The three largest racialized groups, Chinese, South Asian,

and Black, all earn roughly the same average. The fourth largest group, Arab/West Asian, is even lower.[18] However, there are variations within the groups themselves, as some subgroups (both gender and ethnic) sustain lower-than-average incomes and higher-than-average unemployment rates.

By 2000, however, the family income situation had changed dramatically. The gap diminishes when one considers family income (see Table 19.13). The higher average and median incomes for racialized families reported in Table 19.13 may be explained by the higher on-average number of wage earners in racialized families (in many cases three to four wage earners). In 2000, there was a gap in the percentage change in the median after-tax income gap among families with no employment-income earners, from 31.% and 20.1% to 18.6% and 19.35% among families with one income earner; 16.5% and 15.6% among families with two income earners, and 1.5% and 5.5% among families with three income earners. This suggests the significance of the multiple-earner effect among racialized families.

Part of what accounts for this is the increase in average after-tax income of 40.1% between 1997 and 2000 (20.2% median after-tax income increase). Likely because they experienced a benefit from the improved-economy time lag, racialized families experienced the highest average and median after-tax increases between 1997 and 2000.

TABLE 19.13: After-Tax Income of Families, Canada, 2000

	Total Population	Racialized (a)	Non-racialized (b)	Difference (a/b) $	%
Average	53,083	61,266	52,381	– 8,885	–17.0
Median	43,265	50,912	43,080	–7,832	–18.2

Source : Statistics Canada, Income Statistics Division, *Survey of Labour, and Labour and Income Dynamics*, Custom Tables, 1999–2002, 2005.

INEQUALITY IN RACIALIZED GROUP ACCESS TO EMPLOYMENT: UNEMPLOYMENT

The disadvantages experienced by racialized groups and the gap in economic performance become clearer when we focus on the actual employment experience. The labour-market participation patterns reflect the racial differentiation observed in the income data. There are also differentials in unemployment levels. For instance, while racialized groups made up 11% of Canada's population in 1996, they had an average unemployment rate of 16%, compared to 11% for the general population in 1995. The labour-market participation of recent immigrants differs from that of the Canadian population as a whole. In 1996, processing and manufacturing accounted for 15.5% of the recent immigrant population's jobs, compared with 7.6% for the total Canadian population. A third of recent immigrants were in sales and service jobs, compared with just over a quarter of all Canadians.

Historically, racial discrimination in employment has been perpetuated in many ways. With a racialized labour market, racialized group members are often trapped in the low-end jobs and occupations. They are ghettoized in sectors of the economy that pay the least and have the worst workplace conditions. As a group, they continue to be vulnerable to precarious employment. This condition is often multiplied for racialized women, who face a double negative effect.[19] Historically, the dangerous work Chinese immigrants did on the building of the trans-Canada railway westwards typified racialized group work. Blacks were often restricted to occupations such as sleeping car porter.[20] In the early 20th century, South Asian and Japanese immigrants were restricted to such occupations as labourer or domestic under contracts with fixed quotas; they were denied fishing licenses

or access to farmland.[21] To this day, the number of racialized group members working in low-paid occupations is disproportionately higher than their numbers in the population. Various reports dealing with the issue of racial inequity in employment present conclusive evidence to suggest that racial discrimination is not only an endemic feature of the Canadian labour market, but also pervades many of the policies and practices in Canadian workplaces.

An analysis of the unemployment data from the 1996 Census shows the higher levels of low income and unemployment experienced by racialized groups. Statistics Canada shows that in 1996, 36.8% of women and 35% of men in racialized communities were low-income earners compared to 19.2% of other women and 16% of other men.[22] This trend is confirmed by other research. A recently completed study by Edward Harvey and Kathleen Reil titled "Poverty and Unemployment Patterns Among Ethnocultural Groups" compares the socio-economic status of 46 different ethnocultural groups in Canada, including a wide range of racialized ethnocultural groups, for 1986 and 1991. The study considers such socio-economic factors as employment income, unemployment, and incidence of low income as measured by Statistics Canada's Low Income Cut-off (LICO). The study supplemented the census data for 1986 and 1991 with a wide range of Canadian studies of ethnocultural groups and immigrants, the International Migration Data Base (IMDB), maintained by Citizenship and Immigration Canada, as well as three broadly representative focus groups organized by COSTI in Toronto and conducted by Harvey and Reil in June 1998.[23]

The study presented three key findings. First, when 1986 and 1991 data are compared, twice as many ethnocultural groups have higher unemployment rates in 1991. In 1986, 46% of the 46 ethnocultural groups had unemployment rates higher than the national average. In 1991, 76% of the 46 ethnocultural groups (35 groups) had unemployment rates higher than the national average. Second, although the overall national poverty level decreased in 1991 compared with the 1986 level, an increased number of the 46 ethnocultural groups experienced poverty in 1991 (contrary to the national trend). Third, the same ethnocultural groups remain consistently disadvantaged (compared with the national average) when 1986 and 1991 data are compared on the unemployment and poverty dimensions. The study identified a problem of persistent disadvantage for the ethnocultural groups.

In another paper titled "Ethnocultural Groups, Period of Immigration and Socio-economic Situation," Edward Harvey, Bobby Siu, and Kathleen Reil consider the socio-economic situation of immigrants in 17 ethnocultural groups. Immigrants are compared across five periods of immigration: before 1961, 1961–1970, 1971–1980, 1981–1987, and 1988–1991. Taken into account is the fact that of the immigrants coming to Canada, over 70% are members of racialized groups. In this study, both racialized and non-racialized ethnocultural groups are represented across the 17 groups.[24] Their findings confirm studies by the Economic Council of Canada that indicate that more recent immigrants have higher unemployment rates than their Canadian counterparts. The paper assesses the socio-economic situation of immigrants using measures for poverty, employment income, and unemployment, and concludes that:

- Employment experiences of recent immigrants are more diverse than their earlier immigrating counterparts.

- The socio-economic experience of different ethnocultural groups is not homogeneous. Immigrants of visible minority groups experience greater socio-economic disadvantage compared with immigrants of non-visible minority ethnocultural groups.
- Compared with immigrants who immigrated to Canada prior to 1981, immigrants who came to Canada after 1981 have higher unemployment rates, lower employment incomes, and greater incidence of low income.

Data show that despite variations within communities, racialized groups have higher unemployment rates. They represent a growing understanding of the congruence of the phenomenon of racialization and poverty, prompting an increasing number of analysts to draw parallels to the feminization of poverty. In this case, the racial factors disproportionately correlate to the incidence of low income to suggest a racialization of poverty.

More recent data confirms the patterns. As Table 19.14 shows, both the racialized group members and recent immigrants have been losing ground, with their unemployment rates almost twice those of the Canadian labour force by 2001.

INEQUALITY IN RACIALIZED GROUP ACCESS TO EMPLOYMENT: LABOUR FORCE PARTICIPATION

According to Karen Kelly's analysis of 1991 census data, the labour-force participation rate for racialized women was (59%), lower among West Asian and Arab group (50%), while South Asian and Latin American women were at 52%. 1991 census data show that the unemployment rate of racialized groups was 13% (before and after age standardization) higher than that of

TABLE 19.14: **Unemployment Rates for Immigrants, Non-immigrants, and Racialized Groups (%)**

	1981	1991	2001
Total labour force	5.9	9.6	6.7
Canadian-born	6.3	9.4	6.4
All immigrants	4.5	10.4	7.9
Recent immigrants	6.0	15.6	12.1
Racialized groups	n/a	n/a	12.6

Source: Statistics Canada, 2001 Census Analysis Series. *The Changing Profile of Canada's Labour Force*, February, 11, 2000; Human Resource and Development Canada, *2001 Employment Equity Act Report* (Ottawa: HRSDC, 2001).

other adults (10%). The Latin American and Southeast Asian groups, with the lowest labour force participation rates, also had the highest age standardized unemployment rates (19% and 17%, respectively). Unemployment was also high among West Asians and Arabs, and South Asians (each 16%).[25]

Jennifer Chard shows that by 1996, only 53% of racialized women were employed or self-employed, compared to 63% of non-racialized women.[26] Among racialized men, 65% were employed, compared to 74.1% for other men. It is among youth that the figures are the worst: only 36% of women and 36.4% of men aged 15–24 in racialized communities are employed, compared to 52% for other women and 54% for other men. The overall unemployment rates in 1996 were 13.2% for men and 15.3% for women in racialized communities, compared

to 9.4% for women and 9.9% for men in other communities.[27]

According to Harvey et al.'s study discussed above, once the labour force participation rate of the racialized group population is age-standardized, its members have a 66% rate of labour-force participation, lower than that of the non-racialized population. The findings also suggest that immigrants from racialized ethnocultural groups experience economic disadvantage that is persistent over the 30-year period covered during this study. This is also demonstrated by the data in Table 19.15, which shows that racialized groups and immigrants have a persistent labour-market participation disadvantage that grows over the 20-year period analyzed, culminating in the 66% to 80.3% for non-racialized groups.

TABLE 19.15: **Labour Force Participation Rates for Immigrants, Non-immigrants, and Visible Minorities (%)**

	1981	1991	2001
Total labour force	75.5	78.2	80.3
Canadian-born	74.6	78.7	81.8
All immigrants	79.3	77.2	75.6
Recent immigrants	75.7	68.6	65.8
Racialized groups	n/a	70.5	66.0

Source: Statistics Canada, *2003: The Changing Profile of Canada's Labour Force*, 2003; Conference Board of Canada, *Making a Visible Difference: The Contribution of Visible Minorities to Canadian Economic Growth* (April, 2004).

Explaining the Disadvantage: Racialized Groups, Human Capital and Educational Attainment

Various contending explanations have been advanced for the inequalities facing racialized groups in the Canadian labour market. Derek Hum and Wayne Simpson have attempted to show that discrimination is, with one exception, statistically significant only when we examine the case of foreign-born racialized group men. They claim that all racialized group members who are Canadian-born, except Blacks, and all racialized women earn less, but do not suffer from discrimination.[28] This view of course presupposes that factors such as unemployment, the kind of employment, education, and experience, which are used as criteria to measure and examine the differences, are not themselves the product of discrimination! Others explain away the differences using educational achievement. The concept of low quality of human capital among racialized group members remains a persistent explanation for the inequalities.[29] But this is not borne out by analysis of the educational attainment of racialized group members, a key factor for evaluating the quality of human capital. As a recent study by Fernando Mata shows, racialized group members, both Canadian-born and immigrants, do not obtain "fair economic and occupational returns from their educational attainments."[30] This is particularly the case for immigrant and Canadian-born racialized women. Data show that racialized group members under 44 are more likely to have a higher educational attainment than other Canadians.

Hou and Balakrishnan's study also concludes that while racialized group members are more likely to have a higher level of education, they are underrepresented in "high status" occupations and have lower incomes than their educational counterparts.[31] Karen Kelly's work shows that "in 1991, some 18% of the racialized group population aged 15 and over had a university degree, compared with 11% of other adults. As well, while the percentage of those with less than high school education was 33% for racialized groups, it was 39% for other adults." Yet even among those aged 25 to 44 with a university degree, "adults in a racialized groups are less likely than others to be employed in professional or managerial occupations. Instead, many are concentrated in lower-paying clerical, service and manual labour jobs."[32] In 1996 17% of visible minority women had a degree, compared to only 12% for the non-racialized communities.[33] It is important to note that the structures of racial discrimination that generate these inequalities in the workplace also impact access to educational opportunity.

More recent data shows clearly that racialized groups have an educational advantage when one considers average levels of educational attainment based on years of schooling and post-secondary certificates granted.

* * *

Racialized Groups and a Segmented Labour Market

An analysis of HRDC 1996 employment equity data shows that racialized group members were underrepresented in many highly paid occupations, and overrepresented in low-paying sectors of the economy and underrepresented in the higher-paying jobs in those sectors.[34] The sectoral segregation is a major reason for the lower incomes of the racialized group. The underrepresentation in many higher-paid occupational categories, though not in every category, is a key contributor to the racialized income gap.[35] An analysis of a cross-section of key industries confirms the structural nature of the systemic discrimination that racialized groups endure in Canada's workplaces. Industries like clothing and textile (36.2%), and banking services (15%), show the overrepresentation discussed above. On the other hand, racialized minorities are underrepresented in the motor vehicle industry (7%), primary steel (4.2%), and the federal government (5.6%).

Another dimension of the inequality is seen in the occupations within the different industries, especially the ones in which racialized minorities are overrepresented. As an example, in banking, where racialized group members are overrepresented at 15%, and 7% in senior management.

One key category is public-sector employment. As the industry-wide profiles below indicate, in key institutions in the public service, racialized groups are significantly underrepresented. The analysis shows that the importance of these discriminatory patterns goes beyond income. It is directly related to the limited participation of racialized groups in the administration of the Canadian state. Indeed it speaks to the social exclusion that these groups suffer in Canadian society.

Underrepresentation in key public-sector institutions has implications that go beyond compensation inequity. Broad public-sector occupations, such as police officer and judge, are well-paid jobs in Canada. These jobs are concentrated in the major urban areas where most racialized group members live, so that the effect of underrepresentation is magnified. Police officers, for instance, serve a key role in the administration of justice—often mediating the integration of various immigrant communities into the mainstream of Canadian life. They are at the centre of the tensions that often arise between marginalized groups and dominant cultural groups. The seemingly chronic

underrepresentation of racialized groups can only exacerbate the tensions, often leading to charges of racial profiling and racially targeted policing.[36]

Based on 2001 employment equity HRDC data, while some 13.4% of the population are racialized group members, only 10 out of 2,080 fire chiefs are from racialized groups, a percentage of less than 0.5%! Only 2.2% of fire fighters across the country are from racialized group communities (500 out of 25,275). In Ontario, there were 75 racialized commissioned police officers out of 1565, or 4.8%, while in Alberta, there were 230 racialized police officers out of 5,465, or 4.2%.

Another major category in the administration of justice is judging. While figures show a higher-than-average level of contact with the criminal justice system for racialized group members in 2001, only 40 judges out of some 965 are from racialized group members in Ontario, constituting less than 4% of the total.

* * *

RACIALIZED OCCUPATIONAL DIFFERENTIALS: OCCUPATIONAL PROFILES BY INDUSTRIES

Data from a sample section of Canadian industry demonstrate the structural nature of labour-market discrimination against racialized group members. By examining a number of industries by job categories and classifications, we are able to show the effect of differential access to the labour market, which results in overrepresentation in certain sectors and underrepresentation in others, as well as overrepresentation in certain occupations—particularly low-paying occupations—and underrepresentation in well-paying occupations and management-level positions.

An examination of the banking, auto, and steel industries confirms the argument that there is an underrepresentation of racialized group members at the managerial and supervisory levels of important and well-compensated occupations and industrial sectors, and that this is a key contributing factor to the low rates of racialized group incomes and economic performance. Conversely, an examination of the labour structure in the retail and textile industries demonstrates the reverse problem: an overrepresentation of racialized group members in the low-paid occupations.

The discriminatory effect is evident in categories such as senior managers, supervisors of skilled trades, skilled trades, and senior administrative personnel. Figures for the other industries generally show a similar rate of underrepresentation at the management and skilled-trade levels. Some industries such as banking, and especially clothing and textile products, show a larger concentration of racialized group members than exists in the population, while others, such as primary textile and general retail, are about proportional in terms of overall numbers.

In terms of its importance to the socio-political fabric of the country, perhaps the most glaring example of structural employment discrimination is the public sector, and specifically the federal public service. A recent federal government report identified the 5.3% participation rate of racialized groups, less than 50% of their composition in the Canadian population, as indefensible.[37] This finding comes 15 years after the introduction of a federal employment equity program for women, racialized groups, Aboriginal peoples, and persons with disabilities. Perhaps most disappointing is the fact that the lack of progress denies the federal public service the moral authority to act as a leader in implementing employment equity among industries regulated by the federal government.

It also rules out the possibility of redressing employment discrimination through making federal jobs available, a strategy that seemed very effective when francophone exclusion was targeted by the federal government.

Conclusion

The statistical profile of the social economic status of racialized groups shows that the process of economic exclusion persists even after the economic expansion effect is taken into account. There is a gap between the economic performance of racialized and non-racialized groups when one considers such indicators as income, unemployment, and labour-market participation. This inequality leads to increased likelihood of low income or poverty. According to Statistics Canada, the incidence of low income among racialized group members was significantly higher than the national average over the period 1993–1996. Low Income Cut Offs (LICOs) are used by the government to determine the level of income under which a family or an individual is considered to be living in poverty in Canada. Statistics Canada notes that the rate of poverty among racialized groups was 36% in 1995, compared to 19% for the general population. The rate for children under the age of six living in low-income families was an astounding 45%, compared to the overall figure of 26% for all children, a rate of child poverty almost twice that in the population. The poverty gap among those in the over-65 age group is also substantial, at 32% among the racialized groups compared to the national average of 19%.[38] Of those who immigrated to Canada after 1976, more than 15% experienced poverty for four years, compared with 4% of those who were Canadian-born. In Canada's urban centres, while racialized group members account for 21.6% of the population, they account for 33% of the urban poor. In fact, in some cities like Richmond and Vancouver in British Columbia; and Markham, Richmond Hill, Toronto, and Mississauga in Ontario, more than half of those living in poverty are racialized group members.[39]

An analysis of the 1996 data for the City of Toronto by Michael Ornstein breaks the economic performance of racialized groups down by national origin to identify deep pockets of low incomes and unemployment among some African and Caribbean groups, South Asian groups, East Asian groups, Arab and Middle Eastern groups, and Latin American groups in Canada's biggest and most prosperous metropolis. The levels of poverty are most acute among women.[40] Marie Drolet and Rene Morissette's (1999) findings also show that, while 73.1% of the racialized group members lived above the low-income cut-off during the previous four years, the number for non-racialized group members was 86%.[41]

More recent research shows that low-income rates among successive groups of immigrants almost doubled between 1980 and 1995, peaking at 47% before easing up in the late 1990s. In 1980, 24.6% of immigrants who had arrived during the previous five-year period lived below the poverty line. By 1990, the low-income rate among recent immigrants had increased to 31.3%. It rose further to 47.0% in 1995, but fell back somewhat to 35.8% in 2000 (Picot and Hou, 2003).[42]

The data on income attainment, unemployment, skill utilization, and rates of poverty demonstrate in compelling fashion the impact of racialization in the Canadian labour market, and the persistence of social exclusion experienced by racialized groups. In the next chapter, we will consider its impact on particular groups and the extent to which those experiences tell us something new about Canada in the early 21st century.

NOTES

[1] In 1993, government transfers represented 12.9% of family income in Canada. That was down to 11.7% by 1996. Statistics Canada Catalogue 13-207, as cited in A. Yalnyzian, *The Growing Gap: A Report on the Growing Income Inequality between the Rich and Poor in Canada* (Toronto: Centre for Social Justice, 1998), 64.

[2] J. Chard, "Women in a Visible Minority," in *Women in Canada: A Gender-Based Statistical Report* (Ottawa: Statistics Canada, 2000). Cat. No. CS86-503-XPE.

[3] The 1996 census uses the term *visible minority* to denote a group here referred to as a racialized group.

[4] Special run of Statistics Canada Survey of Labour and Income Dynamics (SLID) for the Centre for Social Justice, 2000; 2005. See Galabuzi (2000).

[5] Based on a special run of Statistics Canada Survey of Labour and Income Dynamics (SLID) for the Centre for Social Justice, 1996; 1997.

[6] J. Reitz and A. Verma, *Immigration, Ethnicity and Unionization: Recent Evidence for Canada* (Toronto: Centre for Excellence for Research on Immigration and Settlement (CERIS), May, 2000).

[7] Statistics Canada, *The Daily* (May 12, 1998).

[8] L. Christofides and R. Swidinsky, "Wage Determination by Gender and Visible Minority Status: Evidence from the 1989 LMAS," *Canadian Public Policy* XX, no. 1 (1994): 34–51.

[9] Ibid., 35.

[10] See P. Li, *Ethnicity in Canada* (Toronto: Wall and Thompson, 1988); J. Reitz and R. Breton, *The Illusion of Difference: Realities of Ethnicity in Canada and the United States* (Toronto: C.D. Howe, 1994); K. Gosine, "Revisiting the Notion of a 'Recast' Vertical Mosaic in Canada: Does a Post-Secondary Education Make a Difference?" *Canadian Ethnic Studies* XXXII, no. 30 (2000), 89–104; F. Hou and T.R. Balakrishnan, "The Integration of Visible Minorities in Contemporary Canadian Society," *Canadian Journal of Sociology* 21, no. 3 (1996): 307–325; R. Wanner, "Prejudice, Profit or Productivity: Explaining the Returns to Human Capital among Male Immigrants in Canada," *Canadian Ethnic Studies* 30, no. 3 (1998): 25–55; J. Torczyner, "Diversity, Mobility and Change: The Dynamics of Black Communities in Canada," in *Canadian Black Communities Demographic Project* (Montreal: McGill University Consortium for Ethnic and Strategic Social Planning, 1997).

[11] A. de Wolff, *Breaking the Myth of Flexible Work: Contingent Work in Toronto* (Toronto: Contingent Workers Project Report, September 2000).

[12] F. Mata, "Intergenerational Transmission of Education and Socio-economic Status: A Look at Immigrants, Visible Minorities and Aboriginals" (Ottawa: Statistics Canada, 1997).

[13] Statistics Canada, *The Daily* (May 12, 1998). The situation is different when you discount the variation in the average earnings of immigrants by period of immigration. The much higher incomes of pre-1976 immigrants push the overall average earnings to $27,684, which was 5.7% higher than for non-immigrants ($26,193).

[14] Statistics Canada, "Survey of Labour and Income Dynamics: Encountering Low Income," *The Daily* (March 25, 1999).

[15] Statistics Canada, "1996 Census: Sources of Income, Earnings and Total Income," *The Daily* (May 12, 1998).

[16] Among others, Akbari (1989, 1999); Bloom, Grenier, and Gunderson (1995); L. Christofides and R. Swidinsky, "Wage Determination by Gender and Visible Minority Status: Evidence from the 1989 LMAS," *Canadian Public Policy* 20, no. 1 (1994), pp. 34–51.

[17] Analysis from J. Anderson, "Notes on Visible Minorities and the Income Gap," unpublished paper (Toronto: Centre for Social Justice, 2000).

[18] Ibid.

[19] T. das Gupta, "Political Economy of Gender, Race and Class: Looking at South Asian Immigrant Women in Canada," in *Canadian Ethnic Studies* 26, no. 1 (1994): 59–73; see also, T. das Gupta, *Racism and Paid Work* (Toronto: Garamond Press, 1996); M. Boyd, "At a Disadvantage: The Occupational Attainment of Foreign Born Women in Canada," *International Migration Review* 18. no. 4 (1985): 1091–1119; C. Beach and C. Worswick, "Is There a Double-Negative Effect on the Earnings of Immigrant Women?" *Canadian Public Policy* XIX, no. 1 (1993): 36–53.

[20] S. Grizzle, *My Name's Not George: The Story of the Brotherhood of Sleeping Car Porters in Canada* (Toronto: Umbrella Press, 1998).

[21] Boralia and Li (1988); Adachi (1976); Henry et al. (1995).

[22] Chard, op. cit.

[23] E. Harvey, K. Reil, and B. Siu. "Ethnocultural Groups, Period of Immigration, and Socioeconomic Situation," *Canadian Journal of Ethnic Studies* 31, no. 3 (1999).

[24] E. Harvey, B. Siu. and K. Reil, "Ethnocultural Groups, Period of Immigration and Socio-Economic Situation," *Canadian Journal of Ethnic Studies* 30, no. 3 (1999): 95–103.

[25] K. Kelly, "Visible Minorities: A Diverse Group/Les minorités visibles: une population diversifiée," *Canadian Social Trends/Tendances sociales Canadiennes* 37 (Summer, 1995): 2–8. Published separately in English and French, Statistics Canada Catalogue no. 11008.

[26] Chard (2000).

[27] Chard, op. cit.

[28] D. Hum and W. Simpson, "Wage Opportunities for Visible Minorities in Canada" (Ottawa: Statistics Canada, 1998).

[29] Abbott and Beach (1993); Baker and Benjamin (1994); Chiswick and Miller (1988); De Voretz and Fagnan (1990); De Voretz (1995); Stoffman (1993); Beach and Worswick (1993); Collacott (2002).

[30] Mata (1997).

[31] F. Hou and T.R. Balakrishnan, "The Integration of Visible Minorities in Contemporary Canadian Society," *Canadian Journal of Sociology* 21, no. 3 (1996): 307–325.

[32] Kelly (1995), op. cit.

[33] Chard, op. cit.

[34] Anderson (2000). The sectors chosen for the study were picked in conjunction with Maria Wallis.

[35] For instance, university professors and the post-secondary research and teaching categories show a demographic over-representation of racialized group members.

[36] See Ontario Commission on Systemic Racism in the Criminal Justice System Report (1995); Clare Lewis report (1989), Pitman report (1977), Marshall report (Hickman 1989), Manitoba Aboriginal Justice (1991), Committee to Stop Targeted Policing (2000).

[37] *Report of the Taskforce on the Participation of Visible Minorities in the Federal Public Service 2000: Enforcing Change in the Federal Public Service* (Ottawa: Supply and Services Canada, 2000).

[38] Statistics Canada, "1996 Census: Sources of Income, Earnings," *The Daily* (May 12, 1998).

[39] K. Lee, *Urban Poor in Canada: A Statistical Profile* (Ottawa: Canadian Council on Social Development, 2000), 38.

[40] Ornstein (2000). Some questions have been raised about the group categories used in the report, but these methodological concerns are unlikely to impact the report's major findings.

[41] M. Drolet and R. Morissette, "To What Extent Are Canadians Exposed to Low Income?" (Ottawa: Statistics Canada, March 1999).

[42] G. Picot and F. Hou. *The Rise in Low-Income Rates among Immigrants in Canada*, catalogue no. 11F0019MIE–no. 198 (Ottawa: Statistics Canada, 2003); M. Frenette and R. Morissette, *Will They Ever Converge? Earnings of Immigrants and Canadian-Born Workers over the Last Two Decades*, Analytical Studies paper no. 215 (Ottawa: Statistics Canada, 2003); G. Schellenberg, *Immigrants in Canada's Census Metropolitan Areas*, catalogue no. 89-613-MIE–no. 003 (Ottawa: Statistics Canada, 2004); Statistics Canada, "Earnings of Immigrant and Canadian-Born Workers, 1980–2000," *The Daily* (October 8, 2003).

BIBLIOGRAPHY

Akbari, A. "The Benefits of Immigrants to Canada: Evidence on Tax and Public Services." *Canadian Public Policy* 15, no.4 (Dec 1989): 424–35.

Akbari, A. "Immigrant 'Quality' in Canada: More Direct Evidence of Human Capital Content, 1956–1994." *International Migration Review* 33, no. 1 (Spring 1999): 156–175.

Chard, J., J. Badets, and L. Howatson-Leo. *"Immigrant Women,"Women in Canada, 2000: A Gender-Based Statistical Report.* Ottawa: Statistics Canada, 2000.

Christofides, L., and R. Swidinsky. "Wage Determination by Gender and Visible Minority Status: Evidence from the 1989 LMAS." *Canadian Public Policy* 20, 1 (1994): 34–51.

Gosine, K. "Revisiting the Notion of a 'Recast' Vertical Mosaic in Canada: Does a Post Secondary Education Make a Difference?" *Canadian Ethnic Studies* 32, no. 3 (2000): 89–104.

Grizzle, S. *My Name's Not George: The Story of the Brotherhood of Sleeping Car Porters.* Toronto: Umbrella Press, 1998.

Harvey, E.B., B. Siu, and K. Reil. "Ethnocultural Groups, Periods of Immigration and Social Economic Situation." *Canadian Ethnic Studies* 30, no. 3 (1999): 95–103.

Hou, F., and T. Balakrishnan. "The Integration of Visible Minorities in Contemporary Canadian Society." *Canadian Journal of Sociology* 21, no. 3 (1996): 307–326.

Kelley, K. "Visible Minorities: A Diverse Group/Les minorités visibles: une population diversifiée." *Canadian Social Trends / Tendances sociales Canadiennes* 37 (Summer, 1995): 2–8.

Li, P. *Ethnic Inequality in a Class Society.* Toronto: Wall and Thompson, 1988.

Reitz, J.G. *Immigrant Success in the Knowledge Economy: Institutional Change and the Immigrant Experience in Canada, 1970–1995.* Toronto: Centre for Industrial Relations and Department of Sociology, University of Toronto, March 2000.

Reitz, J. and R. Breton. *The Illusion of Difference: Realities of Ethnicity in Canada and the United States.* Toronto: C. D. Howe Institute, 1994.

Wanner, R. "Prejudice, Profit or Productivity: Explaining Returns to Human Capital among Male Immigrants in Canada." *Canadian Ethnic Studies* 30, no. 3 (1998): 25–55.

FURTHER READING

Backhouse, Constance. *Colour-Coded: A Legal History of Racism in Canada, 1900–1950.* Toronto: University of Toronto Press, 1999.

Canadians, historically, have considered themselves to be free of racial prejudice. In *Colour-Coded,* Backhouse illustrates the tenacious hold white supremacy had on our legal system in the first half of the last century, and underscores the damaging legacy of inequality that continues today. Backhouse presents detailed narratives of six court cases, each giving evidence of blatant racism created and enforced through law. The cases focus on Aboriginal, Inuit, Chinese-Canadian, and African-Canadian individuals. Backhouse has effectively selected studies that constitute central moments in the legal history of race in Canada. This extensive and detailed documentation leaves no doubt the Canadian legal system played a dominant role in creating and preserving racial discrimination.

Galabuzi, Grace-Edward. *Canada's Economic Apartheid: The Social Exclusion of Racialized Groups in the New Century.* Toronto: Canadian Scholars' Press, 2006.

While Canada embraces globalization and romanticizes cultural diversity, there are persistent expressions of xenophobia and racial marginalization that suggest a continuing political and cultural attachment to the concept of a white, settled society. This groundbreaking book calls attention to the growing racialization of the gap between rich and poor, which, despite the dire implications for Canadian society, is proceeding with minimal public and policy attention. This book challenges some common myths about the economic per-formance of Canada's racialized communities. These myths are used to deflect public concern and to mask the growing social crisis. The author points to the role of historical patterns of systemic racial discrimination as essential in understanding the persistent overrepresentation of racialized groups in low-paying occupa-tions.

Tator, Carol, and Frances Henry. *Racial Profiling in Canada: Challenging the Myth of a 'Few Bad Apples.'* Toronto: University of Toronto Press, 2006.

In this controversial and thought-provoking work, Tator and Henry explore the meaning of racial profiling in Canada as it is practised not only by the police, but also by many other social institutions. The authors pro-vide a theoretical framework within which they examine racial profiling from a number of perspectives and in a variety of situations. They analyze the discourses of the media, policing officials, politicians, civil servants, judges, and other public authorities to demonstrate how those in power communicate and produce racialized ideologies and social relations of inequality through their common interactions. This book makes a major con-tribution to the literature and debates on a topic of growing concern.

Hier, Sean P. and B. Singh Bolaria, eds.. *Identity and Belonging: Rethinking Race and Ethnicity in Canadian Society.* Toronto: Canadian Scholars' Press, 2006.

Hier and Bolaria make the claim that Canadian society is rapidly evolving. By 2017, people belonging to a visi-ble minority group will comprise 20 percent of the Canadian population. While Canada has always been cul-turally diverse, the continuing ethno-racial diversification will exercise a profound influence on Canadian culture, as well as on Canadian political and social institutions. As the ethno-racial composition becomes more complex, critical understandings of race, ethnicity, identity, and belonging are increasingly important goals for social jus-tice, fairness, and inclusion.

Provocative and groundbreaking, *Identity and Belonging: Rethinking Race and Ethnicity in Canadian Society* asks some tough universal questions, such as: What is race? And how is it different from ethnicity? Do the meanings of race and ethnicity change through time? How are they reproduced? Why do these markers of identity matter to millions of people? Does globalization influence how people experience self and others? How do ethno-racial identities articulate with other markers of identity, such as gender or nationality?

Iacovetta, Franca., *Gatekeepers: Reshaping Immigrant Lives in Cold War Canada.* Toronto: Between the Lines Press, 2006.

An in-depth study of European immigrants to Canada during the Cold War, *Gatekeepers* explores interactions among these immigrants and the "gatekeepers"—mostly middle-class individuals and institutions whose def-initions of citizenship significantly shaped the immigrant experience. Iacovetta's discussion examines how dom-inant bourgeois gender and Cold War ideologies of the day shaped attitudes toward new Canadians. She shows how the newcomers themselves were significant actors who influenced Canadian culture and society, even as their own behaviour was being modified. *Gatekeepers* explores a side of Cold War history that has been left largely untapped.

Lambertson, Ross. *Repression and Resistance: Canadian Human Rights Activists 1930–1960.* Toronto: University of Toronto Press, 2005.

Repression and Resistance fills a void in our understanding of the emergence and evolution of human rights in Canada. It describes and analyzes the struggles of human rights activists from 1930–1960. It depicts the activ-ities of individual activists who risked social relationships and livelihoods, as well as the formation, develop-ment, and relative levels of success of a number of human rights groups and coalitions. Lambertson illustrates how the human rights community was often brought together through interrelated issues, while at the same time plagued by divisions created by ideological and cultural differences. Lambertson clearly succeeds in demon-strating that 1930–1960 was a critical time for the evolution of human rights in Canada.

Kelley, Ninette, and Michael Trebilcock. *The Making of the Mosaic: A History of Canadian Immigration Policy*. Toronto: University of Toronto Press, 1998.

This book tackles the contentious issues surrounding Canada's immigration policy and examines the ideas, interests, institutions, and rhetoric that have shaped our immigration history. Beginning with the pre-Confederation period, the authors tell of the dramatic transformations that have characterized our attitudes toward immigrants. Then, bringing us right up to date with the expansionary policies of the 1990s, the authors clarify the central issues and attitudes underlying each phase and junction of policy decision through the years.

Walker, James W. St. G. *"Race," Rights and the Law in the Supreme Court of Canada: Historical Case Studies*. Waterloo: Wilfred Laurier University Press, 1998.

Four legal cases, from 1914 to 1955, are intimately examined to explore the role of the Supreme Court of Canada and the law in the racialization of Canadian society. With painstaking research into contemporary attitudes and practices, Walker demonstrates that Supreme Court justices were expressing the prevailing "common sense" about "race" in their legal decisions. He shows that injustice on the grounds of "race" has been chronic in Canadian history, and that the law itself was once instrumental in creating these circumstances. The book concludes with a controversial discussion of current directions in Canadian law and their potential impact on Canada's future as a multicultural society.

COPYRIGHT ACKNOWLEDGEMENTS

CHAPTER 7: Kay J. Anderson, "Creating Outsiders, 1875–1903." From *Vancouver's Chinatown: Racial Discourse in Canada, 1875–1980* by Kay J. Anderson. Copyright © McGill-Queen's University Press 1991. Reprinted by permission of the publisher

CHAPTER 8: Sarah A. Carter, "Two Acres and a Cow: 'Peasant' Farming for the Indians of the Northwest, 1889–97." *Canadian Historical Review* 70, no. 1 (March 1989): 27–52. Reprinted by permission of University of Toronto Press Incorporated (www.utpjournals.com).

CHAPTER 9: Donald Avery, "European Immigrant Workers and Labour Protest in Peace and War, 1896–1919." From *Reluctant Hose: Canada's Response to Immigrant Workers, 1896–1994* by Donald Avery. Copyright © Oxford University Press 1995. Reprinted by permission of the publisher.

CHAPTER 10: Ruth Frager, "'Mixing with People on Spadina': The Tense Relations between Non-Jewish Workers and Jewish Workers." From *Sweatshop Strife: Class, Ethnicity, and Gender in the Jewish Labour Movement of Toronto, 1900–1939* by Ruth Frager. Copyright © University of Toronto Press 1992. Reproduced with permission of the publisher.

CHAPTER 11: Carmela Patrias, "Proletarian Ideology." From *Patriots and Proletarians: Politicizing Hungarian Immigrants in Interwar Canada* by Carmela Patrias. Copyright © McGill-Queen's University Press 2003. Reprinted by permission of the publisher.

CHAPTER 12: Mariana Valverde, "Racial Purity, Sexual Purity, and Immigration Policy." From *The Age of Light, Soap, and Water: Moral Reform in English Canada* by Mariana Valverde. Copyright © University of Toronto Press 1991. Reproduced with permission of the publisher.

CHAPTER 13: Angus McLaren, excerpted from "Stemming the Flood of Defective Aliens." From *Our Own Master Race: Eugenics in Canada 1885–1945* by Angus McLaren. Copyright © 1990 McClelland and Stewart Ltd. Reprinted by permission of the author.

CHAPTER 14: Peter W. Ward, excerpted from "Evacuation." From "British Columbia and the Japanese Evacuation." *Canadian Historical Review* 57, no. 3 (1976): 289–308. Reprinted by permission of University of Toronto Press Incorporated (www.utpjournals.com).

CHAPTER 15: J.L. Granatstein and Gregory A. Johnson, excerpt from "The Evacuation of the Japanese Canadians, 1942: A Realist Critique of the Received Version." From *On Guard for Thee: War, Ethnicity, and the Canadian State, 1939–1945,* edited by Norman Hillmer, Bohdan Kordan, and Lubomyr Luciuk. Copyright © 1998 Canadian Committee for the History of the Second World War. Reprinted by permission of J.L. Granatstein and Gregory A. Johnson.

CHAPTER 16: Dionne Brand, excerpted from "'We weren't allowed to go into factory work until Hitler started the war': The 1920s and the 1940s." From *We're Rooted Here and They Can't Pull Us Up*, edited by Peggy Bristow et al. Copyright © 1994 Dionne Brand. Reprinted by permission of the author.

CHAPTER 17: Franca Iacovetta, "From Contadina to Woman Worker." From *Such Hardworking People: Italian Immigrants in Postward Toronto* by Franca Iacovetta. Copyright © McGill-Queen's University Press 1993. Reprinted by permission of the publisher.